GUIDE TO CONCISE WRITING

Robert Hartwell Fiske

Webster's New World

New York   London   Toronto   Sydney   Tokyo   Singapore

To my parents,
who patiently endured a younger man's polysyllabic words
and worse

First Edition

Copyright © 1990 by Robert Hartwell Fiske

 Webster's New World

Simon & Schuster, Inc.
15 Columbus Circle
New York, NY 10023

WEBSTER'S NEW WORLD and colophons are registered
trademarks of Simon & Schuster, Inc.

DISTRIBUTED BY PRENTICE HALL TRADE SALES

Manufactured in the United States of America

1 2 3 4 5 6 7 8 9

Library of Congress Cataloging-in-Publication Data

Fiske, Robert Hartwell.
    Guide to concise writing / Robert Hartwell Fiske.
        p. cm.
    ISBN 0-13-947855-8
    1. English language—Rhetoric—Dictionaries. 2. English language—
Usage—Dictionaries. I. Title.
PE1460.F47 1990
428.003—dc20   90-31013
                                                                                      CIP

Table of Contents

Robert Hartwell Fiske
Vocabula Communications Company
P.O. Box 611
Andover, Massachusetts 01810

About This Book

This is a reference book and, like all such books, is meant to be referred to, not read through. Although I've long thought works of reference, dictionaries in particular, to be among the most spellbinding books, I cannot expect everyone to agree.

I do wish, as any writer would, that this were a work of creation instead of compilation; still, whether you refer to or read through the book, it will help you write and speak more clearly. It will also help you understand humankind more keenly. You should begin to question more and believe less, to complain more and condemn less, to achieve more and conceal less. With this book, you can become a work of creation.

The *Guide to Concise Writing* consists of two parts. In the first part, I suggest how to identify and correct wordiness. I also discuss why we are wordy. The second part of the book, "The Dictionary of Concision,"* is a compilation of several thousand wordy phrases followed by concise alternative expressions and real-world examples. I show each sentence example in its original, wordy version and then in a revised, concise version.

In replacing a wordy phrase by one less wordy or by a single word or in deleting the phrase altogether, I have tried to show how wordiness can encumber clarity and that it can be corrected. The sentence examples have been edited only to remedy the wordiness diagnosed; rarely are they syntactically and stylistically indefectible.

I don't claim that the entries I've compiled are unfailingly inferior to the alternatives I suggest. All the alternatives are merely proposed; they are not inarguable. In your own writing, you may at times find that an alternative suggested here, though less wordy, does not work so well.

Finally, as sole author of this book, I am solely accountable for any errors or, if I may be so charitable, oversights that these pages may hold. Although I have tried to be as thorough as possible and to include as many entries, and alternatives to them, as time would allow, I don't doubt that I have overlooked some. Anyone who finds an error or omission is welcome to share his discovery with me, and in a revised edition, I will gladly include any correction.

---

*Concision: the quality or state of being concise; conciseness.

PART ONE

Chapter 1

The Perfectibility of Words

Words are flawed, but they can easily be fixed. Words exist to be thought and then formed, to be written and then revised, and even to be said and then denied. They can be misused and neglected or cared for and corrected.

Inadequate though they may be, words distinguish us from all other living things. Only we humans can reflect on the past and plan for the future; it is language that allows us to do so. Indeed, our worth is partly in our words. Effective use of language—clear writing and speaking—is a measure of our humanness.

When they do their work best, words help people communicate; they promote understanding between people. And this, being well understood, is precisely the goal we should all aspire to when writing and speaking. As obvious as this seems, it is not a goal we commonly achieve.

Words often ill serve their purpose. When they do their work badly, words militate against us. Poor grammar, sloppy syntax, abused words, misspelled words, and other infelicities of style impede communication and advance only misunderstanding. But there is another, perhaps less well-known, obstacle to effective communication: too many words.

We often believe that many words are better than few. Perhaps we imagine that the more we say, the more we know or the more others will think we know, or that the more obscure our writing is, the more profound our thoughts are. Seldom, of course, is this so. Wordiness is arguably the biggest obstacle to clear writing and speaking. But it is also more than that.

- Wordiness is an obstacle to success. Almost all professional people know that success in business partly depends on good communications skills, on writing and speaking clearly and persuasively. Businesspeople who cannot express themselves well are often at a disadvantage in the corporate world.

3

- Wordiness is an obstacle to companionship. Few of us enjoy being with someone who speaks incessantly or incoherently. Wordiness in others may make us impatient; it may annoy us, and we may think it rude. Worse than that, when we have difficulty understanding someone, sooner or later we may not care what it is that he tries to convey. We lose interest in what a person says and, ultimately, in who a person is.
- Wordiness is an obstacle to self-knowledge. A superfluity of words conceals more than it reveals. We need time to be silent and still, time to reflect on the past and think about the future; without it, no one is knowable.

Wordiness is an obstacle to these goals and others. Whatever your profession, whatever your personality, wordiness is a condition for which we all should seek a cure.

OF POLISH AND PANACHE

Usually, in reading someone's writing, we see more words than we need to, and in listening to someone speak, we hear more words than we care to. For example, how often have you heard someone say *at this juncture* or, worse still, *at this moment in the history of my life* when a simple *now* would serve? These two phrases are flawed; they are two and eight words longer than they need be. The extra words are not needed to convey the thought; in truth, they interfere with the conveyance of thought.

These are but two of the wordy phrases that we overindulge in when writing and speaking. Though it may be hard to fathom, the English language contains thousands of wordy phrases that dull our understanding of and interest in whatever is being expressed.

Wordiness is a flaw of style—in how we express our language. Today, the style is prevailingly shoddy. In almost everything we read and hear, there is a complexity instead of simplicity and obscurity instead of clarity. This is particularly inexcusable in written material, where words can be reworked.

Few of us write well effortlessly. Typically, we have a thought, and then we write it down in whatever form it first occurred to us. Looking at our sentence further, though, we are usually able to improve on it. By reducing the number of words in a phrase, substituting a single word for a phrase, or deleting extraneous words or phrases, we are able to polish our sentence, to simplify and clarify our thought.

Reducing the number of words in a phrase

- The real test, however, lies in *the degree to which* the man's performance at his regular job improves.

The real test, however, lies in *how much* the man's performance at his regular job improves.

- *Insofar as* the implementation of bank projects *is concerned,* the situation is going back to normal.

  As for the implementation of bank projects, the situation is going back to normal.

- There is ample *evidence to support that* adult services are degrading to women, dangerous to children, and can become an unwitting accomplice to violent crimes and deviant sexual behavior.

  There is ample *evidence that* adult services are degrading to women, dangerous to children, and can become an unwitting accomplice to violent crimes and deviant sexual behavior.

Substituting a single word for a phrase

- The practice *is in violation of* perjury laws requiring candidates to attest that every signature was signed in person.

  The practice *violates* perjury laws requiring candidates to attest that every signature was signed in person.

- *Despite the fact that* Hanson PLC has revenues of over $12 billion, its corporate staff is exceedingly lean.

  Although Hanson PLC has revenues of over $12 billion, its corporate staff is exceedingly lean.

- I think *to a large extent* this kind of problem is a function of our society's inability to talk about sexuality in a reasonable way.

  I think this kind of problem is *largely* a function of our society's inability to talk about sexuality in a reasonable way.

Deleting extraneous words or phrases

- The more sophisticated savings institutions were *located* in places like Boston, New York, and Los Angeles.

  The more sophisticated savings institutions were in places like Boston, New York, and Los Angeles.

- He or she must develop strategies to resolve potentially disruptive or dysfunctional conflict *situations.*

  He or she must develop strategies to resolve potentially disruptive or dysfunctional conflicts.

- The Japanese government is not supplying much *in the way of* guidance concerning comparative advantages involved in investments in particular countries.

  The Japanese government is not supplying much guidance concerning comparative advantages involved in investments in particular countries.

A further benefit of applying some polish, of expressing ourselves more concisely, is that mistakes in grammar and word usage often are corrected as well. For example, we *compare* one person or thing *to* or *with* another, not *against* or *versus* another. The correct phrase is *compare to* or *compare with,* not *compare against* or *compare versus; to* and *with* both have one syllable fewer than *against* and *versus.* Fewer syllables count; life is short.

- The investigators will analyze the new data and *compare* them *against* computer models in an effort to link unequivocally the Arctic's perturbed chemistry to its ozone loss.

  The investigators will analyze the new data and *compare* them *with* computer models in an effort to link unequivocally the Arctic's perturbed chemistry to its ozone loss.

  Likewise, the correct expression is *center on,* not *center around.*

- Much of their behavior *centers around* doing things to please others in an attempt to earn approval.

  Much of their behavior *centers on* doing things to please others in an attempt to earn approval.

  But there are more telling examples.
  Say *the reason is* or simply *because* instead of *the reason is because,* and you are at once concise and correct.

- A common *reason* people join groups *is because* they work near one another.

  A common *reason* people join groups *is* they work near one another.

- *The reason* you explore what-ifs sequentially *is because* few solutions to business problems can be achieved by making a single change.

  You explore what-ifs sequentially *because* few solutions to business problems can be achieved by making a single change.

  The familiar *but rather* or *but instead* is also solecistic. Use *but* or *rather* or *instead,* for each alone does the job.

- It was not lack of sales that led to the downsizing of the project *but rather* the delays caused by a turnover of contractors.

  It was not lack of sales that led to the downsizing of the project *but* the delays caused by a turnover of contractors.

- Ericsson has not reduced its investments in the data processing field, *but* it has, *instead,* obtained greater resources with which to further develop and strengthen the advanced DP technology that constitutes its communications systems.

  Ericsson has not reduced its investments in the data processing field; *instead,* it has obtained greater resources with which to further develop and strengthen the advanced DP technology that constitutes its communications systems.

One final example is using *for example, for instance, like,* or *such as* along with *and others, and so forth, and so on, and such, and the like, et al.,* or *etc.* You don't need both sets of expressions to convey your meaning; use one or the other.

- These codes are used to change formats, *for example,* fonts, printer colors, *etc.*

  These codes are used to change formats, *for example,* fonts and printer colors.

- We have to give it the serious attention that we give illicit drugs *such as* heroin, cocaine, *and so on.*

  We have to give it the serious attention that we give illicit drugs— heroin, cocaine, *and so on.*

I grumble about grammar because mistakes in it invariably vitiate one's style of writing and, like wordiness, often arrest the reader's flow of thought.

A good writing style starts with polish, but it does not stop with it. Style must also have presence and personality. Along with polish, then, a writing style would be a good deal improved by panache, which is as creative as polish is corrective. Panache means writing with variety as well as with balance, writing heedful of sound as well as of sense, and writing interestingly as well as enthusiastically. All this is panache, and it is far more than this.

With a dollop of polish and a dash of panache our words will approach perfection.

CLUES TO CONCISION

There are several clues to realizing a clear and concise writing style. By being vigilant, that is, by rereading and rewriting your material, you will become increasingly adept at identifying superfluous words.

Further, the more words you know and have at your command, the more concise you can be. You will repeatedly discover, in the definition of one word, two or three others that you may have faithfully relied on to express a thought. For example, *like* means *in the same way that, never* means *under no conditions, halve* means *cut in half, share* means *have in common, with* means *in the company of, how* means *the process by which,* and *cynosure* means *center of attention.* By becoming well acquainted with the meanings of words, you will see that a single word often says as much as a string of words.

The key is to question. Ask yourself whether each word in every sentence that you write is needed. More than that, is it vital? Does it contribute to or interfere with the meaning of your sentence? Does it add anything to your meaning that another, perhaps adjacent, word does not?

Eventually, this constant questioning becomes second nature. Not only will you start writing better, you will start speaking better. When you start correcting yourself even as you speak, in midsentence, you are well on your way to achieving the consciousness of a creator.

As you question, be especially aware of phrases containing prepositions, verbs, and nouns and of extraneous adjectives and adverbs. Euphemisms, circumlocutions, clichés, idioms, and polysyllables are also frequent offenders.

Preposition phrases

All preposition phrases are suspect, particularly those longer than two words. A preposition phrase usually can be reduced to a single word or deleted altogether. We depend on these three- and four-word preposition phrases because we are unfamiliar with the meanings of so many one-word prepositions.

Consider a few examples:

Over the duration of the project, we expect there will be some disruption due to noise, dirt, and dust.

Over the duration of is one of those four-word preposition phrases; it is an excrescence. *During* is all that is needed.

As a result of last year's ONA process, a host of new network services will become available to providers of enhanced services *in the very near future.*

In the very near future is certainly a murky preposition phrase. Far better is the more clear *soon* or *shortly.*

> I think it is premature to relinquish our destiny to the hands of fate, for indeed much progress has been made *in the past,* and much more is still possible *in the future.*

In the past, like *in the future,* is often needlessly used. The context of the sentence usually makes the tense clear.

> We have used the MSE and the RMSE *for the purpose of* measuring how much fluctuation remains after a model has been built.

For the purpose of -ing is unpardonably wordy. Use the simpler *to.*

> *In the event that* you are not sure whether a particular problem is an emergency, we encourage you to call the Plan for advice.

In the event that usually can be reduced to *if* or *should.*

> We should be moving *in the direction of* finding psychotherapeutic measures to help correct this sexual disorder whenever the patient wishes it to be corrected.

In the direction of means *toward* in this sentence, though the phrase also can mean a monosyllabic *on, to,* or *with.*

> You can even set these switches *in such a way that* the RAM area can be read from but not written to.

In such a way that is a long-winded way of saying *so* or *so that.*

> There are a number of theories *as to* how firm value is affected by a firm's capital structure design.

As to, like *as regards, in relation to, with reference to,* and other equally dull devices, usually means an unadorned *about, for, in, of,* or *on.*

Verb phrases

Many verb phrases are redundant. In these phrases, two words (generally, a verb followed by a noun) do the work of one (the noun made into a verb).

Consider the following examples.

to arrive at, to come to, and *to reach* phrases

- Space probers are reluctantly *reaching the conclusion* that there is little likelihood that intelligent life is out there in the empty spaces beyond our solar system.

Space probers are reluctantly *concluding* that there is little likelihood that intelligent life is out there in the empty spaces beyond our solar system.

- Several economists predict that the expansion will *come to an end* in what is now its seventh year.

  Several economists predict that the expansion will *end* in what is now its seventh year.

to be phrases

- He *is lacking in* sensitivity.

  He *lacks* sensitivity.

- Unlike computers, which depended on the Cold War and the space race for the funds that drove their development, U.S. biotech *is dependent on* the flow of various health-care payment streams.

  Unlike computers, which depended on the Cold War and the space race for the funds that drove their development, U.S. biotech *depends on* the flow of various health-care payment streams.

to express and *to voice* phrases

- In one letter, dated June 15, 1892, Cather *expresses regret* that friendships between women are looked upon as unnatural.

  In one letter, dated June 15, 1892, Cather *regrets* that friendships between women are looked upon as unnatural.

- The government of Israel *voiced disapproval of* the decision.

  The government of Israel *disapproved of* the decision.

to give phrases

- The rest of the equation is to give people from diverse backgrounds a chance *to give expression to* their different views of the world.

  The rest of the equation is to give people from diverse backgrounds a chance *to express* their different views of the world.

- The continuing strong demand for our products and improving trends in component costs *give us encouragement* that this will be another year of significant growth in revenues and earnings.

  The continuing strong demand for our products and improving trends in component costs *encourage us* that this will be another year of significant growth in revenues and earnings.

to have phrases

• This measure *has the appearance of* reasonableness, but its application would have to be monitored to make sure it did not induce high turnovers by employers to cut labor costs.

This measure *appears* reasonable, but its application would have to be monitored to make sure it did not induce high turnovers by employers to cut labor costs.

• Any disruption of normal computer operations may *have a considerable impact on* the running of the business.

Any disruption of normal computer operations may *considerably affect* the running of the business.

to make phrases

• The code is moved into place by *making use of* the system Monitor block move subroutine, MOVE.

The code is moved into place by *using* the system Monitor block move subroutine, MOVE.

• The column does not *make a distinction* between having chronic pain as a symptom and being a "chronic pain patient," that is, having a chronic pain syndrome.

The column does not *distinguish* between having chronic pain as a symptom and being a "chronic pain patient," that is, having a chronic pain syndrome.

to place and to put phrases

• As a result, the women's groups now *put heavy emphasis on* fielding candidates for open seats and *on* identifying incumbents who might be vulnerable.

As a result, the women's groups now *heavily emphasize* fielding candidates for open seats and identifying incumbents who might be vulnerable.

• Excess supply within the next few years would *place pressure on* the cartel to maintain production restraint and keep average prices low.

Excess supply within the next few years would *pressure* the cartel to maintain production restraint and keep average prices low.

to take phrases

• I would like *to take this opportunity* to thank all of you who aided my candidacy.

I would like to thank all of you who aided my candidacy.

- Their forecasts are best prepared when they *take* the functional area forecasts *into consideration*.

  Their forecasts are best prepared when they *consider* the functional area forecasts.

Noun phrases

These are flaccid phrases that often begin with *a* or *the* followed by a noun and end with *of*. They can easily be made firm, as the following examples show.

(a; the) -ance of and *(a; the) -ence of* phrases

- *Maintenance of* this flow is assured by their willingness to rubber-stamp the decisions of their benefactor.

  Maintaining this flow is assured by their willingness to rubber-stamp the decisions of their benefactor.

- When a number of investment proposals perform essentially the same function so that *the acceptance of* one proposal necessarily means rejecting the others, we are dealing with mutually exclusive investments.

  When a number of investment proposals perform essentially the same function so that *accepting* one proposal necessarily means rejecting the others, we are dealing with mutually exclusive investments.

(a; the) -sion of and *(a; the) -tion of* phrases

- *The inclusion of* families is crucial if nurses are to become a source of help rather than an addition to families' difficulties.

  Including families is crucial if nurses are to become a source of help rather than an addition to families' difficulties.

- *The installation* and testing *of* a new product, *the conversion of* user files, and training users are not small matters.

  Installing and testing a new product, *converting* user files, and training users are not small matters.

(a; the) -ment of phrases

- For more than a decade, Motorola invested in *the development* and marketing *of* cellular systems and phones around the world.

  For more than a decade, Motorola invested in *developing* and marketing cellular systems and phones around the world.

- To the masses, a good government is one that prevents the strong from exploiting the weak, which is best done by *the punishment of* transgression.

  To the masses, a good government is one that prevents the strong from exploiting the weak, which is best done by *punishing* transgression.

(a; the) -ing of phrases

- Personal computers were meant to give people more flexibility in *the processing of* information.

  Personal computers were meant to give people more flexibility in *processing* information.

- Organizing at the middle level means *the making of* specific adjustments in the organizational structure and *the allocating of* the resources acquired by top management.

  Organizing at the middle level means *making* specific adjustments in the organizational structure and *allocating* the resources acquired by top management.

the ... of phrases

- You have to deal with *the issues of* betrayal, anger, rejection—all these things.

  You have to deal with betrayal, anger, rejection—all these things.

- In other situations, *the practice of* rotating managers of work teams on a normal schedule can stimulate a group.

  In other situations, rotating managers of work teams on a normal schedule can stimulate a group.

Adjectives and adverbs

By coupling adjectives and adverbs to perfectly good nouns, verbs, or adjectives, we often diminish the force and effectiveness of our writing. Powerful writing is taut; it admits no weak word, no superfluous adjective or adverb.

Consider these examples.

active; actively

- Individual managers need to be *actively* involved in the human resource planning process.

Individual managers need to be involved in the human resource planning process.

- Suicide attempts by hospitalized patients with "do not resuscitate" orders on their medical charts should be met by *active* resuscitation efforts unless recovery is unlikely.

Suicide attempts by hospitalized patients with "do not resuscitate" orders on their medical charts should be met by resuscitation efforts unless recovery is unlikely.

actual; actually; real; really

- Ideas are exchanged, but there is no *real* closure or plan of action.

Ideas are exchanged, but there is no closure or plan of action.

- My sense is that there is some interest, though it's too early to say how many companies will *actually* submit bids to set up demonstration projects.

My sense is that there is some interest, though it's too early to say how many companies will submit bids to set up demonstration projects.

total; totally; whole; wholly

- I was *totally* overwhelmed by their generosity.

I was overwhelmed by their generosity.

- The *whole* color-coding idea is perfect for marketing the books.

The color-coding idea is perfect for marketing the books.

There are other examples: *full potential* says no more than *potential* does alone; *completely eliminate* no more than *eliminate; possibly may* no more than *may; close scrutiny* no more than *scrutiny; excruciatingly painful* no more than *excruciating; firm commitment* no more than *commitment;* and *exactly identical* no more than *identical.*

Other common phrases to watch for

back with *refer, repay, return, revert,* and the like

- The second section of the booklet, while occasionally *referring back* to ideas discussed in the first section, is more or less independent.

The second section of the booklet, while occasionally *referring* to ideas discussed in the first section, is more or less independent.

- Type the new text, and then press Return to *return* the cursor *back* to the left margin.

  Type the new text, and then press Return to *return* the cursor to the left margin.

mutual with *and, between, both, two,* and the like

- I think this is *mutually* beneficial to *both* sides.

  I think this is beneficial to *both* sides.

- The receiver must share in these responsibilities if the *two* parties are to arrive at a *mutual* understanding.

  The receiver must share in these responsibilities if the *two* parties are to arrive at an understanding.

past, previous, or *prior* with *experience, history,* and the like

- From *previous experience,* we know that a compiler will find many typographical errors.

  From *experience,* we know that a compiler will find many typographical errors.

- *Past history* is full of people who didn't fit in and were left as outcasts.

  History is full of people who didn't fit in and were left as outcasts.

record with *all-time, high, new,* and the like

- "Knots Landing" has been on for nine years, the *all-time record* among prime-time soaps.

  "Knots Landing" has been on for nine years, the *record* among prime-time soaps.

- The number of days in the 90s in Boston and Washington may set a *record high.*

  The number of days in the 90s in Boston and Washington may set a *record.*

separate with *apart, distinct, entity, independent,* and the like

- The public permitting process was *separate and distinct* from the landlord's approval rights under the contract.

  The public permitting process was *separate* from the landlord's approval rights under the contract.

- In the biological world, there are many instances in which the same adaptation has evolved *separately and independently.*

  In the biological world, there are many instances in which the same adaptation has evolved *independently.*

together with *add, combine, join, link,* and the like

- One way of calculating a summary measure of error might be to *add* the error values *together.*

  One way of calculating a summary measure of error might be to *add* the error values.

- We're thousands of Americans who have *joined together* to lower our cost of living and live better on the money we earn.

  We're thousands of Americans who have *joined* to lower our cost of living and live better on the money we earn.

Euphemisms

Euphemisms are inoffensive or tasteful words and phrases that we use in place of offensive or distasteful ones. Many well-known euphemisms deal with sex or death, topics long thought too delicate for candor. Other euphemisms, less well known, are expressions of politeness or deception. During wars or dubious governmental policies, euphemisms abound (like *pacification* and *protective reaction* for *killing* or *bombing*). At other times, euphemisms are less recognizable, but only because we are less watchful.

Consider these euphemisms:

Instead of	Use
advanced in years	old
comfort facilities	bathroom
correctional facility	prison
economic adjustments	price hikes
loss prevention specialist	security guard
negative feelings	hate
no longer with us	dead
put to sleep	destroy
revenue enhancers	taxes
seminal fluid	semen
succumb to injuries	die
unpleasant arousal	depression

Circumlocutions

Circumlocutions are roundabout words and phrases. Often they are simply indirect expressions that say in several words what one or two ably would. Occasionally, however, they are used to evade an issue. When people do not want to commit themselves to a cause, or when they do not want to be held accountable for either supporting or not supporting a position, they hedge by using ambiguous words. Circumlocutions may mean something far different from what almost anyone would imagine.

Consider these circumlocutions:

Instead of	*Use*
a limited number	one
an overwhelming majority of	most
a significant proportion of	some
a sizable percentage of	many
in the near future	soon
is at variance with	differs from
is of the opinion	believes
make a statement saying	say
on more than one occasion	twenty times
over the long term	ultimately
to a certain extent	in part
to a large degree	largely

Clichés

We should never become too attached to a term for fear that it be reduced to a cliché. Once people start using a word or phrase excessively, its meaning is blunted and its usefulness lost. Clichés are words or phrases that no longer effectively express thought or sentiment; they are formulas that we rely on when we are too lazy to express what we think or even to discover how we feel. Clichés keep us in line; the more we use them, the more we conform, in thought and feeling, to everyone else who uses them.

Consider these clichés:

Instead of	*Use*
cautiously optimistic	optimistic
consensus of opinion	consensus
fear and trembling	dread
fly in the face of	defy

Consider these clichés:

Instead of	Use
for all intents and purposes	virtually
goes to show	proves
in a timely fashion	promptly
it is imperative that	must
kinder and gentler	humane
par for the course	typical
sick and tired	annoyed
window of opportunity	opportunity

Idioms

An idiom is an expression that, on the surface, makes little, if any, sense. An idiom's literal meaning, even if decipherable, is frequently different from its actual meaning. Unlike euphemisms and clichés, which usually should be shunned, many popular idioms have their place in the language. Although idioms often say clearly and cleverly what other words cannot, many are wordy expressions for which we can find a more economical phrase or particular word.

Consider these idioms:

Instead of	Use
as a matter of fact	in fact
before long	soon
day in and day out	every day
high and mighty	arrogant
in all probability	most likely
in a nutshell	briefly
in place of	for
on the part of	by
put on an act	pretend
take exception	object
take offense to	resent
the long and the short	the gist

Polysyllables

I am very fond of polysyllabic words and certainly do not wish to discourage their use. Wittgenstein said, "The limits of my language are the limits of my world." The more words you know and can correctly use, the wider your knowledge and understanding of the world and of yourself. Still, there are polysyllabic words that we can, without fear of unrefinement, do well without.

Consider these polysyllables:

Instead of	Use
effectuate	effect
eventuality	event
indebtedness	debt
individuals	people
materialize	happen
methodology	method
multiplicity	many
necessitate	require
parameter	limit
remunerate	pay
stick-to-itiveness	resolve
terminate	end

Couples

A couple is two words, on either side of *and,* that have but one meaning. We often feel that two words do the job twice as well as one, that in a couple, the second word reinforces the first. In truth, the second word enfeebles the first. English contains scores of couples, and most of them should never have met.

Consider these couples:

Instead of	Use
aid and abet	aid or abet
compare and contrast	compare or contrast
fair and equitable	equitable or fair
first and foremost	first or foremost
new and innovative	new or innovative
null and void	null or void
one and only	one or only
peace and quiet	peace or quiet
pick and choose	pick or choose
plain and simple	plain or simple
rules and regulations	rules or regulations
various and sundry	various or sundry

Embarrassments

Embarrassments are found, thankfully, more often in speech than in writing. Of course, these expressions are more embarrassing to the listener than the speaker, who were he embarrassed, wouldn't use them. Embarrassments are best abolished.

Consider these embarrassments:

Instead of	Use
and everything	(delete)
and stuff like that	(delete)
anyway	(delete)
hopefully	I hope
how's it going?	hello
humongous	huge
I'll tell you	(delete)
I mean	(delete)
kind of thing	(delete)
most definitely	yes
or something	(delete)
you know?	(delete)

Chapter 2

The Imperfectibility of People

WORDINESS IS EVERYWHERE

As the several thousand entries in "The Dictionary of Concision" suggest, wordiness is a problem—an omnipresent problem. Though a contagion that nearly all of us suffer from, businesspeople, lawyers, politicians, journalists, and academics seem unusually afflicted with wordiness.

Business jargon

In a 1988 survey, 503 top executives at leading U.S. manufacturing and service firms reported that two-thirds of their entry-level managers and professionals wrote unclearly. Entry level or top level, it seems to matter not. Consider this diffuse phrasing from the president and CEO of a bank, from whom we should expect a more stately style:

> We've enclosed an informative brochure that includes a map and information on the changes occurring February 17. As you will note, you can continue banking just as you have in the past. There is no action required on your part.

Informative and *information* are redundant, *in the past* is superfluous with *as you have,* and *There is no action required on your part* is much inferior to, for example, *You need do nothing.*

From a real-estate professional, we have this unwieldy wording:

> I'm under the impression, due to the fact that I've not heard from the main office, that your application has been accepted.

Had this person written *I believe* instead of *I'm under the impression that* and *since* instead of *due to the fact that,* we might have a bit more confidence in his abilities.

Here is an "explanation" from a credit card company:

> The Minimum Payment Due each month shall be reduced by the amounts paid in excess of the Minimum Payment Due during the previous three months which have not already been so applied in determining the Minimum Payment Due in such earlier months, unless you have exceeded your line of credit or have paid the entire New Balance shown on your billing statement.

This language is so laborious to understand that many people simply wouldn't bother to try; they would disregard it. Of course, the purpose of a statement like this is less to lucidly convey a policy than to legally protect the company.

Businesspeople are also much noted for the expedience of their language. Consider this statement issued by a spokesperson for an insurance company:

> Some letters offering refunds were misdirected due to a computer error.

As many of us know far too well, computers don't make errors, people do. Without the phrase *due to a computer error,* an excuse we frequently hear, human error would be properly implied. Business jargon is as imprecise as it is politic.

Consider this artful sentence from the chairman and CEO of a well-known consulting firm:

> Management, with the participation and concurrence of key professional staff, has determined that we can best serve our shareowners and ourselves by resisting temptation to pursue all of the interesting challenges we are equipped to handle.

This is typical business bombast. It sounds fairly good, and it is meant to (coming as it does from an annual report). But as is often so in business, sound precedes sense. Though phrases like *participation and concurrence, key professional staff, resisting temptation,* and *all of the interesting challenges we are equipped to handle* may sound sweet to shareholders, the sentence means no more than

> We will focus on only some areas of our expertise.

Among the verbose phrases valued by those in the business world are *a high level of, component part, course of action, from the standpoint of, game plan, have an impact on, in a timely fashion, in the not-too-distant future, is in receipt of, plan of action, please be advised that, prioritize, time frame, valuable asset,* and *window of opportunity.*

Legalese

The language of the law is often complicated and unintelligible, but it could be made less so if lawyers would only choose to communicate with laymen in fewer words and syllables.

> Neither party to this Agreement nor any persons to whom either party has disclosed the Proprietary Information pursuant to this paragraph shall disclose the Proprietary Information to any persons, or permit any person access to the Proprietary Information, or use the Proprietary Information or permit it to be used, directly or indirectly, for their own account, or for the account of another, or make any copy of the Proprietary Information without the express prior written consent in each instance of the party from whom it originated, with such consent being granted only by an individual with the capacity to authorize copying, except that each party may disclose and grant access to the Proprietary Information to those members of its staff who (a) need such access in order to effectuate the Arrangement and (b) have agreed not to further disclose or allow access to the Proprietary Information, and not to use it or permit it to be used, directly or indirectly for their own account or for the account of another, but to safeguard the Proprietary Information and treat it as the highly confidential, proprietary and trade secret property of the other party and to use it only to effectuate the Arrangement and only so long as the Arrangement remains in effect.

And that's just one sentence. What it means, I hardly know. What it means, I hardly care. I'd have to hire a lawyer to untangle it.

Here are several shorter, though no less bewildering, illustrations of lawyers' language:

> To the best of my knowledge and belief, the above statements of fact are true and accurate.

If the statements are *of fact,* they are *true and accurate,* which itself is redundant.

> This Agreement shall inure to the benefit of the Agent's successors and assigns, and it shall be binding upon Author's successors, assigns, executors, administrators, heirs, and legal representatives.

Boilerplate like this invariably contains the grandiloquent *inure to the benefit of;* in piecing together their contracts, lawyers should one day learn that *inure to* says no less.

> The trust has agreed that in the event the advisory agreement between the investment adviser and the trust is terminated, or if the affiliation between the investment adviser and its parent company is terminated, the trust will eliminate the name "Allstate" from its name if the investment adviser or its parent company so request.

Legal phraseology frequently is exposed for what it truly is by those who write it. Here the phrase *in the event* on the first line means simply *if,* as the *if* on the second line makes plain.

Lawyers, too, have their preferred wording: *compensate, effectuate, expeditiously, in accordance with, in consideration of, in force and effect, in perpetuity, in the absence of, necessitate, notwithstanding, pursuant to, subsequent to,* and *until such time as.*

Political cant

In a recent poll of 1,513 adults, seventy percent of the respondents considered politicians "not so good" or "poor." The prevailing view was that most politicians make campaign promises they do not intend to fulfill, will lie if the truth would hurt them politically, and are mainly concerned with holding on to power.

Indeed, it is often in the interest of politicians and government bureaucrats to conceal their true thoughts from us. Consider this prize display of evasiveness by a political aide to a city mayor:

> I confirm that I said it, but I will neither confirm nor deny that I meant it.

Equally unsettling is how politicians are forever devising new expressions or redefining old ones to serve their own interests:

> "I misspoke," explained the politico when the committee asked about his stated opinion on abortion.

> **mis · speak** (mis spēk') *vt., vi.* **-spoke', -spok'en, -speak'ing** to speak or say incorrectly; *to lie.*

The danger here is that the euphemism will become synonymous with the word it is used for. When a word like *misspeak* is used euphemistically for a word like *lie,* we must all loudly complain. Lest euphemisms become synonyms, dictionaries become undone, and minds become mangled, we must all complain.

There are other illustrations of euphemism; for example, the wordy *it remains to be seen* and *that's an open question,* favored by politicians and their ilk, so often truly mean the inadmissible *I don't know.*

Allied to euphemism is circumlocution, another stratagem that politicians depend on.

> The senator, who once was seen as wavering, says he now "is supportive of the President's nominee" for secretary of defense.

The verb phrase *is supportive of* is less committing than the verb *supports* and nicely serves the senator his equivocal purpose. Verb phrases are more wordy than verbs, so it seems as though more is being said, but they are less direct and less meaningful. Deception requires more words than truthfulness.

Consider, too, this ineffectual phrasing by a government bureaucrat:

> It remains my hope and cautiously optimistic expectation that necessary legislation may be enacted prior to October 1.

The phrase *hope and expectation* is redundant, but to qualify *expectation* with *cautiously optimistic* is witless. Moreover, *cautiously optimistic*— one of officialdom's favorite phrases—is oxymoronic. But it is surely the incongruity of the words that so appeals to politicians; juxtaposed, they mean nothing, and politicians generally prefer saying nothing to saying something. Still uneasy with his pronouncement, the bureaucrat further tempers it with the *may* preceding *be enacted*. He might have written his words more capably had he used fewer of them:

> I expect legislation will be enacted before October 1.

Journalese

If politicians are attached to euphemism and circumlocution, journalists are surely attached to cliché and slang: *bear a striking resemblance to, despite the fact that, express concern, in connection with, in the meantime, in the midst of, in the wake of, on the condition that, on the part of, on the verge of, stand in sharp contrast to,* and *the vast majority of* are a few of their frightful phrases.

Moreover, despite the confines of their columns, few newspaper and magazine writers have yet to learn much about using the shorter phrase or the single word.

> Oftentimes, the Senate, as well as the White House, struggles with questions involving what is now being described as lifestyle. The problem is that, in effect, the Senate and the White House sometimes are being asked to put their stamp of approval on lifestyles that, while acceptable in Washington, are not acceptable by general standards elsewhere.

If we change *oftentimes* to *often, as well as* to *and, involving what is now being described as* to *of,* the *Senate and the White House* to *both, put their stamp of approval on* to *approve,* and *by general standards* to *generally* and delete *in effect* and *being,* we lose two lines of text but not a word of meaning:

> Often, the Senate and the White House struggle with questions of lifestyle. The problem is that both sometimes are asked to approve lifestyles that, while acceptable in Washington, are not generally acceptable elsewhere.

Journalists furnish their newspapers and magazines with quantities of verbiage. Here, though, are just a few more examples:

> Lack of experience on the part of the firm is also a source of delay and difficulty.

Lack of experience would be better phrased as *the inexperience,* and *on the part of* as, simply, *of.*

> If sea levels rise to the extent that scientists predict, the Marshall Islands, which are composed of two chains of coral islands rising no more than 5 feet above the sea, would be submerged.

A more careful journalist might have written *as much as* instead of *to the extent that,* and *comprise* instead of *are composed of.*

> In the course of the debate, legislators complained that the vote was futile, because the governor had the power to freeze spending regardless of what legislators did.

In the course of can be replaced by *during,* and *regardless of what* by *despite what.*

> The law created the Occupational Safety and Health Administration, a federal agency charged with the responsibility of ensuring the safety of workers.

The phrase *charged with the responsibility of* is repetitious; either *charged with* or *responsible for* is enough.

Academicspeak

Another area known for its reliance on jargon and gibberish is academia. Academics (especially social scientists, administrators, and self-important students) regularly try to give more prestige to their disciplines, and themselves, by breeding their own vocabularies. The author of a recent book on relationships identifies five levels of commitment.

1. dating—no commitment
2. steady dating—some commitment

3. monogamy—seeing yourselves as a couple
4. monogamy plus—you're a couple and everyone around you knows it
5. living together—you're making plans

Monogamy plus (which we might reasonably think is a euphemism for bigamy) is one of their misbegotten idioms. Academics create terms like this so that they may explain the obvious to us. We need them to define their terminology. In fact, most of these words we can happily do without. Academics (and those who would have us think they are) tirelessly create not only idioms but their own spurious systems and subsystems. They categorize what the rest of us have always known and don't need to be reminded of.

From a college preparatory school catalog, here is an entertaining, if perhaps indecorous, description of a course in human sexuality:

Human sexuality is a required skills course that teaches sexuality topics through the framework of values clarification activities.

I think most parents would like further explanation of *required skills course* and *values clarification activities,* but better yet would be a less ambiguous description.

Disturbingly often, the academics' language belies their intellectual standing. Consider this paragraph from the manuscript of a college text on finance:

Mutual savings banks have grown steadily, but relatively slowly. A major reason for their relatively slow growth is that they are geographically limited. There are less than 500 of them operating in only 16 states. They primarily are located only in the Northeastern section of the country—with the sole exception of 6 states, and less than 20 mutual savings banks, that operate in the Far West and Midwest.

There's nothing inherently abstruse about the information in this paragraph. It is the wordiness of the writing, the fuzziness of the thinking, that interferes with our understanding.

Mutual savings banks have grown steadily but slowly. Fewer than 500 of them operate in only 16 states. Except for some 20 mutual savings banks in the Far West and Midwest, they are all in the Northeast.

Finally, here are a few words from a recent college graduate's commencement address.

I think back to freshman year when my parents called in those first couple of weeks, and in the course of the conversation they asked, "Well, what have you learned so far?" I think they were a little worried when I said I've learned to write a sentence—a short, simple, concise sentence that was to the point.

Well they worry.

THE AGE OF SHODDINESS

To say *at this juncture* or *at this moment in the history of my life* instead of *now* signifies more than mere wordiness. It signifies a perversion of society's values. Since how a person speaks and writes is a fair reflection of how a person thinks and feels, shoddy language may imply shoddy people—a public whose ideals have been discarded and whose ideas have been distorted. A society is generally as lax as its language. And in a society of this sort, easiness and mediocrity are much esteemed.

So prevalent is shoddiness that the person who speaks correctly and uses words deliberately is often thought less well of than the person who speaks solecistically and uses slang unreservedly. Today, fluency is in disfavor. Soundness and sense have had their day; shoddiness now has the dais.

But why, we must wonder, are we wordy? Why do we say seven words where two will do or write three instead of only one? Understanding why we are wordy may help us reclaim our command of the language.

Habit, ignorance, and imitation are among the most common reasons for our wordiness.

Habit

Many people who write and speak wordily do so out of habit. Habit, though human, means behaving automatically, without question or deliberation. It means mindlessly maintaining a particular action or reaction. Many of us write and speak habitually, as we always or long have; few of us pay much attention to how we express ourselves. We neither read what we write nor listen to what we say.

Ignorance

Often people are wordy because they know no better. They are unaware that the concise phrase is preferable to the prolix and the precise word to the imprecise; indeed, they may accept the reverse. Moreover, people are generally loath to learn. We embrace what is easy or effortless and avoid what is hard or demanding.

Imitation

As never before, people do as others do, speak as others speak, and think as others think. The cliché is king. Nothing is so reviled as individuality. We imitate one another lest we be left alone. We want to fit in, to be part of the crowd. We want groups to engulf us and institutions to direct us.

Habits must be broken, ignorance overcome, and imitation resisted. But even if we do achieve all this, there are other possible reasons for our wordiness, less understandable and forgivable, perhaps, but human nonetheless.

To enhance our self-importance

Many of us seek to enhance our self-importance by using ostentatious language. We may believe that the more words we use, or the more elaborate our language, the more intelligent we sound and important we are. We may recognize the thinness of our thoughts and try to give them added weight by using polysyllabic words. Or we may chatter endlessly as though each word were further proof of our presence.

To interfere with others' thoughts

Some people, not uncommonly, will try to interfere with other people's thoughts. Through expedient, euphemistic, or circumlocutory language, these people strive to conceal their actions, to becloud what they say and do. With words they do whatever they please and, in so doing, manage to confuse our perception of their deeds and, even, their identity.

To interfere with our own thoughts

If we can interfere with others' thoughts, we can interfere with our own. Some of us do not want to know the meaning of our words. We fear knowing who we truly are, so to shield ourselves from the insight that genuine views and convictions can impart, we write without feeling and speak without thinking. We babble to ward off some bogy of self-knowledge with whom we battle.

We need something to help us create who we can be, to help us question, complain, and achieve more. In this age, the Age of Shoddiness, we need a different kind of dictionary, a dictionary that can catch us unaware, a dictionary that can cast a spell.

PART TWO

The Dictionary of Concision

A

abolish (eliminate) altogether *abolish (eliminate)*. When the market-presence assessment is undertaken with the idea of either reducing the size of the company's presence or eliminating it altogether, management's focus is two-pronged. *When the market-presence assessment is undertaken with the idea of either reducing the size of the company's presence or eliminating it, management's focus is two-pronged.*

about the fact that *because; for; in that; since; that;* delete. She's happy about the fact that she's won $13,000 a day for the past three days. *She's happy because she's won $13,000 a day for the past three days.*

about (around) ... to *about (around); to.* He is about 50 to 60 years old. *He is 50 to 60 years old.* ■ By 1987, about 40 to 50 of the 400-plus foreign banks operating in the United States had become full-service banks. *By 1987, about 45 of the 400-plus foreign banks operating in the United States had become full-service banks.* ■ He works around 10 to 12 hours a day. *He works 10 to 12 hours a day.*

above and beyond *above; besides; beyond; more than; over.* Considering that I managed to save only $100 above and beyond tuition for this year, I really don't see that as an option. *Considering that I managed to save only $100 more than tuition for this year, I really don't see that as an option.* ■ The officers were honored for actions that went above and beyond the call of duty. *The officers were honored for actions that went beyond the call of duty.* ■ Above and beyond that, he's rich. *Besides that, he's rich.*

above (beyond) measure *endless; infinite; limitless; untold.*

(after; for; in; over; within) a brief (limited; little; short) amount of time (length of time; period; period of time: span of time; time; while) *before long; briefly;*

directly; presently; quickly; shortly; soon; straightaway. This anxiety will pass after a short time, and you will then be wondering why you felt it in the first place. *This anxiety will pass quickly, and you will then be wondering why you felt it in the first place.* ■ It snowed for a brief period of time. *It snowed briefly.* ■ *In a short while, he will be making a speech before the convention delegates. He will shortly be making a speech before the convention delegates.* ■ We have one of the finest banking franchises in the country, and within a short period of time our operating results will reflect that. *We have one of the finest banking franchises in the country, and our operating results will soon reflect that.* ■ I have no doubt that within a short period Properties Company will be competing with those players for major property development agreements. *I have no doubt that before long Properties Company will be competing with those players for major property development agreements.*

a (the) broad (extensive; great; vast; wide) array of *an array of; assorted; broad; countless; different; diverse; extensive; many; numerous; scores of; sundry; untold; varied; various; varying; vast;* delete. In any domestic market, a wide array of official and unofficial sources provides information about the chosen market segments. *In any domestic market, numerous official and unofficial sources provide information about the chosen market segments.* ■ Biological and social scientists have offered a wide array of theories in their obsessive search for the "cause" of homosexuality within the individual body or psyche. *Biological and social scientists have offered many theories in their obsessive search for the "cause" of homosexuality within the individual body or psyche.*

a (the) broad (extensive; great; vast; wide) range of *a range of; assorted; broad; countless; different; diverse; extensive; many; numerous; scores of; sundry; untold; varied; various; varying; vast;* delete. A wide range of products is sold by NTIS as subscriptions or standing orders. *Various products are sold by NTIS as subscriptions or standing orders.* ■ Many consumers are intimidated by their lack of knowledge about wines and confused by the wide range of wines available. *Many consumers are intimidated by their lack of knowledge about wines and confused by the countless wines available.* ■ They provide an extensive range of engineering and materials management services to the NYNEX family of companies. *They provide extensive engineering and materials management services to the NYNEX family of companies.* ■ In a political year that otherwise rates mixed reviews, the 100th Congress deserves wholehearted praise for its accomplishments on a broad range of issues. *In a political year that otherwise rates mixed reviews, the 100th Congress deserves wholehearted praise for its accomplishments on diverse issues.*

a (the) broad (extensive; great; vast; wide) spectrum of *a spectrum of; assorted; broad; countless; different; diverse; extensive; many; numerous; scores of; sundry; untold; varied; various; varying; vast;* delete.

a (the) broad (extensive; great; vast; wide) variety of *a variety of; assorted; broad; countless; different; diverse; extensive; many; numerous; scores of; sundry; untold; varied; various; varying; vast;* delete. A wide variety of templates are available for drawing nuts and bolts. *Various templates are available for drawing nuts and bolts.* ■ Researchers have advanced a wide variety of theories about the cause of schizophrenia, including abnormal mother–child relationships, viruses, nervous system injuries during birth, and mutant genes. *Researchers have advanced many theories about the cause of schizophrenia, including abnormal mother–child relationships, viruses, nervous system injuries during birth, and mutant genes.*

(a; the) absence of *dis-; having no; im-; in-; ir-; lacking; -less(ness); mis-; missing; no; non-; not; not any; not having; scant; un-; with no; without.* I wanted to communicate to young people the absence of purpose and how it felt so senseless and wasteful. *I wanted to communicate to young people the purposelessness and how it felt so senseless and wasteful.* ■ Styron sharply criticized America's literati for their absence of passion. *Styron sharply criticized America's literati for their dispassion.* ■ Ward cited the breakdown of communications, the absence of sufficient supervision, and inexperienced police officers as the main reasons the disturbance got out of hand. *Ward cited the breakdown of communications, insufficient supervision, and inexperienced police officers as the main reasons the disturbance got out of hand.* ■ The absence of such "hygiene" factors as good supervisor–employee relations and liberal fringe benefits can make workers unhappy. *Lacking such "hygiene" factors as good supervisor–employee relations and liberal fringe benefits can make workers unhappy.* ■ In this situation, the absence of praise is especially threatening because we know that we are still being evaluated. *In this situation, no praise is especially threatening because we know that we are still being evaluated.*

absolutely *at all; delete.* Rarely am I dissatisfied with purchases of music I know absolutely nothing about. *Rarely am I dissatisfied with purchases of music I know nothing about.* ■ There is absolutely no question that we will not be able to make the necessary investments for our business. *There is no question at all that we will not be able to make the necessary investments for our business.*

absolutely *yes.*

absolutely conclusive *conclusive.*

absolutely essential (indispensable) *essential (indispensable).* I abhor government regulations except where absolutely indispensable. *I abhor government regulations except where indispensable.* ■ In today's age of information, where clarity of expression and understanding are at a premium, and the ability to communicate crisply and accurately becomes more important every day, a good desk dictionary is absolutely essential. *In today's age of information, where clarity of expression and understanding are at a premium, and the ability to communicate crisply and accurately becomes more important every day, a good desk dictionary is essential.*

absolutely not *by no means; no; not at all.*

absolutely positively *absolutely; positively;* delete. Descartes was an introspective man who probed his meditations for things he could be absolutely, positively sure of. *Descartes was an introspective man who probed his meditations for things he could be absolutely sure of.*

a bunch of *many; numerous.*

a case in point *an (one) example; for example; for instance.* Teachers in the trades and industry program at Queen Anne's County High School are a case in point. *Teachers in the trades and industry program at Queen Anne's County High School are an example.*

acclimatize *acclimate.*

accommodations *rooms.*

accompanied by *along with; and; as well as; combined with; coupled with; joined with; paired with; together with; with.* The behavioral implications of this emphasis are an increase in job satisfaction accompanied by a decrease in turnover and absenteeism. *The behavioral implications of this emphasis are an increase in job satisfaction coupled with a decrease in turnover and absenteeism.*

accomplish *achieve; do; perform.* This can be accomplished by assigning consecutive numbers to consecutive periods. *This can be achieved by assigning consecutive numbers to consecutive periods.* ■ Project teams are set up to do a job, and when they have accomplished it, their members return to their departments or are assigned to a new project team. *Project teams are set up to do a job, and when they have done it, their members return to their departments or are assigned to a new project team.* ■ You can use the operating system's utilities to format disks, copy files, and accomplish other file management tasks. *You can use the operating system's utilities to format disks, copy files, and perform other file management tasks.*

accordingly *hence; so; then; therefore; thus.* Accordingly, the board of directors recommends a vote against this stockholder proposal. *Therefore, the board of directors recommends a vote against this stockholder proposal.* ■ Experience under the plan may indicate that changes are desirable; accordingly, the trust reserves the right to amend or terminate the plan. *Experience under the plan may indicate that changes are desirable; thus, the trust reserves the right to amend or terminate the plan.*

according to *by; following; to; under.*

according to *affirm; allege; announce; assert; attest; aver; avow; claim; comment; contend; declare; maintain; note; say; state; suggest; vouch.* According to various estimates, the measure would translate into a 10-percent trimming of insurance rates next year. *Various estimates suggest the measure would translate into a 10-percent trimming of insurance rates next year.* ■ According to those who lived through the strikes of eight years ago, there was a real air of excitement throughout the country then. *Those who lived through the strikes of eight years ago maintain there was a real air of excitement throughout the country then.* ■ Around 60 to 70 percent of all municipal issues are negotiated, according to analysts. *Around 60 to 70 percent of all municipal issues are negotiated, analysts contend.* ■ These forces, according to the authors, have systematically misled Americans about the substance and morality of our foreign policies. *These forces, say the authors, have systematically misled Americans about the substance and morality of our foreign policies.*

according to plan (projections) *as planned (projected).* Kraft is soon to be taken over by Philip Morris if all goes according to plan. *Kraft is soon to be taken over by Philip Morris if all goes as planned.* ■ Officials say the church will continue to pour tens of millions of dollars each year into all four media ventures, at least until it sees signs of whether they will perform according to projections. *Officials say the church will continue to pour tens of millions of dollars each year into all four media ventures, at least until it sees signs of whether they will perform as projected.*

accumulative *cumulative.* The proportions reflect accumulative information as one reads the table from left to right. *The proportions reflect cumulative information as one reads the table from left to right.*

accustomed to *inured to; used to.* These technologies will be considerably different from the ones your applications people are accustomed to. *These technologies will be considerably different from the ones your applications people are used to.* ■ I am accustomed to her sinful ways. *I am inured to her sinful ways.*

a certain amount of *much; some;* delete. There's a certain amount of truth to what you say. *There's much truth to what you say.* ■ He's acquired a certain amount of sophistication from his ex-wife, who's from a wealthier family than he is. *He's acquired some sophistication from his ex-wife, who's from a wealthier family than he is.*

a (the) consequence of *because of; caused by; due to; owing to; resulting from.* The increase is almost entirely the consequence of rising economic activity. *The increase is almost entirely caused by rising economic activity.* ■ He makes it very clear that its success is a consequence of experienced and competent people. *He makes it very clear that its success is due to experienced and competent people.*

a couple of *a few; two.*

(all) across (throughout) the country (nation) *nationwide.*

(all) across (throughout) the world *worldwide.*

act in accord (accordance) with *act on; follow.*

(a; the) ... action delete. Jailing Danilov was retaliatory action against the seizure of a Soviet agent in the United States. *Jailing Danilov was retaliation against the seizure of a Soviet agent in the United States.* ■ Before making such a decision, management needs to review the reasons for unsatisfactory product performance and consider possible remedial action. *Before making such a decision, management needs to review the reasons for unsatisfactory product performance and consider possible remedies.* ■ A series of slides can be made to produce animated action. *A series of slides can be made to produce animation.* ■ We are taking steps to revoke the security clearances of individuals who have been involved in illegal actions. *We are taking steps to revoke the security clearances of individuals who have been involved in illegalities.*

action (attack; battle; game) plan *course; formula; method; plan; policy; procedure; scheme; strategy.* After the optimum alternative has been selected, the manager needs to develop an action plan to implement it. *After the optimum alternative has been selected, the manager needs to develop a plan to implement it.* ■ The legislation calls for a national battle plan to combat the disease on three fronts: education, treatment, and research. *The legislation calls for a national policy to combat the disease on three fronts: education, treatment, and research.* ■ A global distribution strategy is the game plan for simultaneously attaining the company's global- and foreign-market distribution strategy. *A global distribution strategy is the formula for simultaneously attaining the company's global- and foreign-market distribution strategy.* ■ The Democratic leadership's action plan is simple: Delay action as long as possible. *The Democratic leadership's strategy is simple: Delay action as long as possible.*

active (actively) delete. They are learning to actively participate in their own decisions. *They are learning to participate in their own decisions.* ■ To counteract this, the change agent takes an active role in encouraging new solutions and approaches to problems. *To counteract this, the change agent takes a role in encouraging new solutions and approaches to problems.* ■ Citibank is actively pursuing private banking in numerous domestic markets around the world. *Citibank is pursuing private banking in numerous domestic markets around the world.* ■ I wish that both political parties would take an active interest in the captive nations' fate and their struggle for freedom and independence. *I wish that both political parties would take an interest in the captive nations' fate and their struggle for freedom and independence.* ■ It was clear to all of us that the president was going to actively consider our request that this order never be published. *It was clear to all of us that the president was going to consider our request that this order never be published.* ■ The Times said the opposition from AIPAC had been stronger than opposition from Israel, which did not actively resist the sale. The Times *said the opposition from AIPAC had been stronger than opposition from Israel, which did not resist the sale.*

... activity delete. He hasn't been charged with any unlawful activity. *He hasn't been charged with any unlawfulness.* ■ What kind of R&D activity does the firm plan to undertake? *What kind of R&D does the firm plan to undertake?* ■ Unfortunately, countries where counterfeiting activity is widespread are generally not parties to such treaties. *Unfortunately, countries where counterfeiting is widespread are generally not parties to such treaties.* ■ There could be some thunderstorm activity as well. *There could be some thunderstorms as well.*

actual (actually) delete.

add ... additional (further; more) *add.* Companies at the extreme ends of their market's geographical region just add additional cost to their products to cover shipping. *Companies at the extreme ends of their market's geographical region just add cost to their products to cover shipping.* ■ If I can add any additional information, please do not hesitate to contact me. *If I can add any information, please do not hesitate to contact me.* ■ At his suggestion, we will add an additional step to the process. *At his suggestion, we will add a step to the process.*

(an) additional *added; extra; further; more; other.* It supports all Knowledge-Man/2 capabilities and integrates two additional components. *It supports all KnowledgeMan/2 capabilities and integrates two other components.* ■ Four pipe bombs have been found in Needham over the last two weeks, and officials said an additional two have been found in Wellesley. *Four pipe bombs have been found in Needham over the last two weeks, and officials said two more have been found in Wellesley.* ■ Such a transfer has the additional advantage of reducing the donor's income tax in the year of the gift. *Such a transfer has the added advantage of reducing the donor's income tax in the year of the gift.*

additionally *also; and; as well; besides; beyond that (this); even; further; furthermore; moreover; more than that (this); still more; then; too; what is more.* Additionally, he was an authority on butterflies. *He was also an authority on butterflies.* ■ Additionally, in the United States, legislation provided that all financial transactions must be processed through commercial banks. *And in the United States, legislation provided that all financial transactions must be processed through commercial banks.* ■ Additionally, there can be conflicts in terms of loyalty. *More than that, there can be conflicts in terms of loyalty.*

add together *add.* The space you specify in the space-before and space-after command fields are added together. *The space you specify in the space-before and space-after command fields are added.* ■ Add together the first 31 numbers in the sequence 6, 66, 666, 6666, ... *Add the first 31 numbers in the sequence 6, 66, 666, 6666, ...*

add up *add; sum; total.* The assigned points are then added up, and the country is classified on a good-to-poor continuum. *The assigned points are then added, and the country is classified on a good-to-poor continuum.* ■ The program adds up the values of all the ASCII characters in the block and sends the ASCII character for that value last. *The program totals the values of all the ASCII characters in the block and sends the ASCII character for that value last.*

a (a certain; some) degree (of) *a certain; much (of); some (of); somewhat; delete.* The best results will likely be obtained by firms that exercise some degree of restraint in their offshore activities. *The best results will likely be obtained by firms that exercise some restraint in their offshore activities.* ■ California Federal Savings was heavily committed to commercial banking and has achieved a degree of success in this endeavor. *California Federal Savings was heavily committed to commercial banking and has achieved much success in this endeavor.* ■ The new creationists have justifiable grounds for a certain degree of chutzpah. *The new creationists have justifiable grounds for chutzpah.* ■ Each of us has a planning method that works with some degree of effectiveness. *Each of us has a planning method that works somewhat effectively.*

adequate enough *adequate; enough.*

(an; the) adequate number (of) *enough; five (ninety).* Performance tasks appear quite feasible in large-scale assessments as well as in classroom use, provided an adequate number of good tasks are available. *Performance tasks appear quite feasible in large-scale assessments as well as in classroom use, provided enough good tasks are available.*

a (the) diversity of different *assorted; a variety of; broad; countless; different; diverse; extensive; many; numerous; scores of; sundry; varied; various; varying.* The diversity of different types of music that the Society now offers would have been unheard of 20 years ago. *The diverse types of music that the Society now offers would have been unheard of 20 years ago.*

adjacent to *beside; close to; near; next to.*

admit to *admit.* The General Accounting Office found 16 percent of the employers surveyed admitted to engaging in discriminatory hiring practices. *The General Accounting Office found 16 percent of the employers surveyed admitted engaging in discriminatory hiring practices.*

advance ahead (forward; on; onward) *advance; go on; move on; proceed; progress.*

advanced (along) in years *elderly; old.*

advance notice *notice.* Congress is in the thick of a new stage of the battle over my proposal to require businesses to give advance notice to workers before plants are closed or major layoffs are ordered. *Congress is in the thick of a new stage of the battle over my proposal to require businesses to give notice to workers before plants are closed or major layoffs are ordered.*

advance planning (plans) *planning (plans).*

advance preparation *preparation.* In a meeting designed to solve problems or make decisions, you should include in your advance preparations a statement of the problem and your recommended solution. *In a meeting designed to solve problems or make decisions, you should include in your preparations a statement of the problem and your recommended solution.*

advance reservations *reservations.*

advance up *advance.* As the person's needs are met on one level, the person advances up to the next level of needs. *As the person's needs are met on one level, the person advances to the next level of needs.*

advance warning *warning.* Seismologists generally concur that the science of earthquake prediction is such that a region about to be struck by a major quake would have, at best, only a few days' advance warning. *Seismologists generally concur that the science of earthquake prediction is such that a region about to be struck by a major quake would have, at best, only a few days' warning.*

a (the) ... experience delete. Just getting up in the morning is a painful experience for her. *Just getting up in the morning is painful for her.* ■ Overall, we found the launching of IDI a stimulating and enjoyable experience. *Overall, we found the launching of IDI stimulating and enjoyable.* ■ It can be a nerve-racking experience to go to school and find out that your classmates know more about you than you do. *It can be nerve-racking to go to school and find out that your classmates know more about you than you do.*

a (the) ... fact delete. This is an alarming fact, considering that these workers make up the foundation of our service-sector economy. *This is alarming, considering that these workers make up the foundation of our service-sector economy.*

affiliated with *belongs to; employed by; works for.*

affirmative *yes.* If the answer is affirmative, selecting an optimal dividend policy is a valid concern. *If the answer is yes, selecting an optimal dividend policy is a valid concern.*

afford (give; offer; present; provide) ... (an; the) opportunity *allow; give ... (the) chance; let; permit.* Winning the Boston Marathon provided me with an opportunity to make running my career. *Winning the Boston Marathon allowed me to make running my career.* ■ Credit cards offer you the opportunity to purchase goods and services by telephone. *Credit cards let you purchase goods and services by telephone.* ■ Local pets will be afforded the opportunity to do stupid tricks, and there will be remotes from the streets of the city. *Local pets will be given the chance to do stupid tricks, and there will be remotes from the streets of the city.*

afford with *afford.*

a fistful (handful) of *a few; hardly any; not many; two or three (four or five); scarcely any; several; six (ten); some.* The stumbling block is that there are so far only a fistful of programs that take advantage of the features of Presentation Manager. *The stumbling block is that there are so far only twelve programs that take advantage of the features of Presentation Manager.* ■ Since the 1860s, a determined handful of scientists have argued for the feasibility of "sympatric speciation." *Since the 1860s, a few determined scientists have argued for the feasibility of "sympatric speciation."*

after all is said and done *even so; finally; in the end; still; ultimately; yet;* delete.

after ... first *after.* Any model relying on deseasonalized data should be built after the modified Census II method of deseasonalization is first applied to the data. *Any model relying on deseasonalized data should be built after the modified Census II method of deseasonalization is applied to the data.* ■ Each person can speak up for himself only after he has first restated the ideas and feelings of the previous speaker accurately and to that speaker's satisfaction. *Each person can speak up for himself only after he has restated the ideas and feelings of the previous speaker accurately and to that speaker's satisfaction.*

after ... later (subsequently) *after.* After you have created and saved a file on the disk, you can retrieve it later for editing. *After you have created and saved a file on the disk, you can retrieve it for editing.*

after the conclusion (end) of *after.*

after the event (incident; occurrence) *after; afterward; later; next; then.*

after ... then *after.* After making changes, you can then use the transfer command to save the style sheet. *After making changes, you can use the transfer command to save the style sheet.* ■ After a company has decided to sell its products in another country, it must then decide which method of entry to use into that market. *After a company has decided to sell its products in another country, it must decide which method of entry to use into that market.*

again and again *frequently; often; recurrently; regularly; repeatedly.*

again re- *re-.* It's an image that again reinforces my belief that we are more interested in pizzazz than performance. *It's an image that reinforces my belief that we are more interested in pizzazz than performance.*

age (aged) delete. Women reach peak fertility at age 25 and then the ability to get pregnant naturally declines. *Women reach peak fertility at 25 and then the ability to get pregnant naturally declines.* ■ Because people from ages 35 to 54 are in their peak years of earning power, the spending implications are awesome. *Because people from 35 to 54 are in their peak years of earning power, the spending implications are awesome.*

a good (great) deal of *great; much; vast.* There is a great deal of disagreement about generations after the first three. *There is great disagreement about generations after the first three.* ■ In most other respects, the level of your graphics board won't make a great deal of difference. *In most other respects, the level of your graphics board won't make much difference.*

agricultural crop *crop.* To get high carbon dioxide uptake, we end up talking about something that looks more like an agricultural crop than a grove of stately Douglas firs. *To get high carbon dioxide uptake, we end up talking about something that looks more like a crop than a grove of stately Douglas firs.*

ahead of *before.* First names are now listed ahead of last names. *First names are now listed before last names.* ■ The ambassador departed five minutes ahead of the deadline imposed by the State Department. *The ambassador departed five minutes before the deadline imposed by the State Department.*

ahead of schedule *early; too soon.* They arrived in the country two hours ahead of schedule. *They arrived in the country two hours early.*

ahead of time *before; beforehand; earlier; sooner.* The production manager never knew what was in the pipeline, so he could never prepare the materials and staff ahead of time. *The production manager never knew what was in the pipeline, so he could never prepare the materials and staff beforehand.* ■ But once having done so, at least the town should come to the aid of these people by either installing it or informing them ahead of time that the manpower would not be there. *But once having done so, at least the town should come to the aid of these people by either installing it or informing them earlier that the manpower would not be there.*

a (whole) host of *many; numerous.* There are a whole host of reasons why these people resigned from their jobs. *There are many reasons why these people resigned from their jobs.*

aid and abet *abet; aid; help.* Citizens need to persuade the federal government of their support for genuine change in policies that presently aid and abet the tobacco industry. *Citizens need to persuade the federal government of their support for genuine change in policies that presently abet the tobacco* *industry.* ■ The NRC, aided and abetted by the industry and most of the press, has chosen to wink at the law. *The NRC, aided by the industry and most of the press, has chosen to wink at the law.*

aid in -ing *help.* In order to aid in recharging the groundwater, large spreading basins were constructed along the Santa Ana River. *In order to help recharge the groundwater, large spreading basins were constructed along the Santa Ana River.*

a (the) ... job of delete. If common understanding exists after the communication has happened, it can be said that an effective job of communication has taken place. *If common understanding exists after the communication has happened, it can be said that effective communication has taken place.* ■ When the banks offer the products of investment entities with a high market profile, the job of introducing the funds to bank customers is much easier. *When the banks offer the products of investment entities with a high market profile, introducing the funds to bank customers is much easier.*

a ... kind (sort; type) of thing *like;* delete. It became a competition type of thing. *It became like a competition.* ■ It's an unpleasant sort of thing. *It's unpleasant.*

alas and alack *alas.*

albeit *although; though.* This disparity demonstrates very dramatically (albeit crudely) the rapid decline in profit potential for international companies. *This disparity demonstrates very dramatically (though crudely) the rapid decline in profit potential for international companies.* ■ There appears to be enough fuel to propel stocks higher, albeit irregularly, even if the bond market is waylaid by fears of a too robust economy. *There appears to be enough fuel to propel stocks higher, although irregularly, even if the bond market is waylaid by fears of a too robust economy.*

a little bit *a bit; a little; slightly; somewhat.* They're a little bit hesitant. *They're a little hesitant.* ■ They may be fighting soft benefits a little bit, because a lot of this adds more administration and management demands. *They may be fighting soft benefits a bit, because a lot of this adds more administration and management demands.*

all and sundry *all; everybody; everyone; one and all.* He is cheered by all and sundry despite his confession. *He is cheered by everyone despite his confession.*

all done (finished) *complete; done; ended; finished; over; past.* When it is all finished, the commute into town should be much more speedy. *When it is finished, the commute into town should be much more speedy.* ■ Are you all done with your homework? *Are you done with your homework?*

alleged suspect *suspect.*

alleviate *lessen; reduce.* The proposal is designed to alleviate overcrowding at Framingham State Prison. *The proposal is designed to lessen overcrowding at Framingham State Prison.*

all in all *all told; in all; overall.* All in all, it would be difficult to find a less suitable site. *All told, it would be difficult to find a less suitable site.*

all ... long *all.* The president, shop chairman, and entire shop committee of UAW Local 422 worked hard all winter long. *The president, shop chairman, and entire shop committee of UAW Local 422 worked hard all winter.*

all of (the) *all (the).* The mean is the average of all of the data within the time series. *The mean is the average of all the data within the time series.* ■ Can you do all of them? *Can you do them all?* ■ All of that is important, but you have to make a choice. *All that is important, but you have to make a choice.*

all of (us) *(we) all.* All of us practice a kind of inventory control. *We all practice a kind of inventory control.*

all of a sudden *suddenly.* All of a sudden, I began getting memos from the corporate office criticizing my performance. *Suddenly, I began getting memos from the corporate office criticizing my performance.*

all over with *complete; done; ended; finished; over; past.*

allow of *allow; permit.*

allow ... to *let.* Do it in a way that allows you to look the consumer straight in the eye. *Do it in a way that lets you look the consumer straight in the eye.* ■ Light pens are hand-held devices that allow you to draw directly on the screen. *Light pens are hand-held devices that let you draw directly on the screen.*

all that *that.* We didn't find him all that intelligent. *We didn't find him that intelligent.*

all (just) the same *anyhow; even so; still; yet.*

all the time *always; ceaselessly; constantly; endlessly; everyday; forever.*

all things considered *all in all; all told; altogether; in all; on the whole; overall.*

all-time record (high) *record.* Revenues for the quarter will set an all-time record high and will result in a dramatic turnaround of the disappointing first-quarter results. *Revenues for the quarter will set a record and will result in a dramatic turnaround of the disappointing first-quarter results.* ■ International Falls, Minnesota, sometimes called the nation's icebox, tied its all-time record of 98 degrees. *International Falls, Minnesota, sometimes called the nation's icebox, tied its record of 98 degrees.*

all-time record low *record low.* Temperatures in Alaska reached 78 degrees below zero, an all-time record low for the area. *Temperatures in Alaska reached 78 degrees below zero, a record low for the area.*

almost without exception *almost all; almost every; most; nearly all; nearly every.* Almost without exception, those professionals stated that innovation was of major importance to the continued success of the company. *Almost all those professionals stated that innovation was of major importance to the continued success of the company.* ■ Our visitors, almost without exception, are surprised to see for themselves how much less things actually cost through the club. *Nearly all of our visitors are surprised to see for themselves how much less things actually cost through the club.*

alongside of *alongside; among; beside; next to; with.* You will work alongside of experienced workers and see what joys and frustrations they undergo. *You will work with experienced workers and see what joys and frustrations they undergo.* ■ In less affluent markets, a lower quality of product line is sold alongside of the premium product. *In less affluent markets, a lower quality of product line is sold alongside the premium product.*

along that (this) line *about (in; on) that (this).* I don't know what the Twins' thinking was along that line. *I don't know what the Twins' thinking was on that.*

along that (this) line *like that (this).* I can see using TrueScan for some work along that line but only if the documents aren't too complex in fonts or layout. *I can see using TrueScan for some work like that but only if the documents aren't too complex in fonts or layout.*

along the line of *in; with.*

along the lines of *akin to; close to; like; resembling; similar to; such as.* They have no interest in publishing anything along the lines of Microsoft *Bookshelf.* *They have no interest in publishing anything similar to Microsoft Bookshelf.* ■ Such is Connecticut's reputation for good, efficient government, that when a Connecticut official says something along the lines of "New York will probably end up where we are," it would usually be cause for celebration. *Such is Connecticut's reputation for good, efficient government, that when a Connecticut official says something like "New York will probably end up where we are," it would usually be cause for celebration.*

along the same line *alike; likewise; much the same; similar; similarly.* Along the same line, increasing monetary benefits but not expanding opportunities for job variety would be a serious mistake. *Likewise, increasing monetary benefits but not expanding opportunities for job variety would be a serious mistake.*

(for) a long time (while) *long.* It has been around a long time, but has never before been tried in the state. *It has long been around, but has never before been tried in the state.* ∎ She has wanted to travel to Europe for a long time. *She has long wanted to travel to Europe.*

a long time (while) ago *long ago.*

along with (and; combined with; coupled with; plus; together with) the fact that *and that.* U.S. Labor Department figures show that most minimum-wage employees work part time coupled with the fact that 60 percent are between 16 and 24 years old. *U.S. Labor Department figures show that most minimum-wage employees work part time and that 60 percent are between 16 and 24 years old.*

a lot *much.* It also makes assembly-language programs that use GS/OS a lot easier to read. *It also makes assembly-language programs that use GS/OS much easier to read.*

a lot of *many; much; numerous.* In a lot of people's minds, there was no question of his quilt. *In many people's minds, there was no question of his guilt.* ∎ A miniscule market share translates into a lot of opportunity over many years. *A miniscule market share translates into much opportunity over many years.*

a lot of (the) time *frequently; often.* We went into the city a lot of times. *We went into the city often.*

alphabetical *alphabetic.*

alphanumerical *alphameric; alphanumeric.*

also ... as well *also; as well.* I was also physically abused as well. *I was physically abused as well.* ∎ They also agreed to other demands as well. *They also agreed to other demands.*

also ... too *also; too.* We also know that Marilyn Monroe was one of his lovers, too. *We know that Marilyn Monroe was one of his lovers, too.*

alternative choice *alternative.*

a matter of *a; delete.* The issue of automobile insurance has been a matter of concern to me since my early years as a legislator. *The issue of automobile* *insurance has been a concern to me since my early years as a legislator.* ■ Any conclusions at this time would be premature and a matter of conjecture. *Any conclusions at this time would be premature and conjectural.* ■ Even a Public Service proposal to give bonus vacation days to employees has been a matter of contention. *Even a Public Service proposal to give bonus vacation days to employees has been contended.* ■ Just how much of what has been claimed for him is really his is a matter of disputation. *Just how much of what has been claimed for him is really his is disputable.*

a matter of *a few; some;* delete. Within a matter of a day or two, he was dead. *Within a day or two, he was dead.* ■ A streaming tape drive can copy all the data from a hard disk onto a 1/4-inch cartridge tape in a matter of minutes. *A streaming tape drive can copy all the data from a hard disk onto a 1/4-inch cartridge tape in a few minutes.* ■ In a matter of seconds, SpinRite determines the interleave characteristics of the entire system. *In seconds, SpinRite determines the interleave characteristics of the entire system.*

a (a certain; some) measure (of) *a certain; much; some;* delete. With the employer–employee relationship should come a certain measure of understanding. *With the employer–employee relationship should come a certain understanding.* ■ Both provide a measure of feedback control over financial and other activities. *Both provide feedback control over financial and other activities.* ■ Informal conversations provide clients with opportunities to discuss topics that are not stressful and that provide a measure of relief from anxiety. *Informal conversations provide clients with opportunities to discuss topics that are not stressful and that provide some relief from anxiety.*

ameliorate *heal; help; improve; make better.* As medical technology and surgical procedures increase in their ability to ameliorate, they unfortunately also increase in their ability to harm. *As medical technology and surgical procedures increase in their ability to heal, they unfortunately also increase in their ability to harm.*

(8:00) a.m. ... morning *(8:00) a.m.; morning.* I want the cost estimates by 9:00 a.m. tomorrow morning. *I want the cost estimates by 9:00 a.m. tomorrow.* ■ The traditional right expects nothing less than condemnations of such things—especially from an evangelical Presbyterian minister who arises every morning at 5:00 a.m. to pray. *The traditional right expects nothing less than condemnations of such things—especially from an evangelical Presbyterian minister who arises every morning at 5:00 to pray.*

(a; the) amount of delete. If you have any amount of intelligence, you know what's right and what's wrong. *If you have any intelligence, you know what's right and what's wrong.* ■ How he got from the house to Jake's in that short amount of time I'll never know. *How he got from the house to Jake's in that short time I'll never know.* ■ Some amount of stress is necessary. *Some stress is necessary.* ■ The lower the level of a heading, the greater the amount of indent. *The* *lower the level of a heading, the greater the indent.* ■ I understand you've expanded the amount of area available for each animal. *I understand you've expanded the area available for each animal.* ■ Since Properties Company has an extensive amount of expertise in real estate development, the company has in its plans to market its services to companies outside the NYNEX family. *Since Properties Company has extensive expertise in real estate development, the company has in its plans to market its services to companies outside the NYNEX family.*

amount (quantity; sum) of cash (money) *sum.* When the Soviets spent enormous amounts of money improving their antiaircraft systems, the United States responded not by giving up on its bomber program but rather by improving it with cruise missiles, electronic jammers, and so on. *When the Soviets spent enormous sums improving their antiaircraft systems, the United States responded not by giving up on its bomber program but rather by improving it with cruise missiles, electronic jammers, and so on.* ■ To escape the poverty in which they are trapped, the Asian women agree to pay huge sums of money to the purported arrangers of European marriages or jobs. *To escape the poverty in which they are trapped, the Asian women agree to pay huge sums to the purported arrangers of European marriages or jobs.*

(a; the) ... amount of time (length of time; period of time; span of time) *period; time; while; delete.* An option is a contract that conveys the right to buy or sell specified property at a given price for a designated amount of time. *An option is a contract that conveys the right to buy or sell specified property at a given price for a designated period.* ■ They filmed our arguments over a three-month period of time. *They filmed our arguments over three months.* ■ You can get to know someone very well if you date him or her for a long enough period of time. *You can get to know someone very well if you date him or her for a long enough while.* ■ The longer the span of time a forecast covers, the more vulnerable it is to the elements of uncertainty. *The longer the period a forecast covers, the more vulnerable it is to the elements of uncertainty.* ■ But over the same length of time, inflation averaged 3 percent a year. *But over the same period, inflation averaged 3 percent a year.* ■ This is just the start of a new business that, over a period of time, should become a very significant new product. *This is just the start of a new business that, over time, should become a very significant new product.*

amounts to *is; totals.* The number of prisoners released amounts to less than one-third of those held. *The number of prisoners released is less than one-third of those held.*

an (the) abundance of *abundant; ample; copious; countless; legion; liberal; many; myriad; numerous; plentiful; plenty of; profuse.* Among the educated, there is an abundance of people trained in these occupations. *Among the educated, there are plenty of people trained in these occupations.*

an accomplished (established) fact *accomplished (established); a fact; delete.* It is an established fact that reaction times and vision deteriorate with age. *It is* *established that reaction times and vision deteriorate with age.* ■ New, more peaceful Soviet policies are not yet an accomplished fact. *New, more peaceful Soviet policies are not yet a fact.*

an acknowledged (known) fact *acknowledged (known); a fact;* delete. It is an acknowledged fact that well-trained and highly skilled construction craftsmen are not willing to work for wages substandard to the prevailing wage rates. *It is acknowledged that well-trained and highly skilled construction craftsmen are not willing to work for wages substandard to the prevailing wage rates.*

analytical *analytic.*

analyze in depth (in detail) *analyze; detail.* The astronauts have always spent most of their training time practicing responses to almost every imaginable kind of failure, and the contingencies have been analyzed in detail and simulated innumerable times. *The astronauts have always spent most of their training time practicing responses to almost every imaginable kind of failure, and the contingencies have been analyzed and simulated innumerable times.* ■ He analyzes in detail the three nativist eruptions that occurred during the era of mass immigration. *He details the three nativist eruptions that occurred during the era of mass immigration.*

an array of *assorted; countless; different; diverse; extensive; many; numerous; scores of; sundry; varied; various; varying;* delete. Lately, however, an array of new troubles has surfaced—troubles like radon. *Lately, however, many new troubles have surfaced—troubles like radon.*

(a; the) -ance (-ence) of *-ing.* With such asset and liability opportunities, the avoidance of large credit losses was a practical management consideration in ensuring attractive profitability. *With such asset and liability opportunities, avoiding large credit losses was a practical management consideration in ensuring attractive profitability.* ■ This requires the maintenance of special marketing units and the issuance of policies and procedures designed to stimulate the flow of products, resources, and information. *This requires maintaining special marketing units and issuing policies and procedures designed to stimulate the flow of products, resources, and information.* ■ In the performance of their routines, they are acting as extensions of your position. *In performing their routines, they are acting as extensions of your position.*

and ... also *also; and.* Love is an emotion, and it also is a strong emotion. *Love is an emotion; it is also a strong emotion.* ■ The Winters' models are more complex and also more potentially rewarding. *The Winters' models are more complex and more potentially rewarding.* ■ These plans are gaining favor with corporate managements because they limit the employer's retirement plan liability to a known amount, and also, being voluntary, they offer a meaningful benefit to employees at little cost to the employer. *These plans are gaining favor with corporate managements because they limit the employer's retirement plan liability to a known* *amount; being voluntary, they also offer a meaningful benefit to employees at little cost to the employer.* ■ There are various methods for identifying the knowledge of an expert, and there are also methods for codifying that knowledge in a computer. *There are various methods for identifying the knowledge of an expert, and there are methods for codifying that knowledge in a computer.*

and ... as well *and; as well.* It is being done by some of the women whose careers you chronicled and by a growing number of working women as well. *It is being done by some of the women whose careers you chronicled and by a growing number of working women.* ■ A controller card holds a program in ROM that occupies the address space from $Cn00 to $CnFF and, sometimes, from $C800 to $CFFF as well. *A controller card holds a program in ROM that occupies the address space from $Cn00 to $CnFF and, sometimes, from $C800 to $CFFF.*

and etc. (et cetera) *and so forth; and so on; and the like; etc.*

and everything delete.

and everything (stuff; things) like that *and so forth; and so on; and the like; etc.;* delete.

and ... further (furthermore; in addition; moreover; what is more) *also; and; as well; besides; beyond that (this); even; further; furthermore; moreover; more than that (this); still more; then; too; what is more.* The Smart Word Processor can handle large documents and, what's more, it is suitable for heavy-duty word processing needs. *The Smart Word Processor can handle large documents; what's more, it is suitable for heavy-duty word processing needs.* ■ And furthermore, the company is seeking to cooperate with other companies with expertise for mutual advancement. *The company is also seeking to cooperate with other companies with expertise for mutual advancement.* ■ He was calm enough to overcome stressful crises, had the gift for keeping a strict regimen, and in addition possessed outstanding technological knowledge. *He was calm enough to overcome stressful crises, had the gift for keeping a strict regimen, and possessed outstanding technological knowledge.*

and so *and; so.* Thank you for submitting your pieces to *Critical Inquiry;* however, they are inappropriate for our journal, and so we are returning them to you. *Thank you for submitting your pieces to* Critical Inquiry; *however, they are inappropriate for our journal, so we are returning them to you.*

and so as a result *as a result; consequently; hence; so; then; therefore; thus.*

and so on and so forth *and so forth; and so on; and the like; etc.* We believe our neighbor started the conflict with propaganda, espionage, assassinations, bombings, and so on and so forth. *We believe our neighbor started the conflict with propaganda, espionage, assassinations, bombings, and so on.*

and ... too *and; too.* I have become acutely aware of the epidemic of abuse suffered by children in this country—and elsewhere, too. *I have become acutely aware of the epidemic of abuse suffered by children in this country—and elsewhere.*

and yet *and; yet.*

an estimated *about; around; close to; more or less; near; nearly; or so; roughly; some.* An estimated 73 million people, two-thirds of Bangladesh's population, have been affected by the flooding. *Some 73 million people, two-thirds of Bangladesh's population, have been affected by the flooding.* ■ An estimated 50,000 people lined up yesterday to register to vote. *Nearly 50,000 people lined up yesterday to register to vote.* ■ Currently, there are an estimated 300,000 emperor penguins in Antarctica. *Currently, there are roughly 300,000 emperor penguins in Antarctica.*

(after; for; in; over; within) an extended (lengthy; long; prolonged; protracted) amount of time (length of time; period; period of time; span of time; time; while) *at last; at length; eventually; finally; in due time; in time; over the months (years); over time; ultimately; with time.*

an (a certain; some) extent of *a certain; much; some; somewhat;* delete.

an integral part of *a part of; integral to.* Keeping abreast of these developments is an integral part of successful EFT strategy development. *Keeping abreast of these developments is integral to successful EFT strategy development.* ■ Global economic conditions are now in our favor, and all U.S. companies must make exporting an integral part of their corporate plans. *Global economic conditions are now in our favor, and all U.S. companies must make exporting a part of their corporate plans.*

an (the) open question *a (the) question; debatable; moot; questionable; uncertain; unclear; undecided; unknown; unsettled; unsure.* That remains an open question. *That remains questionable.* ■ Whether he can be forced to resign is still very much an open question. *Whether he can be forced to resign is still very much unclear.* ■ But the open question is whether blacks will turn out in numbers big enough to help him squeak by in a close election or whether their bitterness will turn to apathy. *But the question is whether blacks will turn out in numbers big enough to help him squeak by in a close election or whether their bitterness will turn to apathy.* ■ Whether you can increase cure rate by escalating the dose without running into other organ toxicity is still an open question. *Whether you can increase cure rate by escalating the dose without running into other organ toxicity is still unknown.*

an order of magnitude delete. While the first CD-ROM copy costs an order of magnitude more than a WORM disk, subsequent copies cost much less, making

CD-ROM practical for applications requiring many copies of document disks. *While the first CD-ROM copy costs more than a WORM disk, subsequent copies cost much less, making CD-ROM practical for applications requiring many copies of document disks.*

anterior to *before; earlier than.*

anticipate *expect.* It's much longer than I anticipated it to be. *It's much longer than I expected it to be.*

a (a fair; any) number (of) *a few; almost all; dozens (of); hundreds (of); many; most; nearly all; scores (of); several; sixty-seven (twenty); some;* delete. A number of general conclusions about ATMs emerge from our findings. *Several general conclusions about ATMs emerge from our findings.* ■ A number of companies assembled inexpensive copies of the computers and drove prices so low that IBM was eventually forced to retreat from the market. *Scores of companies assembled inexpensive copies of the computers and drove prices so low that IBM was eventually forced to retreat from the market.* ■ There are any number of ways to respond. *There are many ways to respond.* ■ A number of insurance agents sell mutual funds as part of a financial planning approach. *Hundreds of insurance agents sell mutual funds as part of a financial planning approach.* ■ There are a number of points to remember about this definition. *There are a few points to remember about this definition.* ■ A fair number of stores were either sited incorrectly or in the wrong markets and weren't producing the kind of profits they needed to. *Some stores were either sited incorrectly or in the wrong markets and weren't producing the kind of profits they needed to.* ■ People who have changed or plan to change their behavior to avoid the risk of AIDS were asked which of a number of specific precautions they were following. *People who have changed or plan to change their behavior to avoid the risk of AIDS were asked which of seven specific precautions they were following.* ■ I've been wrestling with this for a number of months. *I've been wrestling with this for months.*

any and all *any; all.* This certificate replaces any and all insurance certificates that may have been issued previously to the Insured under the Group Policy and is subject to the terms of the Group Policy. *This certificate replaces all insurance certificates that may have been issued previously to the Insured under the Group Policy and is subject to the terms of the Group Policy.*

anybody (anyone) and everybody (everyone) *all; anybody (anyone); everybody (everyone).* They told anyone and everyone that you are the one we want to use in our ads. *They told everyone that you are the one we want to use in our ads.*

anything and everything *all; anything; anything at all; everything.* These kids lie about anything and everything. *These kids lie about everything.*

anything (something) in the way of *any; some;* delete. It has yet to accomplish anything in the way of practical benefits. *It has yet to accomplish any practical benefits.*

anyway delete.

anywhere (somewhere) between ... and *between ... and.* Upjohn says Minoxidil's success rate ranges anywhere between 24 and 40 percent. *Upjohn says Minoxidil's success rate ranges between 24 and 40 percent.* ■ Stromberg-Carlson recently parlayed that desire for diversity into a 600,000-line order from Bell South valued at somewhere between $100 million and $200 million. *Stromberg-Carlson recently parlayed that desire for diversity into a 600,000-line order from Bell South valued at between $100 million and $200 million.*

anywhere (somewhere) in the range of ... to *in the range of ... to.*

anywhere near *nearly.* You are not anywhere near as dumb as some of this material will make you feel. *You are not nearly as dumb as some of this material will make you feel.*

a (the) ... one delete. This notion of his is not a new one. *This notion of his is not new.* ■ If the former value is lower than the latter one, the tube may overheat. *If the former value is lower than the latter, the tube may overheat.* ■ It remains to be seen, however, if this view will turn out to be the correct one. *It remains to be seen, however, if this view will turn out to be correct.*

apart from *besides; beyond.* Apart from looking like the original, the counterfeit product often performs as well as the original. *Besides looking like the original, the counterfeit product often performs as well as the original.*

apart from ... also (as well) *apart from; besides; beyond.* Apart from being expensive, the international development process is also very risky. *Besides being expensive, the international development process is very risky.* ■ Apart from using its technological prowess, Philips has also used its political clout within the European Community to help it establish desirable joint-venture arrangements. *Beyond using its technological prowess, Philips has used its political clout within the European Community to help it establish desirable joint-venture arrangements.*

a (a certain; some) part (of) *almost all (of); many (of); most (of); much (of); nearly all (of); (a) part (of); some (of).*

a paucity of *few; little; scant.*

a (a certain; some) percentage (of) *almost all (of); many (of); most (of); much (of); nearly all (of); (a) part (of); ... percent (of); some (of).* I own a percentage of Caesar's Palace. *I own some of Caesar's Palace.*

a (the) ... period (of) delete. The FBI conducted its investigation over a two-year period. *The FBI conducted its investigation over two years.* ■ Nothing should be placed around the eyes for a period of eight months. *Nothing should be placed around the eyes for eight months.* ■ Many police officers experience stress after a period of years on the job. *Many police officers experience stress after years on the job.* ■ An inventor granted a patent has the right to exclude others from making, using, or selling the invention for a period of 17 years. *An inventor granted a patent has the right to exclude others from making, using, or selling the invention for 17 years.*

a (the) ... point *a (the);* delete. Identifying a need is the beginning point of the process. *Identifying a need is the beginning of the process.* ■ The country's payment difficulties are approaching a crisis point for major U.S. banks. *The country's payment difficulties are approaching a crisis for major U.S. banks.*

a (the) point of (that) *a (the);* delete. Is this a point of concern for the rest of the pack? *Is this a concern for the rest of the pack?* ■ This is done to illustrate the point that a forecast can be predicted for any number of periods. *This is done to illustrate that a forecast can be predicted for any number of periods.* ■ The hostages are probably near the point of exhaustion. *The hostages are probably near exhaustion.*

a (a certain; some) portion (of) *almost all (of); many (of); most (of); much (of); (a) part (of); nearly all (of); some (of).* To print only a portion of the document, select the block. *To print only part of the document, select the block.* ■ This list covers a portion of the program's capabilities. *This list covers many of the program's capabilities.* ■ Direct marketers of nonfinancial products, like L.L. Bean, were proving that at least a portion of the public was willing to make purchase decisions without face-to-face contact. *Direct marketers of nonfinancial products, like L.L. Bean, were proving that at least some of the public was willing to make purchase decisions without face-to-face contact.*

appear on (upon) the scene *appear.*

appellation *name; title.*

appertain (appertaining) to *pertain to; relate to.* Moneys therefor having been deposited with the Trustee from and after June 12, 1989, interest thereon shall cease to accrue and coupons appertaining to said bonds payable after that date will be void. *Moneys therefor having been deposited with the Trustee from and after June 12, 1989, interest thereon shall cease to accrue and coupons pertaining to said bonds payable after that date will be void.*

appoint as *appoint.*

appreciate *admire; applaud; approve of; enjoy; (be) grateful (for); like; prize; (be) thankful (for); thank you (for); value; welcome.* We appreciate it. *We are grate-*

ful. ■ I appreciate your coming. *I thank you for coming.* ■ Your concern is very much appreciated. *Your concern is very much welcomed.*

appreciate in value *appreciate.* Due to the overall rise of the stock market, many individuals have securities which have appreciated considerably in value. *Due to the overall rise of the stock market, many individuals have securities which have appreciated considerably.*

appreciation *gratefulness; gratitude; thankfulness; thanks.* I would like to express my appreciation for Meals on Wheels. *I would like to express my thanks for Meals on Wheels.*

apprehend *arrest; capture; catch; seize.* Daniel Mahoney, 30, was apprehended near Los Lunas shortly before 1:00 a.m. *Daniel Mahoney, 30, was captured near Los Lunas shortly before 1:00 a.m.* ■ Investigators acknowledge that chances of apprehending a suspect are strongest at the start of an investigation. *Investigators acknowledge that chances of arresting a suspect are strongest at the start of an investigation.*

approbation *approval; praise.*

(for) approximately *about; around; close to; more or less; near; nearly; or so; roughly; some.* It will last for approximately two hours. *It will last about two hours.* ■ Approximately the first 400 characters in the document are automatically displayed. *The first 400 or so characters in the document are automatically displayed.* ■ It said the people in charge of burying the bodies have counted approximately 5,000. *It said the people in charge of burying the bodies have counted roughly 5,000.*

a (the) preponderance (of) *almost all (of); (nine) in (ten) (of); many (of); more (of); most (of); nearly all (of); (43) of (48) (of); ... percent (of);* delete. The preponderance of short selling is done by market professionals engaged in the day-to-day provision of liquidity to the market. *Almost all short selling is done by market professionals engaged in the day-to-day provision of liquidity to the market.* ■ The preponderance of evidence from the national surveys indicates that 20 percent or fewer women in target groups for breast cancer screening have ever had a mammogram. *Most evidence from the national surveys indicates that 20 percent or fewer women in target groups for breast cancer screening have ever had a mammogram.*

a (a certain; some) proportion (of) *almost all (of); many (of); most (of); much (of); nearly all (of); (a) part (of); some (of).*

a (a certain; some) quantity (of) *almost all (of); many (of); most (of); much (of); nearly all (of); (a) part (of); some (of).*

a range of *assorted; countless; different; diverse; extensive; many; numerous; scores of; sundry; varied; various; varying;* delete. It has been tested in a range of working situations in large manufacturing plants, and has been found useful in mending human relations and making them a strong and healthy resource of management. *It has been tested in diverse working situations in large manufacturing plants, and has been found useful in mending human relations and making them a strong and healthy resource of management.*

a ... ratio (of) delete. When you add in those with subsyndromal SAD, the figure is closer to one in four, with women outnumbering men by a ratio of three or four to one. *When you add in those with subsyndromal SAD, the figure is closer to one in four, with women outnumbering men by three or four to one.* ■ A nationwide poll by a major newspaper found that penny lovers outnumbered penny pitchers by almost a two-to-one ratio. *A nationwide poll by a major newspaper found that penny lovers outnumbered penny pitchers by almost two to one.*

(a; the) area (locale; locality; location; place; point; position; region; site; spot) *where; wherever.*

(after; for; in; over; within) a reasonable amount of time (length of time; period; period of time; span of time; time; while) *by next week (tomorrow); fast; in (within) a day (year); promptly; quickly; rapidly; shortly; soon; speedily; swiftly;* delete. If the accident is in Massachusetts, or if it is outside Massachusetts and the injured person does not sue for damages, we will pay benefits within a reasonable time—usually 30 days. *If the accident is in Massachusetts, or if it is outside Massachusetts and the injured person does not sue for damages, we will pay benefits within usually 30 days.* ■ Unlike corporate sales, which can be tied up in a relatively reasonable period of time, government sales tend to be drawn out. *Unlike corporate sales, which can be tied up relatively quickly, government sales tend to be drawn out.* ■ Higher authority should intervene if a professional team cannot set a mediocre school right in a reasonable length of time. *Higher authority should intervene if a professional team cannot set a mediocre school right within a year.*

(a; the) area (locale; locality; location; place; point; position; region; site; spot) where *where; wherever.* The COMSPEC line will show the place where COMMAND.COM is expected. *The COMSPEC line will show where COMMAND.COM is expected.* ■ This is the position where your selection is entered. *This is where your selection is entered.* ■ He said such a "second wave" of transmission is possible in New York and Los Angeles and places where people have been infected with the virus for seven or eight years. *He said such a "second wave" of transmission is possible in New York and Los Angeles and wherever people have been infected with the virus for seven or eight years.*

argumentation *argument; debate; dispute.* Some members may take unyielding positions, leading to unproductive argumentation. *Some members may take* *unyielding positions, leading to unproductive arguments.*

arithmetical *arithmetic.*

around about *about; around.* It was around about then that he left for East Africa. *It was around then that he left for East Africa.*

arrive at (an; the) accord *agree; compromise; concur; decide; resolve; settle.* AT&T and unions representing about 160,000 employees arrived at an accord on a new three-year national contract. *AT&T and unions representing about 160,000 employees agreed on a new three-year national contract.*

arrive at (an; the) agreement *agree; compromise; concur; decide; resolve; settle.*

arrive at (a; the) compromise *agree; compromise; concur; decide; resolve; settle.*

arrive at (a; the) conclusion *conclude; decide; deduce; determine; infer; judge; reason; resolve; settle.* I think they have arrived at the conclusion that he is now a neutralized force. *I think they have concluded that he is now a neutralized force.* ■ He concedes that in terms of sheer numbers, Stalinism may well have been more murderous than Nazism—though he arrives at this conclusion by ruling out of consideration the millions of deaths brought about by the wars the Nazis waged. *He concedes that in terms of sheer numbers, Stalinism may well have been more murderous than Nazism—though he deduces this by ruling out of consideration the millions of deaths brought about by the wars the Nazis waged.*

arrive at (a; the) decision (on; upon) *conclude; decide; deduce; determine; infer; judge; reason; resolve; settle.*

arrive at (a; the) determination (on; upon) *conclude; decide; deduce; determine; infer; judge; reason; resolve; settle.*

arrive at (an; the) estimate (estimation) (of) *approximate; assess; estimate; evaluate; rate.* Since information from subsequent steps in an assessment is needed to arrive at an estimate of what the firm's actual marketing effort will be, the assessment from this point on is reiterative. *Since information from subsequent steps in an assessment is needed to estimate what the firm's actual marketing effort will be, the assessment from this point on is reiterative.*

arrive at (an; the) opinion *conclude; decide; deduce; determine; infer; judge; reason; resolve; settle.*

arrive at (a; the) resolution *agree; conclude; decide; resolve; settle.*

arrive at (a; the) settlement *agree; conclude; decide; resolve; settle.*

arrive at (an; the) understanding *agree; compromise; concur; decide; resolve; settle.*

as a consequence *consequently; hence; so; then; therefore; thus.* As a consequence, there are a lot of charlatans, zealots, and incompetents offering their services. *Thus, there are a lot of charlatans, zealots, and incompetents offering their services.* ■ As a consequence, we do not see obvious opportunities for start-up companies or participants from outside the semiconductor industry. *We therefore do not see obvious opportunities for start-up companies or participants from outside the semiconductor industry.* ■ As a consequence, relative costs of U.S. wheat output are low, and the United States enjoys a comparative advantage in the output of this product. *Consequently, relative costs of U.S. wheat output are low, and the United States enjoys a comparative advantage in the output of this product.*

as a consequence of *after; because of; by; due to; following; for; from; in; out of; owing to; through; with.* This was primarily the result of rationalization measures and high workloads in the Business Area's factories as a consequence of increased activity in a number of markets. *This was primarily the result of rationalization measures and high workloads in the Business Area's factories owing to increased activity in a number of markets.* ■ As a consequence of the 43 million babies born in the years immediately following World War II, a middle-aged bulge is forming and eventually the 35- to-45-year-old age group will increase by 80 percent. *Because of the 43 million babies born in the years immediately following World War II, a middle-aged bulge is forming and eventually the 35-to-45-year-old age group will increase by 80 percent.*

as a consequence of the fact that *because; considering; for; in that; since.*

as against *against; to.* Total investments in property, plant, and equipment amounted to SEK 1,592 m. in 1987, as against SEK 1,643 m. in the preceding year. *Total investments in property, plant, and equipment amounted to SEK 1,592 m. in 1987, against SEK 1,643 m. in the preceding year.*

as a general rule *almost all; as a rule; chiefly; commonly; customarily; generally; greatly; in general; largely; mainly; most; mostly; most often; much; nearly all; normally; overall; typically; usually.* As a general rule, you've gotten your first news of breaking events from television or radio. *As a rule, you've gotten your first news of breaking events from television or radio.* ■ As a general rule, interest payments are made every six months. *Typically, interest payments are made every six months.* ■ As a general rule, new skills develop as a by-product of dealing with new situations or handling familiar ones more effectively. *Most new skills develop as a by-product of dealing with new situations or handling familiar ones more effectively.*

as a matter of course *commonly; customarily; habitually; naturally; normally; ordinarily; regularly; routinely; typically; usually.* If jobs are organized in a proper manner, they reason, the result will be the most efficient job structure, and the most favorable job attitudes will follow as a matter of course. *If jobs are organized in a proper manner, they reason, the result will be the most efficient job structure, and the most favorable job attitudes will follow naturally.* ▪ Most veterinarians do it as a matter of course because it is a money-making procedure. *Most veterinarians do it routinely because it is a money-making procedure.*

as a matter of fact *actually; indeed; in fact; in faith; in reality; in truth; really; truly; delete.* As a matter of fact, there are some rumors of discontent. *In fact, there are some rumors of discontent.*

as a matter of fact *also; and; as well; besides; beyond that (this); even; further; furthermore; moreover; more than that (this); still more; then; too; what is more.*

as a means for (of; to) (-ing) *for (-ing); so as to; to.* I have found the spelling checker extremely useful as a means for proofreading text. *I have found the spelling checker extremely useful for proofreading text.* ▪ The Trust may purchase or sell options on debt securities as a means of achieving additional return or hedging the Trust's portfolio securities. *The Trust may purchase or sell options on debt securities to achieve additional return or hedge the Trust's portfolio securities.* ▪ It is important to recognize the value of structures that draw their strength from the family, the community, and informal associations as a means to create more humane and effective social policy. *It is important to recognize the value of structures that draw their strength from the family, the community, and informal associations so as to create more humane and effective social policy.*

as and when *as; when.* At the same time, they have substantial outflows, ongoing expenses which cannot be shifted but must be paid as and when they become due. *At the same time, they have substantial outflows, ongoing expenses which cannot be shifted but must be paid as they become due.*

as an example *for example; for instance.*

as ... apply to *about; as for; as to; concerning; for; in; of; on; over; regarding; respecting; to; toward; with; delete.* I've always been intrigued by the concept of marketing as it applies to health care. *I've always been intrigued by the concept of health-care marketing.*

as a result *consequently; hence; so; then; therefore; thus.* As a result, file operations occur much more quickly than if unbuffered disk I/O techniques were used. *Hence file operations occur much more quickly than if unbuffered disk I/O techniques were used.* ▪ The IDA was working to make jobs available to the graduates of these schools, and as a result, the educational climate in Ireland has changed dramatically. *The IDA was working to make jobs available to the graduates of these schools, and thus, the educational climate in Ireland has changed dramatically.*

as a result of *after; because of; by; due to; following; for; from; in; out of; owing to; through; with.* Protection and benefits that employees once looked to unions to negotiate for them are now theirs as a result of federal and state legislation. *Protection and benefits that employees once looked to unions to negotiate for them are now theirs through federal and state legislation.* ▪ Much pain and resentment was rekindled as a result of recent political maneuverings between the Turkish and U.S. governments. *Much pain and resentment was rekindled following recent political maneuverings between the Turkish and U.S. governments.* ▪ An objective of a school should be to treat students as clients rather than wards, who as a result of a combination of law and custom are under our supervision. *An objective of a school should be to treat students as clients rather than wards, who owing to a combination of law and custom are under our supervision.* ▪ More people die as a result of drinking alcohol than as a result of smoking marijuana. *More people die from drinking alcohol than from smoking marijuana.* ▪ According to Mr. Chaudhuri, the Bengali Hindu gentry lost their rightful role as the political and cultural leaders of modern India, partly as a result of their own moral limitations, but mostly because of a combination of British racism and the rise of democratic politics. *According to Mr. Chaudhuri, the Bengali Hindu gentry lost their rightful role as the political and cultural leaders of modern India, partly because of their own moral limitations, but mostly because of a combination of British racism and the rise of democratic politics.*

as a result of the fact that *because; considering; for; in that; since.* This is clearly an area of growing importance to BOCs, particularly as a result of the fact that a recent court decision allows them to enter in certain segments of enhanced services. *This is clearly an area of growing importance to BOCs, particularly because a recent court decision allows them to enter in certain segments of enhanced services.*

as a rule *almost all; chiefly; commonly; generally; greatly; in general; largely; mainly; most; mostly; most often; much; nearly all; normally; overall; typically.* As a rule, I wouldn't dream of doing something like this. *Normally, I wouldn't dream of doing something like this.*

as a way for (of; to) (-ing) *for (-ing); so as to; to.* More and more professionals are using dating services as a way of meeting the perfect mate. *More and more professionals are using dating services to meet the perfect mate.*

as a whole *complete; entire; whole;* delete. It's an embarrassment to the administration as a whole. *It's an embarrassment to the administration.* ▪ He was speaking for the democratic party as a whole. *He was speaking for the entire democratic party.* ▪ The comments are wrong, and they are an affront to the black community as a whole. *The comments are wrong, and they are an affront to the whole black community.*

ascend up *ascend.*

as compared to (with) *against; alongside; beside; compared to (with); -(i)er than; less; less than; more; more than; next to; over; than; to; versus; vis-à-vis.* The governments of developing countries give low priority to these skills as compared to technological skills and knowledge. *The governments of developing countries give lower priority to these skills than to technological skills and knowledge.* ■ The Japanese can design and build a car in about 3 1/2 years as compared to U.S. auto makers' average of 5 years. *The Japanese can design and build a car in about 3 1/2 years against U.S. auto makers' average of 5 years.* ■ Data communications is not very familiar ground to the operating companies as compared to their expertise in voice. *Data communications is not very familiar ground to the operating companies compared to their expertise in voice.* ■ Net income for the third quarter of 1988 was $206,000, or 7 cents per share, as compared to income of $917,000, or 28 cents per share, in 1987. *Net income for the third quarter of 1988 was $206,000, or 7 cents per share, versus income of $917,000, or 28 cents per share, in 1987.*

as compared to (with) ... relatively *compared to (with).* As compared to Western Europeans and the Japanese, Americans save a relatively small proportion of their disposable income. *Compared to Western Europeans and the Japanese, Americans save a small proportion of their disposable income.*

as concerns *about; as for; as to; concerning; for; in; of; on; over; regarding; respecting; to; toward; with.*

as contrasted to (with) *against; alongside; beside; compared to (with); -(i)er than; less; less than; more; more than; next to; over; than; to; unlike; versus; vis-à-vis.* Only 27 percent and 15 percent, respectively, believe themselves to be better qualified to teach the life sciences and the physical or earth sciences, as contrasted to 82 percent who consider themselves well qualified to teach reading. *Only 27 percent and 15 percent, respectively, believe themselves to be better qualified to teach the life sciences and the physical or earth sciences, versus 82 percent who consider themselves well qualified to teach reading.* ■ Epidemiologists find that people who eat a lot of fish have much lower rates of both cholesterol-caused heart disease and cholesterol gallstones as contrasted to people who don't. *Epidemiologists find that people who eat a lot of fish have much lower rates of both cholesterol-caused heart disease and cholesterol gallstones than people who don't.*

a (the) score of *delete.* Sweden is on top by a score of 6 to 1. *Sweden is on top by 6 to 1.* ■ Cleveland defeated Baltimore today by a score of 11 to 2. *Cleveland defeated Baltimore today by 11 to 2.*

ascribable to *because of; caused by; due to; owing to; resulting from.*

as (the) days (decades; months; weeks; years) go on *at length; eventually; in time; later; one day; over the months (years); over time; someday; sometime; ultimately; with time; yet;* delete. As the years go on, customers will look to NYNEX and others to give them more than just the transmission of information—they'll also need the software and the systems integration to run their businesses and homes more efficiently. *Over time, customers will look to NYNEX and others to give them more than just the transmission of information—they'll also need the software and the systems integration to run their businesses and homes more efficiently.*

a second time *again; once more.*

as (so) far as ... (goes; is concerned) *about; as for; as to; concerning; for; in; of; on; over; regarding; respecting; to; toward; with;* delete. As far as bonuses go, those are based on year-end results. *As for bonuses, those are based on year-end results.* ▪ As far as I'm concerned, the difference is finding people who know what they're doing. *To me, the difference is finding people who know what they're doing.* ▪ As far as most other possible complications were concerned, one group did about as well as the other. *As to most other possible complications, one group did about as well as the other.* ▪ The effect of lead is particularly traumatic as far as young children are concerned. *The effect of lead is particularly traumatic on young children.* ▪ In fact, as far as the "secrets of entrepreneurial success" go, it's impossible to recognize that a little bit of luck helps and a lot of luck is even better. *In fact, concerning the "secrets of entrepreneurial success," it's impossible to recognize that a little bit of luck helps and a lot of luck is even better.* ▪ The general view seems to be that infectious agents transmitted by rodents are not of particular relevance as far as public health goes. *The general view seems to be that infectious agents transmitted by rodents are not of particular relevance to public health.*

as follows delete. The quote is as follows: "I never met a man who had better motives for all the trouble he's causing." *The quote is "I never met a man who had better motives for all the trouble he's causing."*

as ... for example (for instance) *as; for example (for instance); like; such as.* No such close match is necessary if the intent of the assessment is to monitor the general state of student knowledge and competence in science, as for example in past assessments conducted by NAEP. *No such close match is necessary if the intent of the assessment is to monitor the general state of student knowledge and competence in science, as in past assessments conducted by NAEP.*

as for (in; with) the case of *as for (in; with); like.* Even when countries adopt state religions, as in the cases of the United Kingdom, Spain, and Italy, the religious context of the country is not necessarily monolithic. *Even when countries adopt* *state religions, as in the United Kingdom, Spain, and Italy, the religious context of the country is not necessarily monolithic.*

as how *that.*

aside from *besides; beyond.* Aside from the lack of restraints, there are other differences a foreign investor must get used to. *Besides the lack of restraints, there are other differences a foreign investor must get used to.* ■ Part of Hercules' motive in making the documentary, aside from his love of the game, is to increase public awareness of the historical importance of these baseball parks. *Part of Hercules' motive in making the documentary, beyond his love of the game, is to increase public awareness of the historical importance of these baseball parks.*

aside from ... also (as well) *aside from; besides; beyond.*

as, if, and when *if; when.* The Company will be deemed to have purchased tendered Shares as, if, and when it gives oral and written notice to the Depositary of its acceptance for payment of such Shares. *The Company will be deemed to have purchased tendered Shares when it gives oral and written notice to the Depositary of its acceptance for payment of such Shares.*

a single one *a single; one.* Not a single one of the dire accusations or predictions made in that article has come true. *Not one of the dire accusations or predictions made in that article has come true.*

a single solitary (one) *a single; one.*

(even) as I (we) speak *(just; right) now;* delete. As we speak, New York state is starting a drug education program. *New York state is now starting a drug education program.*

as is the case *as; like.* As is the case with all of our new words, they sound terribly impressive at cocktail parties. *Like all of our new words, they sound terribly impressive at cocktail parties.* ■ As was the case in the previous auction, the government lacked the authority to issue any more long bonds. *As in the previous auction, the government lacked the authority to issue any more long bonds.* ■ As has been the case so often before, the candidates are again trivializing the issues. *As so often before, the candidates are again trivializing the issues.*

as it turned out *by chance; luckily; unluckily.*

ask (a; the) question *ask.* We need to ask ourselves the question if animals are necessary for medical training. *We need to ask ourselves if animals are necessary for medical training.*

as long as (so long as) (that) *if.* This program, as well as others like it, will make a difference as long as we have strong public support for changing the plight of these children. *This program, as well as others like it, will make a difference if we have strong public support for changing the plight of these children.*

as luck would have it *by chance; luckily; unluckily.*

as many (much) as *up to.* There are nearly 300 individual fund managers, ranging from those with a single fund to the very large mutual fund families that offer as many as 100 different funds. *There are nearly 300 individual fund managers, ranging from those with a single fund to the very large mutual fund families that offer up to 100 different funds.*

as of *on;* delete. The plant will shut down as of November 1. *The plant will shut down November 1.*

as often as not *commonly; customarily; generally; normally; often; ordinarily; typically; usually.*

as opposed to *against; alongside; beside; compared to (with); -(i)er than; less; less than; more; more than; next to; over; than; to; versus; vis-à-vis.* Americans were found to be eight times more likely to own a handgun than Canadians—24 percent as opposed to 3 percent. *Americans were found to be eight times more likely to own a handgun than Canadians—24 percent compared to 3 percent.* ▪ Thanks to the recent strength of the dollar, the U.S. markets remain attractive, as opposed to their foreign counterparts. *Thanks to the recent strength of the dollar, the U.S. markets remain more attractive than their foreign counterparts.* ▪ The study found that Boston banks made 24 percent fewer loans in minority neighborhoods as opposed to in nearby white communities. *The study found that Boston banks made 24 percent fewer loans in minority neighborhoods than in nearby white communities.*

as opposed to *instead of; not; rather than; whereas.* You're able to let go of someone you wanted as opposed to someone you needed. *You're able to let go of someone you wanted, not someone you needed.* ▪ All the RamFont cards support 12 fonts, each with 256 characters, as opposed to EGA, which supports only 2 fonts with 256 characters. *All the RamFont cards support 12 fonts, each with 256 characters, whereas EGA supports only 2 fonts with 256 characters.* ▪ Citibank and the customer would be ahead if the customer were served by private banking experts as opposed to branch generalists. *Citibank and the customer would be ahead if the customer were served by private banking experts instead of branch generalists.* ▪ Why do customers choose one brand as opposed to another? *Why do customers choose one brand rather than another?*

a spectrum of *assorted; countless; different; diverse; extensive; many; numerous; scores of; sundry; varied; various; varying;* delete.

as regards *about; as for; as to; concerning; for; in; of; on; over; regarding; respecting; to; toward; with.* He promises to be less tightfisted in the future as regards training. *He promises to be less tightfisted in the future with training.* ■ At the moment, no conclusion has been reached as regards assignment of responsibility. *At the moment, no conclusion has been reached on assignment of responsibility.*

assemble together *assemble.*

assistance *aid; help; succor.*

assist in -ing *help.* This view assists you in visualizing the problem. *This view helps you visualize the problem.* ■ Brainstorming is a group effort at generating ideas and alternatives that can assist a manager in making decisions or solving problems. *Brainstorming is a group effort at generating ideas and alternatives that can help a manager make decisions or solve problems.*

associated with *for; in; linked to; of; -'s; with.* The greater the required accuracy, the greater the cost associated with generating a plan. *The greater the required accuracy, the greater the cost of generating a plan.* ■ There are also many strengths associated with time series analysis. *There are also many strengths in time series analysis.* ■ Unfortunately, many of us slip into the vocabulary associated with our jobs when we are communicating with others who don't know the jargon. *Unfortunately, many of us slip into the vocabulary of our jobs when we are communicating with others who don't know the jargon.* ■ They argue that the technology associated with the program makes it an aircraft whose time has come. *They argue that the program's technology makes it an aircraft whose time has come.*

associated with *belongs to; employed by; works for.*

association *connection; link; relation; tie.* The CDC study concluded there was no association between use of the pill and breast cancer. *The CDC study concluded there was no link between use of the pill and breast cancer.*

as soon as *once; when.* I'll call you as soon as I can. *I'll call you when I can.* ■ If the file contains more text than you want, you can delete unwanted sections as soon as they have been read into the file you are working on. *If the file contains more text than you want, you can delete unwanted sections once they have been read into the file you are working on.*

(most) assuredly *certainly; surely; delete.* That decision may turn out to have been a case of penny-wise and pound-foolish when the time comes—as it most assuredly will—for legislators to vote for new taxes. *That decision may turn out to have been a case of penny-wise and pound-foolish when the time comes—as it surely will—for legislators to vote for new taxes.*

(most; very) assuredly *yes.*

assure (ensure; insure) ... guarantee *ensure; guarantee.* There must be a way to ensure that their privacy is guaranteed. *There must be a way to ensure their privacy.*

a (the) stage of delete. Other products take a long time to gain acceptance and may never reach a stage of widespread adoption. *Other products take a long time to gain acceptance and may never reach widespread adoption.*

as the basis for (-ing) *for (-ing); so as to; to.* Data is any information used as the basis for discussing or deciding something. *Data is any information used for discussing or deciding something.* ■ The claims are the most significant part of the patent since they will be used as the basis for ascertaining the novelty and patentability of an invention. *The claims are the most significant part of the patent since they will be used to ascertain the novelty and patentability of an invention.*

as the case (situation) may be delete. When both are used on the same drawing, the parts list is placed directly above and in contact with the title block or the title strip, as the case may be. *When both are used on the same drawing, the parts list is placed directly above and in contact with the title block or the title strip.*

as the need arises (develops) *as needed.* Corrections and adjustments can be made as the need arises. *Corrections and adjustments can be made as needed.* ■ Teaching on other instruments will be offered as the need arises. *Teaching on other instruments will be offered as needed.*

as the saying goes delete.

as time goes on *at length; in due time; in time; later; one day; over time; someday; sometime; ultimately; with time; yet;* delete. As time goes on, maintenance revenues will rise for the average distributor. *Maintenance revenues will yet rise for the average distributor.* ■ Even frozen at 1986 levels, they will play an increasingly large role in ozone loss as time goes on. *Even frozen at 1986 levels, they will play an increasingly large role in ozone loss over time.* ■ As time went on, he got worse. *Ultimately, he got worse.*

as time progresses (forward; on; onward) *at length; eventually; in due time; in time; later; one day; over the months (years); over time; someday; sometime; ultimately; with time; yet;* delete. As time progressed, she decided to divorce him. *At length, she decided to divorce him.* ■ There may have been a time when he was a man of good deeds, but as time progressed he began to use people to obtain power. *There may have been a time when he was a man of good deeds, but over time he began to use people to obtain power.*

as to *about; for; in; of; on; with;* delete. I'm curious as to why you would choose to be in that situation. *I'm curious why you would choose to be in that situation.* ▪ People have different ideas as to what is sexually acceptable to them. *People have different ideas on what is sexually acceptable to them.* ▪ Once you know your skills, aptitudes, interests, and motivations, you will have a good idea as to what you have going for you and what you want. *Once you know your skills, aptitudes, interests, and motivations, you will have a good idea of what you have going for you and what you want.*

as to whether *whether.* Emotional responses do alter the blood supply to the colon mucosa, but it is unclear as to whether stress is the cause or the effect of the disease process. *Emotional responses do alter the blood supply to the colon mucosa, but it is unclear whether stress is the cause or the effect of the disease process.* ▪ It's too early to speculate as to whether the two stabbings are connected. *It's too early to speculate whether the two stabbings are connected.*

as well as *and.* Banks have added to their capital by retaining a higher share of current earnings, in some cases selling their undervalued real estate as well as business assets. *Banks have added to their capital by retaining a higher share of current earnings, in some cases selling their undervalued real estate and business assets.* ▪ To nurture this customer base as well as to attract new customers, the direct sellers have developed sophisticated telecommunications centers and data processing systems. *To nurture this customer base and attract new customers, the direct sellers have developed sophisticated telecommunications centers and data processing systems.*

as (of) yet *yet.* I haven't mastered the sport as of yet. *I haven't mastered the sport yet.* ▪ Although all questions are not answered as yet, a few basic points are clear. *Although all questions are not yet answered, a few basic points are clear.*

at about (around) *about (around).* We got there at about 7:00. *We got there about 7:00.*

at a certain (any; one; some) point in my history (point in my life; point in the history of my life; point in time) *at one time; ever; once; one day; someday; sometime;* delete. Did you attempt suicide at one point in your life? *Did you ever attempt suicide?* ▪ At one point in the history of my life, I was a high school English teacher. *I was once a high school English teacher.* ▪ I would like a new camera at some point in time. *I would like a new camera one day.*

at a (some) future (later; subsequent) date (time) *at length; eventually; in due time; in time; later; one day; over the months (years); over time; someday; sometime; ultimately; with time; yet.* If you are willing to reconsider your request to cancel your account, either now or at a later date, please let me know. *If you are willing to reconsider your request to cancel your account, either now or later, please let me know.* ▪ They say that if a site isn't going to be excavated professionally, then don't touch it; don't be what might be viewed at some future time as a tomb robber. *They say that if a site isn't going to be excavated professionally, then don't touch it; don't be what might be viewed one day as a tomb robber.*

at all delete. You're unwilling to make any sort of compromise at all. *You're unwilling to make any sort of compromise.* ■ The parent company has rarely issued bonds and issues no CDs at all. *The parent company has rarely issued bonds and issues no CDs.*

at all times *always; ceaselessly; constantly; endlessly; everyday; forever.* The point is that the process must be managed from the top at all times. *The point is that the process must be managed always from the top.* ■ He is at all times a gentleman. *He is always a gentleman.*

at a (the) juncture (juncture in time; moment; moment in time; period; period in time; point; point in time; stage; stage in time; time) *when.* At the point in time this book was published, several other titles were also available. *When this book was published, several other titles were also available.* ■ At the time the DeBraak was found, the Corps believed it was not historically significant enough to merit an archeologist. *When the DeBraak was found, the Corps believed it was not historically significant enough to merit an archeologist.*

at a (the) juncture (juncture in time; moment; moment in time; period; period in time; point; point in time; stage; stage in time; time) when *when.* At the point when the infected person develops clinical symptoms of AIDS, he or she is more likely to infect a sexual partner than at other periods. *When the infected person develops clinical symptoms of AIDS, he or she is more likely to infect a sexual partner than at other periods.* ■ On a computer, the design is created on the screen, and the scale can be decided, and changed, at the time when the final drawing is printed out on a printer or plotter. *On a computer, the design is created on the screen, and the scale can be decided, and changed, when the final drawing is printed out on a printer or plotter.*

at an (some) earlier (former; past; previous) date (time) *before; earlier; formerly; once.*

at an end *complete; done; ended; finished; over; past.* Barring the unexpected, the 25-year search for a new arena is at an end. *Barring the unexpected, the 25-year search for a new arena is over.*

at any date (hour; time) *any time.*

at any minute (moment) *directly; momentarily; momently; presently; soon.*

at any rate *anyhow; even so; still; yet.*

at (from; in; on; to) (a; the) area (locale; locality; location; place; point; position; region; site; spot) *where; wherever.* The program is temporarily interrupted, and can be restarted any time at the exact place it left off. *The program is temporarily interrupted, and can be restarted any time exactly where it left off.*

at (from; in; on; to) (any; each; every; some) area (locale; locality; location; place; point; position; region; site; spot) *anyplace; anywhere; ever; everyplace; everywhere; one day; someday; someplace; sometime; somewhere; where; wherever.* You can insert this information at any point in your document by moving the cursor to the desired spot and playing back the recorded keystrokes. *You can insert this information anywhere in your document by moving the cursor to the desired spot and playing back the recorded keystrokes.* ■ Would you encourage your child to skate competitively at some point? *Would you encourage your child to skate competitively someday?* ■ If at any point I felt I was an embarrassment to the president, I would resign. *If I ever felt I was an embarrassment to the president, I would resign.* ■ Experts estimate 93 percent of these women will become pregnant at some point in their working lives. *Experts estimate 93 percent of these women will become pregnant sometime in their working lives.*

at (from; in; on; to) (a; the) area (locale; locality; location; place; point; position; region; site; spot) where *where; wherever.* The voodoo doctor told me to put them in a location where no one would ever find them. *The voodoo doctor told me to put them where no one would ever find them.* ■ You enter the definition code at the place where you want the table of contents to appear. *You enter the definition code where you want the table of contents to appear.*

at (from; in; on; to) (any; each; every; some) area (locale; locality; location; place; point; position; region; site; spot) where *anyplace; anywhere; ever; everyplace; everywhere; one day; someday; someplace; sometime; somewhere; where; wherever.* To do this, you enter C codes at each point where you want to enter data. *To do this, you enter C codes wherever you want to enter data.* ■ At every place where food was available, people went hungry for lack of dry fuel. *Wherever food was available, people went hungry for lack of dry fuel.*

at (for) (a; the) cost (price; sum) of *at (for).* The Tower was built from 1970 to 1974 at a cost of more than $150 million. *The Tower was built from 1970 to 1974 for more than $150 million.*

at every turn *always; ceaselessly; consistently; constantly; endlessly; eternally; everyday; forever; unfailingly.*

at frequent (periodic; regular) intervals (periods) *frequently; periodically; regularly.* The longer the range in plans, the greater the need to keep them flexible and to review them at frequent intervals. *The longer the range in plans, the* *greater the need to keep them flexible and to review them frequently.* ■ The piece quite plainly belongs to that distinct genre written by and for men with more wits and time than is good for their character and through the reading of which one is supposed to remark, daintily and at regular intervals, "How disgusting, but how sensitive," and keep right on. *The piece quite plainly belongs to that distinct genre written by and for men with more wits and time than is good for their character and through the reading of which one is supposed to remark, daintily and regularly, "How disgusting, but how sensitive," and keep right on.* ■ At periodic intervals, the entries made in the journals are posted to the general ledger. *Periodically, the entries made in the journals are posted to the general ledger.*

at (a; the) ... level *-(al)ly;* delete. Prices at the wholesale level will go up 6 cents per gallon. *Wholesale prices will go up 6 cents per gallon.* ■ The solution lies not with the city but at the state level. *The solution lies not with the city but the state.* ■ If resources are wasted on obtaining information for less valuable situations, they will not be available at adequate levels for more difficult but more valuable studies. *If resources are wasted on obtaining information for less valuable situations, they will not be adequately available for more difficult but more valuable studies.* ■ On average, U.S. students do not master math basics at a level sufficient to sustain our present technologically based society. *On average, U.S. students do not master math basics sufficiently to sustain our present technologically based society.*

at long last *at last; finally.*

at (for) no charge (cost) *free.* It will be available at no charge through Avatar dealers nationwide. *It will be available free through Avatar dealers nationwide.*

at no time *never.* At no time was it this union's position to oppose the Emerson College proposal or deprive fellow workers of jobs made available by this project. *Never was it this union's position to oppose the Emerson College proposal or deprive fellow workers of jobs made available by this project.*

at one time (in the past) *once.*

atop of *atop.*

a (the) total ... (of) delete. From a total of $135 billion at the beginning of 1980, mutual fund assets surged to a total of $716 billion by the end of 1986. *From $135 billion at the beginning of 1980, mutual fund assets surged to $716 billion by the end of 1986.* ■ The United States sent a total of 3.4 million men and women to serve in Southeast Asia during the period. *The United States sent 3.4 million men and women to serve in Southeast Asia during the period.* ■ The status line displays the total number of words that were checked. *The status line displays the number of words that were checked.*

at (a; the) ... pace (of) *at; by; -(al)ly;* delete. We've had fairly stable interest rates and an economy that continues to grow at a moderate pace. *We've had fairly stable interest rates and an economy that continues to grow moderately.*

at (the) present *(just; right) now; nowadays; these days; today; (just) yet;* delete. At present, nothing indicates that South Africa is prepared to completely dismantle apartheid. *Nothing yet indicates that South Africa is prepared to completely dismantle apartheid.* ■ Knowledge-based inference engines have a small market at present. *Knowledge-based inference engines have a small market today.* ■ American businesses are part of a global economy regardless of how large or small they are at present and regardless of where they are located. *American businesses are part of a global economy regardless of how large or small they now are and regardless of where they are located.*

at (a; the) ... rate (of) *at; by; -(al)ly;* delete. Crime on college campuses is growing at a geometric rate. *Crime on college campuses is growing geometrically.* ■ The main danger with carbon monoxide is that it attaches to hemoglobin cells at a rate 210 times faster than oxygen—and the hemoglobin transports the pollutant to the rest of the body, depriving the brain and other organs of oxygen. *The main danger with carbon monoxide is that it attaches to hemoglobin cells 210 times faster than oxygen—and the hemoglobin transports the pollutant to the rest of the body, depriving the brain and other organs of oxygen.* ■ Despite its proximity to the United States, Mexico remains a developing nation burdened by massive external debt and an economy that has shrunk at a rate of 4 percent a year since 1982. *Despite its proximity to the United States, Mexico remains a developing nation burdened by massive external debt and an economy that has shrunk by 4 percent a year since 1982.*

at some point (time) along the line (the way) *at some point; at some time.*

at specific (specified; timed) intervals (periods) *periodically; regularly.*

at (a; the) ... speed (of) *at; by; -(al)ly;* delete. Loosened by rain or melting snow, ordinary soil on a steep hillside can suddenly turn into a lethal wave sweeping downward at speeds of more than 30 miles per hour. *Loosened by rain or melting snow, ordinary soil on a steep hillside can suddenly turn into a lethal wave sweeping downward at more than 30 miles per hour.*

attach together *attach.*

attack by assailants *assail; assault; attack.* They were departing a local discothèque and entering their vehicle when they were attacked by assailants. *They were departing a local discothèque and entering their vehicle when they were attacked.*

attempt *try.* My ex-wife and I attempted to have a child for six years. *My ex-wife and I tried to have a child for six years.* ■ A FILE LOCKED error message appears if you attempt to read the file with a BASIC.SYSTEM command. *A FILE LOCKED error message appears if you try to read the file with a BASIC.SYSTEM command.*

attention ... focused on (upon) *attention on; focus on.* In presidential politics, everyone's attention is now focused on the South. *In presidential politics, everyone is now focused on the South.* ■ Initially, attention is focused on the economic, political, and legal environment in overseas markets and at home. *Initially, attention is on the economic, political, and legal environment in overseas markets and at home.* ■ Thus management attention should now be focused on specific problems in mid- and late-career planning. *Thus management should now be focused on specific problems in mid- and late-career planning.*

at that (this) juncture *at present; at that (this) time; current; currently; (just; right) now; nowadays; present; presently; then; these days; today; (just) yet; delete.* For nimble investors, a little buying may be appropriate at this juncture. *For nimble investors, a little buying may now be appropriate.* ■ At this juncture, we have no further comment. *We have no further comment just yet.* ■ At this juncture, it is appropriate to analyze the nature of Salem Hospital's grievance with the rates established for it. *At this time, it is appropriate to analyze the nature of Salem Hospital's grievance with the rates established for it.*

at that (this) juncture (juncture in time; moment; moment in time; period; period in time; point; point in time; stage; stage in time; time) in my history (in my life; in the history of my life) *at present; at that (this) time; current; currently; (just; right) now; nowadays; present; presently; then; these days; today; (just) yet; delete.* At that point in my life, death seemed vague and romantic. *Death seemed vague and romantic then.* ■ I don't have the desire at this moment in my life to do more acting. *I don't currently have the desire to do more acting.* ■ At this point in time in our history, that can be a subtle and tricky distinction. *Today, that can be a subtle and tricky distinction.* ■ One can't help wondering at this stage in our history whether we are not suffering from entropy of the soul, a general lowering of our emotional or sexual temperature. *One can't help wondering nowadays whether we are not suffering from entropy of the soul, a general lowering of our emotional or sexual temperature.*

at that (this) juncture (moment; period; point; stage) in time *at present; at that (this) time; current; currently; (just; right) now; nowadays; present; presently; then; these days; today; (just) yet; delete.* At this point in time, roughly 20 percent of the people admitted for treatment are women. *At this time, roughly 20 percent of the people admitted for treatment are women.* ■ At this moment in time, he must abide by the way I want things to be. *He now must abide by the way I want things to be.* ■ My chief concern at this moment in time is to try and move the college forward in preparation for the next school year. *My chief concern is to try and move the college forward in preparation for the next school year.* ■ I have no interest in marrying at this point in time. *I have no interest in marrying just yet.*

at that (this) moment *at present; at that (this) time; current; currently; (just; right) now; nowadays; present; presently; then; these days; today; (just) yet;* delete. Did you know at that moment that your father had killed the rest of the family? *Did you know then that your father had killed the rest of the family?*

at that (this) point *at present; current; currently; (just; right) now; nowadays; present; presently; then; these days; today; (just) yet;* delete. How do you feel at this point? *How do you feel now?* ■ At this point, there's nothing the police can do about it. *There's nothing the police can do about it at present.* ■ At that point, we will discontinue our aid to them. *We will then discontinue our aid to them.* ■ We do not know at this point whether an extension of our license from the U.S. government can be obtained. *We do not yet know whether an extension of our license from the U.S. government can be obtained.*

at that (this) stage *at present; at that (this) time; current; currently; (just; right) now; nowadays; present; presently; then; these days; today; (just) yet;* delete. It's hard to tell at this stage. *It's hard to tell now.* ■ At this stage, dozens of cancer research teams around the country are studying the safety and efficiency of CSFs in cancer patients. *Today, dozens of cancer research teams around the country are studying the safety and efficiency of CSFs in cancer patients.*

at that (this) time *at present; current; currently; (just; right) now; nowadays; present; presently; then; these days; today; (just) yet;* delete. The potential return on the investment is uncertain at this time. *The potential return on the investment is presently uncertain.* ■ At that time, the plan in the event of a failure of two main engines was to maneuver the shuttle into level flight and then make an emergency touchdown in the ocean. *Then, the plan in the event of a failure of two main engines was to maneuver the shuttle into level flight and then make an emergency touchdown in the ocean.* ■ Unfortunately, this product does not fit with our marketing strategy at this time. *Unfortunately, this product does not fit with our current marketing strategy.* ■ And, the academics pointed out, some would argue that such a commitment should not be made at this time. *And, the academics pointed out, some would argue that such a commitment should not now be made.*

at (on) the brink of *about to; approaching; close to; near; nearly; verging on.* Some 10,000 Sudanese are on the brink of starving to death in a southern town under siege by armed guerrillas. *Some 10,000 Sudanese are close to starving to death in a southern town under siege by armed guerrillas.* ■ The U.S. is at the brink of a technical crisis, and 3M is one company trying to pull us back from the precipice. *The U.S. is verging on a technical crisis, and 3M is one company trying to pull us back from the precipice.*

at the corner (intersection) of *at.* At the corner of Lake and Union Avenues, you can get all the crack you want. *At Lake and Union Avenues, you can get all the crack you want.* ■ The site is located at the intersection of Buffum and Blake

Streets in the Central Square Historic District. *The site is located at Buffum and Blake Streets in the Central Square Historic District.*

at the current (present) time *at present; at this time; current; currently; (just; right) now; nowadays; present; presently; these days; today; (just) yet;* delete. What is the value of Digital's stock at the present time? *What is the current value of Digital's stock?* ■ At the current time, at least one-quarter of the population of the United States are victims of some kind of crime each year. *Nowadays, at least one-quarter of the population of the United States are victims of some kind of crime each year.* ■ There's no snow in the immediate area at the present time. *There's no snow in the immediate area just yet.*

at the hands of *by; from; through.* Estonians were unwise to seek revenge for 50 years of political, economic, and philosophical rape at the hands of the Soviets. *Estonians were unwise to seek revenge for 50 years of political, economic, and philosophical rape by the Soviets.* ■ I am enraged by the second-class treatment we are receiving at the hands of those who legislate for and govern us. *I am enraged by the second-class treatment we are receiving from those who legislate for and govern us.*

at the (very) minimum *at least.*

at the (current; present) moment *at present; current; currently; (just; right) now; nowadays; present; presently; these days; today; (just) yet;* delete. At the moment, this effort is being left largely to individual state colleges and universities to initiate. *This effort is now being left largely to individual state colleges and universities to initiate.* ■ At the moment, 65 appears to be the traditional age to retire. *Just now, 65 appears to be the traditional age to retire.*

at (on) the point of *about to; approaching; close to; near; nearly; verging on.*

at the same time *as one; at once; collectively; concurrently; jointly; together.* If too many things happened at the same time, data would be lost in the process. *If too many things happened at once, data would be lost in the process.* ■ A given stimulus fed into the network activates all the units at the same time, including feedback mechanisms that stimulate or suppress designated connections. *A given stimulus fed into the network activates all the units together, including feedback mechanisms that stimulate or suppress designated connections.*

(and) at the same time (as; that) *as; while.* In many cases, Soviet interest in smoothing East–West relations has been complicated by conflicting diplomatic priorities, such as improving ties with China and maintaining relations with Vietnam at the same time. *In many cases, Soviet interest in smoothing East–West relations has been complicated by conflicting diplomatic priorities, such as improving ties with China while maintaining relations with Vietnam.* ■ A similar dilemma faces Cray Research Inc., which relies on Japanese-made chips at the same time it fends off Japanese challenges to its role as the world's leading maker of supercomputers. *A similar dilemma faces Cray Research Inc., which relies on Japanese-made chips as it fends off Japanese challenges to its role as the world's leading maker of supercomputers.* ■ At the same time that firms in other cities are examining investment functions for their lawyers, and at the same time that investment subsidiaries may be emerging as harbingers, probate attorneys are taking an especially serious look at taking on investment advice. *While firms in other cities are examining investment functions for their lawyers, and while investment subsidiaries may be emerging as harbingers, probate attorneys are taking an especially serious look at taking on investment advice.*

attired *dressed.*

(a; the) ... attitude (of) delete. He had a very cavalier attitude about money. *He was very cavalier about money.* ■ It is the Plan's policy to settle members' complaints promptly and with an attitude of mutual confidence and respect. *It is the Plan's policy to settle members' complaints promptly and with mutual confidence and respect.*

at (on) (the) top (of) *atop; on.* It removes the dead cells that accumulate on top of the skin. *It removes the dead cells that accumulate on the skin.* ■ Back in the mid-1980s when the dolls were at the top of the toy heap, stores everywhere had lists of customers waiting for them. *Back in the mid-1980s when the dolls were atop the toy heap, stores everywhere had lists of customers waiting for them.*

attributable to *because of; caused by; due to; owing to; result from.* These increases were primarily attributable to a variety of merchant banking activities. *These increases were primarily caused by a variety of merchant banking activities.* ■ His argument that the low U.S. saving rate is attributable to demographics is strengthened if we include the fastest-growing segment of the U.S. population, namely, senior citizens, in his analysis. *His argument that the low U.S. saving rate is due to demographics is strengthened if we include the fastest-growing segment of the U.S. population, namely, senior citizens, in his analysis.* ■ Some of the increase in leasing is attributable to those customers waiting for the new disk system. *Some of the increase in leasing results from those customers waiting for the new disk system.*

attributable to the fact that *because; considering; for; in that; since.* The differing performance of black and white incomes is primarily attributable to the fact that white-married-couple families did significantly better last year than black-married-couple families. *The differing performance of black and white incomes is primarily because white-married-couple families did significantly better last year than black-married-couple families.*

at what (which) juncture (juncture in time; moment; moment in time; period; period in time; point; point in time; stage; stage in time;

time) *when.* At what point will you know if the business is profitable? *When will you know if the business is profitable?* ■ That offer is due to expire Friday, at which point it will revert to BAT's previous $63-a-share tender offer. *That offer is due to expire Friday, when it will revert to BAT's previous $63-a-share tender offer.*

at your earliest convenience *as soon as possible; at once; presently; quickly; right away; shortly; soon; without delay;* delete. Please return the signed and completed application to this office at your earliest convenience. *Please return the signed and completed application to this office.*

audible to the ear *audible.*

authentic replica *replica.*

author *(v) write.*

authoress *author.*

a variety of *assorted; countless; different; diverse; extensive; many; numerous; scores of; sundry; varied; various; varying;* delete. There are a variety of techniques. *There are various techniques.* ■ Today, a variety of pricing approaches are used. *Today, many pricing approaches are used.* ■ The developer interface can make use of graphics in a variety of ways. *The developer interface can make use of graphics in diverse ways.* ■ Scientists may need to compile a large database describing an organism's behavior under a variety of conditions. *Scientists may need to compile a large database describing an organism's behavior under different conditions.*

a (the) variety of different *assorted; a variety of; countless; different; diverse; extensive; many; numerous; scores of; sundry; varied; various; varying.* The children's museum will have a variety of different events. *The children's museum will have a variety of events.* ■ You have to look at these mergers from a variety of different perspectives. *You have to look at these mergers from different perspectives.* ■ A variety of different laws deal with this. *Various laws deal with this.*

B

background of experience *background; experience.* It is, then, from a background of experience in communication that I want to present two ideas. *It is, then, from a background in communication that I want to present two ideas.*

back in *in; last.* My daughter disappeared back in January. *My daughter disappeared last January.* ■ Back in the early 1900s, the U.S. government hired

125,000 people whose only job was to eradicate prairie dogs. *In the early 1900s, the U.S. government hired 125,000 people whose only job was to eradicate prairie dogs.*

back (before) in the past *before; earlier; formerly; in the past; once;* delete. Dealing with irrational people is something my father has done well back in the past and is something he'll do well in the future. *Dealing with irrational people is something my father has done well in the past and is something he'll do well in the future.*

backward and forward *completely; thoroughly.*

badge (mark; sign; symbol) of authenticity (distinction; honor; prestige; rank) *cachet.* Basler says the bumps, which appear on the foot and are regarded as a badge of distinction among serious surfers, result from long hours spent in contact with a surfboard. *Basler says the bumps, which appear on the foot and are regarded as a cachet among serious surfers, result from long hours spent in contact with a surfboard.*

balance out *balance.* Because seasonal forces are relative, they balance each other out by the completion of a full year. *Because seasonal forces are relative, they balance each other by the completion of a full year.*

bald-headed *bald.*

-based *from; in; of; -'s;* delete. At the other end of the spectrum is the niche company, such as Houston-based American General Corporation. *At the other end of the spectrum is the niche company, such as Houston's American General Corporation.* ■ Sharon Howard, an Atlanta-based attorney, has given a lot of thought to the way she is treated in the courtroom. *Sharon Howard, an Atlanta attorney, has given a lot of thought to the way she is treated in the courtroom.* ■ In the first half of 1988, 24.9 million people worked at home compared to 23.3 million last year, according to LINK Resources, a New York-based research and consulting firm. *In the first half of 1988, 24.9 million people worked at home compared to 23.3 million last year, according to LINK Resources, a research and consulting firm in New York.*

based in *from; in; of; -'s;* delete. PCE is a privately held company based in Portland, Oregon. *PCE is a privately held company in Portland, Oregon.* ■ Ms. Rhoades is a free-lance writer based in Cambridge, Massachusetts. *Ms. Rhoades is a free-lance writer from Cambridge, Massachusetts.*

based on (upon) *after; by; for; from; in; on; through; with;* delete. For years, knowledge of the African creature was largely based on speculation. *For years, knowledge of the African creature was largely speculative.* ■ One way to classify operating systems is based on the number of programs they can run at one time and the number of users who can be working on computers or terminals connected to a central computer. *One way to classify operating systems is by the number of programs they can run at one time and the number of users who can be working on computers or terminals connected to a central computer.* ■ Based on what I hear, everyone thinks Fan Pier has lost its moment of opportunity. *From what I hear, everyone thinks Fan Pier has lost its moment of opportunity.*

based on (upon) my personal judgment (opinion) *I assert; I believe; I claim; I consider; I contend; I feel; I hold; I judge; I maintain; I regard; I say; I think; I view; to me;* delete. Based on my personal judgment, I think tax revenues will grow by 8.3 percent. *I think tax revenues will grow by 8.3 percent.*

baseless (groundless; unfounded; unsubstantiated) rumor *hearsay; rumor.* A Foreign Ministry spokesman characterized the reports as unfounded rumors. *A Foreign Ministry spokesman characterized the reports as rumors.* ■ The group also charged that unsubstantiated rumors of homophobia were behind the decision. *The group also charged that rumors of homophobia were behind the decision.*

basic delete. In this section, we introduce you to the basic procedures to control page breaks and page numbers. *In this section, we introduce you to the procedures to control page breaks and page numbers.*

basically *chiefly; largely; mainly; most; mostly;* delete. Basically, the social service groups involved are either indifferent or corrupt. *The social service groups involved are either indifferent or corrupt.* ■ I think you say things that basically make a lot of sense. *I think you say things that make a lot of sense.* ■ Basically, the system involves the calling of tenders. *The system mainly involves the calling of tenders.* ■ Basically, this program is a productivity tool. *This program is largely a productivity tool.*

basic (and) fundamental *basic; fundamental.* As a basic and fundamental question, do you think the trade deficit is a domestic problem or caused by foreign competition? *As a basic question, do you think the trade deficit is a domestic problem or caused by foreign competition?* ■ Our basic, fundamental values are the same. *Our fundamental values are the same.*

basic principle *principle.* We feel there are two basic principles to successful advertising. *We feel there are two principles to successful advertising.* ■ To calculate formulas, you should understand two basic principles: operators and the order of operations. *To calculate formulas, you should understand two principles: operators and the order of operations.*

basis in fact *basis; fact; reason; truth.* In the classic literature, the statement is 50 microns, but as I looked back through the literature there is very little basis in fact for clinically making that statement. *In the classic literature, the statement is 50 microns, but as I looked back through the literature there is very little basis for clinically making that statement.* ■ About the only statement in the article that has any basis in fact is "I want to build the biggest film group in the world." *About the only statement in the article that has any truth is "I want to build the biggest film group in the world."*

bathroom facilities *bathroom; toilet.*

(please) be advised (informed) that delete. Please be advised that we must be notified at least two weeks prior to your closing date in order to issue your 6(d) certificate. *We must be notified at least two weeks prior to your closing date in order to issue your 6(d) certificate.* ■ Be informed that the Department of Social Services will conduct a public hearing regarding the Social Services Block Grant administered by the Department. *The Department of Social Services will conduct a public hearing regarding the Social Services Block Grant administered by the Department.*

bear (have; hold) a grudge (against) *dislike; resent.*

(please) bear in mind *consider; heed; note; realize.*

bear (a; the) ... resemblance (similarity) to *be like; look like; resemble.* The Massachusetts Eye and Ear case bears a striking resemblance to several other frauds that have made headlines in recent years. *The Massachusetts Eye and Ear case strikingly resembles several other frauds that have made headlines in recent years.* ■ The Lumina's body bears a similarity to Chevrolet's Corsica and Beretta. *The Lumina's body resembles Chevrolet's Corsica and Beretta.*

bear witness to *affirm; attest to; certify to; declare; testify to; verify.* A splendid perennial garden surrounds the house and bears witness to the collaboration in the family. *A splendid perennial garden surrounds the house and attests to the collaboration in the family.*

because of *after; by; for; from; in; out of; through; with.* Such a model would be inappropriate because of two reasons. *Such a model would be inappropriate for two reasons.* ■ Often, arguments arise because of too much intimacy. *Often, arguments arise from too much intimacy.*

because of the fact that *because; considering; for; in that; since.* Because of the fact that they are still monopoly suppliers of local exchange, I also see a discouraging prospect for the operating companies in this area. *Since they are still monopoly suppliers of local exchange, I also see a discouraging prospect for the operating companies in this area.*

because why *why.* You say you are a submissive wife, but you are that way because why? *You say you are a submissive wife, but why are you that way?*

become known *emerge; surface; transpire.*

before (earlier; previously) -ed (-en) *-ed (-en).* As we previously noted, the high-cost load funds distributed through a salesperson have dominated the industry. *As we noted, the high-cost load funds distributed through a salesperson have dominated the industry.* ■ The Environmental Protection Agency sounded the alarm September 12, with the announcement that the gas was more widespread than earlier believed. *The Environmental Protection Agency sounded the alarm September 12, with the announcement that the gas was more widespread than believed.* ■ The executive director of a relief organization told Congress that the situation in flood-ravaged Bangladesh is unlike anything he has previously seen. *The executive director of a relief organization told Congress that the situation in flood-ravaged Bangladesh is unlike anything he has seen.*

before ... first *before.* Before you use the delete option, first extract the records you are considering deleting. *Before you use the delete option, extract the records you are considering deleting.* ■ Before I send the manuscript to you, I'd first like to know if there's any interest in it. ■ *Before I send the manuscript to you, I'd like to know if there's any interest in it.*

before (very) long *shortly; soon.*

begin (start) at ... and end (finish) at *(be) between ... and; range from ... to.* Price tags for the condos will start at $350,000 and end at $1.75 million. *Price tags for the condos will range from $350,000 to $1.75 million.*

begin ... first *begin.* You should begin by sketching the centerline and guidelines first. *You should begin by sketching the centerline and guidelines.* ■ Assuming we begin with the data first, how do we go about building a sound, logical model of the business that the system will serve? *Assuming we begin with the data, how do we go about building a sound, logical model of the business that the system will serve?*

behavior pattern *behavior.*

(a; the) ... being *delete.* They won't just assume I'm a nonsexual being. *They won't just assume I'm nonsexual.* ■ What sets teachers apart from other mortal beings is that they never have first names. *What sets teachers apart from other mortals is that they never have first names.*

being (as; as how; that) *because; considering; for; in that; since.* They usually deliver by noontime, and being that you're local, it'll probably be before noon. *They usually deliver by noontime, and since you're local, it'll probably be before noon.*

... being what it is (they are) *delete.* Human nature being what it is, two million square feet in Medford will never get the attention of a Rowes Wharf. *Two million square feet in Medford will never get the attention of a Rowes Wharf.*

besides ... also (as well) *besides; beyond.* Besides providing the high-end AI tools, they have shells for IBM PCs and compatibles as well. *Besides providing the high-end AI tools, they have shells for IBM PCs and compatibles.* ▪ Besides being right about some things and wrong about others, we were also lucky about some things and unlucky about others. *Beyond being right about some things and wrong about others, we were lucky about some things and unlucky about others.*

beside the point *immaterial; inapt; irrelevant; not pertinent.*

best (biggest; greatest; largest; most) ... single *best (biggest; greatest; largest; most).* It was a failure of management, and that is probably the greatest single danger that we face in this industry in the United States at the moment. *It was a failure of management, and that is probably the greatest danger that we face in this industry in the United States at the moment.* ▪ The most important single aspect of quantitatively predicting the movement of groundwater or in determining the yield of a well is accurate knowledge of the aquifer characteristics. *The most important aspect of quantitatively predicting the movement of groundwater or in determining the yield of a well is accurate knowledge of the aquifer characteristics.* ▪ Great Britain, where annual production capacity was increased to 700,000 lines a year, is the largest single market. *Great Britain, where annual production capacity was increased to 700,000 lines a year, is the largest market.*

be that as it may *all (just) the same; anyhow; even so; still; still and all; yet.*

between you and me (us) *between us.* Enclosed is a basic proposal which should lay the groundwork for future discussions between you and us. *Enclosed is a basic proposal which should lay the groundwork for future discussions between us.*

between the two of them (us) *between them (us).*

betwixt and between *in between; undecided.*

beverage *drink.*

beyond (out of) all reason *unreasonable.*

beyond a (the) shadow of a doubt *assuredly; certainly; doubtless; indisputably; irrefutably; no doubt; surely; undoubtedly; unquestionably.*

beyond number *countless; endless; infinite; millions (of); myriad; numberless; untold.*

beyond (outside) the realm of possibility *impossible; inconceivable; undoable; unthinkable.* So it's not beyond the realm of possibility that corporate performance could be improved if directors surveyed other areas of corporate activity, like manufacturing and marketing. *So it's not inconceivable that corporate performance could be improved if directors surveyed other areas of corporate activity, like manufacturing and marketing.*

biased opinion *bias; prejudice.*

big, huge (large) *big; huge; large.* I packed a big, huge picnic lunch for us. *I packed a huge picnic lunch for us.*

biographical *biographic.*

biological *biologic.*

biometrical *biometric.*

biophysiological *biophysiologic.*

bit by bit *gradually; slowly.*

bits and pieces *bits; pieces.* Bits and pieces of segregation have been jettisoned or have rotted away. *Bits of segregation have been jettisoned or have rotted away.* ■ The computations were done in bits and pieces over a number of years and required large amounts of computer time. *The computations were done in pieces over a number of years and required large amounts of computer time.*

blatantly evident (obvious; plain) *blatant; evident (obvious; plain).*

blend of both *blend.* Management is a blend of both science and art. *Management is a blend of science and art.*

blend together *blend.* Blend this WordStar expertise together in a book, and you have the definitive resource to the most widely used word processing software. *Blend this WordStar expertise in a book, and you have the definitive resource to the most widely used word processing software.*

block out *block.* Other conversations, the sound of machinery, and traffic noises can block out messages from being received. *Other conversations, the sound of machinery, and traffic noises can block messages from being received.*

bode (ill; well) for the future *bode (ill; well).* The fact that electric companies had to institute such emergency procedures does not bode well for the future. *The fact that electric companies had to institute such emergency procedures does not bode well.*

botch up *botch.*

both ... agree *agree.* Both of them agree. *They agree.*

both ... alike *alike; both.* The adherence of career-oriented women to the masculine prototype has led both men and women alike to undermine the value of female qualities and responsibilities. *The adherence of career-oriented women to the masculine prototype has led men and women alike to undermine the value of female qualities and responsibilities.*

both ... as well as *as well as; both.*

both equally *both; equally.*

both ... in combination *both; in combination.* Both analytic techniques and judgmental methods might be used in combination to verify each other. *Analytic techniques and judgmental methods might be used in combination to verify each other.*

both of (the) *both.* Both of the boys suffer from Tourette Syndrome. *Both boys suffer from Tourette Syndrome.*

both share *both; share.* We both share a deep commitment to the welfare of the American people. *We share a deep commitment to the welfare of the American people.* ■ But he insists that both movements shared the belief that America is a fragile paradise susceptible to destruction from within. *But he insists that both movements believed that America is a fragile paradise susceptible to destruction from within.*

both together *both; together.* Both of the products together cost $117.95. *Together, the products cost $117.95.*

bound and determined *determined; resolute; resolved.*

brand new *new.* With a brand new product, there is a significant educational need. *With a new product, there is a significant educational need.* ■ Even though most of the inquiries relate to brand-new customers, its need to improve all customer service was paramount. *Even though most of the inquiries relate to new customers, its need to improve all customer service was paramount.*

briefly in passing *briefly; in passing.* Let me say briefly in passing that I am opposed to women not having control of their own bodies. *Let me say briefly that I am opposed to women not having control of their own bodies.*

brief (concise; short; succinct) summary *summary.* A concise summary of the scope of the international product manager's task has been provided by Wind. *A summary of the scope of the international product manager's task has been provided by Wind.* ■ He will be able to exploit a valuable asset that *TV Guide* owns—the succinct summaries and cast descriptions of 150,000 programs and 20,000 movies that already have been shown on television. *He will be able to exploit a valuable asset that* TV Guide *owns—the summaries and cast descriptions of 150,000 programs and 20,000 movies that already have been shown on television.* ■ Some business plans begin with a short summary, but many plans no longer include them. *Some business plans begin with a summary, but many plans no longer include them.*

brief (concise; short; succinct) synopsis *synopsis.* I just wondered if I could give you a brief synopsis of the long-distance services that MCI offers. *I just wondered if I could give you a synopsis of the long-distance services that MCI offers.*

bring about *begin; cause; effect; occasion; produce.* Rather than bring about the death of Yellowstone, the fires triggered natural processes of change that are a normal part of the ecosystem. *Rather than cause the death of Yellowstone, the fires triggered natural processes of change that are a normal part of the ecosystem.*

bring attention to *advertise; announce; disclose; divulge; expose; herald; indicate; make known; make public; mention; point out; point to; present; proclaim; promote; publicize; reveal; show; tell; uncover; unveil.* They were demonstrating at the bank branch in order to bring attention to community lending and banking service issues. *They were demonstrating at the bank branch in order to disclose community lending and banking service issues.*

bring (give) forth *bear; effect; produce; yield.*

bring into being (existence) *conceive; create; devise; fashion; forge; form; invent; make; mold; plan; produce; shape.* He says that reason itself is a ladder that can now be dispensed with—and should be dispensed with—to help bring the liberal utopia into existence. *He says that reason itself is a ladder that can now be dispensed with—and should be dispensed with—to help fashion the liberal utopia.*

bring into question *challenge; contradict; dispute; doubt; question.* The issue goes beyond sexual politics and brings into question how the orthodox verities of an ancient religion fit into the modern world. *The issue goes beyond sexual politics and challenges how the orthodox verities of an ancient religion fit into the modern world.*

bring into the open *advertise; announce; disclose; divulge; expose; herald; indicate; make known; make public; mention; point out; point to; present; proclaim; promote; publicize; reveal; show; tell; uncover; unveil.*

bring into the world *bear; give birth to; produce.*

bring pressure to bear on (upon) *coerce; compel; force; press; pressure.* No matter who is president, the international community must bring pressure to bear on the government to end apartheid. *No matter who is president, the international community must pressure the government to end apartheid.*

bring to account *admonish; censure; chide; rebuke; reprimand; scold.*

bring to a close *cease; close; complete; conclude; end; finish; halt; settle; stop.* How would you bring this meeting to a close? *How would you close this meeting?* ■ The merger of Stellar and Ardent brings to a close a four-year-old battle. *The merger of Stellar and Ardent settles a four-year-old battle.*

bring to a completion *cease; close; complete; conclude; end; finish; halt; settle; stop.*

bring to a conclusion *cease; close; complete; conclude; end; finish; halt; settle; stop.*

bring to a halt *cease; close; complete; conclude; end; finish; halt; settle; stop.* The timber industry said the decision could bring logging to a halt throughout much of the Pacific Northwest within 30 days and cause the loss of as many as 160,000 jobs. *The timber industry said the decision could halt logging throughout much of the Pacific Northwest within 30 days and cause the loss of as many as 160,000 jobs.*

bring to an end *cease; close; complete; conclude; end; finish; halt; settle; stop.* The settlement brings to an end all claims of age discrimination stemming from the firing of 400 salaried employees during the agricultural recession of 1984. *The settlement ends all claims of age discrimination stemming from the firing of 400 salaried employees during the agricultural recession of 1984.*

bring to a standstill *cease; close; complete; conclude; end; finish; halt; settle; stop.* It should seek to bring to a standstill the international flow of arms to the various Khmer factions. *It should seek to halt the international flow of arms to the various Khmer factions.*

bring to ... attention (of) *advertise; announce; disclose; divulge; expose; herald; indicate; make known; make public; mention; point out; point to; present; proclaim; promote; publicize; reveal; show; tell; uncover; unveil.* He was determined to bring to the world's attention the devastation of the innocents. *He was determined to publicize the devastation of the innocents.*

bring to bear (on; upon) *apply; employ; exercise; exert; influence; use.* Whether such influence can be brought to bear now is of vital importance to the bottom half in the schools. *Whether such influence can be applied now is of vital importance to the bottom half in the schools.*

bring together *amass; collect; gather.*

bring to light *advertise; announce; disclose; divulge; expose; herald; indicate; make known; make public; mention; point out; point to; present; proclaim; promote; publicize; reveal; show; tell; uncover; unveil.* A great many uncertainties are brought to light when a bank makes a number of changes. *A great many uncertainties are revealed when a bank makes a number of changes.*

bring (back) to mind *recall; recollect.*

bring to pass *begin; cause; start.*

build a bridge across (between) *bridge.*

(a; the) burgeoning (growing; increasing; rising) amount (degree; extent; number; part; percentage; portion; proportion; quantity) (of) *increasingly; more; more and more.* In recent years, an increasing number of companies have developed global marketing strategies. *In recent years, more and more companies have developed global marketing strategies.* ■ A growing number of attorneys are bringing this up of their own initiative in the course of estate planning reviews. *Increasingly, attorneys are bringing this up of their own initiative in the course of estate planning reviews.* ■ Eastern is now meeting its schedules by using an increasing number of planes and mechanics from its sister airline, Continental. *Eastern is now meeting its schedules by using more planes and mechanics from its sister airline, Continental.*

but all (just) the same *all (just) the same; but.*

but however *but; however.*

but instead *but; instead.* A child's mind is not a tabula rasa, but instead is filled with ideas generated through continuous interaction with the environment. *A child's mind is not a tabula rasa but is filled with ideas generated through continuous interaction with the environment.*

but nevertheless *but; nevertheless.*

but on the other hand *but; on the other hand.*

but rather *but; rather.* Behavior is not an isolated event, but rather it is influenced by the past, present, and future. *Behavior is not an isolated event; rather it is influenced by the past, present, and future.* ■ People think and believe not with their minds alone, but rather with their whole personalities. *People think and believe not with their minds alone but with their whole personalities.*

but whereas *but; whereas.*

by (to) all accounts (appearances; indications) *apparently; ostensibly; seemingly.* By all indications, the T-group was a great success. *Apparently, the T-group was a great success.*

by and large *chiefly; commonly; generally; largely; mainly; most; mostly; normally; typically; usually.* But members involved argue the furor is by and large a phony one. *But members involved argue the furor is largely a phony one.* ■ It is a complication that brings new hazards to many applicants but which, by and large, serves the overall process well. *It is a complication that brings new hazards to many applicants but which usually serves the overall process well.* ■ By and large, ESOPs are started for the purposes Congress intended. *Most ESOPs are started for the purposes Congress intended.*

by any means *at all.*

by (in) comparison *but; however; whereas; yet;* delete. In comparison, about one-third of the patients whose vessels remained partly blocked showed late potentials on their EKGs. *About one-third of the patients whose vessels remained partly blocked showed late potentials on their EKGs.*

by comparison (to; with) *against; alongside; beside; compared to (with); -(i)er than; less; less than; more; more than; next to; over; than; to; versus; vis-à-vis.* While mentoring is institutionalized in Japan, mentoring in the United States, by comparison, is a rare and random phenomenon. *While mentoring is institutionalized in Japan, mentoring in the United States is a more rare and random phenomenon.* ■ Even MiniScribe's quarterly results, strong by comparison to others, did not receive rave reviews. *Even MiniScribe's quarterly results, stronger than others, did not receive rave reviews.*

by consequence of *after; because of; by; due to; following; for; from; in; out of; owing to; through; with.*

by (a; the) considerable (good; great; huge; large; overwhelming; sizable; vast; wide) margin *by far; far and away; much.* It already was ranked as one of the top five malls in the country, with sales per square foot of $480, and by a great margin the most successful in New England. *It already was ranked as one of the top five malls in the country, with sales per square foot of $480, and by far the most successful in New England.* ■ The leader by a considerable margin was the deep-water lake trout. *The leader by far was the deep-water lake trout.*

by (in) contrast *but; however; whereas; yet;* delete. In contrast, in the longer term, both quadratic models may lead to poor results. *But in the longer term, both quadratic models may lead to poor results.* ■ Post-modernism, by contrast, is indifferent to consistency and continuity altogether. *Yet post-modernism is indifferent to consistency and continuity altogether.*

by contrast to (with) *against; alongside; beside; compared to (with); -(i)er than; less; less than; more; more than; next to; over; than; to; unlike; versus; vis-à-vis.* And, by contrast with the governor and some younger politicians, Crane has always seen politics as an essential part of the job. *And, unlike the governor and some younger politicians, Crane has always seen politics as an essential part of the job.*

by definition delete. For all the fanfare, post-modernism is, by definition, known by the company it follows. *For all the fanfare, post-modernism is known by the company it follows.* ■ Collaboration, by definition, is a two-way venture. *Collaboration is a two-way venture.*

(all) by itself (themselves) *alone.* Each microcomputer has its own computational ability, so it can function either by itself or as a part of the network. *Each microcomputer has its own computational ability, so it can function either alone or as a part of the network.*

by (a; the) little (narrow; nominal; slender; slight; slim; small; tiny) margin *marginally; narrowly; nominally; slightly.* Blue-chip stocks closed higher by a small margin in a listless session as many participants were absent because of the Jewish New Year holiday. *Blue-chip stocks closed marginally higher in a listless session as many participants were absent because of the Jewish New Year holiday.*

by (a; the) ... margin (of) *by; -(al)ly;* delete. Advancing issues outpaced losers by a margin of more than 2 to 1 among issues listed on the New York Stock Exchange. *Advancing issues outpaced losers by more than 2 to 1 among issues listed on the New York Stock Exchange.*

by (the) means of *by; from; in; on; over; through; with.* It retains control over product decisions and generally markets a standardized product and attempts to influence local decisions by means of persuasion. *It retains control over product decisions and generally markets a standardized product and attempts to influence local decisions through persuasion.* ■ He was convicted of assault and battery by means of a dangerous weapon. *He was convicted of assault and battery with a dangerous weapon.* ■ In 1976, he established the first "superstation," a television station that distributes its signal to a wide area by means of satellites. *In 1976, he established the first "superstation," a television station that distributes its signal to a wide area over satellites.*

by (its; their) nature delete. Researchers at MGH and Harvard University reported they have found that children who are extremely shy and inhibited at an early age are much more likely to exhibit irrational anxieties and fears than children who are, by nature, outgoing and spontaneous. *Researchers at MGH and Harvard University reported they have found that children who are extremely shy* *and inhibited at an early age are much more likely to exhibit irrational anxieties and fears than children who are outgoing and spontaneous.* ■ Attempts at comprehensive historical accounts of this sort are by their nature incomplete and much better on some things than others. *Attempts at comprehensive historical accounts of this sort are incomplete and much better on some things than others.* ■ The truth is that genuine debt crises are, by their nature, almost impossible to predict. *The truth is that genuine debt crises are almost impossible to predict.* ■ Some words are vague and unclear by nature: function, in terms of, eventuate, expeditious. *Some words are vague and unclear: function, in terms of, eventuate, expeditious.*

by no means *far from; hardly; scarcely.* Though this advice is extremely helpful to many families, it is by no means the only thing they need to know. *Though this advice is extremely helpful to many families, it is far from the only thing they need to know.*

by occupation delete. He's a day laborer by occupation. *He's a day laborer.*

by one means or another *anyhow; anyway; by some means; however; in any way; in some way; in whatever way; somehow; somehow or another; someway(s).*

by reason of *after; because of; by; due to; following; for; from; in; out of; owing to; through; with.* Nomura, by reason of its size, capital, research abilities, and leading position in the largest creditor nation, should certainly be in the top group. *Nomura, because of its size, capital, research abilities, and leading position in the largest creditor nation, should certainly be in the top group.* ■ If the taxpayer pays the third and fourth installments in full as herein specified, the taxpayer will not be liable for any penalty for the underpayment of estimated tax by reason of the enactment of Chapter 202. *If the taxpayer pays the third and fourth installments in full as herein specified, the taxpayer will not be liable for any penalty for the underpayment of estimated tax owing to the enactment of Chapter 202.*

by reason of the fact that *because; considering; for; in that; since.* Property the decedent had interest in includes dividends payable to the decedent by reason of the fact that, on or before the date of death, the decedent was a shareholder of record. *Property the decedent had interest in includes dividends payable to the decedent because, on or before the date of death, the decedent was a shareholder of record.*

(all) by -self (-selves) *alone.* She lives all by herself. *She lives alone.*

by ... standards *-(al)ly;* delete. By historical standards, these relative prices for thrifts are extremely low. *Historically, these relative prices for thrifts are extremely low.* ■ By legal standards, we are an independent nation. *Legally, we are an independent nation.*

by the fact that *because; considering; for; in that; since.* The chore is simplified by the fact that the parameter tables for READ_BLOCK and WRITE_BLOCK are identical. *The chore is simplified because the parameter tables for READ_BLOCK and WRITE_BLOCK are identical.* ■ By the fact that they are using state capital, there can be no free competition. *Considering they are using state capital, there can be no free competition.*

by the same token *also; and; as well; besides; beyond that (this); even; further; furthermore; likewise; moreover; more than that (this); similarly; still more; then; too; what is more;* delete. By the same token, northeastern and southeastern banks, which have been the fastest growing, could witness slower loan growth. *Similarly, northeastern and southeastern banks, which have been the fastest growing, could witness slower loan growth.* ■ That face-to-face presence may upset the truthful rape victim or abused child; by the same token, it may confound and undo the false accuser or reveal the child coached by a malevolent adult. *That face-to-face presence may upset the truthful rape victim or abused child; moreover, it may confound and undo the false accuser or reveal the child coached by a malevolent adult.*

by (in) virtue of *after; because of; by; due to; following; for; from; in; out of; owing to; through; with.* The U.S. hockey team is up by one by virtue of their win over Austria. *The U.S. hockey team is up by one following their win over Austria.* ■ By virtue of its relatively selective action on beta2-adrenoceptors, albuterol relaxes smooth muscle of the bronchi, uterus, and vascular supply to skeletal muscles. *Owing to its relatively selective action on beta2-adrenoceptors, albuterol relaxes smooth muscle of the bronchi, uterus, and vascular supply to skeletal muscles.* ■ Conifers survive the winter not only through this adaptation but also by virtue of the design of their leaves, which keeps them from drying out. *Conifers survive the winter not only through this adaptation but also through the design of their leaves, which keeps them from drying out.*

by (in) virtue of the fact that *because; considering; for; in that; since.* People who can be helpful to you are attracted to you by virtue of the fact that you're a person who is doing interesting things and initiating activity yourself. *People who can be helpful to you are attracted to you because you're a person who is doing interesting things and initiating activity yourself.*

by (the) way of *by; from; in; on; over; through; with;* delete. A worm is a self-contained computer program that enters by way of a communications channel and then generates its own commands. *A worm is a self-contained computer program that enters through a communications channel and then generates its own commands.*

by way of (-ing) *for (-ing); so as to; to.* By way of summarizing, I have tried to depict prospective new roles for the Bell Operating Companies. *To summarize, I have tried to depict prospective new roles for the Bell Operating Companies.* ■ All of this is by way of making a point. *All of this is to make a point.*

by way of being delete. *Today's column is by way of being a commentary on a column that appeared in this space a week ago.* *Today's column is a commentary on a column that appeared in this space a week ago.*

by way of comparison (contrast) *but; however; whereas; yet.* The volume directory for a ProDOS-formatted disk can hold up to 51 files; by way of contrast, a DOS 3.3 directory can hold 105. *The volume directory for a ProDOS-formatted disk can hold up to 51 files, whereas a DOS 3.3 directory can hold 105.*

by way of example (illustration) *for example; to illustrate.* By way of illustration, he examines a number of inventions that were allegedly produced *ex nihilo* but which in fact had antecedents. *To illustrate, he examines a number of inventions that were allegedly produced ex nihilo but which in fact had antecedents.*

by whatever (whichever) manner (means) *despite how; however.* By whatever means they have been brought to our attention, they have been corrected. *However they have been brought to our attention, they have been corrected.*

by what (which) means (mechanism) *how.* Still a mystery is by what mechanism insulin resistance might cause heart disease. *Still a mystery is how insulin resistance might cause heart disease.*

C

call a halt to *cease; close; complete; conclude; end; finish; halt; settle; stop.* We asked them to call a halt to the violence and harassment. *We asked them to stop the violence and harassment.*

call an end to *cease; close; complete; conclude; end; finish; halt; settle; stop.*

call a stop to *cease; close; complete; conclude; end; finish; halt; settle; stop.*

call attention to *advertise; announce; disclose; divulge; expose; herald; indicate; make known; make public; mention; point out; point to; present; proclaim; promote; publicize; reveal; show; tell; uncover; unveil.* She said the sole purpose of the program was to call attention to what happened in Mexico. *She said the sole purpose of the program was to disclose what happened in Mexico.* ■ For one thing, the letter-writers call attention to errors or misinterpretations and are largely critical. *For one thing, the letter-writers point out errors or misinterpretations and are largely critical.* ■ My review did not in any way denigrate Dr. Karl or his achievements; rather, it called attention to what in my judgment was an inadequate job of historical editing. *My review did not in any way denigrate Dr. Karl or his achievements; rather, it revealed what in my judgment was an inadequate job of historical editing.*

called delete. A set is a collection of objects, and the objects in the set are called the elements. *A set is a collection of objects, and the objects in the set are the elements.* ■ The person who wants to send the message or signal to another is called the sender, and the person for whom the message is intended is called the receiver. *The person who wants to send the message or signal to another is the sender, and the person for whom the message is intended is the receiver.*

call into being (existence) *conceive; create; devise; fashion; forge; form; invent; make; mold; plan; produce; shape.*

call into question *challenge; contradict; dispute; doubt; question.* It calls into question the no-threshold theory—because if there is no threshold, average county measurements should correlate directly with observed lung-cancer incidence. *It challenges the no-threshold theory—because if there is no threshold, average county measurements should correlate directly with observed lung-cancer incidence.* ■ As basic assumptions about the therapy are called into question, some investigators wonder aloud about the wisdom of pursuing more widespread human trials. *As basic assumptions about the therapy are questioned, some investigators wonder aloud about the wisdom of pursuing more widespread human trials.* ■ Whether the magazine has accurately interpreted what those interests are is a point some former staffers call into question. *Whether the magazine has accurately interpreted what those interests are is a point some former staffers dispute.*

call to ... attention (of) *advertise; announce; disclose; divulge; expose; herald; indicate; make known; make public; mention; point out; point to; present; proclaim; promote; publicize; reveal; show; tell; uncover; unveil.* The results were called to the attention of the town's building inspector, who forced the ferry service to shut down. *The results were shown to the town's building inspector, who forced the ferry service to shut down.* ■ I would like to call to your attention that coverage will not be bound until we approve the application. *I would like to mention that coverage will not be bound until we approve the application.*

call to mind *recall; recollect.*

call up *call.*

calm, cool, and collected *calm; collected; cool.* She is calm, cool, and collected now, but you should have seen her Friday night. *She is calm now, but you should have seen her Friday night.*

candor and frankness *candor; frankness.*

capability *ability.* No two managers are equal in their abilities, and their subordinates will have differing capabilities and levels of experience. *No two managers are equal in their abilities, and their subordinates will have differing abilities and levels of experience.*

capacity *job; position.*

cast about for *look for; search for; seek.* Toymakers have been casting about for something exciting enough to pull parents and children back into the toy stores. *Toymakers have been searching for something exciting enough to pull parents and children back into the toy stores.*

cast doubt on (upon) *challenge; contradict; dispute; doubt; question.*

catch by surprise *startle; surprise.* He says the association was caught by surprise by the House's action. *He says the association was surprised by the House's action.*

cause ... to be (become) *make; render.* Reading his performance appraisal caused him to become angry. *Reading his performance appraisal made him angry.*

cause to happen (occur; take place) *bring about; cause; effect; produce.* Although policy cannot in and of itself cause improvement to happen in the classroom, it can impede or facilitate improvement. *Although policy cannot in and of itself cause improvement in the classroom, it can impede or facilitate improvement.*

cease and desist *cease; desist.*

center around *center on.* All these fears center around the loss of control, which may result in being embarrassed or ridiculed by others. *All these fears center on the loss of control, which may result in being embarrassed or ridiculed by others.* ▪ The investigation appears to center around a handful of top defense officials and consultants. *The investigation appears to center on a handful of top defense officials and consultants.*

center of attention (attraction) *cynosure; focus.*

(of) central (critical; vital) importance *central; critical; important; vital.* One point that was expressed often and eloquently was the necessity for government at every level to address the serious challenges we face on issues of vital importance to all of us. *One point that was expressed often and eloquently was the necessity for government at every level to address the serious challenges we face on issues vital to all of us.* ▪ Although these contextual factors are often ignored by domestic firms, they are of central importance to international firms. *Although* *these contextual factors are often ignored by domestic firms, they are central to international firms.* ■ This information will be critically important to researchers and to the quality of health care for all Americans well into the next century. *This information will be critical to researchers and to the quality of health care for all Americans well into the next century.*

(a; the) central ... in (of; to) *central to.* His experience, including heading various task forces, is a central part of the resume on which he is running for office. *His experience, including heading various task forces, is central to the resume on which he is running for office.* ■ As such, religion (or its traces) is a central element of a culture. *As such, religion (or its traces) is central to a culture.*

characterize as *call; name; term.*

charge with the responsibility for (of) *charge with; responsible for.* The organization might have a management information system that is charged with the responsibility for gathering and processing data. *The organization might have a management information system that is responsible for gathering and processing data.* ■ While the town manager is basically charged with the responsibility of budget preparation, selectmen, as his overseers, should be taking sufficient time to review his proposals. *While the town manager is basically charged with budget preparation, selectmen, as his overseers, should be taking sufficient time to review his proposals.*

check to see *check; examine; see; verify.* You should also check to see if the original warranty is still in effect. *You should also check if the original warranty is still in effect.* ■ The best instructional strategies involve repetition, reinforcement, and coaching—that is, checking to see if the child has actually learned anything. *The best instructional strategies involve repetition, reinforcement, and coaching—that is, verifying if the child has actually learned anything.*

christen as *christen.*

climb up *climb.* Young Americans have become increasingly disillusioned with their ability to successfully climb up the corporate ladder. *Young Americans have become increasingly disillusioned with their ability to successfully climb the corporate ladder.*

close (near; rough) approximation (estimate; estimation) *approximation (estimate; estimation).* A close approximation of the optimal value can be estimated on a computer spreadsheet. *An approximation of the optimal value can be estimated on a computer spreadsheet.* ■ Powers of two roughly approximate powers of ten. *Powers of two approximate powers of ten.*

close (near) at hand *close by; close to; near; nearby.*

close down *close.* Both health plans will close down as of December 31 because of projected financial losses. *Both health plans will close as of December 31 because of projected financial losses.*

close scrutiny *scrutiny.* The interest deduction is likely to receive close scrutiny when the chairman of the House Ways and Means Committee looks into the matter. *The interest deduction is likely to receive scrutiny when the chairman of the House Ways and Means Committee looks into the matter.*

cluster together *cluster.* The report points out that 189.4 million Americans—77 percent of the population—are clustered together in metropolitan areas. *The report points out that 189.4 million Americans—77 percent of the population—are clustered in metropolitan areas.*

cognizant *aware.*

cohabit together *cohabit.*

collaborate together *collaborate.*

collect together *collect.* If you want to collect together your word processing, desktop publishing, document conversion, and text search programs under one main menu entry, you may do so. *If you want to collect your word processing, desktop publishing, document conversion, and text search programs under one main menu entry, you may do so.*

(a; the) combination (of) *both;* delete. Which sources to use for forecasting (internal, external, or a combination) depends on the particular organization, its resources, degree of sophistication in forecasting, and the type of forecast needed. *Which sources to use for forecasting (internal, external, or both) depends on the particular organization, its resources, degree of sophistication in forecasting, and the type of forecast needed.* ■ You experience a combination of relief at having gotten the hard part behind you and satisfaction at making the program do your bidding. *You experience both relief at having gotten the hard part behind you and satisfaction at making the program do your bidding.* ■ Architects use a combination of feet and inches, but the inch units are omitted (e.g., 7′2). *Architects use feet and inches, but the inch units are omitted (e.g., 7′2).*

(a; the) combination of ... along with (combined with; coupled with; joined with; paired with; together with) *along with (combined with; coupled with; joined with; paired with; together with).* The combination of the Relaxation Response coupled with the person's particular belief will work. *The Relaxation Response coupled with the person's particular belief will work.*

(a; the) combination of both *both (of them); combination.* A combination of both whites and blacks are members of these groups. *Both whites and blacks are* *members of these groups.* ■ Most economic output embodies some combination of both goods and services. *Most economic output embodies some combination of goods and services.*

(a; the) combination of the two *both (of them); combination.* You may use either technique or a combination of the two. *You may use either or both techniques.* ■ These programming languages include true fourth-generation languages, process-oriented languages, or a combination of the two. *These programming languages include true fourth-generation languages, process-oriented languages, or a combination.* ■ The meeting's objective could be to convey product knowledge, selling skills, or a combination of the two. *The meeting's objective could be to convey product knowledge, selling skills, or both.*

combine both *combine.* The latest development is to combine both record and programming so you can record and then edit macros. *The latest development is to combine record and programming so you can record and then edit macros.*

combine into one *combine.* The single justice noted that combining the two motions into one was a minor procedural discrepancy. *The single justice noted that combining the two motions was a minor procedural discrepancy.*

combine together *combine.*   .

come about *befall; happen; occur; result; take place.*

come as a disappointment (to) *disappoint.* I know this may come as a disappointment to some of you, but my husband is not going to be running for office. *I know this may disappoint some of you, but my husband is not going to be running for office.*

come as a relief (to) *relieve.* The pronunciation system of the former OED, a frequent source of criticism, has been replaced by the International Phonetic Alphabet, which should come as a relief to many. *The pronunciation system of the former OED, a frequent source of criticism, has been replaced by the International Phonetic Alphabet, which should relieve many.*

come as a surprise (to) *startle; surprise.* It wouldn't come as a surprise to any woman schooled in the ways of womanizers to learn that he is alleged to share his bed not only with many women but with a variety of defense contractors as well. *It wouldn't surprise any woman schooled in the ways of womanizers to learn that he is alleged to share his bed not only with many women but with a variety of defense contractors as well.*

come close (near) to *approach; resemble.* The results of a true national probability sample would most likely come close to these findings. *The results of a true national probability sample would most likely approach these findings.*

come equipped (furnished) with *come with; equipped (furnished) with.* All computers come equipped with a keyboard. *All computers come with a keyboard.* ▪ Equipment manufacturers like to sell general-purpose machines, the ones that come equipped with a dazzling array of cranks, switches, knobs, buttons, cams, and dials. *Equipment manufacturers like to sell general-purpose machines, the ones equipped with a dazzling array of cranks, switches, knobs, buttons, cams, and dials.*

come in contact (with) *come across; contact; discover; encounter; find; locate; meet (with); spot; touch.* The attached memorandum from the California Highway Patrol implies that members of the Sandinista National Liberation Front will utilize deadly force against law enforcement officers who come in contact with them. *The attached memorandum from the California Highway Patrol implies that members of the Sandinista National Liberation Front will utilize deadly force against law enforcement officers who encounter them.* ▪ She tried to pass on her love of learning to the many thousands of young persons she came in contact with over the years. *She tried to pass on her love of learning to the many thousands of young persons she met over the years.* ▪ If the part is designed to come in contact with another surface, the rough surface must be machined. *If the part is designed to touch another surface, the rough surface must be machined.*

come into being *appear; arise; evolve; exist.*

come into existence *appear; arise; evolve; exist.* In the chain network, the possibility of screening by levels comes into existence. *In the chain network, the possibility of screening by levels arises.* ▪ Scientific discoveries are the basis for development of practical applications that may not come into existence until years after discovery. *Scientific discoveries are the basis for development of practical applications that may not exist until years after discovery.*

come into play *appear; arise; come about; develop; emerge; happen; occur; result; surface; take place; turn up; unfold.* When they act out their depression, thoughts of suicide can come into play. *When they act out their depression, thoughts of suicide can surface.* ▪ Dirty tricks—or at least dubious methods—can also come into play in the final days of a campaign, and they have this year. *Dirty tricks—or at least dubious methods—can also emerge in the final days of a campaign, and they have this year.*

come into (to) (a; the) ... (of) *delete.* Eventually they came to the recognition that the supercomputer business is a high-stakes poker game. *Eventually they recognized that the supercomputer business is a high-stakes poker game.* ▪ It neither glosses over the true historical picture nor attempts to come to the defense of any individuals. *It neither glosses over the true historical picture nor attempts to defend any individuals.* ▪ I can only hope that other industries will come to the realization that by protecting the environment, they are also protecting their profits. *I can only hope that other industries will realize that by protecting the* *environment, they are also protecting their profits.* ■ Because it's now cheaper to violate the law than to come into compliance with it, many owners of these underground tanks have simply ignored the state regulations. *Because it's now cheaper to violate the law than to comply with it, many owners of these underground tanks have simply ignored the state regulations.*

come to (an; the) accord *agree; compromise; concur; decide; resolve; settle.*

come to a close *cease; close; complete; conclude; end; finish; halt; stop.*

come to a (the) conclusion *cease; close; complete; conclude; end; finish; halt; stop.* In August, the first wave of exploration of the solar system came to a conclusion with Voyager 2's swoop past the present outermost planet, Neptune. *In August, the first wave of exploration of the solar system concluded with Voyager 2's swoop past the present outermost planet, Neptune.*

come to (an; the) agreement *agree; compromise; concur; decide; resolve; settle.* The parents and the school board have not yet come to an agreement on whether the child should be in regular classes. *The parents and the school board have not yet agreed on whether the child should be in regular classes.*

come to a halt *cease; close; complete; conclude; end; finish; halt; stop.* Suddenly, all activity came to a halt. *Suddenly, all activity stopped.*

come to an end *cease; close; complete; conclude; end; finish; halt; stop.* He sees himself as the last survivor of the so-called Bengal Renaissance, the vital and creative cultural movement that was initiated by Ram Mohan Roy (c. 1774–1833) and that came to an end with the death of Rabindranath Tagore in 1941. *He sees himself as the last survivor of the so-called Bengal Renaissance, the vital and creative cultural movement that was initiated by Ram Mohan Roy (c. 1774–1833) and that ceased with the death of Rabindranath Tagore in 1941.* ■ We would like to extend our sincere gratitude to all of you in the community for everything you've done for us in the passing of our beloved husband and father, whose life came to an end suddenly on October 14. *We would like to extend our sincere gratitude to all of you in the community for everything you've done for us in the passing of our beloved husband and father, whose life ended suddenly on October 14.*

come to a standstill *cease; close; complete; conclude; end; finish; halt; stop.* A spokesman for the Export-Import Bank of Japan said talks with China have come to a standstill. *A spokesman for the Export-Import Bank of Japan said talks with China have ceased.*

come to (a; the) compromise *agree; compromise; concur; decide; resolve; settle.*

come to (a; the) conclusion *conclude; decide; deduce; determine; infer; judge; reason; resolve; settle.* We came to the conclusion that she should start with antibiotics. *We decided that she should start with antibiotics.* ■ We feel something has happened to her, and we think the police are coming to the same conclusion. *We feel something has happened to her, and we think the police are concluding the same.* ■ He also made the supreme sacrifice and started eating English-style food, having come to the conclusion that "good English cannot be written on [an Indian] diet." *He also made the supreme sacrifice and started eating English-style food, having reasoned that "good English cannot be written on [an Indian] diet."* ■ The only conclusion I can come to is that they're trying to frighten us into abandoning our bid. *I can only infer that they're trying to frighten us into abandoning our bid.*

come to (a; the) decision (on; upon) *conclude; decide; deduce; determine; infer; judge; reason; resolve; settle.* It was during the counseling session that we came to the decision to let Allison move in with us. *It was during the counseling session that we decided to let Allison move in with us.*

come to (a; the) determination (on; upon) *conclude; decide; deduce; determine; infer; judge; reason; resolve; settle.*

come to discover (find; find out) *discover; find; learn.*

come to (an; the) estimate (estimation) (of) *approximate; assess; estimate; evaluate; rate.*

come to find out *discern; discover; find out.*

come together *assemble; congregate; converge; gather.* In the days before mass immunizations when compulsory education began, disease could spread quickly as large numbers of children came together in unsanitary, poorly heated, poorly ventilated buildings. *In the days before mass immunizations when compulsory education began, disease could spread quickly as large numbers of children gathered in unsanitary, poorly heated, poorly ventilated buildings.*

come to grips with *accept; comprehend; cope with; deal with; face; struggle with; understand.* The systems software maker is now coming to grips with a period of rapid growth. *The systems software maker is now struggling with a period of rapid growth.* ■ The legislature has failed to come to grips with the budget or pare state spending sufficiently. *The legislature has failed to deal with the budget or pare state spending sufficiently.*

come to light *emerge; surface; transpire.* In the past year, a few new clues have come to light. *In the past year, a few new clues have transpired.*

come to (a; the) opinion *conclude; decide; deduce; determine; infer; judge; reason; resolve; settle.* I came to the opinion that it was an electrical fire, not arson. *I deduced that it was an electrical fire, not arson.*

come to pass *befall; happen; occur; result; take place.* If this should come to pass, it would benefit everybody. *If this should happen, it would benefit everybody.* ■ Beyond that, no one can predict what will come to pass. *Beyond that, no one can predict what will occur.*

come to (a; the) resolution (about; on) *agree; conclude; decide; determine; resolve; settle.* I don't understand why they did what they did, and I hope we can come to a resolution about it. *I don't understand why they did what they did, and I hope we can resolve it.*

come to (a; the) settlement *agree; conclude; decide; resolve; settle.*

come to terms (on; upon) *agree; arbitrate; compromise; concur; decide; settle.* What they can't come to terms on is whether selling the profitable Eastern Shuttle will cure the airline or kill it. *What they can't agree on is whether selling the profitable Eastern Shuttle will cure the airline or kill it.*

come to terms with *accept; comprehend; cope with; deal with; face; struggle with; understand.* An executive who has difficulty in coming to terms with a competitive environment will be relatively ineffective. *An executive who has difficulty in coping with a competitive environment will be relatively ineffective.* ■ Fitzwater said the president has come to terms with the constant attention. *Fitzwater said the president has accepted the constant attention.*

come to (an; the) understanding *agree; compromise; concur; decide; resolve; settle.*

come up with *craft; create; design; devise; draft; fashion; find; form; make; map (out); mold; plan; plot; prepare; produce; propose; shape; sketch; suggest.* The NRC has given the nuclear plant a month to come up with a workable plan. *The NRC has given the nuclear plant a month to devise a workable plan.* ■ The New York Stock Exchange and the Chicago Mercantile Exchange have come up with plans for "circuit breakers" designed to prevent breakdowns in runaway markets. *The New York Stock Exchange and the Chicago Mercantile Exchange have created plans for "circuit breakers" designed to prevent breakdowns in runaway markets.* ■ Identifying resource conflicts and coming up with possible solutions isn't always enough. *Identifying resource conflicts and forming possible solutions isn't always enough.*

comfortably ensconced *ensconced.* He is comfortably ensconced as head of the national guard of Panama. *He is ensconced as head of the national guard of Panama.*

comfort facilities *bathroom; toilet.* It seems to me that the required visitor-information services, tour departments, and comfort facilities could be provided in a leased ground-floor space in an existing nearby building. *It seems to me that the required visitor-information services, tour departments, and bathrooms could be provided in a leased ground-floor space in an existing nearby building.*

comical *comic.*

commence *begin; start.* If the candidate accepts the employment offer, the next phase commences. *If the candidate accepts the employment offer, the next phase begins.*

commencement *start.* Investment of the net proceeds will take place during a period which will not exceed six months from the commencement of operations. *Investment of the net proceeds will take place during a period which will not exceed six months from the start of operations.*

commit (a; the) ... (of) delete. You could not give it to your spouse without committing a violation of federal law. *You could not give it to your spouse without violating federal law.*

common (and) everyday *common; everyday.*

communicate (with) *call; call or write; phone; speak (with); talk (to); write (to).* Please communicate with us at your first opportunity. *Please call us at your first opportunity.* ■ To reserve a space, please communicate with Mr. Rigby, 1384 Arthur Road, Plano, TX 75075—(214) 432-3775. *To reserve a space, please call or write Mr. Rigby, 1384 Arthur Road, Plano, TX 75075—(214) 432-3775.*

communicate in writing *write.*

communication *dialogue; letter; message; note; report; speech; talk; text; words.* Nurses frequently make the assumption that their communication has been listened to and understood by patients. *Nurses frequently make the assumption that their words have been listened to and understood by patients.*

comparatively *-(i)er; less; more.* Computing what happens to stars and gas in a galactic cube, 100 cells on a side, turns out to be comparatively straightforward. *Computing what happens to stars and gas in a galactic cube, 100 cells on a side, turns out to be more straightforward.*

comparatively -(i)er than (less than; more than) *-(i)er than (less than; more than).* U.S. experts say the Soviet budget deficit that Moscow has finally acknowledged is comparatively larger than that of America. *U.S. experts say the Soviet budget deficit that Moscow has finally acknowledged is larger than that of America.*

compare against (versus) *compare to (with).* Compare the printout carefully against Figure 50. *Compare the printout carefully with Figure 50.* ■ Comparing the cost of owning versus renting will provide those who would have chosen home ownership with a firmer knowledge of their housing costs. *Comparing the cost of owning to renting will provide those who would have chosen home ownership with a firmer knowledge of their housing costs.*

compare and contrast *compare; contrast.* Perhaps it should have appeared in the Living section, where lifestyles of women from other Arab populations could be compared and contrasted to those living in the occupied territories under Israeli control. *Perhaps it should have appeared in the Living section, where lifestyles of women from other Arab populations could be contrasted to those living in the occupied territories under Israeli control.* ■ After finishing this topic, you will be able to compare and contrast different word processing programs. *After finishing this topic, you will be able to compare different word processing programs.*

compared to (with) *against; alongside; beside; -(i)er than; less; less than; more; more than; next to; over; than; to; versus.* Smoking prevalence has declined across all educational groups, but the decline has occurred five times faster among the higher-educated compared with the less educated. *Smoking prevalence has declined across all educational groups, but the decline has occurred five times faster among the higher-educated than the less educated.* ■ Volume on the Big Board averaged 153.57 million shares a day compared to 153.39 million in the first week of 1989. *Volume on the Big Board averaged 153.57 million shares a day against 153.39 million in the first week of 1989.* ■ Compared with children who died from trauma and with infants who died suddenly of known causes, the SIDS victims had much higher hypoxanthine levels. *The SIDS victims had much higher hypoxanthine levels than children who died from trauma and infants who died suddenly of known causes.* ■ But the combination aspirin/ heparin treatment showed no particular benefit compared with aspirin alone or heparin alone. *But the combination aspirin/heparin treatment showed no particular benefit over aspirin alone or heparin alone.* ■ Heavy buying of dollars by traders, or governments, on exchange markets drives up its price, making it strong compared to other currencies. *Heavy buying of dollars by traders, or governments, on exchange markets drives up its price, making it stronger than other currencies.* ■ He cited studies that show consumers get almost 20 percent of their initial claim in arbitration compared with less than 3 percent in the courts. *He cited studies that show consumers get almost 20 percent of their initial claim in arbitration versus less than 3 percent in the courts.*

compared (contrasted) to (with) ... relatively *compared (contrasted) to (with).* A number of researchers have suggested that the rings of Uranus—compared with the solar system, which has been around for some 4.6 billion years—look relatively young, perhaps less than a billion years old. *A number of researchers have suggested that the rings of Uranus—compared with the solar system, which has been around for some 4.6 billion years—look young, perhaps less than a billion* *years old.* ■ Compared to the advantages, there are relatively few disadvantages for a sole proprietorship. *Compared to the advantages, there are few disadvantages for a sole proprietorship.*

compartmentalized *compartmented.*

compensate *pay.*

compensation *cash; fee; money; pay; payment; reward; wage.*

competency *competence.* I feel this would be a good way of assessing his competency. *I feel this would be a good way of assessing his competence.* ■ The message of competency is one the American people are eager to hear. *The message of competence is one the American people are eager to hear.*

complete and utter *complete; utter.* It is going to be a complete and utter mess for people to figure out. *It is going to be an utter mess for people to figure out.*

completely *delete.* The car was completely destroyed in the fire. *The car was destroyed in the fire.* ■ An independent auditor will begin reviewing 10,000 claims ranging from minor dents to completely totaled cars. *An independent auditor will begin reviewing 10,000 claims ranging from minor dents to totaled cars.*

completely (entirely; exclusively; fully; solely; thoroughly; totally; utterly; wholly) dedicated to *dedicated to.* SDS recently moved into a new facility exclusively dedicated to EWSD development for the U.S. market. *SDS recently moved into a new facility dedicated to EWSD development for the U.S. market.*

completely (entirely; exclusively; fully; solely; thoroughly; totally; utterly; wholly) devoted to *devoted to.* The store was devoted entirely to consumer-oriented systems of racks, shelves, bins and hooks, largely of European manufacture, all designed to make a small space more serviceable. *The store was devoted to consumer-oriented systems of racks, shelves, bins and hooks, largely of European manufacture, all designed to make a small space more serviceable.*

completely (entirely; fully; thoroughly; totally; utterly; wholly) eliminate *eliminate.* Computer specialists at MIT said it would take several more days to entirely eliminate the virus. *Computer specialists at MIT said it would take several more days to eliminate the virus.* ■ But because of intense pressure from its 11 million farmers, the EEC has been unwilling to agree to their total elimination. *But because of intense pressure from its 11 million farmers, the EEC has been unwilling to agree to their elimination.*

completely (entirely; fully; thoroughly; totally; utterly; wholly) eradicate *eradicate.* Dr. Carlos said he expects the trend to continue, although completely eradicating the decay is probably not possible. *Dr. Carlos said he expects the trend to continue, although eradicating the decay is probably not possible.*

completely (entirely; fully; thoroughly; totally; utterly; wholly) unanimous *unanimous.*

complete monopoly *monopoly.*

component *part.* Two-tier coverage was cited as an important component of successful marketing. *Two-tier coverage was cited as an important part of successful marketing.* ■ Flexible integration of commercial and investment banking services is a major component of Westpac Banking Corporation's strategy for future expansion. *Flexible integration of commercial and investment banking services is a major part of Westpac Banking Corporation's strategy for future expansion.*

component (and) part *component; part.* If the firm intends to deliver finished products, component parts, or other inputs to the market under review, it needs to review its sourcing and delivery alternatives. *If the firm intends to deliver finished products, components, or other inputs to the market under review, it needs to review its sourcing and delivery alternatives.* ■ The plants manufacture electrical appliances or component parts for the appliances. *The plants manufacture electrical appliances or parts for the appliances.* ■ Other Johnstone services include a 500-page catalog of components and parts, which it issues three times a year along with a direct-mail promotion. *Other Johnstone services include a 500-page catalog of parts, which it issues three times a year along with a direct-mail promotion.*

conceive (of) an (the) idea (for) *conceive (of).* While a student at Cambridge University, he conceived an idea for a calculator that would calculate and print logarithmic tables. *While a student at Cambridge University, he conceived of a calculator that would calculate and print logarithmic tables.*

concentrate ... attention on (upon) *concentrate on; focus on.* Eastern has decided to concentrate most of its attention on keeping its shuttle going. *Eastern has decided to concentrate on keeping its shuttle going.* ■ Had he recognized this fact, he could have concentrated his attention on the glorious history of the frustrated Red Sox. *Had he recognized this fact, he could have focused on the glorious history of the frustrated Red Sox.*

concentrate (media; people's; public) attention on (upon) *advertise; announce; disclose; divulge; expose; herald; indicate; make known; make public; mention; point out; point to; present; proclaim; promote; publicize; reveal; show; tell;*

uncover; unveil. She never became president of the American Economics Association—perhaps because of her relentless work concentrating attention on the low status of women in the profession. *She never became president of the American Economics Association—perhaps because of her relentless work exposing the low status of women in the profession.*

concentrate … effort on (upon) *concentrate on; focus on.* If we concentrate our effort on the areas of most need, we might be able to make a difference. *If we concentrate on the areas of most need, we might be able to make a difference.*

concentrate … energy on (upon) *concentrate on; focus on.* Students need to concentrate their energies on their studies, extracurricular activities, and work. *Students need to focus on their studies, extracurricular activities, and work.*

concentrate … time and energy on (upon) *concentrate on; focus on.* We still have 10 million gallons of oil in the water, and we ought to be concentrating our time and energy on minimizing the damage that that does. *We still have 10 million gallons of oil in the water, and we ought to be concentrating on minimizing the damage that that does.*

concerning *about; as for; as to; for; in; of; on; over; to; toward; with;* delete. The Federal Reserve Board makes available various indexes, including one concerning industrial production. *The Federal Reserve Board makes available various indexes, including one about industrial production.* ■ We surveyed the evidence concerning how firms finance their assets. *We surveyed the evidence on how firms finance their assets.* ■ Concerning price, key factors include the point at which the exporting firm ceases to be responsible for the products, the currency of settlement, and the terms of payment. *As for price, key factors include the point at which the exporting firm ceases to be responsible for the products, the currency of settlement, and the terms of payment.*

conclusive end *conclusion; end.*

concurrently *as one; at once; jointly; together.*

concurrent (concurrently) with *while; with.* Concurrent with rejecting the tender offer, Prime's directors approved a series of defensive measures. *While rejecting the tender offer, Prime's directors approved a series of defensive measures.*

(a; the) … condition delete. I'm telling the truth now partly because of my health condition. *I'm telling the truth now partly because of my health.* ■ Congruency is a necessary condition for clients to develop trust in nurses. *Congruency is necessary for clients to develop trust in nurses.*

conduct (a; the) ... (into; of; on; to; with) delete. We conducted interviews with EFT industry experts early in the study. *We interviewed EFT industry experts early in the study.* ■ The company conducts surveys of employers' hiring plans quarterly. *The company surveys employers' hiring plans quarterly.* ■ Another method of collecting information is to conduct research on hunters' opinions about the merits of introducing a hunting seat on the market. *Another method of collecting information is to research hunters' opinions about the merits of introducing a hunting seat on the market.* ■ They should conduct an investigation into how these scholarships were awarded with no set criteria for selection, and explain why linguistic minorities are seemingly underrepresented. *They should investigate how these scholarships were awarded with no set criteria for selection, and explain why linguistic minorities are seemingly underrepresented.*

congregate together *congregate.* We feel that the five baby dinosaurs were congregating together behind a sand dune in a sandstorm. *We feel that the five baby dinosaurs were congregating behind a sand dune in a sandstorm.*

connected with *for; in; linked to; of; -'s; with.* Before getting involved with a coverup, consider the costs connected with such a move. *Before getting involved with a coverup, consider the costs of such a move.* ■ Obviously, the most profitable method of investing would be to buy low and sell high; however, there are several problems connected with this method. *Obviously, the most profitable method of investing would be to buy low and sell high; however, there are several problems with this method.*

connect together *connect; link.* A network is two or more computers connected together with cables so that they can exchange files and share resources. *A network is two or more computers connected with cables so that they can exchange files and share resources.* ■ They want everything from telephone equipment to computers to local networks that connect all the pieces together. *They want everything from telephone equipment to computers to local networks that link all the pieces.*

consecutive *straight.*

consensus (of) opinion *consensus.* There is a consensus of opinion in this country against executing our young criminals. *There is a consensus in this country against executing our young criminals.*

consequence *import; moment.*

consequence *effect; outcome; result.*

consequence (effect; outcome) resulting from *consequence (effect; outcome) of; result of.* The potential long-term outcomes resulting from their reactions are destroyed creativity and stifled initiative. *The potential long-term outcomes of their reactions are destroyed creativity and stifled initiative.*

consequently *hence; so; then; therefore; thus.* They were victims of misfortune or of circumstances beyond their control, and consequently, they live in shelters or on the streets. *They were victims of misfortune or of circumstances beyond their control, and thus, they live in shelters or on the streets.* ■ The beliefs and practices that flow from Catholicism and Protestantism also appear to have differing influences on economic activity and, consequently, economic development. *The beliefs and practices that flow from Catholicism and Protestantism also appear to have differing influences on economic activity and, hence, economic development.*

considerable *ample; big; grand; great; heavy; huge; immense; large; many; most; much; vast.* This is a source of considerable uneasiness for them. *This is a source of much uneasiness for them.* ■ The cause of the fire is not known, but it did cause considerable damage. *The cause of the fire is not known, but it did cause great damage.*

(a; the) considerable (good; great; huge; large; sizable; vast) amount (of) *a good (great) deal (of); a good (great) many (of); almost all (of); considerable; many (of); most (of); much (of); nearly all (of); vast;* delete. It's operationally complex and requires a large amount of resources. *It's operationally complex and requires vast resources.* ■ A vast amount of time and effort is wasted in solving the wrong problems. *Much time and effort is wasted in solving the wrong problems.* ■ A considerable amount of political power is being transferred to the local level. *Considerable political power is being transferred to the local level.*

(a; the) considerable (good; great; huge; large; sizable; vast) degree (of) *a good (great) deal (of); considerable; great; much (of); vast;* delete. We would expect to see a large degree of individuality in these sets of twins. *We would expect to see much individuality in these sets of twins.* ■ They now realize they showed a considerable degree of insensitivity toward small businesses. *They now realize they showed great insensitivity toward small businesses.*

(a; the) considerable (good; great; huge; large; sizable; vast) element (of) *a good (great) deal (of); considerable; great; much (of); vast;* delete. True to the spirit of covert operations, there was a large element of deception and dissembling in this struggle. *True to the spirit of covert operations, there was much deception and dissembling in this struggle.*

(a; the) considerable (good; great; huge; large; overwhelming; vast; sizable; wide) majority (of) *a good (great) deal (of); a good (great) many (of); almost all (of); (nine) in (ten) (of); many (of); most (of); much (of); nearly all (of); (43) of (48) (of); ... percent (of); three-fourths (two-thirds) (of);* delete. The truth must remain that the overwhelming majority of the decisions on what to produce, and how and where to produce it, have been made by private persons and businesses. *The truth must remain that 70 percent of the decisions on what to produce, and how and where to produce it, have been made by private persons and businesses.* ■ A large majority of them also favors shortening the length of the primary campaign. *Two-thirds of them also favor shortening the length of the primary campaign.* ■ Not all patients with brain tumors die although the vast majority of them do. *Not all patients with brain tumors die although most of them do.* ■ The overwhelming majority of Americans agree that alcoholism is a disease. *Eight in ten Americans agree that alcoholism is a disease.* ■ A very large majority—95 to 97 percent—of those who try to quit smoking on their own, without any help, fail the first time. *Of those who try to quit smoking on their own, without any help, 95 to 97 percent fail the first time.* ■ The two own the vast majority of the stock. *The two own almost all the stock.*

(a; the) considerable (good; great; huge; large; overwhelming; sizable; vast) number (of) *a good (great) many (of); almost all (of); countless; dozens (of); hundreds (of); many (of); millions (of); most (of); nearly all (of); numerous; scores (of); six hundred (twelve hundred); thousands (of).* The language provides a large number of primitive data types. *The language provides dozens of primitive data types.* ■ This faction is epitomized by kids who came of age in the 1960s, but includes vast numbers of citizens who came both before and after. *This faction is epitomized by kids who came of age in the 1960s, but includes thousands of citizens who came both before and after.* ■ Not every car torched is insurance fraud, but a large number are. *Not every car torched is insurance fraud, but many are.* ■ Various government agencies offer advisory services along with a huge number of useful publications. *Various government agencies offer advisory services along with countless useful publications.* ■ That would show a blatant disregard for the opinions of a vast number of people. *That would show a blatant disregard for the opinions of millions of people.* ■ Reports from northern Burundi indicated that hundreds died, including large numbers of women and children. *Reports from northern Burundi indicated that hundreds died, including scores of women and children.*

(a; the) considerable (good; great; huge; large; sizable; vast) part (of) *a good (great) deal (of); a good (great) many (of); almost all (of); (nine) in (ten) (of); many (of); most (of); much (of); nearly all (of); (43) of (48) (of); ... percent (of); three-fourths (two-thirds) (of); delete.* What may surprise you, however, is that a large part of this analysis is within your reach at little or no cost. *What may surprise you, however, is that much of this analysis is within your reach at little or no cost.*

(a; the) considerable (good; great; huge; large; overwhelming; sizable; vast) percentage (of) *a good (great) deal (of); a good (great) many (of); almost all (of); (nine) in (ten) (of); many (of); most (of); much (of); nearly all (of); (43) of (48) (of); ... percent (of); three-fourths (two-thirds) (of); delete.* Airway obstruction is the primary cause of death in a large percentage of head trauma victims. *Airway obstruction is the primary cause of death in most head trauma* *victims.* ■ A sizable percentage of men cheat on their wives. *A good many men cheat on their wives.* ■ The large percentage of people will experiment with alcohol and drugs when they're young. *Three in five people will experiment with alcohol and drugs when they're young.* ■ We know that a large percentage of IRA contributors had been saving very little before IRAs were created. *We know that one-third of IRA contributors had been saving very little before IRAs were created.*

(a; the) considerable (good; great; huge; large; sizable; vast) portion (of) *a good (great) deal (of); a good (great) many (of); almost all (of); (nine) in (ten) (of); many (of); most (of); much (of); nearly all (of); (43) of (48) (of); ... percent (of); three-fourths (two-thirds) (of);* delete. It will be unseasonably cool over a considerable portion of the United States today. *It will be unseasonably cool over much of the United States today.* ■ A large portion of the blame must be placed squarely at the door of corporate management. *Most of the blame must be placed squarely at the door of corporate management.* ■ While a vast portion of the pie in 1985 might have gone to specialty hardware vendors and generic AI tool vendors, today the picture looks different. *While two-thirds of the pie in 1985 might have gone to specialty hardware vendors and generic AI tool vendors, today the picture looks different.*

(a; the) considerable (good; great; huge; large; sizable; vast) proportion (of) *a good (great) deal (of); a good (great) many (of); almost all (of); (nine) in (ten) (of); many (of); most (of); much (of); nearly all (of); (43) of (48) (of); ... percent (of); three-fourths (two-thirds) (of);* delete. These precautions also are common in other nations in which a large proportion of people are altering their behavior because of AIDS. *These precautions also are common in other nations in which many people are altering their behavior because of AIDS.* ■ I don't believe that the vast proportion of creative people are or were psychotic. *I don't believe that most creative people are or were psychotic.* ■ They may squander huge proportions of their purchasing power by paying high instead of low prices on each purchase. *They may squander much of their purchasing power by paying high instead of low prices on each purchase.*

(a; the) considerable (good; great; huge; large; sizable; vast) quantity (of) *a good (great) deal (of); a good (great) many (of); almost all (of); dozens (of); hundreds (of); many (of); millions (of); most (of); nearly all (of); scores (of); six hundred (twelve hundred) (of); thousands (of).* There are vast quantities of transactions that are still processed slowly and manually. *There are many transactions that are still processed slowly and manually.* ■ Students often fail to remember or understand large quantities of their elementary calculus. *Students often fail to remember or understand most of their elementary calculus.*

considerably *a good (great) deal; amply; far; greatly; largely; mostly; much; vastly.* This is considerably different from the past, when information was printed and approved before being passed up the hierarchy. *This is far different from the past, when information was printed and approved before being passed up the* *hierarchy.* ■ Most contracts are bid, signed, delivered, and paid for in 14–16-week cycles, but some can be drawn out considerably longer than that. *Most contracts are bid, signed, delivered, and paid for in 14–16-week cycles, but some can be drawn out much longer than that.*

consider as *consider.* It could be considered as false advertising. *It could be considered false advertising.* ■ Buddhism's world-denying orientation is considered by many as an obstacle to economic development. *Buddhism's world-denying orientation is considered by many an obstacle to economic development.*

consider as being *consider.* In many ways, software engineering may be considered as being similar to various other sciences and branches of engineering. *In many ways, software engineering may be considered similar to various other sciences and branches of engineering.* ■ Problems in Class P, therefore, may be considered as being solvable. *Problems in Class P, therefore, may be considered solvable.*

considering the fact that *because; considering; for; in that; since; when.* Considering the fact that the average person uses 77 gallons of water a day, we can estimate that each person uses close to 26 gallons of water every day simply by flushing the toilet. *Since the average person uses 77 gallons of water a day, we can estimate that each person uses close to 26 gallons of water every day simply by flushing the toilet.*

consider to be *consider.* We considered him to be a milksop. *We considered him a milksop.* ■ Most consultants consider effective presentation to be essential. *Most consultants consider effective presentation essential.*

consolidate together *consolidate.*

constitute *be; compose; form; make up.* Corporate debt issues constitute the largest segment, totaling more than $341 billion in 1986. *Corporate debt issues make up the largest segment, totaling more than $341 billion in 1986.* ■ And the fact that he remains in power, so high in the line of succession to the presidency, constitutes a national embarrassment. *And the fact that he remains in power, so high in the line of succession to the presidency, is a national embarrassment.* ■ While the beneficiaries of the system constitute a minority of the public, they are well organized and politically powerful. *While the beneficiaries of the system form a minority of the public, they are well organized and politically powerful.*

contact *call; phone; reach; write (to).* She contacted the state agency that helps welfare recipients. *She called the state agency that helps welfare recipients.* ■ Please do not hesitate to contact me if you have further questions. *Please do not hesitate to phone me if you have further questions.*

contagious disease *contagion.*

contain (a; the) ... of delete. Figure 12.1 contains a graphical representation of these factors. *Figure 12.1 graphically represents these factors.* ▪ Chapter 15 contains a formal discussion of the theoretical underpinnings of these formulas. ▪ *Chapter 15 formally discusses the theoretical underpinnings of these formulas.* ▪ Table 4-3 contains a list of all 26 ProDOS commands and command numbers. *Table 4-3 lists all 26 ProDOS commands and command numbers.*

continue in existence (to exist) *continue; endure; exist; last; persevere; persist; prevail; remain; survive.* I believe that nuclear reactions are taking place, and that possibility continues to exist until proven otherwise. *I believe that nuclear reactions are taking place, and that possibility exists until proven otherwise.* ▪ The possibility of becoming an independent company continues to exist. *The possibility of becoming an independent company persists.*

continue into the future *continue.* The rate of growth in the market is expected to continue into the future. *The rate of growth in the market is expected to continue.*

continue on *continue.* If he doesn't raise enough money, he won't be able to continue on. *If he doesn't raise enough money, he won't be able to continue.* ▪ The three dots in 1, 2, 3, 4, 5, ... mean the list continues on and on. *The three dots in 1, 2, 3, 4, 5, ... mean the list continues.*

continue to be *be still; remain; stay.* This was the case before the New York state law and continues to be the case after the New York state law. *This was the case before the New York state law and remains the case after the New York state law.* ▪ Working out continues to be a popular pastime. *Working out is still a popular pastime.*

continue to remain *be still; remain; stay.* Sex stereotypes continue to remain a problem in the military. *Sex stereotypes remain a problem in the military.* ▪ As a result, both anorexia nervosa and obesity are characteristic of modern life, and will continue to remain so. *As a result, both anorexia nervosa and obesity are characteristic of modern life, and will remain so.*

contractual agreement *agreement; contract.* Contractual agreements with independent distributors in Indonesia are required by law to be for a minimum of three years. *Contracts with independent distributors in Indonesia are required by law to be for a minimum of three years.* ▪ Under a variety of contractual agreements, the institution will permit a mutual fund provider to sell funds directly to its customers. *Under a variety of agreements, the institution will permit a mutual fund provider to sell funds directly to its customers.*

contrariwise *but; conversely; however; instead; not so; rather; still; whereas; yet.*

contrary to *after all; apart; aside; despite; even with; for all; with all.* Contrary to some of the things you've heard, I am the same man I was when I came to Washington. *Despite some of the things you've heard, I am the same man I was when I came to Washington.* ■ Contrary to his allegations, AARP does not "profit" when insurance claims are less than projected. *For all his allegations, AARP does not "profit" when insurance claims are less than projected.*

contrasted to (with) *against; alongside; beside; compared to (with); -(i)er than; less; less than; more; more than; next to; over; than; to; unlike; versus; vis-à-vis.*

contribute to *add to.*

converge together *converge.*

(in) conversation *talk.*

converse *speak; talk.* She has multiple personalities, and I was able to converse with all of them. *She has multiple personalities, and I was able to talk with all of them.*

convicted felon *felon.* There are concerns over the fact that the bank loaned money to convicted felons. *There are concerns over the fact that the bank loaned money to felons.*

cooperate together *cooperate.*

core essence *core; crux; essence; gist; pith; substance.* Issues are supposed to be the core essence of a political convention. *Issues are supposed to be the core of a political convention.*

correctional (prison) facility *jail; prison.* Opponents complained that a prison facility for 500 inmates and several hundred staff members would overwhelm the town of barely 800 people. *Opponents complained that a prison for 500 inmates and several hundred staff members would overwhelm the town of barely 800 people.* ■ The reduction was necessary because state law limits the number of male and female prisoners who can be accommodated in correctional facilities. *The reduction was necessary because state law limits the number of male and female prisoners who can be accommodated in jails.*

correspondence *letter; memo; note; report.*

(a; the) countless number (of) *countless; endless; infinite; millions (of); myriad; numberless; untold.* The congestion has resulted in interminable delays and countless numbers of accidents for motorists. *The congestion has resulted in interminable delays and countless accidents for motorists.* ■ These so-called pro-lifers try to force their views on countless numbers of women. *These so-called pro-lifers try to force their views on untold women.*

couple together *couple.*

course of action *action; course; direction; intention; method; move; plan; policy; procedure; route; scheme; strategy.* The coalition has urged a boycott of tuna, but strengthening existing laws—and enforcing them—would be a better course of action. *The coalition has urged a boycott of tuna, but strengthening existing laws—and enforcing them—would be a better course.* ■ Not surprisingly, the defendant denied that he had agreed to this course of action or that he knew of the statement prior to the time he received a transcript. *Not surprisingly, the defendant denied that he had agreed to this scheme or that he knew of the statement prior to the time he received a transcript.* ■ He declined to say definitely whether that was the course of action he would take but pointed out that a bankruptcy filing is an option. *He declined to say definitely whether that was the direction he would take but pointed out that a bankruptcy filing is an option.* ■ Management perceived the surface manifestations of the problem correctly but failed to thoroughly explore the cause before deciding on a course of action. *Management perceived the surface manifestations of the problem correctly but failed to thoroughly explore the cause before deciding on a plan.*

cover over *cover.*

criminal act *crime.* Certainly if a public official commits a criminal act, he or she must face full consequences. *Certainly if a public official commits a crime, he or she must face full consequences.*

criminal offense *crime; offense.* Mr. Hurd said he had misgivings about making drinking on the streets a criminal offense. *Mr. Hurd said he had misgivings about making drinking on the streets an offense.*

criminal record *record.*

criminal wrongdoing *crime; wrongdoing.* McNamara may not be guilty of any criminal wrongdoing, but he is a terrible U.S. attorney. *McNamara may not be guilty of any crime, but he is a terrible U.S. attorney.*

(a; the) critical ... in (of; to) *critical to.* A critical ingredient in a manager's philosophy of change is how much emphasis is placed on trust in the work environment. *Critical to a manager's philosophy of change is how much emphasis is placed on trust in the work environment.* ■ A critical element in the development of these competitive advantages is the creation of a global marketing management process capable of coordinating, integrating, and controlling all marketing efforts. *Critical to the development of these competitive advantages is the creation of a global marketing management process capable of coordinating, integrating, and controlling all marketing efforts.* ■ Active cooperation among all industry groups is a critical factor to the success of EFT. *Active cooperation among all industry groups is critical to the success of EFT.*

(a; the) crucial ... in (of; to) *crucial to.* He believes hostility is a crucial component of the Type A personality and a potent predictor of heart trouble. *He believes hostility is crucial to the Type A personality and a potent predictor of heart trouble.* ▪ Social Security is a crucial aspect of retirement income for the vast majority of Americans, and financing the system is a crucial aspect of how the country saves and invests. *Social Security is crucial to retirement income for the vast majority of Americans, and financing the system is crucial to how the country saves and invests.*

currently *(just; right) now; today; (just) yet;* delete. He is currently unemployed. *He is unemployed.* ▪ It's the only spreadsheet currently on the market that has the look and feel of WordPerfect. *It's the only spreadsheet now on the market that has the look and feel of WordPerfect.* ▪ Currently, the industry seems to be concentrating on developing more AI applications rather than on developing better AI tools. *Today, the industry seems to be concentrating on developing more AI applications rather than on developing better AI tools.*

current (present) status *status.* Nothing material to date can be reported on the current status of these negotiations. *Nothing material to date can be reported on the status of these negotiations.* ▪ The Software Carousel includes a special menu used to control the operation of the system and to provide helpful information about the system's present status. *The Software Carousel includes a special menu used to control the operation of the system and to provide helpful information about the system's status.*

custom-built *custom; tailored.* At least one vendor uses a custom-built database system in addition to a commercial one to speed up operations. *At least one vendor uses a custom database system in addition to a commercial one to speed up operations.*

custom-made *custom; tailored.* Our courses are custom-made to meet the training needs of each client. *Our courses are tailored to meet the training needs of each client.* ▪ The Hitachi system incorporates a proprietary operating system and relational database running on custom-made Intel workstations. *The Hitachi system incorporates a proprietary operating system and relational database running on custom Intel workstations.*

custom-tailored *custom; customized; tailored.* We provide on-site courses that are custom-tailored to reflect our clients' specific needs and objectives. *We provide on-site courses that are tailored to reflect our clients' specific needs and objectives.* ▪ Customers today demand custom-tailored solutions to communications problems. *Customers today demand customized solutions to communications problems.*

cut by (in) half *halve.* A cooperative agreement was announced that could cut by half the amount of ozone-destroying chemicals released in the service and repair of auto air conditioners. *A cooperative agreement was announced that could halve the amount of ozone-destroying chemicals released in the service and repair of auto air conditioners.*

cyclical *cyclic.* The lengths of time within cyclical periods tend to vary. *The lengths of time within cyclic periods tend to vary.*

D

date back to *date from; date to.* Rogation Days date back at least to the 13th century and probably to the days before the Norman Conquest. *Rogation Days date to at least the 13th century and probably to the days before the Norman Conquest.* ■ The firm is still paying claims that date back to the 1930s, '40s, and '50s. *The firm is still paying claims that date from the 1930s, '40s, and '50s.*

day in (and) day out *always; ceaselessly; consistently; constantly; daily; endlessly; eternally; everlastingly; every day; forever; invariably; never ending; perpetually; routinely; unfailingly.* I was doing portraits day in and day out. *I was doing portraits every day.*

day-to-day routine *routine.* I am greatly tired of the day-to-day routine. *I am greatly tired of the routine.*

dead body *body.* They found a dead body in the river. *They found a body in the river.*

(a) decade's (year's) history of *(a) decade (year) of.* In spite of over a year's history of unusual trading in "Inside Wall Street" highlighted stocks, BW amazingly did not alert the New York Stock Exchange or the Securities & Exchange Commission. *In spite of over a year of unusual trading in "Inside Wall Street" highlighted stocks, BW amazingly did not alert the New York Stock Exchange or the Securities & Exchange Commission.*

decapitate ... head *behead; decapitate.* She hired a hit man to decapitate her husband's head. *She hired a hit man to decapitate her husband.*

(a; the) declining (decreasing; diminishing; dwindling) amount (degree; extent; part; percentage; portion; proportion) (of) *decreasingly; less; less and less.*

(a; the) declining (decreasing; diminishing; dwindling) number (quantity) (of) *decreasingly; few; fewer and fewer.*

decrease down *decrease.*

decreasing in *decreasingly.*

deductive reasoning *deduction.*

deem as *deem.*

(most) definitely *certainly; surely;* delete. Blocking out information will definitely limit communication. *Blocking out information will limit communication.*

(most; very) definitely *yes.*

(a; the) ... degree of delete. He provides a healthy and thoughtful degree of skepticism about prospects for positive change at the national level. *He provides a healthy and thoughtful skepticism about prospects for positive change at the national level.* ■ Competitor reaction cannot be predicted with any degree of accuracy. *Competitor reaction cannot be predicted with any accuracy.* ■ The development of the market that has taken place, characterized by an increasing degree of standardization, has made it possible to connect terminals and computers of different makes to telecommunications systems. *The development of the market that has taken place, characterized by increasing standardization, has made it possible to connect terminals and computers of different makes to telecommunications systems.*

demise *death; end.* While smoking may cause my demise, an individual's alcohol abuse can kill innocent people on our nation's roads. *While smoking may cause my death, an individual's alcohol abuse can kill innocent people on our nation's roads.* ■ That access is hastening the demise of many U.S. industries. *That access is hastening the end of many U.S. industries.*

demonstrate *show.*

depart *leave.* The president departs for Moscow this morning. *The president leaves for Moscow this morning.*

dependency *dependence.* It may also be difficult for these people to make the decision to marry because of the dependency and commitment required in an intimate relationship. *It may also be difficult for these people to make the decision to marry because of the dependence and commitment required in an intimate relationship.*

depreciate in value *depreciate.* He was carrying several hundred condos that depreciated between 10 and 30 percent in value. *He was carrying several hundred condos that depreciated between 10 and 30 percent.*

derive benefit (from) *benefit.* This suggests that many people would derive benefit from "stand-up-and-stretch" work breaks. *This suggests that many people would benefit from "stand-up-and-stretch" work breaks.* ■ Those 65 and older derived every bit as much benefit as quitters between 35 and 55—a reduction of 40 to 50 percent in their heart-attack/early-death risk. *Those 65 and older benefited every bit as much as quitters between 35 and 55—a reduction of 40 to 50 percent in their heart-attack/early-death risk.*

derive enjoyment from *admire; delight in; enjoy; rejoice in; relish; savor.*

derive pleasure from *admire; appreciate; delight in; enjoy; rejoice in; relish; savor.* We derived great pleasure from their performance. *We delighted in their performance.*

derive satisfaction from *admire; appreciate; delight in; enjoy; rejoice in; relish; savor.* If you derive genuine satisfaction from being in a leadership role, you will obviously bring that attitude to your role as a meeting leader. *If you genuinely enjoy being in a leadership role, you will obviously bring that attitude to your role as a meeting leader.*

descend down *descend.*

describe (explain) in ... detail *detail.* The proposal should describe in detail the procedure to be used to obtain data. *The proposal should detail the procedure to be used to obtain data.* ■ The enclosed résumé describes my background and experience in detail. *The enclosed résumé details my background and experience.*

desideratum *need.*

designate as *designate.*

despite the fact that *although; but; even though; still; though; yet.* Despite the fact that all the charts are on paper rather than on-line, the bank reports that departments competed to improve their performance. *Although all the charts are on paper rather than on-line, the bank reports that departments competed to improve their performance.* ■ Despite the fact that the logarithms are approximate values, it is customary to use the equals sign rather than the approximately equals sign when writing logarithms. *Though the logarithms are approximate values, it is customary to use the equals sign rather than the approximately equals sign when writing logarithms.* ■ Despite the fact that the crew was preparing the spinnaker for hoisting, they managed to replace the jib and keep the lead. *The crew was preparing the spinnaker for hoisting, but they managed to replace the jib and keep the lead.* ■ Despite the fact that many of his sources were admittedly very close to the Shah, few of the main players here emerge unscathed. *Even though many of his sources were admittedly very close to the Shah, few of the main players here emerge unscathed.*

detailed (in-depth) analysis *analysis; detail.* Apparently there are some who would discourage any detailed analysis of these weaknesses. *Apparently there are some who would discourage any analysis of these weaknesses.* ■ His original clinical research tracks people through 40 years of life, and provides a valuable in-depth analysis of adult development. *His original clinical research tracks people through 40 years of life, and provides a valuable analysis of adult development.*

determine the truth (truthfulness; validity; veracity) of *verify.*

devoid of *dis-; il-; im-; in-; ir-; lack; -less(ness); mis-; no; non-; not; un-; want; with no; without.* Your editorial makes the term censorship somewhat devoid of meaning. *Your editorial makes the term censorship somewhat meaningless.* ■ TV today is devoid of strong role models. *TV today lacks strong role models.*

diametrical *diametral.* The diametrical pitch is the number of teeth about the circumference divided by the diameter. *The diametral pitch is the number of teeth about the circumference divided by the diameter.*

(five; many; several) different *(five; many; several); different.* My parents own five different homes. *My parents own five homes.* ■ That can mean so many different things. *That can mean so many things.* ■ Identifying a problem and solving it are two different tasks. *Identifying a problem and solving it are different tasks.* ■ The company has learned that several different brokers in at least two different firms have employed various manipulative techniques to force the value of SSOA's stock down. *The company has learned that several brokers in at least two firms have employed various manipulative techniques to force the value of SSOA's stock down.*

(a; the) difficult task *difficult; task.* The difficult task of obtaining information for marketing decisionmaking presents two overriding challenges. *The task of obtaining information for marketing decisionmaking presents two overriding challenges.* ■ Given the differences between the languages, you might imagine that learning English is a difficult task for Japanese students. *Given the differences between the languages, you might imagine that learning English is difficult for Japanese students.*

difficulty in (of) -ing *difficulty -ing.* She has great difficulty in falling asleep. *She has great difficulty falling asleep.* ■ People afflicted with Parkinson's have tremors and difficulty in moving, and they may become demented. *People afflicted with Parkinson's have tremors and difficulty moving, and they may become demented.*

diminish down *diminish.*

direct ... attention to *advertise; announce; disclose; divulge; expose; herald; indicate; make known; make public; mention; point out; point to; present;*

proclaim; promote; publicize; reveal; show; tell; uncover; unveil. The Draper award is seen by some engineering leaders as a way of directing attention to the profession and making sure engineers share the spotlight with scientists. *The Draper award is seen by some engineering leaders as a way of promoting the profession and making sure engineers share the spotlight with scientists.*

disassociate *dissociate.* It set off calls by the faculty for nationally known conservatives to disassociate themselves from alleged Jew-baiting by the *Review,* which in the past has been accused of race-baiting and unfair characterization of women and homosexuals. *It set off calls by the faculty for nationally known conservatives to dissociate themselves from alleged Jew-baiting by the* Review, *which in the past has been accused of race-baiting and unfair characterization of women and homosexuals.*

discomfiture *discomfit; discomfort.*

(in) discussion *speaking; talking.* At Honda, managers spend up to 50 percent of their time in discussions with dealers and distributors. *At Honda, managers spend up to 50 percent of their time talking with dealers and distributors.*

display (a; the) ... (of; to) delete. The Task Manager displays a list of the programs that are currently running. *The Task Manager lists the programs that are currently running.*

distinct difference (distinctly different) *different;   distinct;   distinction.* We wanted to do something distinctly different. *We wanted to do something distinct.* ■ These contracts are explicitly authorized by state law—a distinct and major difference between MMWEC and WPPSS. *These contracts are explicitly authorized by state law—a major distinction between MMWEC and WPPSS.*

divide in half *halve.*

divide up *divide.* He suggested we divide up the money between us. *He suggested we divide the money between us.* ■ It also makes extensive use of "X windows," which allow a computer user to divide up the screen into multiple panels and look at two or more programs at once. *It also makes extensive use of "X windows," which allow a computer user to divide the screen into multiple panels and look at two or more programs at once.*

do (a; the) ... (about; in; of; on; to) *-(al)ly;* delete. We did a thorough search of the area and found nothing. *We thoroughly searched the area and found nothing.* ■ They'd rather build a roadway than provide a program that prevents someone from doing harm to someone else. *They'd rather build a roadway than provide a program that prevents someone from harming someone else.* ■ By setting demanding targets and strictly enforcing them, corporate management constantly challenges plans that are identified early and weeded out before they do damage to the company. *By setting demanding targets and strictly enforcing them, corporate management constantly challenges plans that are identified early and weeded out before they damage the company.*

do away with *cancel; destroy; end; kill; stop.*

does not ... any *no; none; nothing.* I don't see any reason to allow the sale of Saturday Night Specials. *I see no reason to allow the sale of Saturday Night Specials.* ■ I do not understand any of this. *I understand none of this.*

does not have to *needs not.* You do not have to specify extensions when you save or load files. *You need not specify extensions when you save or load files.* ■ Private banking premises should be tastefully decorated, but they do not have to be lavish. *Private banking premises should be tastefully decorated, but they need not be lavish.*

does not necessarily *needs not.* A long waiting time does not necessarily mean that your doctor is smart, successful, busy, dedicated, or involved in saving lives. *A long waiting time need not mean that your doctor is smart, successful, busy, dedicated, or involved in saving lives.*

does not pay attention to *ignores.*

does not remember *forgets.*

$... dollar *$....* A heavy fine of, say, $100 million dollars imposed on a company does very little good, as it is paid by the shareholders and not by those who have committed the crime. *A heavy fine of, say, $100 million imposed on a company does very little good, as it is paid by the shareholders and not by those who have committed the crime.*

dollar amount *delete.* The daily maximum price change is 50 basis points, which is equivalent to a dollar amount of $1,250. *The daily maximum price change is 50 basis points, which is equivalent to $1,250.*

dollar value *value.*

domicile *(n) home; house.*

domicile *(v) dwell; live; reside.*

done (finished; over) with *done (finished; over).*

doomed to fail (failure) *doomed.* A vocal element in the United States insists that any attempt to counter armed Soviet insurgency is doomed to failure and is evil in its inception. *A vocal element in the United States insists that any attempt to* *counter armed Soviet insurgency is doomed and is evil in its inception.* ■ The governor said the president's strategy is doomed to fail. *The governor said the president's strategy is doomed.*

dosage *dose.* If the recommended dosage does not provide relief of symptoms or symptoms become worse, seek immediate medical attention. *If the recommended dose does not provide relief of symptoms or symptoms become worse, seek immediate medical attention.*

doubt but that *doubt that.*

(on) down the line (road; way) *from now; later.* Ten years down the line where are you going to be? *Ten years from now where are you going to be?*

down to a minimum of *down to.*

dramatical *dramatic.*

draw attention to *advertise; announce; disclose; divulge; expose; herald; indicate; make known; make public; mention; point out; point to; present; proclaim; promote; publicize; reveal; show; tell; uncover; unveil.* Our goal is to draw attention to what has been accomplished in improving the world food situation, and what can be done to better it in the future. *Our goal is to publicize what has been accomplished in improving the world food situation, and what can be done to better it in the future.* ■ *Cézanne and America* draws attention to the need for similar studies of the reception of Cézanne's contemporaries in the United States. *Cézanne and America uncovers the need for similar studies of the reception of Cézanne's contemporaries in the United States.*

draw (a; the) conclusion *conclude; deduce; draw; infer; reason.* It would be wrong to draw the conclusion that the British tend to underreact to incest. *It would be wrong to infer that the British tend to underreact to incest.* ■ What conclusions were you able to draw from your experience? *What were you able to conclude from your experience?* ■ Using your logic, one would draw the conclusion that our system of justice doesn't work. *Using your logic, one would deduce that our system of justice doesn't work.*

draw (a; the) inference *conclude; deduce; draw; infer; reason.*

draw to a close *cease; close; complete; conclude; end; finish; halt; stop.* Scientists expect to feel in the next few days a real sense of letdown as the first phase of humanity's exploration of the Earth's neighborhood draws to a close. *Scientists expect to feel in the next few days a real sense of letdown as the first phase of humanity's exploration of the Earth's neighborhood concludes.*

draw to a conclusion *cease; close; complete; conclude; end; finish; halt; stop.*

driving force *drive; energy; force; impetus; motivation; power.* He is especially concerned about young people and is the driving force behind Catholic Schools United. *He is especially concerned about young people and is the impetus behind Catholic Schools United.* ■ Capital spending is the main driving force in the economy at the present time, and there are no signs that it is going to ease off. *Capital spending is the main force in the economy at the present time, and there are no signs that it is going to ease off.*

drop down *down; drop.*

dualistic *dual.* They have dualistic meanings. *They have dual meanings.*

due to the fact that *because; considering; for; in that; since.* Due to the fact that the deposit requirements in the futures markets are less onerous than margin requirements in the cash market, increased participation by speculators in the futures market could cause distortions. *Since the deposit requirements in the futures markets are less onerous than margin requirements in the cash market, increased participation by speculators in the futures market could cause distortions.*

duplicate copy *copy; duplicate.* When a drawing is traced with one of the pens, the other pen moves in the same pattern, making a duplicate copy of the original drawing. *When a drawing is traced with one of the pens, the other pen moves in the same pattern, making a duplicate of the original drawing.* ■ When you want a duplicate copy of one or more files, you use the COPY command. *When you want a copy of one or more files, you use the COPY command.*

during the course (length) of *during; for; in; over; throughout; when; while; with.* During the course of the analysis, we suppose the array or list contains *n* elements. *Throughout the analysis, we suppose the array or list contains n elements.* ■ During the course of 350 years, the building was renovated several times. *Over 350 years, the building was renovated several times.* ■ Sooner or later during the course of the year, we expect the balance sheet and the cash situation to be in sync. *Sooner or later during the year, we expect the balance sheet and the cash situation to be in sync.* ■ During the course of the campaign, there was a lot of rhetoric and a lot of empty talk. *In the campaign, there was a lot of rhetoric and a lot of empty talk.*

during (for; over) the decade (period; period of time; span of time; time; years) (from) ... through (till; to; until) *between ... and; from ... through (to).* During the period from October 31 to March 20, the entire flood-control space is reserved for flood control. *Between October 31 and March 20, the entire flood-control space is reserved for flood control.* ■ During the period November 26, 1986 to October 31, 1987, the maximum borrowings outstanding and the average daily borrowings outstanding amounted to $77,229,000 and $19,982,105, respectively. *From November 26, 1986 to October 31, 1987, the maximum borrowings outstanding and the average daily borrowings outstanding* *amounted to $77,229,000 and $19,982,105, respectively.* ■ The fees and expenses of the non-interested Trustees for the period November 26, 1986 to October 31, 1987 amounted to $3,731. *The fees and expenses of the non-interested Trustees from November 26, 1986 to October 31, 1987 amounted to $3,731.*

during the period (period of time; span of time; time; years) (that) *while.*

during the rule of *under.*

dwindle down *dwindle.* A $10,000 gross bonus can dwindle down to a surprisingly small amount with income tax deductions. *A $10,000 gross bonus can dwindle to a surprisingly small amount with income tax deductions.*

dynamical *dynamic.*

E

each and every (one) *all; each; every (one).* Each and every one of the candidates understands that. *All the candidates understand that.* ■ Each and every one of these crimes was committed by a pathological killer. *Each of these crimes was committed by a pathological killer.* ■ It takes some time to set up an atomic database, but it eliminates the need to consolidate each and every report. *It takes some time to set up an atomic database, but it eliminates the need to consolidate every report.*

each one *each.* My method is to introduce the key elements of office automation and explain each one in concrete terms. *My method is to introduce the key elements of office automation and explain each in concrete terms.* ■ We are opening six plants today for each one that closes, and the layoff rate is lower than it's been in 20 years. *We are opening six plants today for each that closes, and the layoff rate is lower than it's been in 20 years.*

(from) each other *delete.* When you first load the program, the highlight and end mark overlap each other. *When you first load the program, the highlight and end mark overlap.* ■ The two dates on the printout differ from each other because the first was entered as text and the second as a code. *The two dates on the printout differ because the first was entered as text and the second as a code.*

early beginnings *beginnings.*

-ed (-en) before (earlier; previously) *-ed (-en).* As we noted earlier, Equation 3-8, and thus Darcy's law, are valid only for laminar flow. *As we noted, Equation 3-8, and thus Darcy's law, are valid only for laminar flow.* ■ Actually the term was used previously by Thomas Edison. *Actually the term was used by Thomas Edison.* ▪ As I stated before, even in the binary format, Golden Retriever came through like a champ. *As I stated, even in the binary format, Golden Retriever came through like a champ.*

edifice *building.*

effectuate *bring about; carry out; effect; execute.* In order to effectuate this policy, the legislature imposed strict liability for all damages resulting from a failure to remove such materials on the owners of residential premises. *In order to effect this policy, the legislature imposed strict liability for all damages resulting from a failure to remove such materials on the owners of residential premises.*

either one *either.* The vice president doesn't like either one of them. *The vice president doesn't like either of them.* ▪ I've done both, so I have no problem doing either one. *I've done both, so I have no problem doing either.*

elect as *elect.*

electrical *electric.*

(a; the) ... element (in; of; to) *some;* delete. At that age, there's no element of fear. *At that age, there's no fear.* ▪ There will always be an element of doubt. *There will always be some doubt.* ▪ The florid phrases and poor editing suggest some element of haste in the booklet's concoction. *The florid phrases and poor editing suggest some haste in the booklet's concoction.* ▪ A common element to any system is the need for continuous top-management involvement. *Common to any system is the need for continuous top-management involvement.*

elliptical *elliptic.*

emblematical *emblematic.*

emerge out *emerge.* Part (d) corresponds to a time when the reflected shock waves have emerged out from the dust cloud. *Part (d) corresponds to a time when the reflected shock waves have emerged from the dust cloud.*

employ *use.* Not only did the Indians use words from their languages while speaking English, but English speakers also employed words of Indian origin. *Not only did the Indians use words from their languages while speaking English, but English speakers also used words of Indian origin.* ▪ Fewer than one-tenth of the small business prospects worldwide employ computers today. *Fewer than one-tenth of the small business prospects worldwide use computers today.*

employment *use.* The consistent employment of particular defenses leads to the development of personality traits. *The consistent use of particular defenses leads to the development of personality traits.*

enable ... to *let.* This enables analysts to sense the need for changes in methods. *This lets analysts sense the need for changes in methods.*

encapsulate *encapsule.* The responses provide a snapshot view of current U.S. efforts to use Japanese information and encapsulate some of the challenges faced by both providers and users. *The responses provide a snapshot view of current U.S. efforts to use Japanese information and encapsule some of the challenges faced by both providers and users.*

encircle *circle.*

enclosed herein (herewith) is (please find) *enclosed is; here is.* Enclosed herewith please find a letter from our client, Mr. Edward Price, which is self-explanatory. *Here is a letter from our client, Mr. Edward Price, which is self-explanatory.*

enclosed is *here is.*

encounter *find; have; meet;* delete. This support usually consists of a technical representative you can call if you encounter a problem. *This support usually consists of a technical representative you can call if you have a problem.* ▪ A particular (and fortunately infrequently encountered) bias in published league tables is gerrymandering to suit advertising or editorial policy. *A particular (and fortunately infrequently found) bias in published league tables is gerrymandering to suit advertising or editorial policy.*

encourage *urge.*

endeavor *try.*

end product *product.*

end (final; net; ultimate) result *result.* The end result was a series of consolidations that lasted until a single company was left to serve the market. *The result was a series of consolidations that lasted until a single company was left to serve the market.* ▪ Even though word processing and desktop publishing can lead to the same ultimate result, the paths to that result are completely different. *Even though word processing and desktop publishing can lead to the same result, the paths to that result are completely different.* ▪ He said states have broad discretion over how they go about regulating utilities, as long as the final result is a reasonable system. *He said states have broad discretion over how they go about regulating utilities, as long as the result is a reasonable system.*

engage in ... (a; the) delete. I appreciate the straightforward way in which you've engaged in this discussion. *I appreciate the straightforward way in which you've* *discussed this.* ■ Known as an active force in the labor movement, the unions at the Gillette France plant are engaged in a nationwide campaign to shape public opinion. *Known as an active force in the labor movement, the unions at the Gillette France plant are campaigning nationwide to shape public opinion.* ■ In that case, Drexel, the head of its junk bond department, Michael Milken, and others were charged with engaging in a scheme to defraud Drexel customers, and with committing a variety of other securities laws violations including insider trading. *In that case, Drexel, the head of its junk bond department, Michael Milken, and others were charged with scheming to defraud Drexel customers, and with committing a variety of other securities laws violations including insider trading.*

enter into a contract *agree; contract.*

enter into an agreement *agree; contract.* Courier Dispatch Group Inc. said it has entered into an agreement in principle to acquire the assets of J.A. Finn Inc. *Courier Dispatch Group Inc. said it has agreed in principle to acquire the assets of J.A. Finn Inc.*

entirely delete. Our competition introduced an entirely new product. *Our competition introduced a new product.* ■ In some cases, villages are entirely surrounded and in urgent need of drinking water. *In some cases, villages are surrounded and in urgent need of drinking water.*

entitle *title;* delete. The report is entitled "Outlook for EFT/POS: An Executive Summary." *The report is titled "Outlook for EFT/POS: An Executive Summary."*

enumerate *count; list; name; numerate.*

epidemical *epidemic.*

epidemiological *epidemiologic.*

epigrammatical *epigrammatic.*

epigraphical *epigraphic.*

equally as *equally; as.* It was equally as difficult for me. *It was equally difficult for me.* ■ Preserving our past is equally as important as building our future. *Preserving our past is as important as building our future.* ■ The emotional component of the nurse–client relationship is equally as important as the physical component. *The emotional component of the nurse–client relationship is as important as the physical component.*

equitable *fair.*

(the) -(i)er ... of the two *(the) -(i)er; (the) more.* Direct exporting is the riskier of the two, but the potential rewards are also greater. *Direct exporting is riskier, but the potential rewards are also greater.*

essentially *chiefly; largely; mainly; most; mostly;* delete. This is essentially the idea behind classical deseasonalization. *This is the idea behind classical deseasonalization.* ▪ Essentially, the university experts act as information gatekeepers. *The university experts chiefly act as information gatekeepers.*

essential core *core; crux; essence; gist; pith; substance.* The reviewer let himself be diverted by the book's feminist frame and missed its essential core. *The reviewer let himself be diverted by the book's feminist frame and missed its essence.*

(an; the) essential ... for (in; of; to) *essential to.* Homeownership is an essential part of the American dream. *Homeownership is essential to the American dream.* ▪ His point is that physical contact is an essential element in everyone's life, and most people don't get enough. *His point is that physical contact is essential to everyone's life, and most people don't get enough.* ▪ Toughness is not an essential ingredient for getting ahead, and it isn't the same as resolve. *Toughness is not essential to getting ahead, and it isn't the same as resolve.*

essential prerequisite *essential; prerequisite.* Categorizing a given product is an essential prerequisite for a successful marketing effort. *Categorizing a given product is essential for a successful marketing effort.*

establish *set up.*

establish conclusive evidence (proof) of *prove.*

established standard *standard.* Over the past few years, a number of spreadsheet, database, and word processing programs have become established standards in their areas of application. *Over the past few years, a number of spreadsheet, database, and word processing programs have become standards in their areas of application.*

established tradition *tradition.* IBM broke established traditions and set up a special group at Boca Raton, Florida, to develop their own microcomputer. *IBM broke traditions and set up a special group at Boca Raton, Florida, to develop their own microcomputer.*

establishment *business; club; firm.* The state supreme court will decide whether to allow nude dancing to continue at that establishment. *The state supreme court will decide whether to allow nude dancing to continue at that club.*

-est ever *-est.* That amount is the largest ever paid by the city in a civil rights action. *That amount is the largest paid by the city in a civil rights action.*

et cetera, et cetera, et cetera *and so forth; and so on; and the like; etc.*

eventuality *event; occurrence; outcome;* delete. We all must prepare for this unpleasant eventuality. *We all must prepare for this unpleasantness.* ▪ Potential buyers of its stock, looking for quick run-ups engendered by takeover artists, but knowing that the directing family could prevent such an eventuality, have instead backed likelier candidates for soaring prices. *Potential buyers of its stock, looking for quick run-ups engendered by takeover artists, but knowing that the directing family could prevent such an event, have instead backed likelier candidates for soaring prices.* ▪ Kodak should have prepared for this eventuality. *Kodak should have prepared for this outcome.*

eventuate *befall; come about; happen; occur; result; take place.*

ever and anon *at times; now and again; now and then; occasionally; once in a while; on occasion; sometimes.*

every day (month; week; year) *daily (monthly; weekly; yearly).*

every now and then *at times; from time to time; now and again; now and then; occasionally; once in a while; on occasion; sometimes.*

every once in a while *at times; from time to time; now and again; now and then; occasionally; once in a while; on occasion; sometimes.* Every once in a while, I was struck by how hot it was. *Now and then, I was struck by how hot it was.*

every single (solitary) *every.* Every single solitary juvenile in these four states was examined. *Every juvenile in these four states was examined.* ▪ And that commitment is good jobs and economic opportunity for every single citizen in this country. *And that commitment is good jobs and economic opportunity for every citizen in this country.*

evidence in (to) support of (that) *evidence of (that).* The great pay-raise debate is on, and we see little evidence to support that higher salaries will attract higher-quality candidates. *The great pay-raise debate is on, and we see little evidence that higher salaries will attract higher-quality candidates.* ▪ There is no evidence to support that those new mortgages are any more likely to default than those insured by F.H.A. under current law. *There is no evidence that those new mortgages are any more likely to default than those insured by F.H.A. under current law.*

exact (exactly) duplicate *duplicate; exact; identical; match; (the) same.* This one-to-one correspondence between pixels on the document and pixels on the screen allows an exact duplicate of the original to be read into the computer and displayed. *This one-to-one correspondence between pixels on the document and pixels on the screen allows a duplicate of the original to be read into the computer and displayed.* ▪ Nothing could exactly duplicate what we just heard. *Nothing could match what we just heard.*

exact (exactly) equivalent *duplicate; equivalent; exact; identical; match; (the) same.* This situation is exactly equivalent to our usual neglect of the Earth's rotation when we do experiments in laboratories. *This situation is equivalent to our usual neglect of the Earth's rotation when we do experiments in laboratories.*

exact (exactly) identical *duplicate; exact; identical; match; (the) same.* This pattern, though not exactly identical, tends to recur every year. *This pattern, though not identical, tends to recur every year.*

exactly sure *sure.* I'm not exactly sure of her name. *I'm not sure of her name.*

exact (exactly) match *duplicate; exact; identical; match; (the) same.* When you enter a value that doesn't exactly match one of those listed on the lookup table, the function will find the value equal to or less than the value being looked up. *When you enter a value that doesn't match one of those listed on the lookup table, the function will find the value equal to or less than the value being looked up.*

exact (exactly) (the) same *duplicate; exact; identical; just; match; (the) same.* He used those exact same words. *He used those exact words.* ■ We should not assume that these people enter the line at a uniform rate or that the service always requires exactly the same amount of time. *We should not assume that these people enter the line at a uniform rate or that the service always requires the same amount of time.* ■ The construction of a drawing of a square nut or a hexagon nut across corners is exactly the same as the construction of a drawing of a bolt head across corners. *The construction of a drawing of a square nut or a hexagon nut across corners is identical to the construction of a drawing of a bolt head across corners.* ■ If things are going badly, do exactly the same as you would in a department store. *If things are going badly, do just as you would in a department store.*

examination *exam.*

(an) example that illustrates (to illustrate) *example (of); (to) illustrate.* Sears, Roebuck provides an example that illustrates how several retailers are entering the financial services market. *Sears, Roebuck provides an example of how several retailers are entering the financial services market.* ■ The design of a hunting seat is used as an example to illustrate the decision step of the design process. *The design of a hunting seat is used to illustrate the decision step of the design process.* ■ Here are some examples to illustrate the benefits of word processing on a network. *Here are some examples of the benefits of word processing on a network.*

excerption *excerpt.*

(a; the) excessive amount (of) *excessive; too much.*

(a; the) excessive number (of) *excessive; too many.* If your failure to detect errors in the proofing stage results in a published text that contains an excessive number of errors, the costs of making these corrections in a subsequent printing will be charged against your royalties. *If your failure to detect errors in the proofing stage results in a published text that contains excessive errors, the costs of making these corrections in a subsequent printing will be charged against your royalties.*

excess verbiage *verbiage.*

excruciatingly painful *excruciating; painful.* To always be the largest woman in exercise classes is excruciatingly painful. *To always be the largest woman in exercise classes is painful.* ■ It has been an excruciatingly painful experience for the town's 8,000 residents. *It has been an excruciating experience for the town's 8,000 residents.*

(that) exist *delete.* Ample evidence exists to support the differences in investment tax shields across industries. *Ample evidence supports the differences in investment tax shields across industries.* ■ The degree of such emphasis will depend upon market conditions existing at the time of investment. *The degree of such emphasis will depend upon market conditions at the time of investment.* ■ Exhibit 15-1 shows examples of the variations in shopping hours that exist among five European countries. *Exhibit 15-1 shows examples of the variations in shopping hours among five European countries.*

expect (expectation) and hope *expect (expectation); hope; trust.* We're pleased with our progress and expect and hope that it will continue as our initiatives take hold. *We're pleased with our progress and expect that it will continue as our initiatives take hold.*

expediency *expedience.*

expeditiously *fast; promptly; quickly; rapidly; speedily; straightaway.* This problem must be dealt with expeditiously. *This problem must be dealt with quickly.*

expenditure (of money) *cost; expense.* He deplored the long electoral campaigns that involved heavy expenditures of money and brought the country to a virtual standstill for months. *He deplored the long electoral campaigns that involved heavy costs and brought the country to a virtual standstill for months.*

experience *feel; find; go through; have; know; see.* According to this book, many people have experienced boredom and alienation. *According to this book, many people have known boredom and alienation.* ■ Needs are deficiencies a person is experiencing at a particular time. *Needs are deficiencies a person is* *feeling at a particular time.* ■ Clerical workers in Boston experienced the highest annual rate of increase since 1983. *Clerical workers in Boston saw the highest annual rate of increase since 1983.* ■ Siemens reasons that it will experience difficulty maintaining the economies of scale necessary to remain globally competitive. *Siemens reasons that it will have difficulty maintaining the economies of scale necessary to remain globally competitive.*

experience   delete. This magazine has experienced tremendous growth in the past two years. *This magazine has grown tremendously in the past two years.* ■ If SDS experiences success in the corporate sector, more packet switching will ultimately be placed on BOCs' networks to interconnect disparate private systems. *If SDS succeeds in the corporate sector, more packet switching will ultimately be placed on BOCs' networks to interconnect disparate private systems.* ■ It is a very dangerous drug; it causes every woman who takes it to experience a miscarriage. *It is a very dangerous drug; it causes every woman who takes it to miscarry.* ■ The only sardine industry in the United States is in Maine, and it has experienced a significant decline over the last 70 years. *The only sardine industry in the United States is in Maine, and it has declined significantly over the last 70 years.* ■ All nurses at times experience feelings of anxiety, anger, and resentment toward some clients. *All nurses at times feel anxiety, anger, and resentment toward some clients.*

express ... (about; for; of; to)   delete. He expressed doubt whether the issue would be much of a headache on the campaign trail this fall. *He doubted whether the issue would be much of a headache on the campaign trail this fall.* ■ Many express open admiration for women who are healthy, well-groomed, and confident. *Many openly admire women who are healthy, well-groomed, and confident.* ■ Most top executives seem to believe strongly in the need for better human relations, but they often express distrust of the training program itself. *Most top executives seem to believe strongly in the need for better human relations, but they often distrust the training program itself.* ■ We wish to express our sincere thanks to our special representative for her responsiveness. *We wish to sincerely thank our special representative for her responsiveness.* ■ Though solar physics rather than comet-finding is Solar Max's primary role, some scientists are expressing outrage at NASA's recent decision not to send astronauts to refurbish the satellite's instruments and raise its orbit before the drag of Earth's uppermost atmosphere sends it plunging to its destruction. *Though solar physics rather than comet-finding is Solar Max's primary role, some scientists are outraged at NASA's recent decision not to send astronauts to refurbish the satellite's instruments and raise its orbit before the drag of Earth's uppermost atmosphere sends it plunging to its destruction.*

express concern (about)   *agonize (over; about); brood (on; over); dread; fear; fret (about; over); regret; stew (about; over); worry (about; over).* Some scientists express concern about the implications of splicing the genes for certain insecticides into plants. *Some scientists worry about the implications of splicing the* *genes for certain insecticides into plants.* ■ Alumni and students express concern that this will shift the school's focus from personal interactions in business to a more traditional, theoretical, and analytical approach to management. *Alumni and students fret that this will shift the school's focus from personal interactions in business to a more traditional, theoretical, and analytical approach to management.* ■ Company analysts expressed concern about the level of debt that the combined companies would carry if the hostile bid succeeds. *Company analysts stewed over the level of debt that the combined companies would carry if the hostile bid succeeds.*

express opposition to *contest; criticize; disagree with; disapprove of; dispute; object to; oppose; protest.*

express skepticism (about) *disbelieve; distrust; doubt; mistrust; question.* But others express skepticism about those results, with some scientists' questions verging upon accusations of exaggeration. *But others distrust those results, with some scientists' questions verging upon accusations of exaggeration.*

express sorrow (about) *bemoan; deplore; grieve; lament; moan; mourn; regret.* At a press conference earlier in the day, he had expressed sorrow that American writers and American politics seem to occupy two different worlds. *At a press conference earlier in the day, he had bemoaned that American writers and American politics seem to occupy two different worlds.*

extend (issue) an invitation to *invite.* The Open Software Foundation would like to extend an invitation to you to explore the OSF/Motif user environment. *The Open Software Foundation would like to invite you to explore the OSF/Motif user environment.*

extend out *extend.* Press the right arrow until the highlight extends out to cell F4, and then press Return. *Press the right arrow until the highlight extends to cell F4, and then press Return.*

extensively throughout *all through; extensively in (through); throughout.* Our reporter has traveled extensively throughout South America. *Our reporter has traveled throughout South America.*

(a; the) ... extent of delete.

F

face up to *face.*

facilitate *ease; help.*

facility *bathroom; building; factory; hospital; jail; office; place; plant; prison; school;* delete. In 1986, hospital executives estimated that 21 percent of their facilities might close. *In 1986, hospital executives estimated that 21 percent of their hospitals might close.* ▪ The report calls for increased AIDS testing of prisoners in state and local facilities, bringing them in line with federal testing in prisons. *The report calls for increased AIDS testing of prisoners in state and local jails, bringing them in line with federal testing in prisons.* ▪ The Singapore plant, a 140,000-square-foot facility, employs 220 people. *The 140,000-square-foot Singapore plant employs 220 people.* ▪ In the United States, FTZs have been established mainly near primary ports of entry, industrial parks, and major warehouse facilities. *In the United States, FTZs have been established mainly near primary ports of entry, industrial parks, and major warehouses.*

(a; the) ... factor (in; of; to) delete. The fact that we could not have children was a contributing factor to our divorce. *The fact that we could not have children contributed to our divorce.* ▪ What will be the deciding factor that will make young people slow down their automobiles? *What will make young people decide to slow down their automobiles?* ▪ Customer demand for practical solutions to communications problems—rather than technology for the sake of technology—is the determining factor in the development work that is taking place. *Customer demand for practical solutions to communications problems—rather than technology for the sake of technology—determines the development work that is taking place.* ▪ Knowing the consequences of obesity should be a motivating factor in losing weight. *Knowing the consequences of obesity should be a motivation in losing weight.* ▪ Researchers indicate, however, that after age 50 life-style becomes a less influential factor in physiological change than aging itself. *Researchers indicate, however, that after age 50 life-style becomes less influential in physiological change than aging itself.*

facts and information *facts; information.* Request a full disclosure statement highlighting all the pertinent facts and information about them. *Request a full disclosure statement highlighting all the pertinent facts about them.*

factual basis *basis; fact; reason; truth.* People who know me know there's no factual basis to the story. *People who know me know there's no truth to the story.*

fair (just) and equitable *fair; just; equitable.* I support fair and equitable taxes to insure human services are funded. *I support equitable taxes to insure human services are funded.* ▪ The church affirmed commitment to a just and equitable welfare system. *The church affirmed commitment to a just welfare system.*

fair and square *fair; honest; just; square.*

false and misleading *deceptive; false; misleading.*

false illusion *illusion.*

false pretense *pretense.*

far and away *by far; much.* The judgment was for $10.3 billion, far and away the biggest ever in American commerce. *The judgment was for $10.3 billion, by far the biggest ever in American commerce.* ■ As for silhouette, maillots remain far and away the best sellers. *As for silhouette, maillots remain much the best sellers.*

far and wide *broadly; widely.*

far away from *far from.* The pressure is greatest near the outer wall (farthest away from the center of the curvature). *The pressure is greatest near the outer wall (farthest from the center of the curvature).* ■ These blocks are usually physically located far away from the file's data blocks. *These blocks are usually physically located far from the file's data blocks.*

fasten together *fasten.* Screw threads provide a fast and easy method of fastening two parts together and of exerting a force that can be used for adjustment of movable parts. *Screw threads provide a fast and easy method of fastening two parts and of exerting a force that can be used for adjustment of movable parts.*

favor ... as opposed to (instead of; rather than) *favor ... over; favor ... to.* Lager is a pale, American-style beer favored by the young as opposed to the dark, traditional "bitter" English beer. *Lager is a pale, American-style beer favored by the young over the dark, traditional "bitter" English beer.*

fear and trembling *anxiety; dismay; dread; fear; foreboding; horror; terror; trembling.*

(a; the) ... feeling(s) (of) *delete.* We describe the intensity of the feeling of anger along a four-point scale. *We describe the intensity of anger along a four-point scale.* ■ Neither of us has any guilt feelings about it. *Neither of us has any guilt about it.* ■ The moderately anxious person may verbalize subjective experiences such as a dry mouth, upset stomach, anorexia, tension headache, stiff neck, feelings of tiredness, and inability to relax. *The moderately anxious person may verbalize subjective experiences such as a dry mouth, upset stomach, anorexia, tension headache, stiff neck, tiredness, and inability to relax.*

feel inside *feel.* What's most important is how you feel inside about it. *What's most important is how you feel about it.*

fervency *fervor.*

few and far between *few; infrequent; meager; rare; scant; scanty; scarce; scattered; seldom; sparse; uncommon; unusual.* Since then the shooting stars have been few and far between. *Since then the shooting stars have been infrequent.* ■ Efforts by the government, foundations, academic institutions, and business to stimulate and/or support systematic studies of the problem have been few and far between. *Efforts by the government, foundations, academic institutions, and business to stimulate and/or support systematic studies of the problem have been sparse.*

few (small) in number *few; not many.*

fifty (50) percent (of) *half (of); one-half (of).* Nearly fifty percent of the town's population is associated with the university. *Nearly half the town's population is associated with the university.*

figuratively speaking *as it were; in a sense; in a way; so to speak.*

(a; the) ... figure delete. Alan Paton has become something of a legendary figure. *Alan Paton has become something of a legend.*

figure in *add; include.*

figure on (upon) *expect; plan on.*

figure out *decide; determine; discern; discover; think.* Now, at the age of 50, I have to figure out what I'm going to do with the rest of my life. *Now, at the age of 50, I have to decide what I'm going to do with the rest of my life.*

figure up *add; total.*

fill up *fill.* Fill up the tank when you're in town. *Fill the tank when you're in town.*

fill to capacity *fill.*

filter out *filter.* It's very hard to filter out fact from fiction. *It's very hard to filter fact from fiction.*

filthy dirty *dirty; filthy.*

final and irrevocable *final; irrevocable.* His decision not to seek a fourth term as governor is final and irrevocable. *His decision not to seek a fourth term as governor is final.*

final (ultimate) completion *completion.* Because the order, timing, and costs of the individual tasks are interrelated, they all affect the total cost of the project and its final completion date. *Because the order, timing, and costs of the individual* *tasks are interrelated, they all affect the total cost of the project and its completion date.*

final (ultimate) conclusion *conclusion.*

final (ultimate) culmination *culmination.*

finalize *complete; conclude; finish.* After five or ten successful projects, you should review guidelines and begin to finalize the procedure. *After five or ten successful projects, you should review guidelines and begin to complete the procedure.*

final (ultimate) outcome *outcome.* We were saddened by the final outcome. *We were saddened by the outcome.*

final (ultimate) resolution *resolution.* The outcome of these matters is not presently determinable, but the ultimate resolution of such matters will not have a material adverse impact on NYNEX's financial position. *The outcome of these matters is not presently determinable, but the resolution of such matters will not have a material adverse impact on NYNEX's financial position.*

final (ultimate) settlement *settlement.*

financial (monetary) resources *assets; capital; money; resources.*

financial wherewithal *assets; cash; funds; means; money; wherewithal.* The commission also is considering whether owners have the financial wherewithal to operate the plant. *The commission also is considering whether owners have the money to operate the plant.* ■ That strength has permitted us time, and provided financial wherewithal, to "build out" and augment that core with above-average growth. *That strength has permitted us time, and provided means, to "build out" and augment that core with above-average growth.*

find out *find; learn.* We found out that there is a great deal of teenage prostitution going on. *We learned that there is a great deal of teenage prostitution going on.*

(all) fine (good) and well *all right; fine; good; great; nice; pleasant; pleasing; welcome; well.*

finish up *finish.*

firm (strong) commitment *commitment.* Voters are not firmly committed to any of the candidates. *Voters are not committed to any of the candidates.*

firm (strong) conviction *conviction.* This participative process has enabled us to develop a strong conviction throughout the Company that our strategy is the right one. *This participative process has enabled us to develop a conviction through-out the Company that our strategy is the right one.*

firmly establish *establish; firm.* We should have resolved them earlier in the implementation of the reorganization, before structure and behavior patterns became firmly established. *We should have resolved them earlier in the implementation of the reorganization, before structure and behavior patterns became firm.* ■ Once the reserves were firmly established, the accounting issues became less problematic because the accounting firms felt more comfortable, and the banks felt more flexible. *Once the reserves were established, the accounting issues became less problematic because the accounting firms felt more comfortable, and the banks felt more flexible.*

firm (strong) resolution *resolution.*

first and foremost *chief; chiefly; first; foremost; main; mainly; mostly; primarily; primary; principal; principally;* delete. Football is first and foremost a running game. *Football is primarily a running game.* ■ Our loyalties are first and foremost to our families and friends, then to our communities, the state and nation. *Our loyalties are first to our families and friends, then to our communities, the state and nation.* ■ All breached science's code of ethics, which is based, first and foremost, on an absolute commitment to the truth. *All breached science's code of ethics, which is chiefly based on an absolute commitment to the truth.* ■ We can't speak for others, but at Arthur Young, quality is our first and foremost principle. *We can't speak for others, but at Arthur Young, quality is our foremost principle.*

first and last *only; sole.*

first and only *only; sole.* Was he the first and only person to have superheated ice, yet whose work has fallen into obscurity? *Was he the only person to have superheated ice, yet whose work has fallen into obscurity?*

first ... before *before.* You cannot print a document on the disk that has been fast-saved unless you first positioned the cursor at the end of the document before you saved it. *You cannot print a document on the disk that has been fast-saved unless you positioned the cursor at the end of the document before you saved it.*

first begin *begin; start.*

first (initially) coined *coined.* The term *psychic distance* was initially coined by Swedish researchers at the University of Uppsala. *The term* psychic distance *was coined by Swedish researchers at the University of Uppsala.*

first come into being *arise; begin; start.* When Social Security first came into being, relatively few people lived to the retirement age of 65, so the many were supporting the few. *When Social Security began, relatively few people lived to the retirement age of 65, so the many were supporting the few.*

first created *created.*

first ever *first.* This was the first-ever congressional review of the condition of wilderness areas protected from development under a landmark 1964 law. *This was the first congressional review of the condition of wilderness areas protected from development under a landmark 1964 law.*

first initially *first; initially.* When he first initially got the complaint, he wrote a letter to the Human Rights Commission admitting his guilt. *When he first got the complaint, he wrote a letter to the Human Rights Commission admitting his guilt.*

first introduced *introduced.* He built on some ideas first introduced by Leibniz almost 200 years earlier. *He built on some ideas introduced by Leibniz almost 200 years earlier.* ■ Surprisingly, when microcomputers were first introduced, large corporations were not the first to adopt them. *Surprisingly, when microcomputers were introduced, large corporations were not the first to adopt them.* ■ When the Tucker was first introduced, owners displayed signs in the back window reading, "You've just been passed by a Tucker." *When the Tucker was introduced, owners displayed signs in the back window reading, "You've just been passed by a Tucker."*

first invented *invented.*

firstly *first.*

first of all *first.* I would first of all ask how many of you are going to help us. *I would first ask how many of you are going to help us.* ■ First of all, most departments that have already invested in PCs are happy with them. *First, most departments that have already invested in PCs are happy with them.*

first off *first.* First off, these price and yield figures are for multimillion-dollar dealer-to-dealer negotiated transactions at any given hour or day. *First, these price and yield figures are for multimillion-dollar dealer-to-dealer negotiated transactions at any given hour or day.*

first start *begin; start.* It may well be that when they first started getting the stuff they needed it. *It may well be that when they started getting the stuff they needed it.* ■ The market share of Searle's Calan was fairly low when we first started. *The market share of Searle's Calan was fairly low when we began.*

first time ever *first time.* It's the first time ever that disabled skiers were represented at the Olympics. *It's the first time that disabled skiers were represented at the Olympics.* ■ For the first time ever, the school district has dismissed a child in the third grade for erratic behavior caused by hyperactivity. *For the first time, the school district has dismissed a child in the third grade for erratic behavior caused by hyperactivity.*

flood over *flood.*

fly in the face of *challenge; contradict; defy; dispute; disregard.* Although it may be morally reassuring, this tale flies in the face of historical fact. *Although it may be morally reassuring, this tale defies historical fact.*

focal point *center; focus.* The U.S.–Canada trade agreement has been the focal point of the campaign. *The U.S.–Canada trade agreement has been the focus of the campaign.*

focus ... attention on (upon) *concentrate on; focus on.* It's time we focus our attention on the plight of the poor. *It's time we focus on the plight of the poor.* ■ I was too wrapped up in my own concerns to be able to focus my attention on him. *I was too wrapped up in my own concerns to be able to concentrate on him.* ■ Perhaps if the media focused their attention on long-term investment rather than short-term blips, the investment community would feel less compelled to predict daily fluctuations. *Perhaps if the media focused on long-term investment rather than short-term blips, the investment community would feel less compelled to predict daily fluctuations.*

focus (media; people's; public) attention on (upon) *advertise; announce; disclose; divulge; expose; herald; indicate; make known; make public; mention; point out; point to; present; proclaim; promote; publicize; reveal; show; tell; uncover; unveil.* All this has helped us focus attention on the problem. *All this has helped us publicize the problem.* ■ Arbitrary as such an approach may be, at least it is an effort to focus attention on people as resources, not just expenses. *Arbitrary as such an approach may be, at least it is an effort to present people as resources, not just expenses.*

focus ... effort on (upon) *concentrate on; focus on.* It was also agreed to reduce the number of items on the control list and focus efforts on truly sensitive goods and technology. *It was also agreed to reduce the number of items on the control list and focus on truly sensitive goods and technology.* ■ He said the crew would focus efforts on saving baby penguins. *He said the crew would concentrate on saving baby penguins.*

focus ... energy on (upon) *concentrate on; focus on.* If production focuses its energies on manufacturing a product at the lowest possible cost, but the sales department is willing to accept unprofitable orders, conflict will arise. *If production focuses on manufacturing a product at the lowest possible cost, but the sales department is willing to accept unprofitable orders, conflict will arise.* ■ When those discussions failed to lead to an acceptable transaction, we focused our energies on the profitable value-added solutions market. *When those discussions failed to lead to an acceptable transaction, we focused on the profitable value-added solutions market.*

focus in *focus.* We're focusing in on what we have to do to achieve this. *We're focusing on what we have to do to achieve this.* ■ We focused in on the area of price. *We focused on the area of price.*

focus of attention *cynosure; focus.*

focus ... time and energy on (upon) *concentrate on; focus on.*

fold up *fold.* The commission folded up because we voted to have it fold up. *The commission folded because we voted to have it fold.*

follow after *follow.*

follow along the lines of *duplicate; imitate; match; resemble.* There might be a settlement on rates by the end of this year; however, we doubt it will follow along the lines of the New York rate case moratorium. *There might be a settlement on rates by the end of this year; however, we doubt it will resemble the New York rate case moratorium.*

for (to) all intents and purposes *essentially; in effect; in essence; practically; virtually.* The file name is removed from the directory so that the file appears, for all intents and purposes, to be deleted. *The file name is removed from the directory so that the file appears, in effect, to be deleted.* ■ Following the treatment with interleukin-2, the nodule for all intents and purposes disappeared. *Following the treatment with interleukin-2, the nodule virtually disappeared.*

for (all) practical purposes *essentially; in effect; in essence; practically; virtually.* For all practical purposes, there will be no expansion in existing programs. *There will be virtually no expansion in existing programs.* ■ For all practical purposes, last month's rent and a security deposit are the same. *In essence, last month's rent and a security deposit are the same.* ■ So round one, for practical purposes, is over. *So round one, in effect, is over.*

for an extended (prolonged; protracted) amount of time (length of time; period; period of time; span of time; time; while) *awhile; for a long time (while); for a time (while); for days (hours; weeks; years); for six months (three years); long.* The reason for not turning a computer off is that the surge of electricity that goes through it when you turn it on can cause more damage than leaving the computer on for an extended period. *The reason for not turning a computer off is that the surge of electricity that goes through it when you turn it on can cause more damage than leaving the computer on for hours.* ■ It is recommended to "test spray" into the air before using for the first time and in cases where the aerosol has not been used for a prolonged period of time. *It is recommended to "test spray" into the air before using for the first time and in cases where the aerosol has not been used for a long time.* ▪ We had observed this family for a prolonged period of time. *We had long observed this family.*

for another (thing) *second.* For another thing, there is still ample legal precedent for highly effective affirmative action programs that stop short of specific quotas. *Second, there is still ample legal precedent for highly effective affirmative action programs that stop short of specific quotas.*

forasmuch as *because; considering; for; in that; since.*

for a while *awhile.* After this program executes for a while, procedure B is called. *After this program executes awhile, procedure B is called.* ▪ Team A will serve for a while, and then Team B will serve. *Team A will serve awhile, and then Team B will serve.*

for awhile *awhile.* If the program continues to run for awhile, the answer may not be so clear. *If the program continues to run awhile, the answer may not be so clear.*

forecast ... future *forecast; foretell; predict.* After a model is identified as being a good predictor, it is used to forecast future sales. *After a model is identified as being a good predictor, it is used to forecast sales.*

foretell ... future *forecast; foretell; predict.*

for ever and a day *always; ceaselessly; consistently; constantly; endlessly; eternally; everlastingly; everyday; forever; invariably; never ending; perpetually; routinely; unfailingly.*

forevermore *always; evermore; forever.* I am not naive enough to think that we will forevermore walk hand in hand with the business community to clean the environment. *I am not naive enough to think that we will forever walk hand in hand with the business community to clean the environment.*

forewarn *warn.*

for example (for instance) *say.* When the scanner reads the bar code on, for example, a can of beans, the computer looks up the product number the bar code represents and returns its name and price to the register. *When the scanner reads the bar code on, say, a can of beans, the computer looks up the product number the bar code represents and returns its name and price to the register.*

for example ... and others (and so forth; and so on; and such; and the like; et al.; etc.) *and others (and so forth; and so on; and such; and the like; et al.; etc.); for example.* Many other examples of the influence religion has on buyer behavior—for example, on values and norms, time, sense of self, and so forth—will be found in the following sections. *Many other examples of the influence religion has on buyer behavior—on values and norms, time, sense of self, and so forth—will be found in the following sections.* ■ For example, you may create one directory to hold word processing documents, another to hold Applesoft programs, etc. *For example, you may create one directory to hold word processing documents and another to hold Applesoft programs.* ■ For example, the first field in each record is field 1, the second field in each record is field 2, and so on. *The first field in each record is field 1, the second field in each record is field 2, and so on.*

for fear (that; of) ... can (could; may; might; shall; should; will; would) *lest.* IBM also wants its message to reach Europe's governments ahead of 1992 for fear that they might favor national flagships as trade barriers come down across the European Community. *IBM also wants its message to reach Europe's governments ahead of 1992 lest they favor national flagships as trade barriers come down across the European Community.* ■ Public officials are being discouraged from seeking psychological care for fear the very fact of seeking care will subject them to being labeled mentally ill and unfit for public service. *Public officials are being discouraged from seeking psychological care lest the very fact of seeking care subject them to being labeled mentally ill and unfit for public service.* ■ Few of us know what to say to friends who are mourning, so we may avoid them for fear we'll say the wrong thing. *Few of us know what to say to friends who are mourning, so we may avoid them lest we say the wrong thing.*

for free *free.* Purchasers of 1.0 versions will receive 1.1 upgrades for free from IBM. *Purchasers of 1.0 versions will receive free 1.1 upgrades from IBM.* ■ Now through November 13, whenever you buy a pair of Reeboks, you can get them painted for free. *Now through November 13, whenever you buy a pair of Reeboks, you can get them painted free.*

for (in; to) (the) furtherance of *for; to advance; to further; to promote.* Neither the conspiracy itself nor the overt acts allegedly done in furtherance of it were directed toward Boisjoly. *Neither the conspiracy itself nor the overt acts allegedly done to further it were directed toward Boisjoly.* ■ They shall administer the affairs of the Corporation, have the general direction, control, and management of the property of the Corporation, and employ personnel for the furtherance of the business of the Corporation. *They shall administer the affairs of the Corporation, have the general direction, control, and management of the property of the Corporation, and employ personnel to advance the business of the Corporation.*

for (an) indefinite (indeterminate) amount of time (length of time; period; period of time; span of time; time; while) *briefly; for a time; for a while; indefinitely; temporarily.* We can't have an open agenda of unknowns that frustrates private development for an indefinite period of time. *We can't have an open agenda of* *unknowns that frustrates private development indefinitely.* ■ We are freezing prices and wages for an indefinite period. *We are freezing prices and wages temporarily.*

for instance ... and others (and so forth; and so on; and such; and the like; et al.; etc.) *for instance; and others (and so forth; and so on; and such; and the like; et al.; etc.).* Use one of these labels to assign a number and perhaps a descriptive title to each disk, for instance, Disk 1: Letters, Disk 2: Spreadsheet Files, Disk 3: Reports, and so on. *Use one of these labels to assign a number and perhaps a descriptive title to each disk, for instance, Disk 1: Letters, Disk 2: Spreadsheet Files, and Disk 3: Reports.*

for long *long.* If top executives cannot control their responsibilities, they usually do not remain in their positions for long. *If top executives cannot control their responsibilities, they usually do not remain long in their positions.*

form (a; the) judgment *conclude; decide; deduce; determine; infer; judge; reason; resolve; settle.*

form (a; the) opinion *conclude; decide; deduce; determine; infer; judge; reason; resolve; settle.*

form (a; the) resolution *conclude; decide; determine; resolve; settle.*

formulate *devise; form; make.* Have you formulated no opinion about her? *Have you formed no opinion about her?* ■ Conrail is already providing service via conventional trains and plans are being formulated for double-stack trains to serve those lines. *Conrail is already providing service via conventional trains and plans are being made for double-stack trains to serve those lines.*

for obvious reasons *obviously.* For obvious reasons, he wants to announce his choice at the convention. *Obviously, he wants to announce his choice at the convention.*

for one ... (be) an example (an instance) *(be) an example (an instance); for one; one example (one instance).* The Massachusetts Industrial Services Program, for one, is an example of the kind of broad industrial extension service we think is needed to retool manufacturing facilities. *The Massachusetts Industrial Services Program is one example of the kind of broad industrial extension service we think is needed to retool manufacturing facilities.*

for one (thing) *first.* For one thing, a national program would have to be tailored to each state because the delivery of health-care services can differ significantly. *First, a national program would have to be tailored to each state because the delivery of health-care services can differ significantly.*

for ... purposes (of) *for; so as to; to.* The trust may enter into futures contracts and options on futures contracts transactions only for purposes of hedging a part or all of its portfolio. *The trust may enter into futures contracts and options on futures contracts transactions only to hedge a part or all of its portfolio.* ■ The money we receive from licensing John Wayne's image is used entirely for charitable purposes. *The money we receive from licensing John Wayne's image is used entirely for charity.* ■ The Iranian oil rigs have radar installations on them that are used for surveillance purposes. *The Iranian oil rigs have radar installations on them that are used for surveillance.*

for reasons of *after; because of; by; for; from; in; out of; through.* When airlines have replaced older planes, they have done so primarily for reasons of economics—newer aircraft cost less to inspect and repair. *When airlines have replaced older planes, they have done so primarily because of economics—newer aircraft cost less to inspect and repair.* ■ For reasons of compatibility, BASIC.SYSTEM also permits the use of the ,S# and ,D# parameters. *For compatibility, BASIC.SYSTEM also permits the use of the ,S# and ,D# parameters.*

for some time (now) *long.* I have enjoyed reading your articles for some time now. *I have long enjoyed reading your articles.* ■ The telephone companies have been managing their buildings for some time. *The telephone companies have long been managing their buildings.*

for that matter *also; and; as well; besides; beyond that (this); even; further; furthermore; moreover; more than that (this); still more; then; too; what is more; delete.* How can they speak up and tell the South Africans what they should do with their people or, for that matter, what the Soviet Union should do with its Jewish population? *How can they speak up and tell the South Africans what they should do with their people, or even what the Soviet Union should do with its Jewish population?* ■ Saint-Saens, who was born in 1835 and did not die until 1921, outlived Debussy; so, for that matter, did Indy, who was born 11 years before Debussy but lived on until 1931. *Saint-Saens, who was born in 1835 and did not die until 1921, outlived Debussy; so, too, did Indy, who was born 11 years before Debussy but lived on until 1931.*

for that (this) reason *consequently; hence; so; then; therefore; thus.* For that reason, I wouldn't do it again. *I therefore wouldn't do it again.* ■ You can receive but not send; for this reason, simplex is rarely used. *You can receive but not send; hence, simplex is rarely used.*

for the first (last) time *first (last).* The series of studies were presented for the first time at the three-day conference. *The series of studies were first presented at the three-day conference.*

for the foreseeable future *for a time; for a while; for now; for many (several) months (years); for six (two) months (years); for some time; for the present; for the* *time being; temporarily.* For the foreseeable future, participation in the stock market by small investors will remain depressed. *For a time, participation in the stock market by small investors will remain depressed.* ▪ He said the company would continue to operate Wright Line for the foreseeable future. *He said the company would continue to operate Wright Line for the time being.* ▪ If it succeeds, it could mark the end for the foreseeable future of serious attempts to build a toxic waste disposal facility. *If it succeeds, it could mark the end for a while of serious attempts to build a toxic waste disposal facility.* ▪ He is one of those who believes that a recession can be avoided for the foreseeable future. *He is one of those who believes that a recession can be avoided for now.*

for the immediate future *for a time; for a while; for now; for many (several) months (years); for six (two) months (years); for some time; for the present; for the time being; temporarily.* Several said they were canceling planned business trips for the immediate future. *Several said they were canceling planned business trips for the present.*

for the most part *almost all; chiefly; commonly; generally; greatly; in general; largely; mainly; most; mostly; most often; much; nearly all; normally; overall; typically; usually.* Those problems for the most part have been overcome. *Those problems have been largely overcome.* ▪ Doctors for the most part agree that circumcision is not necessary. *Most doctors agree that circumcision is not necessary.* ▪ For the most part, readers like the new investment page. *Readers generally like the new investment page.* ▪ For the most part, post-modernist writing confesses (or celebrates!) helplessness. *Typically, post-modernist writing confesses (or celebrates!) helplessness.* ▪ He forces people to make practical decisions, and for the most part it results in justice being done. *He forces people to make practical decisions, and usually it results in justice being done.*

for the (very) near future *for a time; for a while; for now; for many (several) months (years); for six (two) months (years); for some time; for the present; for the time being; temporarily.* While the analysts expected Kraft and General Foods to exist as separate entities for the near future, they said they did not expect the honeymoon to last forever. *While the analysts expected Kraft and General Foods to exist as separate entities for now, they said they did not expect the honeymoon to last forever.*

for the not-so-distant (not-too-distant) future *for a time; for a while; for now; for many (several) months (years); for six (two) months (years); for some time; for the present; for the time being; temporarily.*

for the present *for now; delete.* Perhaps one day we shall find an Etruscan library, buried deep in the Italian countryside, but for the present, we have to make do with what we have, which is precious little. *Perhaps one day we shall find an Etruscan library, buried deep in the Italian countryside, but for now, we have to make do with what we have, which is precious little.*

for the purpose of (-ing) *for (-ing); so as to; to.* All deposited items are received for the purpose of collection, and all credits for deposited items are provisional. *All deposited items are received for collection, and all credits for deposited items are provisional.* ■ He purchased a hunting knife for the purpose of killing the victims and to protect him from others he believed were out to do him harm. *He purchased a hunting knife to kill the victims and to protect him from others he believed were out to do him harm.* ■ The trust may not invest for the purpose of exercising control or management of any other issuer. *The trust may not invest so as to exercise control or management of any other issuer.*

for the (simple) reason that *because; considering; for; in that; since.* Normally, short-term Treasuries yield less than longer-term Treasuries, for the simple reason that investors demand to be rewarded for tying up their money in longer-term instruments. *Normally, short-term Treasuries yield less than longer-term Treasuries because investors demand to be rewarded for tying up their money in longer-term instruments.* ■ Even children who attend the same school and have the same teachers experience different realities, for the simple reason that they are genetically different in temperament. *Even children who attend the same school and have the same teachers experience different realities, for they are genetically different in temperament.*

for the sake of *for; so as to; to.* Most serial killers kill for the sake of sexual pleasure. *Most serial killers kill for sexual pleasure.* ■ I have never found it necessary to practice "defensive medicine," if that means doing that which would not otherwise be done solely for the sake of protecting oneself against possible legal action. *I have never found it necessary to practice "defensive medicine," if that means doing that which would not otherwise be done solely to protect oneself against possible legal action.*

for the time (while) being *for now; for the moment; for the present; delete.* For the time being, look at the current PLOT ORIGIN and the SCALE. *For the moment, look at the current PLOT ORIGIN and the SCALE.* ■ For the time being, AFSCME has garnered itself a win—but a small one. *For now, AFSCME has garnered itself a win—but a small one.*

for ... to come *for.* Each man, in his own way, will carry on the conservative viewpoint for years to come. *Each man, in his own way, will carry on the conservative viewpoint for years.* ■ This can go on for generations to come. *This can go on for generations.* ■ Now that the museum's mummies are preserved not only in sealed coffins but on film, their images, properly stored, should last for millennia to come. *Now that the museum's mummies are preserved not only in sealed coffins but on film, their images, properly stored, should last for millennia.*

forward in (into) the future *in (into) the future; later.*

for (many; several) years (now) *long.* The few policies I was able to get from SBLI have, for many years now, paid me an annual dividend, with no payment of any premium. *The few policies I was able to get from SBLI have long paid me an annual dividend, with no payment of any premium.*

for your information delete.

fourthly *fourth.*

frame of mind *attitude; belief; opinion; position; posture; stand; standpoint; vantage; view; viewpoint;* delete.

fraught with meaning (significance) *meaningful (significant).* If nothing else, the question is fraught with significance for Democrats trying to figure out whether to mount a campaign today that will peak three years from now. *If nothing else, the question is significant for Democrats trying to figure out whether to mount a campaign today that will peak three years from now.*

free and gratis *free.*

free gift *gift.* For your free gift, fill out this form today. *For your gift, fill out this form today.*

free of charge *free.* The energy audit and the weatherization services are provided free of charge to eligible households, and all work is performed by licensed contractors or agency crews. *The energy audit and the weatherization services are provided free to eligible households, and all work is performed by licensed contractors or agency crews.* ■ All meetings are free of charge and open to the public. *All meetings are free and open to the public.*

free pass *pass.*

free up *free.* On some programs, rows and columns can be deleted to free up memory for new data on a model. *On some programs, rows and columns can be deleted to free memory for new data on a model.*

freezing cold *cold; freezing.* It's freezing cold outside. *It's freezing outside.*

frequently *often.* Prosecutors and defense lawyers frequently call on psychologists and psychiatrists for opinions. *Prosecutors and defense lawyers often call on psychologists and psychiatrists for opinions.* ■ It is frequently altered by the activities of both man and nature. *It is often altered by the activities of both man and nature.*

from (a; the) ... aspect (of) *as (does); as for; as to; for; from; in; in that; -(al)ly; since; to;* delete. From a legal aspect, the joint venture falls under local company or corporation law when participation is in the form of equity. *Legally, the* *joint venture falls under local company or corporation law when participation is in the form of equity.* ■ From the aspect of quality of technology, there are hardly any differences between the top sellers in the industry. *In quality of technology, there are hardly any differences between the top sellers in the industry.*

from beginning to end *all through; completely; entirely; thoroughly; throughout; totally; wholly.*

from (a; the) ... distance of *from; from ... away.* Most of the spectators watched from a distance of 1,300 feet, while the Soviet observers viewed the firings from a concrete bunker. *Most of the spectators watched from 1,300 feet away, while the Soviet observers viewed the firings from a concrete bunker.*

from hence *hence.*

from minute (moment) to minute (moment) *directly; momentarily; presently; soon.* I expect them from moment to moment. *I expect them momentarily.*

from now (on) *hence.*

from ... on (onward) *since.* Other researchers had already confirmed that from 200 A.D. onward there had been human sacrifices of varying kinds. *Other researchers had already confirmed that since 200 A.D. there had been human sacrifices of varying kinds.*

from one ... to another *between.* Moving your funds from one institution to another is easy to do, and there is no tax liability or IRS penalty at all, if you follow the correct procedures. *Moving your funds between institutions is easy to do, and there is no tax liability or IRS penalty at all, if you follow the correct procedures.*

from (a; the) ... perspective (of) *as (does); as for; as to; for; from; in; in that; -(al)ly; since; to;* delete. From my perspective, trashing my system makes a lot of sense. *Trashing my system makes a lot of sense to me.* ■ From an economic and educational perspective, life in the "territories" is better now than during Jordan's 19-year rule. *Economically and educationally, life in the "territories" is better now than during Jordan's 19-year rule.* ■ From the investment banker's perspective, the private sector represents the most desirable clientele. *For the investment banker, the private sector represents the most desirable clientele.*

from (a; the) ... point of view (of) *as (does); as for; as to; for; from; in; in that; -(al)ly; since; to;* delete. From a scientific point of view, there is no adequate definition of stress. *There is no adequate scientific definition of stress.* ■ It was an adventurous sort of life from my point of view. *To me, it was an adventurous sort of life.* ■ From our point of view, my losing my job was a blessing. *For us, my losing my job was a blessing.* ■ From moral and humanistic points of view, receiving this information became more crucial as we watched SDI appropriations weighed against federal allocations for housing, education, transportation, and so on. *Morally and humanistically, receiving this information became more crucial as we watched SDI appropriations weighed against federal allocations for housing, education, transportation, and so on.* ■ You've got to look at it from an optimistic point of view. *You've got to look at it optimistically.* ■ I try to see things from the customer's point of view. *I try to see things as the customer does.*

from (a; the) ... standpoint (of) *as (does); as for; as to; for; from; in; in that; -(al)ly; since; to;* delete. From a statistical standpoint, who is most vulnerable to colon-rectal cancer? *Statistically, who is most vulnerable to colon-rectal cancer?* ■ We should analyze each of the candidates from an ethical standpoint. *We should analyze the ethics of each candidate.* ■ I have had some experience with grief from a personal standpoint. *I have had some personal experience with grief.* ■ The proposed purchase price is indeed a good value from the city's standpoint. *The proposed purchase price is indeed a good value for the city.* ■ The deal makes great sense for us both from a strategic standpoint and an operating standpoint. *The deal makes great sense for us both strategically and operationally.* ■ A move to Jacksonville will be highly profitable for the club and would be smart from a business standpoint. *A move to Jacksonville will be highly profitable for the club and would be smart business.* ■ From a medical standpoint, we don't have any evidence that the senator abuses alcohol. *We don't have any medical evidence that the senator abuses alcohol.*

from start to finish *all through; completely; entirely; thoroughly; throughout; totally; wholly.*

from that day (moment; point; time) (forward; on; onward) *from then (on); since; since then;* delete. From that point on, she hasn't said a word to me. *Since then, she hasn't said a word to me.* ■ But from that moment forward, everything moves more quickly. *But from then on, everything moves more quickly.*

from the beginning (start) *always.* From the start, it has been a haven for those whose religions or political beliefs were not tolerated in their homelands. *It has always been a haven for those whose religions or political beliefs were not tolerated in their homelands.* ■ From the beginning, the first principle of those devising the bailout of the Federal Savings and Loan Insurance Corp. has been to stick the bill as close to the industry as possible. *The first principle of those devising the bailout of the Federal Savings and Loan Insurance Corp. has always been to stick the bill as close to the industry as possible.*

from (in) the following year *from (in) (1991).*

from (in) the preceding year *from (in) (1989).* At year-end 1987, 70,893 persons were employed within Ericsson, a decrease of 1,682 from the preceding year. *At* *year-end 1987, 70,893 persons were employed within Ericsson, a decrease of 1,682 from 1986.*

from the time of *since.*

from this day (moment; point; time) (forward; on; onward) *from now (on); hence; henceforth; henceforward;* delete. From this point on, elected students and faculty will be running the affairs of the school. *Henceforth, elected students and faculty will be running the affairs of the school.* ■ That's up to the American people to decide from this point forward. *That's up to the American people to decide from now on.*

from ... until *from ... to.* This book is intriguing because it also concerns the role of that on-again, off-again colonial revival in popular culture from 1876 until the present. *This book is intriguing because it also concerns the role of that on-again, off-again colonial revival in popular culture from 1876 to the present.*

from (a; the) ... viewpoint (of) *as (does); as for; as to; for; from; in; in that; -(al)ly; since; to;* delete. Its Category II products should be of respectable quality and, from the user's viewpoint, virtually indistinguishable from comparable products offered by competitors. *Its Category II products should be of respectable quality and, to the users, virtually indistinguishable from comparable products offered by competitors.* ■ From a business viewpoint, it makes good sense to free minds from the drudgery of processing data and to engage them in finding new ways to apply that data. *It makes good sense for business to free minds from the drudgery of processing data and to engage them in finding new ways to apply that data.*

from whence *whence.* From whence did he draw his strength? *Whence did he draw his strength?*

full capacity *capacity.* Demand for petroleum products was so strong that refineries were operating at or near full capacity. *Demand for petroleum products was so strong that refineries were operating at or near capacity.* ■ The Large Electron-Positron collider should be operating at full capacity by October. *The Large Electron-Positron collider should be operating at capacity by October.*

full (maximum) potential (potentiality) *potential (potentiality).* If we are to achieve our full potential, we must see beyond the routine. *If we are to achieve our potential, we must see beyond the routine.* ■ We have not yet pushed the instrument to its maximum potential. *We have not yet pushed the instrument to its potential.* ■ It is an acceptance of one's strengths and limitations while at the same time struggling to grow toward one's full potentialities. *It is an acceptance of one's strengths and limitations while at the same time struggling to grow toward one's potentialities.*

full satisfaction *satisfaction.*

fundamental *basic;* delete.

fundamental (and) basic *basic; fundamental.* These are fundamental and basic rights. *These are basic rights.*

fundamental basis *basis.* Siemens sees this ISDN capability as providing the fundamental basis for a new generation of Centrex services, and the company views Centrex as a cornerstone EWSD service. *Siemens sees this ISDN capability as providing the basis for a new generation of Centrex services, and the company views Centrex as a cornerstone EWSD service.*

fundamental principle *principle.*

furiously angry *angry; furious.* She's furiously angry. *She's furious.*

further *more.* For further information, or free form samples, contact Deluxe at their toll-free number. *For more information, or free form samples, contact Deluxe at their toll-free number.*

furthermore *also; and; as well; besides; even; further; still more; then; too.* Furthermore, foreign words may occasionally be used to convey an idea or attitude that is not readily served by an English translation. *Foreign words may also occasionally be used to convey an idea or attitude that is not readily served by an English translation.* ■ Furthermore, some of the changes may reduce the extent to which issuers may issue tax-exempt bonds. *Further, some of the changes may reduce the extent to which issuers may issue tax-exempt bonds.*

fuse together *fuse.* Most metals, except for low- and medium-carbon steels, require fluxes to aid in the process of melting and fusing the metals together. *Most metals, except for low- and medium-carbon steels, require fluxes to aid in the process of melting and fusing the metals.* ■ Their laboratory experiments show that hydrogen atoms can be forced to fuse together inside a solid material rather than in the superhot gases that fusion researchers have used heretofore. *Their laboratory experiments show that hydrogen atoms can be forced to fuse inside a solid material rather than in the superhot gases that fusion researchers have used heretofore.*

future developments *developments.*

future plans *plans.* He said future plans call for the introduction of 2-Mb/s service in the switched network by 1992, which would mean videoconferences could be switched like normal phone calls. *He said plans call for the introduction of 2-Mb/s service in the switched network by 1992, which would mean videoconferences could be switched like normal phone calls.*

future projections *projections.*

future prospects *prospects.* Proponents of the information center concept, Atre Consultants are not overly romantic about its future prospects. *Proponents of the information center concept, Atre Consultants are not overly romantic about its prospects.*

G

gather together *gather.* Various fields of a record are gathered together in a buffer before being sent out to the file on a single operation. *Various fields of a record are gathered in a buffer before being sent out to the file on a single operation.* ■ In Dubai, about 400 relatives of the dead and their supporters gathered together for a memorial service at a large Shiite mosque. *In Dubai, about 400 relatives of the dead and their supporters gathered for a memorial service at a large Shiite mosque.*

general consensus *consensus.* The general consensus among corporations is to be cautious about 1989. *The consensus among corporations is to be cautious about 1989.*

general public *public.*

general rule *rule.*

general vicinity *area; vicinity.*

gentleman *man.* Nothing would give me greater pleasure than to see these gentlemen put out of business. *Nothing would give me greater pleasure than to see these men put out of business.*

geographical *geographic.* Several large commercial banks provide economic data and forecasts for the geographical area they serve. *Several large commercial banks provide economic data and forecasts for the geographic area they serve.*

geological *geologic.* On-site geological studies would be needed to confirm an impact origin. *On-site geologic studies would be needed to confirm an impact origin.*

geometrical *geometric.*

get across *convey; explain.* There's an important element here that we need to get across. *There's an important element here that we need to convey.*

get divorced *divorce.*

get in touch with *call; contact; phone; reach; visit; write (to).* Agency representatives with reports to enter can get in touch with him at (703) 323-5711. *Agency representatives with reports to enter can reach him at (703) 323-5711.*

get married *marry.* We plan to get married in the fall. *We plan to marry in the fall.* ■ An estimated 738,000 divorced women got married again last year, but a study suggests that remarriage will come late or never for many women who recently separated. *An estimated 738,000 divorced women married again last year, but a study suggests that remarriage will come late or never for many women who recently separated.*

give (a; the) ... (for; of; to) delete. Give an estimate on the amount of time it will take and the number of people you will need. *Estimate the amount of time it will take and the number of people you will need.* ■ The Book of Leviticus gives a list of the women who are not available to marry certain men. *The Book of Leviticus lists the women who are not available to marry certain men.* ■ The main purpose of choosing an outside auditor is to guarantee to insiders and interested outsiders that the financial data presented in financial documents give an accurate representation of events. *The main purpose of choosing an outside auditor is to guarantee to insiders and interested outsiders that the financial data presented in financial documents accurately represent events.* ■ They work hard; they deserve to be given compensation. *They work hard; they deserve to be compensated.* ■ Did he give any indication of what he plans to do? *Did he indicate what he plans to do?* ■ I'll give you a call at the end of the week. *I'll call you at the end of the week.* ■ I hope you will give me consideration for diverse projects. *I hope you will consider me for diverse projects.* ■ Once the source of conflict is cleared up, top managers can better evaluate whether the bank is giving the appropriate emphasis to each of its different units. *Once the source of conflict is cleared up, top managers can better evaluate whether the bank is appropriately emphasizing each of its different units.*

give birth to *bear.*

given at (in) *at (in).* Since all limits are given in thousandths, the values can be converted by moving the decimal point three places to the left. *Since all limits are in thousandths, the values can be converted by moving the decimal point three places to the left.*

given the fact that *because; considering; for; in that; since; when.* Given the fact that the leadership here has been galvanized to action for some time, Boston is likely to remain the world capital of the biomedical sciences. *Since the leadership here has been galvanized to action for some time, Boston is likely to remain the world capital of the biomedical sciences.* ■ Given the fact that she only read 400 pages of the book, she didn't do too badly. *Considering she only read 400 pages of the book, she didn't do too badly.* ■ He said he will continue to seek the $59 million originally targeted for the state, but he stressed it will be a hard sell given the fact that other cities are also clamoring for cash. *He said he will con-*

tinue to seek the $59 million originally targeted for the state, but he stressed it will be a hard sell because other cities are also clamoring for cash.

give rise to *bear; cause.* The researchers concluded that abnormalities in the neurotransmitter system may give rise to the depression in demented patients. *The researchers concluded that abnormalities in the neurotransmitter system may cause the depression in demented patients.*

give ... consideration (thought; weight) to *consider; examine; ponder; reflect on; study; weigh.* Many small businesses and private individuals are giving serious consideration to their energy and resource needs for the year ahead. *Many small businesses and private individuals are seriously considering their energy and resource needs for the year ahead.* ■ One might also give thought to the possibility that whatever energetic process produced the flash photolytic "burn" in the cloth might have dramatically altered both the atomic and molecular structure of the linen, thus resulting in faulty or artifactual carbon-14 readings. *One might also examine the possibility that whatever energetic process produced the flash photolytic "burn" in the cloth might have dramatically altered both the atomic and molecular structure of the linen, thus resulting in faulty or artifactual carbon-14 readings.*

go along with *agree with; back; endorse; favor; support.* She absolutely would have gone along with the idea. *She absolutely would have agreed with the idea.* ■ He was unwilling to say whether he would go along with such a recommendation. *He was unwilling to say whether he would support such a recommendation.*

(just) goes to show *attests; proves; reveals; shows; supports; verifies; delete.* It just goes to show that safety in driving is most important. *It shows that safety in driving is most important.* ■ It just goes to show what a difference there can be between people. *It proves what a difference there can be between people.*

(it) goes without saying (that) *clearly; naturally; obviously; of course; plainly; delete.* It goes without saying that the heart of constitutional democracy lies in public debate by an informed electorate. *The heart of constitutional democracy lies in public debate by an informed electorate.* ■ It goes without saying that in the case of purchasing equipment from abroad, it's a question of modern and high-technology equipment. *Obviously, in the case of purchasing equipment from abroad, it's a question of modern and high-technology equipment.* ■ This may go without saying, but I also look at a person's motivation, commitment, and energy. *Naturally, I also look at a person's motivation, commitment, and energy.*

go forward *advance; go on; move on; proceed; progress.* There are too many negative effects on the immediate neighborhood to allow this to go forward. *There are too many negative effects on the immediate neighborhood to allow this to progress.* ■ We want the project to go forward as soon as possible, and we are confident that these issues can be addressed. *We want the project to proceed as soon as possible, and we are confident that these issues can be addressed.*

good and sufficient *adequate; good; sufficient.* We think that the safety of present plants is good and sufficient. *We think that the safety of present plants is adequate.*

go through ... experience *experience; go through.* I think I'm a much better person for having gone through that experience. *I think I'm a much better person for having experienced that.*

grateful thanks *gratitude; thanks.*

(a; the) great (large) fraction (of) *a good (great) deal (of); a good (great) many (of); almost all (of); (nine) in (ten) (of); many (of); most (of); much (of); nearly all (of); (43) of (48) (of); ... percent (of); three-fourths (two-thirds) (of).* Of the numerous complete fossils discovered in this quarry, a large fraction are either babies or mothers carrying young. *Of the numerous complete fossils discovered in this quarry, most are either babies or mothers carrying young.* ■ We are sacrificing a large fraction of our young people along the way. *We are sacrificing many of our young people along the way.*

H

had ... then *had.* Had he exhibited the kind of behavior that would have warranted such a recommendation, then it would have been made. *Had he exhibited the kind of behavior that would have warranted such a recommendation, it would have been made.*

hale and hearty *hale; healthy; hearty; well.*

half of *half.* More than half of the nearly 3 million women-owned businesses had total annual sales of less than $5000. *More than half the nearly 3 million women-owned businesses had total annual sales of less than $5000.* ■ The menus occupy almost half of the screen display. *The menus occupy almost half the screen display.*

harbinger of the future (of things to come) *harbinger; omen; sign.* I hope it is a harbinger of the future. *I hope it is an omen.* ■ The mass gatherings and push-and-shove clashes following last week's abortion ruling appear to be harbingers of things to come. *The mass gatherings and push-and-shove clashes following last week's abortion ruling appear to be harbingers.*

hard and fast *firm; fixed; steadfast; strict.*

has (a; the) ... (about; for; of; on; over) delete. Maria and I will be having a talk in a few minutes. *Maria and I will be talking in a few minutes.* ∎ Boston has the need for a new harbor tunnel. *Boston needs a new harbor tunnel.* ∎ The complete strategic partnering lawyer must also have a firm grasp of the fundamentals of the legal principles in Europe and in the Far East. *The complete strategic partnering lawyer must also firmly grasp the fundamentals of the legal principles in Europe and in the Far East.* ∎ He has control over the entire program. *He controls the entire program.* ∎ If you have intentions of going, you should make your reservations now. *If you intend to go, you should make your reservations now.* ∎ A lot of new jobs for people who want them is a goal worth having. *A lot of new jobs for people who want them is a worthy goal.*

has a bearing on (upon) acts on; affects; bears on; influences. What we are learning about primates and other social species has a direct bearing on our own species. *What we are learning about primates and other social species directly bears on our own species.* ∎ The global company's management has attitudes toward doing business overseas that have a bearing on the strategy formulation process used. *The global company's management has attitudes toward doing business overseas that act on the strategy formulation process used.* ∎ The degree of stability or uncertainty in the economic and political dimensions of the environment has a direct bearing on the form of market presence to be established. *The degree of stability or uncertainty in the economic and political dimensions of the environment directly affects the form of market presence to be established.*

has a (the) capability to can; is able to.

has a difference of opinion with differs; disagrees with; disputes; objects to; opposes. We have a difference of opinion with the decision the judge made. *We disagree with the decision the judge made.*

has a (the) habit of (-ing) tends to; will. He has a habit of biting his nails. *He tends to bite his nails.*

has an (the) ability to can; is able to. Eighty percent of the retail deposit accounts have the ability to be accessed by a debit card even though actual usage is much less. *Eighty percent of the retail deposit accounts can be accessed by a debit card even though actual usage is much less.* ∎ Almost all body cells have the ability to accommodate environmental demands by two primary mechanisms: cell hypertrophy and cell hyperplasia. *Almost all body cells are able to accommodate environmental demands by two primary mechanisms: cell hypertrophy and cell hyperplasia.*

has an (the) appreciation for appreciates; approves of; cherishes; enjoys; esteems; likes; prizes; treasures; understands; values. Most people don't have an appreciation for esoteric beliefs. *Most people don't appreciate esoteric beliefs.*

has a (the) preference for *favors; prefers.* By now, you will have gathered that I have a strong preference for organization along functional lines. *By now, you will have gathered that I strongly prefer organization along functional lines.* ▪ In a survey of management executives, 67 percent of the respondents have a preference for the rational/logical decision model. *In a survey of management executives, 67 percent of the respondents favor the rational/logical decision model.*

has a (the) tendency (to) *tends to; will.* In one respect, market share is synonymous with published league tables because clients have a tendency to read them. *In one respect, market share is synonymous with published league tables because clients tend to read them.* ▪ As a community, the Basques have a tendency to be healthy and long-lived. *As a community, the Basques tend to be healthy and long-lived.* ▪ Narcissistic people also have a tendency to be extremely ambitious. *Narcissistic people also tend to be extremely ambitious.*

has (a) ... effect on (upon) *acts on; affects; bears on; influences;* delete. Inaccurate information on costs, capital, personnel, time needed, historical performances, or potential developments in the economy can have devastating effects on plans. *Inaccurate information on costs, capital, personnel, time needed, historical performances, or potential developments in the economy can devastate plans.* ▪ Human activity is changing the composition of the atmosphere in ways that could have profound effects upon life on the Earth. *Human activity is changing the composition of the atmosphere in ways that could profoundly affect life on the Earth.* ▪ Over the past twenty years, the U.S. economy has had a significant effect on the Amish way of life. *Over the past twenty years, the U.S. economy has significantly influenced the Amish way of life.*

has got *has.*

has (a) ... impact (on; upon) *acts on; affects; bears on; influences;* delete. It has a direct impact on the majority of the American people. *It directly affects the majority of the American people.* ▪ Your tone of voice, expression, and apparent receptiveness to others' responses all have a tremendous impact upon those you wish to reach. *Your tone of voice, expression, and apparent receptiveness to others' responses all tremendously influence those you wish to reach.* ▪ The global marketing manager must be sensitive to fundamental institutions and systems that transcend national boundaries and have an impact on international business activities. *The global marketing manager must be sensitive to fundamental institutions and systems that transcend national boundaries and bear on international business activities.*

has (a) ... influence on (upon) *acts on; affects; bears on; influences;* delete. Management was alerted to the fact that the social environment of employees had a great influence on productivity. *Management was alerted to the fact that the social environment of employees greatly affected productivity.* ▪ In combination, these three components of the global marketing mission have a strong influ-ence on the structure and content of the company's core marketing strategy. *In combination, these three components of the global marketing mission strongly influence the structure and content of the company's core marketing strate-gy.* ▪ This will have an influence on the college labor market since two-thirds of all college graduates work in the service industry. *This will bear on the college labor market since two-thirds of all college graduates work in the service indus-try.*

has only to *need only.* To view any of the channels available, you have only to switch between channels. *To view any of the channels available, you need only switch between channels.*

has reference to *concerns; deals with; is about; pertains to; regards; relates to.*

has the effect of -ing delete. The trust presently has certain antitakeover provi-sions in its declaration that could have the effect of limiting the ability of other entities or persons to acquire control of the trust. *The trust presently has certain antitakeover provisions in its declaration that could limit the ability of other entities or persons to acquire control of the trust.* ▪ Such a slowdown would have the effect of easing inflationary fears. *Such a slowdown would ease inflationary fears.*

has (got) to *must.* I have to be going. *I must be going.* ▪ The empty labs are a problem that hospitals and patients alike have got to deal with. *The empty labs are a problem that hospitals and patients alike must deal with.*

(that) has to do with *concerns; deals with; is about; pertains to; regards; relates to.* The key to their maintaining a high degree of competitiveness has to do with how effective they are in leveraging via others. *The key to their maintaining a high degree of competitiveness concerns how effective they are in leveraging via others.* ▪ The more interesting issue has to do with what Europe gained during those 15 years of zero employment growth. *The more interesting issue deals with what Europe gained during those 15 years of zero employment growth.* ▪ You raise another question that has to do with the confusion patients experience when their doctors don't agree. *You raise another question about the confusion patients experience when their doctors don't agree.* ▪ The first has to do with the relative merits of CD versus analog. *The first pertains to the relative merits of CD versus analog.*

have (possess) ... in common *share.* We have no interests in common. *We share no interests.* ▪ Her philosophy had more in common with the neo-radicalism of American politics than with European traditions of social or Christian democra-cy. *Her philosophy shared more with the neo-radicalism of American politics than with European traditions of social or Christian democracy.*

have ... in (my) possession *have; possess.* I have made it my practice not to ask a grand jury to indict a case unless I have evidence in my possession that would permit me to argue in good faith to the trial jury that they should find the defendant guilty beyond a reasonable doubt. *I have made it my practice not to ask a grand jury to indict a case unless I have evidence that would permit me to argue in good faith to the trial jury that they should find the defendant guilty beyond a reasonable doubt.* ∎ We now have in our possession a class of machines that are right around energy breakeven. *We now possess a class of machines that are right around energy breakeven.*

head up *direct; head; lead.* George Bush headed up the committee that eliminated those regulations. *George Bush headed the committee that eliminated those regulations.*

heat up *heat.* I just threw it all together and then heated it up. *I just threw it all together and then heated it.*

(a; the) height of delete. The stratosphere is one of the middle layers of the atmosphere that starts some 15 kilometers above Earth's surface and extends to a height of about 50 kilometers. *The stratosphere is one of the middle layers of the atmosphere that starts some 15 kilometers above Earth's surface and extends to about 50 kilometers.*

help in (of) -ing *help (-ing).* Those who have no diversions or hobbies may need help in selecting appropriate activities. *Those who have no diversions or hobbies may need help selecting appropriate activities.* ∎ The work may also help in tracking down inherited influences in mental diseases. *The work may also help track down inherited influences in mental diseases.*

help out *help.* They're very eager to help out. *They're very eager to help.*

help ... to *help.* Following these guidelines may help to cut down on the amount of aspirin you need. *Following these guidelines may help cut down on the amount of aspirin you need.* ∎ International business is not a panacea that will help a firm with a weak domestic base to pull itself up into the major leagues. *International business is not a panacea that will help a firm with a weak domestic base pull itself up into the major leagues.*

henceforth (henceforward) *hence.*

here delete. These examples here were borrowed from Fowler. *These examples were borrowed from Fowler.*

hereafter *hence.*

(the) here and now *(just; right) now; presently; the present.*

high and dry *alone; helpless; powerless.*

high and low *everywhere.*

high and mighty *arrogant; dogmatic; domineering; haughty.*

(a; the) high degree (of) *abundant; a good (great) deal (of); a good (great) many (of); ample; great; high; many (of); marked; most (of); much (of); salient; striking; vast;* delete. We recognize that banks retain a close and often emotional link to the consumer, offering traditional services and a very high degree of trust. *We recognize that banks retain a close and often emotional link to the consumer, offering traditional services and much trust.* ■ One of the distinguishing characteristics of the Eurobond market is its high degree of competitiveness. *One of the distinguishing characteristics of the Eurobond market is it marked competitiveness.* ■ He surveyed 510 high school juniors and seniors and found a high degree of anxiety about making the right career decisions and earning enough money. *He surveyed 510 high school juniors and seniors and found high anxiety about making the right career decisions and earning enough money.* ■ This kind of lifestyle requires that you have a high degree of self-esteem. *This kind of lifestyle requires that you have ample self-esteem.*

(a; the) high level (of) *abundant; a good (great) deal (of); a good (great) many (of); ample; great; high; many (of); marked; most (of); much (of); salient; striking; vast;* delete. The London merchant banks have a very high level of expertise. *The London merchant banks have vast expertise.* ■ In less than 20 years, this product has achieved a high level of visibility in the industry. *In less than 20 years, this product has achieved much visibility in the industry.* ■ It has also suffered from a high level of passenger complaints over its service. *It has also suffered from many passenger complaints over its service.*

(a; the) high number (of) *a good (great) many (of); almost all; countless; dozens (of); hundreds (of); many (of); millions (of); most (of); nearly all (of); numerous; scores (of); six hundred (twelve hundred) (of); thousands (of).* Hampton's high number of published recordings further supports the idea that he has spent several decades sharing his vibe playing with those who would listen. *Hampton's numerous published recordings further supports the idea that he has spent several decades sharing his vibe playing with those who would listen.*

(a; the) high percentage (of) *a good (great) deal (of); a good (great) many (of); almost all (of); (nine) in (ten) (of); many (of); most (of); much (of); nearly all (of); (43) of (48) (of); ... percent (of); three-fourths (two-thirds) (of).* A high percentage of those who test positive do develop the AIDS antibody. *Most of those who test positive do develop the AIDS antibody.* ■ That probably is excellent advice, if these bonds represent a high percentage of your total investments. *That probably is excellent advice, if these bonds represent much of your total investments.* ■ A high percentage of the people in this community have seen a nurse practitioner at one time or another. *Forty percent of the people in this community have seen a nurse practitioner at one time or another.*

(a; the) high proportion (of) *a good (great) deal (of); a good (great) many (of); almost all (of); (nine) in (ten) (of); many (of); most (of); much (of); nearly all (of); (43) of (48) (of); ... percent (of); three-fourths (two-thirds) (of).* In the pharmaceutical industry, most companies devote a high proportion of their budgets to R&D expenditures. *In the pharmaceutical industry, most companies devote much of their budgets to R&D expenditures.* ■ A high proportion of Americans view the prospect of speaking in public as a fate worse than death. *Nearly all Americans view the prospect of speaking in public as a fate worse than death.*

hired mercenary *mercenary.*

historical experience *experience; history.* The quote could be misconstrued to leave the impression that we made an explicit assumption that was at odds with recent historical experience. *The quote could be misconstrued to leave the impression that we made an explicit assumption that was at odds with recent experience.* ■ A person's, or a nation's, historical experience and the degree to which either has confronted evil apparently play major roles in determining perspective. *A person's, or a nation's, history and the degree to which either has confronted evil apparently play major roles in determining perspective.* ■ Marriage, like growing old, can be among the most relentless historical experiences. *Marriage, like growing old, can be among the most relentless experiences.*

historical precedent *history; precedent.* We are unaware of any historical precedent that has seen a nation indefinitely borrow and consume its way to prosperity. *We are unaware of any precedent that has seen a nation indefinitely borrow and consume its way to prosperity.*

historical record *history; record.* Mr. Macdonald is too young to have known this, but neither youth nor filial piety justifies distorting the historical record. *Mr. Macdonald is too young to have known this, but neither youth nor filial piety justifies distorting the record.* ■ Given the historical record of the PLO and its commitment to terrorism, Arafat's allies in the United Nations do not deny his support of terrorism in the Middle East. *Given the history of the PLO and its commitment to terrorism, Arafat's allies in the United Nations do not deny his support of terrorism in the Middle East.*

hoist up *hoist.*

hold a meeting *meet.*

hold (to) the view (that) *assert; believe; claim; consider; contend; feel; hold; judge; maintain; regard; say; think; to; view.* Most utility regulators and economists hold to the view that electric utilities are "natural monopolies." *Most* *utility regulators and economists hold that electric utilities are "natural monopolies."*

hold (to) the opinion (that) *assert; believe; claim; consider; contend; feel; hold; judge; maintain; regard; say; think; to; view.*

hold true *hold.* As we age, our muscles become weaker and more easily tired, and the same holds true for polio victims. *As we age, our muscles become weaker and more easily tired, and the same holds for polio victims.* ■ If the latter conclusion holds true, a 3,000-year span separated early cultivation efforts and the appearance of full-scale agriculture in the same region. *If the latter conclusion holds, a 3,000-year span separated early cultivation efforts and the appearance of full-scale agriculture in the same region.*

hollow tube *tube.*

honestly and truly *honestly; truly; truthfully.*

(the) honest truth *honestly; truly; (the) truth; truthfully.* The person you're interviewing doesn't want you to discover the honest truth. *The person you're interviewing doesn't want you to discover the truth.*

hope and expect (expectation) *expect (expectation); hope; trust.* With the reputation that ABC has earned in the past decade, we hope and expect it will be more than song and dance. *With the reputation that ABC has earned in the past decade, we trust it will be more than song and dance.* ■ We hope and expect that we can put together a good, solid plan. *We expect that we can put together a good, solid plan.*

hopefully *(I; we) hope; delete.* Today, hopefully, we have some answers to these problems. *Today, I hope, we have some answers to these problems.* ■ Hopefully, the governor will feel enough heat to sign the bill. *We hope the governor will feel enough heat to sign the bill.*

how do (you) go about (-ing) *how do (you).* How do you go about getting an income tax extension? *How do you get an income tax extension?*

however *but; still; though; yet; delete.* When you use these programs, however, you do not always have to use all the commands. *But when you use these programs, you do not always have to use all the commands.* ■ However, in reality, most prisons are notorious for corrupting what is left of an inmate's virtue and allow little opportunity for free exercise of individual will. *Yet in reality, most prisons are notorious for corrupting what is left of an inmate's virtue and allow little opportunity for free exercise of individual will.*

how in God's (heaven's) name *however; how ever.*

how in the world (on earth) *however; how ever.* How in the world did you manage that? *However did you manage that?* ■ How on earth did matters reach this sorry point, and what might the repercussions be? *How did matters ever reach this sorry point, and what might the repercussions be?*

how is it (that) *how come; why.*

howsoever *however.*

hue and cry *clamor; hubbub; outcry.* He moved to stem the hue and cry by saying that the House would vote next week on trimming the raise to 30 percent. *He moved to stem the outcry by saying that the House would vote next week on trimming the raise to 30 percent.*

huge throng *throng.*

human being *being; female; human; male; man; person; woman.* Such a statement is beneath the dignity of any civilized human being. *Such a statement is beneath the dignity of any civilized person.*

human resources *employees; people; persons; workers.* If the company does not have enough human resources to meet future needs, it must begin hiring them. *If the company does not have enough employees to meet future needs, it must begin hiring them.*

humongous *big; giant; grand; great; huge; immense; large; mammoth; mighty; monstrous.* It's a humongous amount, oceans and oceans of material. *It's a huge amount, oceans and oceans of material.*

hurry up *hurry.*

I

identical (identically) match *duplicate; exact; identical; match; (the) same.*

identical (identically) (the) same *duplicate; exact; identical; match; (the) same.* The operating system assumes they are the same file because the first eight characters are identically the same. *The operating system assumes they are the same file because the first eight characters are identical.*

I do not think so *I think not.*

I don't think *I doubt; I think;* delete. If Dole doesn't act more civilized, he's not going to make it, I don't think. *If Dole doesn't act more civilized, he's not going to make it.* ■ Technology is not now being taxed, and I don't think it will ever be taxed in the supply of these services. *Technology is not now being taxed, and I doubt it will ever be taxed in the supply of these services.*

if and only if *if; only if.* It is agreed that the premiums stated in the Coverage Selections page are subject to recomputation if, and only if, the rates fixed and established are found not to meet the requirements of state law. *It is agreed that the premiums stated in the Coverage Selections page are subject to recomputation only if the rates fixed and established are found not to meet the requirements of state law.*

if and (or) when *if; when.* To use a program, it is not necessary for you to know all the commands because many of them are for advanced features that you learn if and when you need them. *To use a program, it is not necessary for you to know all the commands because many of them are for advanced features that you learn if you need them.*

if by way of hypothesis (supposition) *assuming (that); supposing (that).*

if ... had *had.* It would be unrealistic to claim that all the employees are as well off today as they would have been if the brewery had stayed open. *It would be unrealistic to claim that all the employees are as well off today as they would have been had the brewery stayed open.*

if in return *if.* I would guess that most of us would happily compromise our abstract essence of moral agency if, in return, we were allowed to avoid a prison term. *I would guess that most of us would happily compromise our abstract essence of moral agency if we were allowed to avoid a prison term.* ■ I will ask him if you in return will stop talking about him. *I will ask him if you will stop talking about him.*

if it were not for *but for; except for.* The loss would have been $261 million if it were not for an accounting change related to the treatment of income taxes. *The loss would have been $261 million but for an accounting change related to the treatment of income taxes.*

ifs, ands, or buts *conditions.*

if ... should *should.* We will be alert to other opportunities if this one should collapse. *We will be alert to other opportunities should this one collapse.*

if ... then *if.* If he tells you he doesn't ever want to have children, then you will have to make a decision. *If he tells you he doesn't ever want to have children, you will have to make a decision.* ■ If you want the government to disapprove a given merger, then you must ask the government to make sure that neither party in the merger goes out of business. *If you want the government to disapprove a given merger, you must ask the government to make sure that neither party in the merger goes out of business.*

if that (this) is the case (situation) *if so.*

if that (this) is true *if so.*

if ... were *should; were.* We have never experienced the slightest hint of pressure from any of our funders and would immediately reject both the pressure and the money if that were ever to occur. *We have never experienced the slightest hint of pressure from any of our funders and would immediately reject both the pressure and the money should that ever occur.* ■ If that were the only penalty, I would settle for keeping 22 cents on the dollar. *Were that the only penalty, I would settle for keeping 22 cents on the dollar.*

I'll (let me) tell you (something) delete.

illustrative example *example.* From the Software Library, you can download illustrative code examples and the latest technical specifications. *From the Software Library, you can download code examples and the latest technical specifications.*

I'm curious why *why.* I'm curious why you want to see him. *Why do you want to see him?* ■ I am curious why Fidelity is requiring me to give them confidential information on my employment history and income. *Why is Fidelity requiring me to give them confidential information on my employment history and income?*

I mean delete.

immunological *immunologic.*

impact (on; upon) *(v) act on; affect; bear on; influence.* It's the numbers that impact on all of us. *It's the numbers that influence all of us.* ■ Stress most often impacts upon people who have an all-or-nothing achievement perspective, a low-frustration tolerance, limited coping skills, a limited support group, and a cutthroat approach toward others. *Stress most often affects people who have an all-or-nothing achievement perspective, a low-frustration tolerance, limited coping skills, a limited support group, and a cutthroat approach toward others.*

implement *achieve; complete; effect; fulfill; make; perform; produce; realize.*

importance *import; moment.*

important essentials *essentials.*

(an; the) important ... for (in; of; to) *important for (to).* Because decision making is an important element of a manager's job, we need to discover anything that can improve the quality of decision making. *Because decision making is important to a manager's job, we need to discover anything that can improve the* *quality of decision making.* ■ Their willingness to commit capital was an important factor for success. *Their willingness to commit capital was important for success.* ■ Because we organize our activities well in advance, the schedule is an important aspect in the preparation of an article. *Because we organize our activities well in advance, the schedule is important to the preparation of an article.* ■ Certainly, overall physical health is an important component in any society. *Certainly, overall physical health is important to any society.*

important significance *consequence; importance; significance.*

in (on; with) (a; the) ... (of; that) *-ing (that).* Now researchers are testing a promising vaccine given to pregnant women in the hope that maternal antibodies passed on to the developing fetus will protect it from GBS infection during the first months of life outside the womb. *Now researchers are testing a promising vaccine given to pregnant women hoping that maternal antibodies passed on to the developing fetus will protect it from GBS infection during the first months of life outside the womb.* ■ Since 1973, the United States has gotten almost all of its supply from volunteers, in the belief that an unpaid donor is unlikely to offer blood if he or she is sick. *Since 1973, the United States has gotten almost all of its supply from volunteers, believing an unpaid donor is unlikely to offer blood if he or she is sick.* ■ These same people are making significant international dispositions on the expectation that Japan will continue to be the world's largest creditor. *These same people are making significant international dispositions expecting that Japan will continue to be the world's largest creditor.* ■ In the 1980s, many people made plans on the assumption that oil prices would exceed $75 per barrel by 1990. *In the 1980s, many people made plans assuming that oil prices would exceed $75 per barrel by 1990.*

in a bad mood *angry; dejected; depressed; displeased; downcast; glum; grouchy; sad; unhappy; vexed.*

in (a; the) ... capacity (function; position; role) as *as (a; the).*

in accord (accordance) with *according to; by; following; in keeping with; in line with; in step with; to; under.* Working drawings describe the details of a part or project so that construction can be performed in accordance with specifications. *Working drawings describe the details of a part or project so that construction can be performed to specifications.* ■ The net proceeds of the offering will be invested in accordance with the trust's investment objectives and policies. *The net proceeds of the offering will be invested in keeping with the trust's investment objectives and policies.* ■ Once accurate forecasts of sales income are available, money can be allocated to the various parts of the enterprise in accordance with some formula. *Once accurate forecasts of sales income are available, money can be allocated to the various parts of the enterprise following some formula.* ■ This document shall be governed and construed in accordance with the laws of the State of Utah. *This document shall be governed and construed under the laws of the State of Utah.*

in a class by itself *matchless; novel; peerless; singular; special; unequaled; unique; unmatched; unrivaled.*

in a (the) ... condition delete. The Tenant must keep the Apartment in a clean and sanitary condition, free of garbage, rubbish, and other filth. *The Tenant must keep the Apartment clean and sanitary, free of garbage, rubbish, and other filth.*

in actual fact *actually; indeed; in fact; in faith; in reality; in truth; really; truly;* delete. And, in actual fact, the copywriter who created the spots and several other people who worked on it are also Catholic. *And, in fact, the copywriter who created the spots and several other people who worked on it are also Catholic.*

in actuality *actually; indeed; in fact; in faith; in truth; really; truly;* delete. It is possible that each member might do parts of jobs that each thought important to meet the objectives, whereas in actuality, the members might be working in opposite directions. *It is possible that each member might do parts of jobs that each thought important to meet the objectives, whereas in truth, the members might be working in opposite directions.* ■ This looks like a very simple process, but in actuality it is very sensitive. *This looks like a very simple process, but actually it is very sensitive.* ■ In actuality, such a situation seldom occurs. *In fact, such a situation seldom occurs.*

in addition *also; and; as well; besides; beyond that (this); even; further; furthermore; moreover; more than that (this); still more; then; too; what is more.* In addition, we reviewed several net present value models. *We even reviewed several net present value models.* ■ In addition, Lotus 1-2-3 Release 3 gives users more spreadsheet power with several new features. *And Lotus 1-2-3 Release 3 gives users more spreadsheet power with several new features.* ■ In addition, direct communication between countries is not always easy. *What's more, direct communication between countries is not always easy.* ■ In addition, the chart is a trouble-shooting tool. *The chart is a trouble-shooting tool as well.*

in addition to *besides; beyond.* In addition to widening the marketplace, deregulation has provided increased opportunities for diversification and development of new revenue sources. *Beyond widening the marketplace, deregulation has provided increased opportunities for diversification and development of new revenue sources.* ■ In addition to using words to communicate, all of us talk with our body poses and facial expressions. *Besides using words to communicate, all of us talk with our body poses and facial expressions.*

in addition to ... also (as well) *besides; beyond; in addition to.* In addition to measuring a computer in terms of its memory and processing speed, we must also analyze the computer's ability to handle list processing. *In addition to measuring a computer in terms of its memory and processing speed, we must analyze the computer's ability to handle list processing.* ■ In addition to its marketing strategy responsibilities, the global marketing management is also responsible for the development and maintenance of the company's overall competitive advantages across and within all its markets. *Besides its marketing strategy responsibilities, the global marketing management is responsible for the development and maintenance of the company's overall competitive advantages across and within all its markets.*

in a (the) ... direction delete. Vertical lines are drawn along the left side of a triangle in an upward direction. *Vertical lines are drawn upward along the left side of a triangle.* ■ Ribs are not section-lined when the cutting plane passes in a flatwise direction through them. *Ribs are not section-lined when the cutting plane passes flatwise through them.* ■ Flow in the horizontal direction is affected by at least two types of boundaries. *Horizontal flow is affected by at least two types of boundaries.*

in advance *before; beforehand; earlier; sooner;* delete. If I'd known in advance that out of every 100 books published, only one becomes a best seller, I wouldn't have started a book. *If I'd known sooner that out of every 100 books published, only one becomes a best seller, I wouldn't have started a book.* ■ Because of inflation, there is no way of telling in advance how much purchasing power these dollars will have. *Because of inflation, there is no way of telling beforehand how much purchasing power these dollars will have.*

in advance of *ahead of; before.* In advance of our first break, let me introduce Thomas Armstrong, Ph.D., a learning and education specialist. *Before our first break, let me introduce Thomas Armstrong, Ph.D., a learning and education specialist.* ■ The Department of Elder Affairs should distribute material about coping with climate extremes well in advance of the change of seasons. *The Department of Elder Affairs should distribute material about coping with climate extremes well before the change of seasons.*

inadvertent (unintended; unintentional) oversight *oversight.*

in a (the) fashion (manner; way) (in which; that) *as; like.* It seems to make more sense to be positioned as a responsive communications expert, with capability to serve the customer's needs in the manner in which the customer desires. *It seems to make more sense to be positioned as a responsive communications expert, with capability to serve the customer's needs as the customer desires.* ■ Zeus allows you to work intuitively in the way that you think best. *Zeus allows you to work intuitively as you think best.* ■ But such a scientific inquiry already took place years ago, in the manner provided for by law. *But such a scientific inquiry already took place years ago, as provided for by law.*

in a (the) fashion (manner; way) characteristic of *as; like.*

in a (the) fashion (manner; way) similar to *alike; as; like; much as; much like; much the same (as); rather like; resembling; similar to; similarly to.* Problems involving formulas of the type F_1 x $F_2 = F_3$ can be solved in a manner similar to the example given in Fig. 34.1 when logarithmic scales are used. *Problems involving formulas of the type F_1 x $F_2 = F_3$ can be solved much like the example given in Fig. 34.1 when logarithmic scales are used.* ■ In a manner similar to modern-day whales, ichthyosaurs seem to have frequented breeding or birthing areas. *Like modern-day whales, ichthyosaurs seem to have frequented breeding or birthing areas.*

in a few minutes (moments) *briefly; directly; momentarily; presently; quickly; shortly; soon; straightaway.* Press any key, and in a few moments, the Lotus 1-2-3 spreadsheet will appear on the screen. *Press any key, and the Lotus 1-2-3 spreadsheet will directly appear on the screen.*

in a good mood *cheerful; glad; gleeful; happy; joyful; joyous; merry; pleased.*

in agreement with *according to; by; following; in keeping with; in line with; in step with; to; under.*

in (almost) all (every) cases (circumstances; instances; situations) *all; almost all; almost always; always; consistently; constantly; invariably; nearly all; nearly always; unfailingly.* In almost all cases, the expert system assists or advises, as opposed to replacing problem solvers. *Almost always, the expert system assists or advises, as opposed to replacing problem solvers.* ■ The actual percentage should be given in all cases. *The actual percentage should always be given.* ■ In all cases, the bodies have been there since last spring or summer. *All the bodies have been there since last spring or summer.*

in all likelihood *likely; most (very) likely; probably; most (very) probably.* If you don't have this kind of sponsorship, you should not even attempt a project because, in all likelihood, it is doomed to fall far short of the intended objectives. *If you don't have this kind of sponsorship, you should not even attempt a project because it is probably doomed to fall far short of the intended objectives.* ■ In all likelihood, it will get extended until there is a determination of the ESOP litigation. *Most likely, it will get extended until there is a determination of the ESOP litigation.*

in all probability *likely; most (very) likely; probably; most (very) probably.* A telephone call to the coordinator keeps the bank from stepping on its own toes by duplicating efforts and, in all probability, makes the call more effective. *A telephone call to the coordinator keeps the bank from stepping on its own toes by duplicating efforts and, most probably, makes the call more effective.* ■ If declines in groundwater levels do not make the use of the water uneconomical, pumping will in all probability continue despite the declines. *If declines in groundwater levels do not make the use of the water uneconomical, pumping will probably continue despite the declines.*

in a lot of cases (circumstances; instances; situations) *frequently; most often; often; sometimes; usually.* In a lot of cases, serial killers seek power over others. *Often, serial killers seek power over others.*

in a (the) majority of cases (circumstances; instances; situations) *frequently; most often; often; usually.*

in a manner of speaking *as it were; in a sense; in a way; so to speak.*

in a (some) measure *partially; partly; somewhat.*

in a minute (moment) *briefly; directly; momentarily; presently; quickly; shortly; soon; straightaway.*

in an attempt to *in trying to; to try to.* In an attempt to satisfy the informal group, the employee may come in conflict with the formal organization. *In trying to satisfy the informal group, the employee may come in conflict with the formal organization.* ■ In an attempt to solve these problems, IBM and Microsoft introduced OS/2 when IBM introduced their IBM PS/2 computers. *To try to solve these problems, IBM and Microsoft introduced OS/2 when IBM introduced their IBM PS/2 computers.*

in and of itself (themselves) *as such; in itself (in themselves).* The mere claim of protection asserted by a witness of his constitutional rights does not in and of itself constitute the admission of a crime. *The mere claim of protection asserted by a witness of his constitutional rights does not in itself constitute the admission of a crime.* ■ In fact, no panelist argued that abortion in and of itself is anything to praise. *In fact, no panelist argued that abortion as such is anything to praise.*

in an effort to *in trying to; to try to.* The trust may invest up to 10 percent of the value of its total assets in municipal obligations denominated and payable in foreign currency in an effort to increase the income of the trust. *The trust may invest up to 10 percent of the value of its total assets in municipal obligations denominated and payable in foreign currency to try to increase the income of the trust.* ■ In an effort to contain the spiraling cost of automobile insurance, a number of legislative changes have been proposed. *In trying to contain the spiraling cost of automobile insurance, a number of legislative changes have been proposed.* ■ They often drink before sleeping at night in an effort to prevent nightmares. *They often drink before sleeping at night to try to prevent nightmares.*

in a nutshell *briefly; concisely; succinctly; tersely.* That, in a nutshell, explains the financial community's attitude toward the crash. *That briefly explains the financial community's attitude toward the crash.*

in any case (event) *all (just) the same; anyhow; even so; still; still and all; yet.*

in any fashion (manner; way) *at all; in the least;* delete. And he personally is not obligated in any way to stand behind the $675 million bond offering, or any other debt of the project. *And he personally is not at all obligated to stand behind the $675 million bond offering, or any other debt of the project.*

in any way, shape, or form *at all; in any way; in the least; in the slightest;* delete. We're not interested in emulating men in any way, shape, or form. *We're not interested in emulating men at all.* ■ I don't feel put upon in any way, shape, or form by my kids' having come back home. *I don't feel in the least put upon by my kids' having come back home.*

in a position to *able to; ready to.* By the end of the year, we will be in a position to hire another person. *By the end of the year, we will be ready to hire another person.* ■ But, we hasten to add, we are not in a position to pay for any of it. *But, we hasten to add, we are not able to pay for any of it.*

in appearance delete.

in a row *straight.* Whether the bill dies on Beacon Hill for the third year in a row or becomes law in some form, the advocates of acupuncture are pressing their case with a gentle insistence. *Whether the bill dies on Beacon Hill for the third straight year or becomes law in some form, the advocates of acupuncture are pressing their case with a gentle insistence.*

in arrears *late; overdue.*

in a (the) ... sense *-(al)ly;* delete. In a broad sense, office automation is the incorporation of technology to help people manage information. *Broadly, office automation is the incorporation of technology to help people manage information.* ■ In this case, Equations 7-9 converge uniformly or in an asymptotic sense. *In this case, Equations 7-9 converge uniformly or asymptotically.* ■ Some variables are not quantifiable in a strict sense. *Some variables are not strictly quantifiable.* ■ Although there is a significant relationship in a statistical sense, the association is not strong. *Although there is a significant statistical relationship, the association is not strong.* ■ I don't mean this in a pejorative sense. *I don't mean this pejoratively.* ■ There was really nothing which could be called communication in any genuine sense. *There was really nothing which could be called genuine communication.*

in a similar fashion (manner; way) (to) *alike; as; like; much as; much like; much the same (as); rather like; resembling; similar (to); similarly (to).* There is no guarantee that the prices of taxable securities will move in a similar manner to the prices of tax-exempt securities. *There is no guarantee that the prices of taxable securities will move like the prices of tax-exempt securities.* ■ These companies are interested in identifying target markets that have similar needs and wants and that will respond in a similar fashion to particular marketing programs. *These* *companies are interested in identifying target markets that have similar needs and wants and that will respond similarly to particular marketing programs.* ■ My guess is 99 percent of the customers will behave in a similar manner. *My guess is 99 percent of the customers will behave similarly.*

inasmuch (insomuch) as *as far as; as much as; so far as; so much as.*

inasmuch (insomuch) as *because; considering; for; in that; since.* Inasmuch as part of each premium is invested in the economy, the life insurance industry is a major source of capital for the country. *Since part of each premium is invested in the economy, the life insurance industry is a major source of capital for the country.* ■ All seemed to share the conviction that the American educational system is far superior inasmuch as it focuses on the individual student. *All seemed to share the conviction that the American educational system is far superior because it focuses on the individual student.*

in association with *along with; and; as well as; combined with; coupled with; joined with; paired with; together with; with.*

in a (the) ... state (of) ... *in;* delete. I'm in a state of uncertainty about how to travel. *I'm uncertain about how to travel.* ■ People aren't always going to be in a state of total involvement. *People aren't always going to be totally involved.* ■ But while men's wear has been doing pretty well, women's wear storeowners are in a state of shock. *But while men's wear has been doing pretty well, women's wear storeowners are in shock.* ■ Forecasting in situations that are stable requires less attention than those that are in a state of flux. *Forecasting in situations that are stable requires less attention than those that are in flux.* ■ All of this has happened at a time when IBM is in a state of disarray. *All of this has happened at a time when IBM is in disarray.*

in a timely fashion (manner; way) *by next week (tomorrow); fast; in (within) a day (year); in time; promptly; quickly; rapidly; right away; shortly; soon; speedily; swiftly; timely.* Please give me your response in a timely manner. *Please give me your response by tomorrow.* ■ Sarrouf said he was particularly concerned about whether the courts would be able to assemble the tribunals in a timely manner under the new standards. *Sarrouf said he was particularly concerned about whether the courts would be able to assemble the tribunals quickly under the new standards.* ■ It's unlikely that we can come to an agreement on this in a timely fashion. *It's unlikely that we can come to an agreement on this in time.* ■ We got it done in a reasonably timely fashion. *We got it done reasonably fast.* ■ It allows us to bring other services to the market in a timely manner and in a way that reflects competitive circumstances. *It allows us to bring other services to the market by next year and in a way that reflects competitive circumstances.* ■ The DOJ's failure to act upon our request in a timely manner is regrettable. *The DOJ's failure to act upon our request promptly is regrettable.*

in attendance *present.* Also in attendance were key attorneys and representatives on both sides of the lawsuit. *Also present were key attorneys and representatives on both sides of the lawsuit.*

in a way *rather; somehow; someway(s); somewhat.* In a way, I find it intimidating. *I somehow find it intimidating.*

in back of *after; behind.*

in ... behalf (of) *by; for.*

(something; somewhere) in between *between; in; within.* The bonds are selling at $2 bid, $4 offered for a $100 face value bond, which means that the selling price would probably fall somewhere in between that range. *The bonds are selling at $2 bid, $4 offered for a $100 face value bond, which means that the selling price would probably fall in that range.*

in (a; the) bigger (greater; higher; larger) amount (degree; number; quantity) *more; more often; more so.* Apple must wait until high-quality flat-panel screens are available in greater numbers before it can release a lap-top Macintosh. *Apple must wait until more high-quality flat-panel screens are available before it can release a lap-top Macintosh.* ■ Women who never graduated from college took up the habit in greater numbers than they dropped it. *Women who never graduated from college took up the habit more often than they dropped it.* ■ Openness is already here, in a much greater degree than any of the myopic critics can bear to admit. *Openness is already here, much more than any of the myopic critics can bear to admit.*

in big (great; high; huge; large; overwhelming; sizable; vast) numbers *a good (great) many; almost all; dozens (of); hundreds (of); many; millions (of); most; nearly all; scores (of); six hundred (twelve hundred); thousands (of).* Riot police in large numbers were called in to stop the protestors. *Scores of riot police were called in to stop the protestors.* ■ The candidate is pursuing a risky strategy that could lead to a Democratic defeat if blacks are not motivated to vote in large numbers. *The candidate is pursuing a risky strategy that could lead to a Democratic defeat if many blacks are not motivated to vote.* ■ Americans, in vast numbers, consider this pay hike to be scandalous in size. *Millions of Americans consider this pay hike to be scandalous in size.* ■ Children were abandoned throughout Europe in great numbers by parents of every social standing. *Hundreds of children were abandoned throughout Europe by parents of every social standing.*

in both cases (circumstances; instances; situations) *both; for (in) both;* delete. In both cases, about 10 percent of the sales force accounted for about 90 percent of the revenues. *For both, about 10 percent of the sales force accounted for about 90 percent of the revenues.* ■ In both cases, the companies were unable to change the habits and beliefs of Brazilian cooks and mothers concerning the preparation and nutritional benefits of their products. *Both companies were unable to change the habits and beliefs of Brazilian cooks and mothers concerning the preparation and nutritional benefits of their products.*

in brief (concise; succinct) summary *briefly (concisely; succinctly); in brief; in fine; in short; in sum.* In brief summary, those are some of the reasons why original intention cannot be a neat solution to the problem of expounding our Constitution—and living under it. *In sum, those are some of the reasons why original intention cannot be a neat solution to the problem of expounding our Constitution—and living under it.*

incarcerate *jail.*

in case *if; lest; should.* In case you've just joined us, we're talking about men's perception of the Women's Movement. *If you've just joined us, we're talking about men's perception of the Women's Movement.* ▪ This establishes the ownership of the ideas and dates their development in case this becomes an issue in obtaining a patent. *This establishes the ownership of the ideas and dates their development should this become an issue in obtaining a patent.*

in (a; the) ... case (circumstance; instance; situation) *-(al)ly.* In a typical situation, the MLI command will have stored important information in an MLI data area that is used by all MLI commands. *Typically, the MLI command will have stored important information in an MLI data area that is used by all MLI commands.*

in (the) ... case (of) *about; as for; as to; concerning; for; in; of; on; over; regarding; respecting; to; toward; with;* delete. It is especially true that judgment is required in the case of new products where there is little history to draw on. *It is especially true that judgment is required for new products where there is little history to draw on.* ▪ In case of a disaster, it would help verify insurance claims. *In a disaster, it would help verify insurance claims.* ▪ In the case of the airport, that role is performed by the air traffic controller and each airline's operations center. *As to the airport, that role is performed by the air traffic controller and each airline's operations center.* ▪ In the case of services, there is the additional problem that most thrifts are new to these businesses and must spend significant sums for systems. *Concerning services, there is the additional problem that most thrifts are new to these businesses and must spend significant sums for systems.* ▪ In the case of Campbell Soups, the decision to withdraw came after three years and an advertising campaign costing $2 million. *Campbell Soups' decision to withdraw came after three years and an advertising campaign costing $2 million.*

in cases (circumstances; instances; situations) in which *if; when; where.* In cases in which improperly tested blood products had been released, Dr. Sandler said the donors were contacted for retesting to assure that no tainted blood had been transmitted. *Where improperly tested blood products had been released, Dr. Sandler said the donors were contacted for retesting to assure that no tainted blood had been transmitted.*

in cases when (where) *if; when; where.* In cases where the equity in the property is "thin," a default and subsequent foreclosure by the first mortgage lender could easily consume all of the equity for the payment of the expenses of the foreclosure proceedings. *When the equity in the property is "thin," a default and subsequent foreclosure by the first mortgage lender could easily consume all of the equity for the payment of the expenses of the foreclosure proceedings.* ■ In cases where one topic requires knowledge of another, the required topic is cross-referenced. *Where one topic requires knowledge of another, the required topic is cross-referenced.* ■ In cases where another firm is already using the brand name independently, the issue is more complex. *If another firm is already using the brand name independently, the issue is more complex.*

in certain (some) cases *at times; now and then; occasionally; on occasion; some; sometimes;* delete. In some cases, banks and thrifts have formed new entities to act as conduits in marketing mutual funds as well as other investment products provided by third parties. *Some banks and thrifts have formed new entities to act as conduits in marketing mutual funds as well as other investment products provided by third parties.* ■ In some cases, the end user can develop the application without using an expert system builder per se. *At times, the end user can develop the application without using an expert system builder per se.* ■ In some cases, smoking does affect mental acuity. *Smoking sometimes does affect mental acuity.* ■ In some cases, your boss can be a big help in the quest for knowledge. *Now and then, your boss can be a big help in the quest for knowledge.* ■ In some cases, attorneys didn't bother to obtain clinical evaluations for their clients. *Some attorneys didn't bother to obtain clinical evaluations for their clients.*

in certain (some) circumstances *at times; every so often; now and again; now and then; occasionally; on occasion; some; sometimes;* delete. In some circumstances, the computer can augment or replace many of the engineer's other tools. *Now and then, the computer can augment or replace many of the engineer's other tools.*

in certain (some) instances *at times; every so often; now and again; now and then; occasionally; on occasion; some; sometimes;* delete. In some instances, a physician's practice may be full, so you may have to select another physician. *Sometimes a physician's practice may be full, so you may have to select another physician.* ■ In some instances, we lost the customer to the competition. *We lost some customers to the competition.* ■ Signed medical statements from physicians are also required in some instances. *At times, signed medical statements from physicians are also required.* ■ In some instances, houses are worth 10 times the original payment. *Some houses are worth 10 times the original payment.*

in certain (some) regards *rather; somehow; someway(s); somewhat.*

in certain (some) respects *rather; somehow; someway(s); somewhat.* The finding is somewhat surprising since auditory information processing seems in some respects quite different from the operations required to sense visual patterns. *The finding is somewhat surprising since auditory information processing seems somehow quite different from the operations required to sense visual patterns.* ■ In some respects, yesterday's closing arguments resembled a dispute by doctors over the treatment of a terminal patient. *Yesterday's closing arguments somewhat resembled a dispute by doctors over the treatment of a terminal patient.*

in certain (some) situations *at times; every so often; now and again; now and then; occasionally; on occasion; some; sometimes;* delete. In some situations, change threatens security. *Sometimes change threatens security.* ■ In certain situations, your selector code may be permitted to pass the name of a file to the system program it selects so that the system program can work with it when it first starts up. *At times, your selector code may be permitted to pass the name of a file to the system program it selects so that the system program can work with it when it first starts up.* ■ In some situations, it may be possible to replace a toxic item with a harmless one. *On occasion, it may be possible to replace a toxic item with a harmless one.*

in character delete. As the market becomes more institutional in character, it will be easier for foreign companies to enter the U.S. market. *As the market becomes more institutional, it will be easier for foreign companies to enter the U.S. market.* ■ Islam is also fatalistic in character. *Islam is also fatalistic.* ■ These companies seek to satisfy some need or want that is uniquely national in character. *These companies seek to satisfy some uniquely national need or want.*

in ... circumstances (conditions) *-(al)ly;* delete. The attack was a carefully planned military operation that ended in tragic circumstances. *The attack was a carefully planned military operation that ended tragically.*

in circumstances when (where) *if; when; where.* Independent counsel might well be required prior to accepting a defendant's waiver of important constitutional rights in circumstances where there is reason to believe that independent legal advice is reasonably necessary in order to permit the defendant knowingly and intelligently to decide whether to waive or to exercise his rights. *Independent counsel might well be required prior to accepting a defendant's waiver of important constitutional rights where there is reason to believe that independent legal advice is reasonably necessary in order to permit the defendant knowingly and intelligently to decide whether to waive or to exercise his rights.*

in close proximity (to) *close by; close to; in proximity; near; nearby.* A LAN is used to share peripherals and data among computers in close proximity. *A LAN is used to share peripherals and data among computers in proximity.* ■ When Tower Records opened its $7 million megastore last December, the initial effect was devastating for some record retailers, particularly those in close proximity. *When Tower Records opened its $7 million megastore last December, the initial effect was devastating for some record retailers, particularly those nearby.* ■ Some who have worked in close proximity to the Oval Office in recent years support his major propositions. *Some who have worked close to the Oval Office in recent years support his major propositions.* ■ Our strong view is that discharging firearms on and in close proximity to the island is a threat to our students and to the more than 20 staff members who inhabit the island. *Our strong view is that discharging firearms on and near the island is a threat to our students and to the more than 20 staff members who inhabit the island.*

including everything *in all; overall.*

(red) in color *(red).*

in combination with *along with; and; as well as; combined with; coupled with; joined with; paired with; together with; with.* By using the 30°–60° triangle in combination with the 45° triangle, angles can be drawn at 15° intervals. *By using the 30°–60° triangle and the 45° triangle, angles can be drawn at 15° intervals.* ■ This risk is now avoided by using estrogen in combination with progesterone. *This risk is now avoided by using estrogen along with progesterone.* ■ On the left side is a double bank of five keys marked F1 through F10 which, when pressed alone or in combination with another key, perform certain functions. *On the left side is a double bank of five keys marked F1 through F10 which, when pressed alone or together with another key, perform certain functions.* ■ At issue is what the federal government needs to do in combination with the states to make sure people aren't quitting their jobs and spending into poverty simply to get access to expensive drugs. *At issue is what the federal government needs to do with the states to make sure people aren't quitting their jobs and spending into poverty simply to get access to expensive drugs.*

in (over) (the) coming days (decades; months; weeks; years) *at length; before long; eventually; in time; later; one day; over time; presently; quickly; shortly; someday; sometime; soon; ultimately; with time; yet;* delete. Other schemes could emerge in coming months. *Other schemes could emerge before long.* ■ Some analysts predicted that without positive news to move the market in coming days, prices could begin weakening. *Some analysts predicted that without positive news to move the market, prices could soon begin weakening.* ■ For this reason, many economists predicted the Federal Reserve will be forced in coming weeks to begin pushing interest rates higher in the United States. *For this reason, many economists predicted the Federal Reserve will shortly be forced to begin pushing interest rates higher in the United States.* ■ Each form of wildlife feels the effects of fire in its own way, and researchers will be monitoring how the animals react in the coming months and years. *Each form of wildlife feels the effects of fire in its own way, and researchers will be monitoring how the animals react over time.* ■ These approaches still need refining, but they could reduce the expense and increase the effectiveness of cleanup work in coming decades. *These approaches still need refining, but they could ultimately reduce the expense and increase the effectiveness of cleanup work.*

in common with *like.* You are quite right in pointing out that I, in common with other cultural historians, have singled out but one out of several possible Adams lines. *You are quite right in pointing out that I, like other cultural historians, have singled out but one out of several possible Adams lines.* ■ In common with Siemens, Ericsson is a leading contender for third-supplier status with the regional Bell operating companies. *Like Siemens, Ericsson is a leading contender for third-supplier status with the regional Bell operating companies.*

in company with *along with; and; as well as; together with; with.* If anything, the Reagan administration, in company with the Kremlin and the other big powers, has waited too long to denounce the use of chemical weapons. *If anything, the Reagan administration, as well as the Kremlin and the other big powers, has waited too long to denounce the use of chemical weapons.*

in comparison to (with) *against; alongside; beside; compared to (with); -(i)er than; less; less than; more; more than; next to; over; than; to; versus; vis-à-vis.* Klein's firm claims it can tell a manufacturer how many people will like the car, how great the car is in comparison to another car, and how many cars will likely sell. *Klein's firm claims it can tell a manufacturer how many people will like the car, how great the car is compared to another car, and how many cars will likely sell.* ■ The ratio of demand deposits to total deposits in Texas as a whole was high in comparison with those of money center banks and other major regional banks. *The ratio of demand deposits to total deposits in Texas as a whole was higher than those of money center banks and other major regional banks.* ■ The reunion was large in comparison to other reunions. *The reunion was larger than other reunions.* ■ U.S. students are inferior in their spelling ability in comparison to the other nations' students. *U.S. students are inferior in their spelling ability to the other nations' students.*

in comparison (in contrast) to (with) ... relatively *compared (contrasted) to (with).* In comparison to earlier years, inflation has been relatively moderate over the last half decade. *Compared to earlier years, inflation has been moderate over the last half decade.*

incompetency *incompetence.* Hospitalization often makes clients vulnerable to thoughts of inadequacy and incompetency. *Hospitalization often makes clients vulnerable to thoughts of inadequacy and incompetence.*

in compliance with *according to; by; following; in keeping with; in line with; in step with; to; under.* In compliance with the new order, all participants now receive a 2-percent discount from market prices on shares made available direct-ly from the company. *Under the new order, participants now receive a 2-percent discount from market prices on shares made available directly from the company.*

in conclusion *finally; in closing; lastly.*

in conformance to (with) *according to; by; following; in keeping with; in line with; in step with; to; under.* Certain terms of this Agreement shall be completed in conformance with the terms of the successful proposal. *Certain terms of this Agreement shall be completed according to the terms of the successful proposal.*

in conformity to (with) *according to; by; following; in keeping with; in line with; in step with; to; under.* The consolidated financial statements on the following pages have been prepared in conformity with generally accepted accounting principles. *The consolidated financial statements on the following pages have been prepared according to generally accepted accounting principles.* ■ The law says a product is presumed to be free of defects when it is produced in conformity to government standards. *The law says a product is presumed to be free of defects when it is produced to government standards.*

in conjunction *combined; together.* The primary evidence with which the War-ren Report failed to deal consists of the ballistics report, the Zapruder film, and the autopsy report, taken in conjunction. *The primary evidence with which the Warren Report failed to deal consists of the ballistics report, the Zapruder film, and the autopsy report, taken together.*

in conjunction with *along with; and; as well as; combined with; coupled with; joined with; paired with; together with; with.* The results of the interviews in conjunction with other supporting data are contained in the report. *The results of the interviews and other supporting data are contained in the report.* ■ In con-junction with the operating system, the CPU coordinates all the computer's activ-ities. *Together with the operating system, the CPU coordinates all the computer's activities.* ■ Surgery is generally used in conjunction with other therapies to cure and control cancer. *Surgery is generally used along with other therapies to cure and control cancer.* ■ The ACCJ has long worked in conjunction with the U.S. government through the American embassy to open the Japanese market to U.S. products and services. *The ACCJ has long worked with the U.S. government through the American embassy to open the Japanese market to U.S. products and services.* ■ These new findings, in conjunction with records from other oceans, indicate that Earth's climate cooled immediately before the boundary. *These new findings, coupled with records from other oceans, indicate that Earth's climate cooled immediately before the boundary.*

in connection with *along with; and; as well as; combined with; coupled with; joined with; paired with; together with; with.*

in connection with *about; as for; as to; concerning; for; in; of; on; over; regarding; respecting; to; toward; with;* delete. Police in Holyoke are questioning a suspect in connection with the brutal rape of a 7-year-old boy. *Police in Holyoke are questioning a suspect about the brutal rape of a 7-year-old boy.* ■ The bank with sufficient presence and skills may be asked to work with the client's own local advisors in connection with purely domestic transactions. *The bank with sufficient presence and skills may be asked to work with the client's own local advisors on purely domestic transactions.* ■ Sein Win, formerly publisher of the English-language daily *The Guardian,* was jailed for three years in Burma in the 1960s in connection with his journalistic activities. *Sein Win, formerly publisher of the English-language daily* The Guardian, *was jailed for three years in Burma in the 1960s for his journalistic activities.* ■ A suspect was captured and charged yesterday in connection with the abduction, robbery, and shooting of two Charlotte County prosecutors. *A suspect was captured and charged yesterday with the abduction, robbery, and shooting of two Charlotte County prosecutors.* ■ In connection with the Lord Geller case, I said: "Given the circumstances, there was nothing else we could do but sue." *Regarding the Lord Geller case, I said: "Given the circumstances, there was nothing else we could do but sue."*

in consequence *consequently; hence; so; then; therefore; thus.*

in consequence of *after; because of; by; due to; following; for; from; in; out of; owing to; through; with.* The defendants cannot claim to have suffered damage in consequence of the plaintiffs' early entry onto premises they had already vacated pursuant to a notice to quit for nonpayment of rent. *The defendants cannot claim to have suffered damage from the plaintiffs' early entry onto premises they had already vacated pursuant to a notice to quit for nonpayment of rent.*

in consequence of the fact that *because; considering; for; in that; since.*

in consideration of (payment of; sum of) *because of; due to; for; in return for; in view of; on account of; owing to; through.* In consideration of the foregoing and of the mutual promises contained herein, the parties mutually agree as follows. *In view of the foregoing and the mutual promises contained herein, the parties mutually agree as follows.* ■ In consideration of payment of the License fee, Microsoft grants to you a nonexclusive right to use and display this copy of a Microsoft software program on a single computer at a single location. *In return for the License fee, Microsoft grants to you a nonexclusive right to use and display this copy of a Microsoft software program on a single computer at a single location.*

in consideration of the fact that *because; considering; for; in that; since.* In consideration of the fact that Medicare payments are already deducted from my Social Security checks, am I entitled to a credit for this further deduction? *Since Medicare payments are already deducted from my Social Security checks, am I entitled to a credit for this further deduction?*

in consonance to (with) *according to; by; following; in keeping with; in line with; in step with; to; under.*

in contempt of *despite.*

in contrast to (with) *against; alongside; beside; compared to (with); -(i)er than; less; less than; more; more than; next to; over; than; to; unlike; versus; vis-à-vis.* In contrast to last month, September sales of government debt are expected to be light. *Compared to last month, September sales of government debt are expected to be light.* ■ Both capital assets have changed in real value, and the landowner is better off in contrast to the stockholder. *Both capital assets have changed in real value, and the landowner is better off than the stockholder.*

in conversation with *conversing with; speaking to (with); talking to (with).* The doctor is in conversation with the woman who tried to kill her son. *The doctor is speaking to the woman who tried to kill her son.* ■ I don't know what happened; I was in conversation with my friend. *I don't know what happened; I was talking with my friend.*

in copious profusion *copiously; in profusion.* As naturally and spontaneously as the notes that issue from the throat of a thrush, the melodies poured forth from Schubert's pen in copious profusion. *As naturally and spontaneously as the notes that issue from the throat of a thrush, the melodies poured forth from Schubert's pen in profusion.*

incorporate in(to) *add; contain; have; include.*

in correspondence to (with) *according to; by; following; in keeping with; in line with; in step with; to; under.*

(a) ... increase over *more than.* That's a 33-percent increase over last year. *That's 33 percent more than last year.* ■ In 1986, some 4,000 women gave birth for the first time, a 26 percent increase over the 1985 figure. *In 1986, some 4,000 women gave birth for the first time, 26 percent more than the 1985 figure.*

increasing in *increasingly.* The seaweed treatments are increasing in popularity with both men and women. *The seaweed treatments are increasingly popular with both men and women.*

increasingly more *increasingly; more and more.* Information processing is becoming increasingly more automated through the use of machines. *Information processing is becoming increasingly automated through the use of machines.* ■ As you gain experience with a program, the ease with which the commands can be executed becomes increasingly more important. *As you gain experience with a program, the ease with which the commands can be executed becomes more and more important.*

incremental increase *minute (nominal; slight; small) increase; increase.* The incremental increase in the possibility of pregnancy is not significant. *The increase in the possibility of pregnancy is not significant.*

in (over) (the) days (decades; months; weeks; years) ahead *at length; before long; eventually; in time; later; one day; over time; presently; quickly; shortly; someday; sometime; soon; ultimately; with time; yet;* delete. The men and women who build America's bridges, design spacecraft, and keep nuclear power plants running will be in short supply in the years ahead unless more college students study engineering. *The men and women who build America's bridges, design spacecraft, and keep nuclear power plants running will soon be in short supply unless more college students study engineering.* ■ While these changes will be automatic, we recognize that the decision to continue banking with us in the months and years ahead is entirely yours. *While these changes will be automatic, we recognize that the decision to continue banking with us is entirely yours.* ■ In the years ahead, it simply will not be possible to keep up with demands if our company remains what it once was. *Over time, it simply will not be possible to keep up with demands if our company remains what it once was.* ■ We expect prospects will improve over the years ahead. *We expect prospects will improve in time.*

in (the) days (decades; months; weeks; years) gone by *before; earlier; formerly; once;* delete. In years gone by, much has been written about perceived gains in the powers of the presidency compared with the powers of the Congress and vice versa. *Much has been written about perceived gains in the powers of the presidency compared with the powers of the Congress and vice versa.*

in (the) days (decades; months; weeks; years) of old *before; earlier; formerly; once;* delete. The world must have seemed a larger place in days of old. *The world must have once seemed a larger place.*

in (the) days (decades; months; weeks; years) past *before; earlier; formerly; once;* delete. Police academy training is more extensive for new officers, providing extensive computer training, whereas in years past only a few officers would have had any experience with computers. *Police academy training is more extensive for new officers, providing extensive computer training, whereas before only a few officers would have had any experience with computers.*

in (the) days (decades; months; weeks; years) since *since; since then.* In the years since, the number of women in jail has increased and the nature of the crimes they commit has changed. *Since then, the number of women in jail has increased and the nature of the crimes they commit has changed.* ■ However, in the years since 1970, the same continent has experienced precipitation levels above the mean measurements for the reference period. *However, since 1970, the same continent has experienced precipitation levels above the mean measurements for the reference period.*

in (over) ... days' (decades'; hours'; minutes'; months'; weeks'; years') time *in (over) ... days (decades; hours; minutes; months; weeks; years)*. I'm going to be visiting some Navy bases in a few months' time. *I'm going to be visiting some Navy bases in a few months.* ■ The only concern I had with First Service is that they had doubled the size of the loan portfolio in 12 months' time. *The only concern I had with First Service is that they had doubled the size of the loan portfolio in 12 months.* ■ Over a year's time, the manual will likely be reprinted two or three times, and interim releases will be issued perhaps five or six times. *Over a year, the manual will likely be reprinted two or three times, and interim releases will be issued perhaps five or six times.*

in (over) (the) days (decades; months; weeks; years) to come *at length; before long; eventually; in time; later; one day; over time; presently; quickly; shortly; someday; sometime; soon; ultimately; with time; yet;* delete. We are deadly serious about making changes that will allow us to remain a viable competitor in the years to come. *We are deadly serious about making changes that will allow us to remain a viable competitor.* ■ He estimated that the change would have little impact in the current quarter but would boost margins in months to come. *He estimated that the change would have little impact in the current quarter but would boost margins in time.*

indebtedness *debt(s)*. Sales-tax revenues are down because people are spending less, paying off their indebtedness, and saving more. *Sales-tax revenues are down because people are spending less, paying off their debts, and saving more.*

in defense of *for; with*. May I please put in a word in defense of poor Livia Budai, who has been lambasted out of all proportion in your articles? *May I please put in a word for poor Livia Budai, who has been lambasted out of all proportion in your articles?*

in defiance of *against; despite*. Responsibility for the tragedy rests exclusively on the war criminals in the Iranian government who have elected, in defiance of the rules of warfare established for many centuries, to make regular murderous attacks on neutral merchant ships on the high seas. *Responsibility for the tragedy rests exclusively on the war criminals in the Iranian government who have elected, despite the rules of warfare established for many centuries, to make regular murderous attacks on neutral merchant ships on the high seas.*

in depth *deep*.

in despite of *after all; apart; aside; despite; even with; for all; with all*. In despite of his good looks, he has never married. *For all his good looks, he has never married.*

indicate *feel; disclose; hint; imply; mention; reveal; say; show; suggest; tell*. He indicated that he would be fine. *He said that he would be fine.* ■ I indicated to her that I wasn't happy. *I told her I wasn't happy.* ■ Have they indicated what kinds of cancer are prevalent in the Soviet Union? *Have they mentioned what kinds of cancer are prevalent in the Soviet Union?*

indication *clue; cue; hint; inkling; sign.* There are indications that Iran may have its own chemical weapons. *There are clues that Iran may have its own chemical weapons.* ■ Is this an indication of things to come? *Is this a hint of things to come?* ■ The demonstrations were another indication of ferment in the Baltic republics under Mikhail S. Gorbachev's policies of greater openness and more local control. *The demonstrations were another sign of ferment in the Baltic republics under Mikhail S. Gorbachev's policies of greater openness and more local control.*

individual *(adj)* delete. I think there are individual exceptions. *I think there are exceptions.* ■ In my individual case, time seemed to stand still. *In my case, time seemed to stand still.*

individual(s) *(n) anybody; anyone; everybody; everyone; man; men; people; person; somebody; someone; those; woman; women; you;* delete. The dominant behavioral characteristic of phobic individuals is avoidance. *The dominant behavioral characteristic of phobic persons is avoidance.* ■ Unless you're a very callous individual, their pain begins to affect you. *Unless you're very callous, their pain begins to affect you.* ■ Individuals who are likely to make the grade in the foreseeable future are often included. *Those who are likely to make the grade in the foreseeable future are often included.* ■ The type of individual who becomes addicted to alcohol is often the same type of individual who becomes addicted to cigarettes or drugs. *The type of person who becomes addicted to alcohol is often the same type who becomes addicted to cigarettes or drugs.* ■ Advertising philosophies are highly subjective; virtually every individual has his or her own approach. *Advertising philosophies are highly subjective; virtually everyone has his or her own approach.* ■ There is no evidence that experts are any better equipped to make those judgments than are lay individuals. *There is no evidence that experts are any better equipped to make those judgments than are lay people.*

individuals (men; people; persons; women) in (a; the) business *businessmen (businesspeople; businesspersons; businesswomen).* Most people in a business, however, do not actually use the database file itself. *Most businesspeople, however, do not actually use the database file itself.* ■ When people in a business disagree or see things from opposing perspectives, a meeting provides a safe and sanctioned setting for resolution. *When businesspeople disagree or see things from opposing perspectives, a meeting provides a safe and sanctioned setting for resolution.*

individuals (men; people; persons; women) who are delete. People who are obsessive-compulsive have difficulty making decisions. *Obsessive-compulsives have difficulty making decisions.* ■ We conducted a brainstorming session with

15 individuals who are well-known specialists in payment systems. *We conducted a brainstorming session with 15 well-known specialists in payment systems.*

inductive reasoning *induction.*

in due course (time) *at length; in time; later; one day; over time; someday; sometime; with time; yet.* He was the CEO of a large corporation and in due course the secretary of state. *He was the CEO of a large corporation and at length the secretary of state.* ▪ In due course, the family bought the house and moved in. *In time, the family bought the house and moved in.* ▪ We will consider your statement in due time. *We will yet consider your statement.*

in duration *last; long;* delete. Girls are at far greater risk for sexual abuse than boys, and their sexual abuse apparently is more common and longer in duration than the physical abuse boys are more likely to experience. *Girls are at far greater risk for sexual abuse than boys, and their sexual abuse apparently is more common and lasts longer than the physical abuse boys are more likely to experience.*

in each (every) case (circumstance; instance; situation) *all; always; consistently; constantly; each; each time; for (in) each; for (in) every; every one; every time; invariably; unfailingly;* delete. In each case, the affected company had to find solutions to a sudden change in its local environment. *Each affected company had to find solutions to a sudden change in its local environment.* ▪ Although some of the previous examples have been somewhat complex, in each case we could predict what the code would produce. *Although some of the previous examples have been somewhat complex, in each we could predict what the code would produce.* ▪ In each case, multiply the result by 10 to give you a per share dollar cost of each regional share. *Multiply each result by 10 to give you a per share dollar cost of each regional share.* ▪ In every instance, the acquirer selected is the one with the best bid. *The acquirer selected is always the one with the best bid.*

in earlier (former; prior) times *before; earlier; formerly; once.* There was plenty of weekend ticketing in prior times. *There once was plenty of weekend ticketing.*

in either (neither) case (circumstance; instance; situation) *either (neither) way;* delete. In either case, a veto would have provided Democratic opponents with powerful rhetorical ammunition in light of the 80 percent approval for the legislation in public opinion polls. *Either way, a veto would have provided Democratic opponents with powerful rhetorical ammunition in light of the 80 percent approval for the legislation in public opinion polls.* ▪ In either situation, GS/OS sets the A, D, and SP registers to the following values before passing control to the program. *Either way, GS/OS sets the A, D, and SP registers to the following values before passing control to the program.*

in either (neither) event *either (neither) way;* delete. In either event, it is not likely that AT&T and Northern, aware of customer desire for greater software control, will allow Ericsson and others to win business on this point alone. *Either way, it is not likely that AT&T and Northern, aware of customer desire for greater software control, will allow Ericsson and others to win business on this point alone.* ■ In either event, you have a few options. *Either way, you have a few options.*

in error *wrong.* He will not listen, nor will he back down even when he knows he is in error. *He will not listen, nor will he back down even when he knows he is wrong.* ■ If my information is in error, I stand corrected. *If my information is wrong, I stand corrected.*

in (the) event (of; that) *if (there were); if ... should; should (there); were (there; ... to); when;* delete. In the event that any liquid or solid object falls into the cabinet, unplug the unit and have it checked by qualified personnel. *Should any liquid or solid object fall into the cabinet, unplug the unit and have it checked by qualified personnel.* ■ Palau has long been regarded as a possible fallback site in event the United States loses its military bases in the Philippines. *Palau has long been regarded as a possible fallback site were the United States to lose its military bases in the Philippines.* ■ In the event of my death, I wish to be cremated and have my ashes scattered into the Tennessee River. *When I die, I wish to be cremated and have my ashes scattered into the Tennessee River.* ■ Such information would be vital in the event they chose to have children. *Such information would be vital if they choose to have children.* ■ WGBH officials insisted that they were prepared to remain on the air in the event of a union walkout. *WGBH officials insisted that they were prepared to remain on the air were there a union walkout.*

in evidence *apparent; conspicuous; evident; obvious; plain.* Little of that has been in evidence among the thrifts. *Little of that has been evident among the thrifts.*

in excess of *above; better than; beyond; greater than; larger than; more than; over; stronger than.* Annually, retailers lose in excess of $1.5 billion, and only about 30 percent of those losses are to shoplifters and other outsiders. *Annually, retailers lose more than $1.5 billion, and only about 30 percent of those losses are to shoplifters and other outsiders.* ■ The basic filing fee is $65; an additional $2 is required for each claim in excess of ten on any one application. *The basic filing fee is $65; an additional $2 is required for each claim over ten on any one application.* ■ Sales in excess of 10,000 units result in profit. *Sales above 10,000 units result in profit.* ■ The term *piping* is considered to apply to rigid pipes that are larger than tubes, usually in excess of 2 inches in diameter. *The term* piping *is considered to apply to rigid pipes that are larger than tubes, usually larger than 2 inches in diameter.* ■ Winds were in excess of 150 mph. *Winds were stronger than 150 mph.* ■ The closings will have no impact on the nation's military strength, since the Pentagon has already acquired a redundant arsenal far in excess of rational requirements for many years to come. *The closings will have no impact on the nation's military strength, since the Pentagon has already acquired a redundant arsenal far beyond rational requirements for many years to come.*

in exchange (for) *for.* The deal would involve his gaining credibility with the administration in exchange for his helping Nicaraguan Contras in their fight against the Sandinistas. *The deal would involve his gaining credibility with the administration for his helping Nicaraguan Contras in their fight against the Sandinistas.* ■ In exchange for their 10-percent minority position in the publicly traded shares of Southland, the Thompsons got almost 100-percent control of their empire. *For their 10-percent minority position in the publicly traded shares of Southland, the Thompsons got almost 100-percent control of their empire.*

in (the) face of *after all; apart; aside; despite; even with; for all; with all.* He persevered in the face of strong pressure within his agency. *He persevered despite strong pressure within his agency.* ■ In the face of their education, few managers see the possibilities of applying their business knowledge at home. *Their education aside, few managers see the possibilities of applying their business knowledge at home.* ■ In face of the uncertainty, they are still struggling to keep the native way of life alive. *With all the uncertainty, they are still struggling to keep the native way of life alive.*

in fact *delete.* Women not able to have power in the external world have in fact developed a secondary power. *Women not able to have power in the external world have developed a secondary power.* ■ If it is determined that drug use did in fact take place, the agency has several options, ranging from rehabilitation to firing. *If it is determined that drug use did take place, the agency has several options, ranging from rehabilitation to firing.* ■ Were it in fact true that the governor had sought assistance at such times from a mental health professional, it would speak highly of his courage and self-awareness. *Were it true that the governor had sought assistance at such times from a mental health professional, it would speak highly of his courage and self-awareness.*

in (a; the) ... fashion *-(al)ly; delete.* It is true that the records are stored in a sequential fashion. *It is true that the records are stored sequentially.* ■ They want you to do it in a safe and fast fashion. *They want you to do it safely and fast.* ■ I don't think I was treated in a loyal fashion by the president. *I don't think I was treated loyally by the president.* ■ Your story quotes antismokers 11 times and tobacco industry representatives only twice—and then in a disdainful fashion. *Your story quotes antismokers 11 times and tobacco industry representatives only twice—and then disdainfully.*

in favor (of) *for; with.* Five circuit courts of appeal have ruled in favor of testing without individualized suspicion. *Five circuit courts of appeal have ruled for testing without individualized suspicion.* ■ IBM has shed its old way of doing business in favor of a more competitive approach. *IBM has shed its old way of* *doing business for a more competitive approach.* ■ Many women forfeit one in favor of the other, yet end up feeling regret for missing out on the path not taken. *Many women forfeit one for the other, yet end up feeling regret for missing out on the path not taken.*

(an; the) infinite number (of) *countless; endless; infinite; millions (of); myriad; numberless; untold.* The voice is capable of an infinite number of sounds and pitches. *The voice is capable of countless sounds and pitches.* ■ You may obtain an infinite number of views of each part by selecting VPOINTS. *You may obtain endless views of each part by selecting VPOINTS.* ■ We are surrounded by an infinite number of mechanical, electrical, magnetic, thermal, nuclear, and other kinds of gadgets that our technological culture puts at our disposal to make our lives easier, faster, cheaper, safer, and at times even pleasanter. *We are surrounded by numberless mechanical, electrical, magnetic, thermal, nuclear, and other kinds of gadgets that our technological culture puts at our disposal to make our lives easier, faster, cheaper, safer, and at times even pleasanter.*

inflammable *flammable.*

in force and effect *active; at work; effective; in action; in effect; in force; in play; working.* Tenant agrees to pay Landlord at the rate of $1200 per month on the first day of each and every month in advance so long as this lease is in force and effect. *Tenant agrees to pay Landlord at the rate of $1200 per month on the first day of each and every month in advance so long as this lease is in effect.*

inform *tell; write.* She informed me that she wants a divorce. *She told me that she wants a divorce.* ■ The authors of the paper were not invited to testify, nor were they informed that the investigation was underway. *The authors of the paper were not invited to testify, nor were they told that the investigation was underway.*

in (a; the) ... form *in; -(al)ly; delete.* An analyst must be able to state the assumption in explicit form. *An analyst must be able to explicitly state the assumption.* ■ The movie tells the same story in a spare but elegant form. *The movie sparely but elegantly tells the same story.* ■ The remaining specifications are given in tabular form. *The remaining specifications are given in a table.* ■ This subroutine will print out the GS/OS version number in ASCII form. *This subroutine will print out the GS/OS version number in ASCII.* ■ Specifications of a patent must be attached to the application in written form describing the invention in detail so that a person skilled in the field can produce the item. *Written specifications of a patent must be attached to the application describing the invention in detail so that a person skilled in the field can produce the item.*

in ... from now *from now; in.* In about seven years from now, OPEC will once again be able to capture 50 percent of the world market. *In about seven years, OPEC will once again be able to capture 50 percent of the world market.*

in front of *before.* Each person was tested four times during a two-hour period while sitting or standing in front of a computer monitor. *Each person was tested four times during a two-hour period while sitting or standing before a computer monitor.* ■ We have tough challenges in front of us. *We have tough challenges before us.* ■ It is folly to stand up in front of a group and hope to pull off your show without a hitch if this is your first run-through. *It is folly to stand up before a group and hope to pull off your show without a hitch if this is your first run-through.*

in fulfillment of *to complete; to finish; to fulfill; to satisfy.* In fulfillment of its open-ended agreement, Saatchi & Saatchi will also advise the Soviets on how much they should charge for TV spots that could reach some 180 million Soviet citizens and another 30 million viewers in Eastern Europe. *To fulfill its open-ended agreement, Saatchi & Saatchi will also advise the Soviets on how much they should charge for TV spots that could reach some 180 million Soviet citizens and another 30 million viewers in Eastern Europe.*

in general *delete.* Women in general have a responsibility to one another. *Women have a responsibility to one another.*

(a; the) -ing of *-ing.* The taking of drugs is bad for people. *Taking drugs is bad for people.* ■ Often the initial development of a program focuses on the obtaining of some correct solution to the given problem. *Often the initial development of a program focuses on obtaining some correct solution to the given problem.* ■ It has several verification problems that can only be appreciated by a careful reading of the treaty. *It has several verification problems that can only be appreciated by carefully reading the treaty.* ■ An understanding of these terms allows you to describe a sloping plane. *Understanding these terms allows you to describe a sloping plane.* ■ When you are working with hundreds of files, the limitations that the operating system imposes make the naming of files a difficult task. *When you are working with hundreds of files, the limitations that the operating system imposes make naming files a difficult task.*

in good time *at length; in time; later; one day; over time; someday; sometime; with time; yet.*

in great (large) measure *almost all; chiefly; commonly; generally; greatly; in general; largely; mainly; most; mostly; most often; much; nearly all; normally; overall; typically; usually.* Your today is in large measure a result of your yesterdays. *Your today is largely a result of your yesterdays.* ■ Success in winning the war on drugs depends in large measure on our ability to set the correct priorities among these areas and fund them accordingly. *Success in winning the war on drugs depends mostly on our ability to set the correct priorities among these areas and fund them accordingly.* ■ Most Americans understand that the ability of our nation to compete depends in large measure on its scientific and technological advances. *Most Americans understand that the ability of our* *nation to compete greatly depends on its scientific and technological advances.*

in great (large) part *almost all; chiefly; commonly; generally; greatly; in general; largely; mainly; most; mostly; most often; much; nearly all; normally; overall; typically; usually.* The lower cost of U.S. labor was due in large part to the drop in value of the dollar compared with most other currencies. *The lower cost of U.S. labor was largely due to the drop in value of the dollar compared with most other currencies.* ■ Learning-disabled kids in large part are not being encouraged and rewarded enough for their strengths. *Most learning-disabled kids are not being encouraged and rewarded enough for their strengths.* ■ Your choice of language predetermines in large part the reactions of your listeners. *Your choice of language commonly predetermines the reactions of your listeners.* ■ They said the increase was in large part a rebound from May, when the index had dropped by a sharp 0.8 percent. *They said the increase was chiefly a rebound from May, when the index had dropped by a sharp 0.8 percent.*

in great (large) quantities *a good (great) deal (of); a good (great) many (of); almost all; dozens (of); hundreds (of); many; millions (of); most; nearly all; scores (of); six hundred (twelve hundred); thousands (of).* The $2 bills are not being ordered by area banks even though the Federal Reserve has them in large quantities. *The $2 bills are not being ordered by area banks even though the Federal Reserve has millions of them.*

in height *high;* delete. They should be at least 1/8 inch in height, not encircled, and placed close to the parts they apply to. *They should be at least 1/8 inch high, not encircled, and placed close to the parts they apply to.* ■ The mountain gorilla is the largest and most endangered of the great apes; the adult males often reach six feet in height and weigh 375 pounds or more. *The mountain gorilla is the largest and most endangered of the great apes; the adult males often reach six feet and weigh 375 pounds or more.*

in (the) history (of the world) *ever.* Original plans called for a fleet of 132 bombers with the cost of each plane estimated at $500 million, making it the most expensive plane in history. *Original plans called for a fleet of 132 bombers with the cost of each plane estimated at $500 million, making it the most expensive plane ever.*

in honor of *after; for; to.*

in imitation of *after; follow.*

in instances when (where) *if; when; where.* In instances where the products and services being traded within the firm are unique, the cost-plus method seems appropriate. *When the products and services being traded within the firm are unique, the cost-plus method seems appropriate.*

in isolation (from) *alone; apart (from); by itself; separate (from).* It makes no sense to discuss one issue in isolation from the other. *It makes no sense to discuss one issue separate from the other.* ▪ Companies would never make high-quality products if the manufacturing department were forced to pursue quality in isolation. *Companies would never make high-quality products if the manufacturing department alone were forced to pursue quality.*

initial (initially) *at first; first.* Initially, a problem is noticed. *First, a problem is noticed.* ▪ Initially, the key was successfully marketing the fund to commercial banks. *At first, the key was successfully marketing the fund to commercial banks.* ▪ A just-released second-quarter financial report indicates that the situation may be more serious than initially thought. *A just-released second-quarter financial report indicates that the situation may be more serious than first thought.*

initially ... begin (start) *begin (start).* I believe he initially started as a stand-up comic. *I believe he started as a stand-up comic.* ▪ Initially, it started out as a polarization problem. *It started out as a polarization problem.* ▪ Savings and loan associations initially started as building associations and were designed to provide members with funds for housing construction. *Savings and loan associations started as building associations and were designed to provide members with funds for housing construction.*

in its (their) entirety *all (the); (the) complete; completely; (the) entire; entirely; every; (the) full; fully; (the) whole; wholly;* delete. Any entity that is crossed by the window is removed in its entirety. *Any entity that is crossed by the window is wholly removed.* ▪ When you read the book in its entirety, you will understand my position. *When you read the entire book, you will understand my position.* ▪ As we read the testimony of Janice in its entirety (her account of the shooting and her denials that she ever said it was an accident), the excluded evidence would have been a plain contradiction of her testimony on the main issue before the jury. *As we read the complete testimony of Janice (her account of the shooting and her denials that she ever said it was an accident), the excluded evidence would have been a plain contradiction of her testimony on the main issue before the jury.* ▪ The three candidates for majority leader have embraced the freshman's demands in their entirety. *The three candidates for majority leader have embraced all the freshman's demands.*

(be) in jeopardy *endangered; imperiled; jeopardized.* None of us can avoid the responsibility of working in all ways open to us to shore up the democracy that is so clearly in jeopardy. *None of us can avoid the responsibility of working in all ways open to us to shore up the democracy that is so clearly jeopardized.* ▪ This outlook was reinforced by the Gaither Committee's 1957 report, drafted in part by Mr. Nitze, which concluded that American nuclear deterrence and the country's survival were in jeopardy. *This outlook was reinforced by the Gaither Committee's 1957 report, drafted in part by Mr. Nitze, which concluded that American nuclear deterrence and the country's survival were imperiled.* ▪ Already several thousand jobs have been lost or are in jeopardy since the free-trade vote was taken, even though 1.5 million more Canadians voted no than voted yes. *Already several thousand jobs have been lost or are endangered since the free-trade vote was taken, even though 1.5 million more Canadians voted no than voted yes.*

in length *last; long;* delete. Vehicle owners may choose any combination of letters and numbers between two and seven characters in length for their plates. *Vehicle owners may choose any combination of letters and numbers between two and seven characters for their plates.* ▪ The snakes, which can grow to 13 feet in length, seem to be everywhere. *The snakes, which can grow to 13 feet, seem to be everywhere.* ▪ The panel discussion itself will be two hours in length. *The panel discussion itself will last two hours.* ▪ To get your company some free, positive public exposure, issue press releases (three to four paragraphs in length). *To get your company some free, positive public exposure, issue press releases (three to four paragraphs).* ▪ Each of these sonatas is approximately 45 minutes in length. *Each of these sonatas is approximately 45 minutes long.* ▪ A one-semester text envisioned to be 300 pages in length may have no market if the author's final version runs to 900 pages. *A one-semester text envisioned to be 300 pages may have no market if the author's final version runs to 900 pages.*

in (the) light of the fact that *because; considering; for; in that; since; when.* This is clumsy by comparison to the Macintosh file system's embedded information about files, especially in light of the fact that you might have MultiMate, Word, and DisplayWrite on the same disk—and they all use .DOC extensions on their files. *This is clumsy by comparison to the Macintosh file system's embedded information about files, especially because you might have MultiMate, Word, and DisplayWrite on the same disk—and they all use .DOC extensions on their files.* ▪ She called her husband to their lower road home, which is interesting in light of the fact that she killed him and not herself. *She called her husband to their lower road home, which is interesting considering she killed him and not herself.* ▪ In light of the fact that abortion is legal and that the research in question is intended to achieve significant medical goals, the Panel concludes that the use of such tissue is acceptable public policy. *Since abortion is legal and the research in question is intended to achieve significant medical goals, the Panel concludes that the use of such tissue is acceptable public policy.*

in like fashion (manner) *likewise; similarly.* In like fashion, managers need to know how they are doing from the viewpoints of those they are paid to serve. *Likewise, managers need to know how they are doing from the viewpoints of those they are paid to serve.* ▪ In like manner, the corporate budget office will consolidate and prepare a corporate office under the overall supervision of the chief financial officer. *Similarly, the corporate budget office will consolidate and prepare a corporate office under the overall supervision of the chief financial officer.*

in (a; the) ... manner *-(al)ly;* delete. In killing her abusive husband, she did not deal with his behavior in an appropriate manner. *In killing her abusive husband, she did not deal appropriately with his behavior.* ■ American businesses, as virtual extensions abroad of the United States itself, should conduct their foreign operations in an ethical and moral manner. *American businesses, as virtual extensions abroad of the United States itself, should conduct their foreign operations ethically and morally.* ■ When carried out in a professional and systematic manner, personal contact in banking relationships has enabled some banks to differentiate themselves through relationship management. *When carried out professionally and systematically, personal contact in banking relationships has enabled some banks to differentiate themselves through relationship management.* ■ I hope future stories dealing with sensitive issues such as this will be handled in a more responsible and accurate manner. *I hope future stories dealing with sensitive issues such as this will be handled more responsibly and accurately.*

in many (most) cases *almost all; almost always; commonly; frequently; many; many times; most; most often; much; nearly all; nearly always; normally; often; typically; usually.* In most cases, the pitch can be approximated or laid off with a scale or dividers. *Usually, the pitch can be approximated or laid off with a scale or dividers.* ■ In most cases, the drug has been beneficial and has solved more problems than it created. *Most often, the drug has been beneficial and has solved more problems than it created.* ■ In most cases, LBO operators are paying huge premiums to gain control of their target companies. *Most LBO operators are paying huge premiums to gain control of their target companies.* ■ In many cases, networks are either too expensive or too complicated for users. *Many networks are often either too expensive or too complicated for users.* ■ In many cases, their growth rates are larger than those for whites, whose numbers have declined. *Commonly, their growth rates are larger than those for whites, whose numbers have declined.* ■ In too many cases, U.S. businesses that should be competitive by world standards have been hurt. *Too often, U.S. businesses that should be competitive by world standards have been hurt.*

in many (most) circumstances *almost all; almost always; commonly; frequently; many; many times; most; most often; much; nearly all; nearly always; normally; often; ordinarily; typically; usually.* RISC microprocessors operate faster than CISC microprocessors in many circumstances. *RISC microprocessors often operate faster than CISC microprocessors.* ■ Death certificates are public records and information about how people died should be available in most circumstances. *Death certificates are public records and information about how people died should usually be available.*

in many (most) instances *almost all; almost always; commonly; frequently; many; many times; most; most often; much; nearly all; nearly always; normally; often; ordinarily; typically; usually.* In many instances, the family is in a state of dysfunction and disrepair. *Often, the family is in a state of dysfunction and disrepair.* ■ In most instances, change is resisted. *Change is usually resisted.* ■ In most instances, the contracts are closed out before the settlement date without the making or taking of delivery of the securities. *Typically, the contracts are closed out before the settlement date without the making or taking of delivery of the securities.* ■ With inflation held to moderate levels, shoppers are opting in many instances for store brands, which cost a little more than generics. *With inflation held to moderate levels, many shoppers are opting for store brands, which cost a little more than generics.* ■ Such a license is merely a formality and, in most instances, is as easy to acquire as a Social Security card. *Such a license is merely a formality and, normally, is as easy to acquire as a Social Security card.*

in many (most) regards *almost always; largely; many; most; mostly; most often; nearly always; often; usually.*

in many (most) respects *almost always; largely; many; most; mostly; most often; nearly always; often; usually.* We're dealing with an illness that is medical in many respects. *We're dealing with an illness that is mostly medical.* ■ In most respects, competition among banks has been polite. *Competition among banks has been largely polite.* ■ This body of information in many respects represents the most personal and intimate details of a person's being. *This body of information represents many of the most personal and intimate details of a person's being.*

in many (most) situations *almost all; almost always; commonly; frequently; many; many times; most; most often; much; nearly all; nearly always; normally; often; ordinarily; typically; usually.* The speed with which a modem can transmit and receive data is important in many situations. *The speed with which a modem can transmit and receive data is usually important.* ■ This is helpful in many situations, but when executing commands, holding a function key down too long can cause problems. *This is often helpful, but when executing commands, holding a function key down too long can cause problems.*

in (our) midst *among (us).*

in much the same fashion (manner; way) (as; that) *much as; much like.* Though similar in size, material, and color and fabricated in much the same way as their plainer cousins, the new tokens bore various kinds of surface markings and showed a greater variety of shapes. *Though similar in size, material, and color and fabricated much like their plainer cousins, the new tokens bore various kinds of surface markings and showed a greater variety of shapes.* ■ Many analysts maintain that natural, fully integrated companies run by Saudis or Kuwaitis will operate in much the same manner that the U.S. and European oil majors do, guided more by the bottom line than politics. *Many analysts maintain that natural, fully integrated companies run by Saudis or Kuwaitis will operate much as the U.S. and European oil majors do, guided more by the bottom line than politics.* ■ At the heart of the problem is an educational system that has failed to keep pace with a changing national economy and that has been teaching math and science in much the same way they have been taught for decades. *At the heart of the problem is an educational system that has failed to keep pace with a changing national economy and that has been teaching math and science much as they have been taught for decades.*

in my assessment *I assert; I believe; I claim; I consider; I contend; I feel; I hold; I judge; I maintain; I regard; I say; I think; I view; to me;* delete. In my assessment, the most desirable changes for commercial banks to incorporate are as follows. *To me, the most desirable changes for commercial banks to incorporate are as follows.*

in my estimation *I assert; I believe; I claim; I consider; I contend; I feel; I hold; I judge; I maintain; I regard; I say; I think; I view; to me;* delete. In my estimation, the treatment is suitable to Mr. Ross's case. *I feel the treatment is suitable to Mr. Ross's case.* ■ Why was it necessary, in your estimation, to occupy the New Africa House? *Why do you think it was necessary to occupy the New Africa House?* ■ The traffic, in my estimation, will be heavier this year than last year. *I believe the traffic will be heavier this year than last year.*

in my judgment *I assert; I believe; I claim; I consider; I contend; I feel; I hold; I judge; I maintain; I regard; I say; I think; I view; to me;* delete. The most critical issue confronting America, in my judgment, is how we match educational accessibility and opportunity to the demographic change. *The most critical issue confronting America, I contend, is how we match educational accessibility and opportunity to the demographic change.* ■ In my judgment, what they have done—declare that the unborn child is not a person—is shocking. *To me, what they have done—declare that the unborn child is not a person—is shocking.*

in my (own) mind *for myself;* delete. I had to find out in my own mind if quiet diplomacy would work. *I had to find out for myself if quiet diplomacy would work.* ■ In his mind, he thought he had a full bottle. *He thought he had a full bottle.*

(to) ... in my (own) mind's eye *envisage; envision; imagine; visualize;* delete. Once you get to the gate, you need to review in your mind's eye where the engines are. *Once you get to the gate, you need to visualize where the engines are.*

in my opinion *I assert; I believe; I claim; I consider; I contend; I feel; I hold; I judge; I maintain; I regard; I say; I think; I view; to me;* delete. In my opinion, the cruelest aggression is nonverbal, passive aggression. *To me, the cruelest aggression is nonverbal, passive aggression.* ■ If your final manuscript is not acceptable to us, or if it is not delivered on schedule, and if in our opinion an extension of time is not advisable, we may at any time thereafter and at our option terminate this agreement by notice in writing mailed to your last known address. *If your final manuscript is not acceptable to us, or if it is not delivered on schedule, and if we believe an extension of time is not advisable, we may at any* *time thereafter and at our option terminate this agreement by notice in writing mailed to your last known address.*

in my view *I assert; I believe; I claim; I consider; I contend; I feel; I hold; I judge; I maintain; I regard; I say; I think; I view; to me;* delete. In my view, most of these principles were narrow in scope. *I believe most of these principles were narrow in scope.* ▪ In my view, we should appraise the education system chiefly in terms of demonstrated skills and knowledge gained by those who have passed through it. *I feel we should appraise the education system chiefly in terms of demonstrated skills and knowledge gained by those who have passed through it.*

in nature delete. One of the problems is that workloads are so diverse in nature. *One of the problems is that workloads are so diverse.* ▪ Many of these pieces of clothing are ceremonial in nature. *Many of these pieces of clothing are ceremonial.* ▪ Christianity is theistic and revelatory in nature; the New Age is humanistic and generally solipsistic in nature. *Christianity is theistic and revelatory; the New Age is humanistic and generally solipsistic.* ▪ This technique can be used when the misbehavior is seen by the supervisor as temporary in nature, nontypical, and not serious. *This technique can be used when the misbehavior is seen by the supervisor as temporary, nontypical, and not serious.* ▪ There was an accident, minor in nature, on Route 495. *There was a minor accident on Route 495.* ▪ Her evaluations are very subjective and judgmental in nature. *Her evaluations are very subjective and judgmental.*

in no case *never; not; not ever; not once.* In no case would I recommend anything that could lead to the situation at Agawam. *Never would I recommend anything that could lead to the situation at Agawam.*

in normal (ordinary; typical; usual) practice *commonly; customarily; normally; ordinarily; typically; usually.* In normal practice, the party chairman is nominated, and the voting delegation then stands in unison to express its support. *Normally, the party chairman is nominated, and the voting delegation then stands in unison to express its support.*

in no small measure *almost all; chiefly; commonly; generally; greatly; in general; largely; mainly; most; mostly; most often; much; nearly all; normally; overall; typically; usually.* Our continued success is due in no small measure to their contribution on a daily basis. *Our continued success is greatly due to their contribution on a daily basis.*

in no small part *almost all; chiefly; commonly; generally; greatly; in general; largely; mainly; most; mostly; most often; much; nearly all; normally; overall; typically; usually.* And I continue to feel that his lifelong feelings of inadequacy and frustration stemmed in no small part from the limitations that he imposed upon his work. *And I continue to feel that his lifelong feelings of inadequacy and frustration stemmed largely from the limitations that he imposed upon his work.*

in no time (at all) *promptly; quickly; rapidly; right away; shortly; soon; speedily; swiftly.*

innovative new *innovative; new.* An innovative new product combining the latest in communications technology is being installed in courthouses and recording offices throughout the country for public use. *A new product combining the latest in communications technology is being installed in courthouses and recording offices throughout the country for public use.* ■ The oven's innovative new single burner design performs bake, broil, and self-clean functions thanks to a novel flame switching technique that creates a low radiant flame for baking and a high radiant flame required for broiling. *The oven's innovative single burner design performs bake, broil, and self-clean functions thanks to a novel flame switching technique that creates a low radiant flame for baking and a high radiant flame required for broiling.*

in no way *never; not; not ever; not once.* In no way are they meant to represent the official position of NYNEX. *They are not meant to represent the official position of NYNEX.*

in no way, shape, or form *in no way; never; not; not ever; not once.* In no way, shape, or form did we aid anyone or offer incentives to anyone to go to the town meeting. *Never did we aid anyone or offer incentives to anyone to go to the town meeting.*

in number delete. Characteristics of the collaborative phase include team actions to solve problems, reduction of headquarters staff in number, and simplification of formal systems. *Characteristics of the collaborative phase include team actions to solve problems, reduction of headquarters staff, and simplification of formal systems.* ■ Nineteenth-century sweatshops are once again increasing in number. *Nineteenth-century sweatshops are once again increasing.* ■ Since 1987, nongroup Blue Cross subscribers dropped in number from 162,000 to 147,000. *Since 1987, nongroup Blue Cross subscribers dropped from 162,000 to 147,000.*

innumerable *countless; endless; infinite; millions (of); myriad; numberless; untold.*

in (March) of (1992) *in (March) (1992).* The second moving year begins in February of 1984 and extends through January of 1985. *The second moving year begins in February 1984 and extends through January 1985.* ■ I had my surgery in June of 1979. *I had my surgery in June 1979.*

in (the) olden days *before; earlier; formerly; once.*

in operation *active; functioning; in place; running; set up; working;* delete. A large midwestern bank has had a performance monitoring program in operation since 1981. *A large midwestern bank has had a performance monitoring program since 1981.*

in opposition to *against; with.* Based on records of northeast Japan earthquakes since 1600, two geophysicists now propose this scenario in opposition to a long-held theory suggesting offshore earthquakes instead generate onshore quakes. *Based on records of northeast Japan earthquakes since 1600, two geophysicists now propose this scenario against a long-held theory suggesting offshore earthquakes instead generate onshore quakes.*

in ... order *-(al)ly;* delete. We examine, in alphabetical order, all the MLI commands that make up GS/OS and ProDOS 8. *We examine, alphabetically, all the MLI commands that make up GS/OS and ProDOS 8.* ■ Press N to have endnotes continue in sequential order. *Press N to have endnotes continue sequentially.* ■ The available diskettes are listed in *Data Files,* in alphabetical order. *The available diskettes are alphabetically listed in* Data Files.

in order for *for.* If you have the therapy, you have to use it in order for it to work. *If you have the therapy, you have to use it for it to work.* ■ Is it necessary that animals die in order for humans to live? *Is it necessary that animals die for humans to live?* ■ In order for communication to be effective, both the receiver and sender must attribute one symbolic meaning to a word. *For communication to be effective, both the receiver and sender must attribute one symbolic meaning to a word.*

in order that *for; so; so that; that.* In order that the bully boss can score a kill, you have to play the part of the victim. *For the bully boss to score a kill, you have to play the part of the victim.* ■ Past coping behavior must be assessed in order that current behavior is supported or more effective patterns are established. *Past coping behavior must be assessed so that current behavior is supported or more effective patterns are established.* ■ The overall dimension and the radii are given in order that their centers may be located. *The overall dimension and the radii are given so that their centers may be located.*

in order to *so as to; to.* In order to qualify for a heart transplant, certain criteria must be met, one of which is having less than a year to live. *To qualify for a heart transplant, certain criteria must be met, one of which is having less than a year to live.* ■ Sometimes quite a bit of background information, as well as context, is necessary in order to interpret a reference. *Sometimes quite a bit of background information, as well as context, is necessary to interpret a reference.* ■ Every good marketer knows that in order to sell successfully, you must first understand your customers and their needs. *Every good marketer knows that to sell successfully, you must first understand your customers and their needs.*

in other cases (circumstances; instances; situations) *at times; other; (at) other times; some; sometimes;* delete. In other cases, the application may be more mundane, like helping users set up newly delivered microcomputers. *Other applications may be more mundane, like helping users set up newly delivered microcomputers.* ■ In other instances, where the job is creative or where the work is the result of a team-centered environment, a participative style is indicated. *Where the job is creative or where the work is the result of a team-centered environment, a participative style is indicated.* ■ Growths can obstruct the ovaries or tubes, but in other cases there is no blockage. *Growths can obstruct the ovaries or tubes, but sometimes there is no blockage.*

in other words *namely; that is; to wit.* The directory names in the chain must define a continuous path; in other words, each directory specified must be contained within the preceding directory. *The directory names in the chain must define a continuous path; that is, each directory specified must be contained within the preceding directory.*

in partial fulfillment of *toward.*

in (over) (the) past days (decades; months; weeks; years) *before; earlier; formerly; once.*

in payment for (of) *for.* Connoisseurs of the region cannot help wondering what Assad could offer Washington in payment for such a favor. *Connoisseurs of the region cannot help wondering what Assad could offer Washington for such a favor.*

in perpetuity *always; ceaselessly; constantly; endlessly; eternally; everlastingly; forever; never ending; perpetually.* It promised to preserve the rest of the farm in perpetuity as farm or forest. *It promised to preserve the rest of the farm forever as farm or forest.*

in place of *for.* Table 11.1 can be used for the UNR thread form by substituting UNR in place of UN. *Table 11.1 can be used for the UNR thread form by substituting UNR for UN.* ■ No reasonably literate person of my acquaintance says "sunk" in place of "sank." *No reasonably literate person of my acquaintance says "sunk" for "sank."*

in point of *about; as for; as to; concerning; for; in; of; on; over; regarding; respecting; to; toward; with;* delete.

in point of fact *actually; indeed; in fact; in faith; in reality; in truth; really; truly;* delete. The U.S. government said he wasn't working for them, but in point of fact, he was a military attaché. *The U.S. government said he wasn't working for them, but in truth he was a military attaché.* ■ You may have assumed that sectors are numbered sequentially around the track, and in point of fact, many times they are. *You may have assumed that sectors are numbered sequentially around the track, and indeed, many times they are.*

in preference to *over.* Mile's new product emphasis is on performance in preference to fashion. *Mile's new product emphasis is on performance over fashion.*

in proportion to *for; with.*

in proximity (to) *close by; close to; near; nearby.* The property is in proximity to metropolitan Boston. *The property is near metropolitan Boston.*

in punishment for (of) *for.*

in pursuit of *exploring; probing; pursuing; searching; seeking.* One would think they could better spend their time in pursuit of the pressing problems which beset the Redevelopment Authority and the city's development plans. *One would think they could better spend their time pursuing the pressing problems which beset the Redevelopment Authority and the city's development plans.*

input *clout; pull; say; voice.* I have a lot of input into what I'll wear on the set. *I have a lot of say about what I'll wear on the set.* ■ It has some input in long-term strategy and certainly in the selection of senior management but little in the day-to-day running of the business. *It has some voice in long-term strategy and certainly in the selection of senior management but little in the day-to-day running of the business.*

input *thoughts; views.* These style alternatives do not solicit employee input. *These style alternatives do not solicit employee views.* ■ Do you have any more input about his predicament? *Do you have any more thoughts about his predicament?*

(the) ... in question *the; that; this;* delete. Neither Phillips nor any of its subsidiaries has ever sold the chemical in question to Libya. *Neither Phillips nor any of its subsidiaries has ever sold this chemical to Libya.* ■ He did not acknowledge that decree violations had occurred, but said that Nynex had or would discontinue the practice in question. *He did not acknowledge that decree violations had occurred, but said that Nynex had or would discontinue the practice.* ■ Actually there is nothing embarrassing about this discovery unless the passions in question are masked in pretended objectivity and are themselves embarrassing. *Actually there is nothing embarrassing about this discovery unless these passions are masked in pretended objectivity and are themselves embarrassing.*

in quick (short) order *directly; presently; promptly; quickly; shortly; soon; straightaway.* IBM's major (.0) releases often have these problems, sometimes bugs, and sometimes simply changes, and they are followed in short order by the .1 versions. *IBM's major (.0) releases often have these problems, sometimes bugs, and sometimes simply changes, and they are followed shortly by the .1 versions.* ■ The first volume of *The Feynman Lectures on Physics* was published the previous year, and two more volumes followed in quick order. *The first volume of* The Feynman Lectures on Physics *was published the previous year, and two more volumes soon followed.*

inquire (about; of) *ask.* May I inquire how you were able to do that? *May I ask how you were able to do that?* ■ Everyone has been inquiring about the status of cable installation. *Everyone has been asking about the status of cable installation.* ■ I inquired of the doctor why these children have distended stomachs. *I asked the doctor why these children have distended stomachs.*

in reaction to *after; because of; by; due to; following; for; from; in; out of; owing to; through; with.*

in reality *actually; indeed; in fact; in faith; in truth; really; truly;* delete.

in recent days (decades; months; weeks; years) *lately; of late; recent; recently;* delete. In recent years, much discussion has taken place about opening central office switching markets to increased competition. *Lately, much discussion has taken place about opening central office switching markets to increased competition.* ■ Some officials had suggested in recent days that the meeting might lead to some interim agreement—or "confidence-building measures"— on at least some aspects of the treaty under negotiation in Geneva. *Some officials had recently suggested that the meeting might lead to some interim agreement— or "confidence-building measures"—on at least some aspects of the treaty under negotiation in Geneva.* ■ In recent decades, subpopulations of Rhagoletis have developed a clear preference for one kind of tree or the other. *Of late, subpopulations of Rhagoletis have developed a clear preference for one kind of tree or the other.* ■ But events have not been kind to the university in recent weeks. *But recent events have not been kind to the university.*

in recent history (memory; times) *in days (months; weeks; years); lately; of late; recent; recently;* delete. *The Wall Street Journal* earlier this month noted that Macmillan tried more defenses and pushed them further than almost any company in recent memory. The Wall Street Journal *earlier this month noted that Macmillan tried more defenses and pushed them further than almost any company of late.* ■ It is the largest drop in auto insurance rates in recent memory. *It is the largest drop in auto insurance rates in years.* ■ He concedes that the ratio of reserves in the FDIC to deposits in banks is at its lowest level in recent history. *He concedes that the ratio of reserves in the FDIC to deposits in banks is at its lowest level in months.* ■ New breeds of animals and plants have, of course, arisen throughout the planet's history through evolution and, in recent times, through the selective mating of individuals with desired characteristics. *New breeds of animals and plants have, of course, arisen throughout the planet's history through evolution and, recently, through the selective mating of individuals with desired characteristics.*

in recorded history *on record; recorded.* Though final figures aren't yet in, as of November 1 this has been the hottest year in recorded history. *Though final figures aren't yet in, as of November 1 this has been the hottest year on record.*

in reference to *about; as for; as to; concerning; for; in; of; on; over; regarding; respecting; to; toward; with;* delete. Never make any assumptions or promises in reference to product flaws, but report all instances either to customer service or the appropriate management personnel for corrective action. *Never make any assumptions or promises about product flaws, but report all instances either to customer service or the appropriate management personnel for corrective action.*

in regard(s) to *about; as for; as to; concerning; for; in; of; on; over; regarding; respecting; to; toward; with;* delete. They questioned me in regard to a 1986 rape and murder case. *They questioned me about a 1986 rape and murder case.* ■ The U.S. government is currently pushing hard for greater international protection of intellectual property rights, particularly in regard to patents, copyrights, and trademarks. *The U.S. government is currently pushing hard for greater international protection of intellectual property rights, particularly for patents, copyrights, and trademarks.*

in relation to *about; as for; as to; concerning; for; in; of; on; over; regarding; respecting; to; toward; with;* delete. But how high a cholesterol level is too high and how you evaluate those levels in relation to the individual have not been answered. *But how high a cholesterol level is too high and how you evaluate those levels in the individual have not been answered.* ■ The researchers interviewed the survivors in relation to six areas of postwar life. *The researchers interviewed the survivors regarding six areas of postwar life.*

in relation (relationship) to *against; alongside; beside; compared to (with); -(i)er than; less; less than; more; more than; next to; over; than; to; versus; vis-à-vis.* The small-business computer market has been accelerating slowly in relation to the overall information processing market. *The small-business computer market has been accelerating slower than the overall information processing market.* ■ When this information is considered in relation to the magnitude and direction of planned company growth, future manpower needs can be predicted. *When this information is considered alongside the magnitude and direction of planned company growth, future manpower needs can be predicted.*

in repetition *again; over.*

in resistance to *against; with.*

in respect of (to) *about; as for; as to; concerning; for; in; of; on; over; regarding; respecting; to; toward; with;* delete. Some additional perspective is needed in respect to South Korea. *Some additional perspective is needed on South Korea.* ▪ Its power to effect major policy changes, particularly in respect to foreign affairs, is now exceedingly limited. *Its power to effect major policy changes, particularly in foreign affairs, is now exceedingly limited.*

in response to *after; because of; by; due to; following; for; from; in; out of; owing to; through; with.* It became the object of widespread screening in the United States in the early 1970s, partly in response to demands by the black community for better health care. *It became the object of widespread screening in the United States in the early 1970s, partly because of demands by the black community for better health care.* ▪ The dollar yesterday fell against most major currencies in response to renewed dollar sales by central banks and a bearish statement by a West German banking official. *The dollar yesterday fell against most major currencies following renewed dollar sales by central banks and a bearish statement by a West German banking official.*

in return (for) *for.* Switch traders are specialized third-party trading houses that have developed extensive international networks of contracts and are willing, in return for a fee, to find buyers for countertraded goods. *Switch traders are specialized third-party trading houses that have developed extensive international networks of contracts and are willing, for a fee, to find buyers for countertraded goods.* ▪ Agency officials speculate that is why residents who completed the survey, when asked, focused on the little things—for example, the letters that promised so much in return for so little. *Agency officials speculate that is why residents who completed the survey, when asked, focused on the little things— for example, the letters that promised so much for so little.*

(the) ins and (the) outs *details; features; particulars; specifics.*

in scale delete.

in scope delete. Competition for these foreign opportunities has become more intense and global in scope. *Competition for these foreign opportunities has become more intense and global.* ▪ Smokeless tobacco is becoming a problem large in scope. *Smokeless tobacco is becoming a large problem.*

in shape delete. The true-size surface is elliptical in shape. *The true-size surface is elliptical.* ▪ The section gives the impression that the part is conical in shape. *The section gives the impression that the part is conical.* ▪ The only rule is that the range must be rectangular in shape. *The only rule is that the range must be rectangular.*

in short supply *meager; rare; scant; scarce; sparse.*

inside of *inside.*

inside (and) out *completely; thoroughly.*

inside the boundaries (limits; parameters) of *within.*

in situations when (where) *if; when; where.* In situations where there is an even number of seasons in a year, the first period in the trend is estimated as the intercept plus one-half the estimated slope. *If there is an even number of seasons in a year, the first period in the trend is estimated as the intercept plus one-half the estimated slope.* ■ In situations where market heterogeneity limits opportunity for uniformity, the firm should actively promote global convergence of market segments. *Where market heterogeneity limits opportunity for uniformity, the firm should actively promote global convergence of market segments.* ■ Individuals with eczema tend to be emotionally sensitive, especially in situations where they perceive the loss of approval or love. *Individuals with eczema tend to be emotionally sensitive, especially when they perceive the loss of approval or love.* ■ Nuts can be drawn across flats in situations where doing so improves the drawing. *Nuts can be drawn across flats if doing so improves the drawing.*

in size delete. The sides range from 4 to 24 inches in size. *The sides range from 4 to 24 inches.* ■ We are a studio small enough in size to be able to offer excellent coverage and follow-through. *We are a studio small enough to be able to offer excellent coverage and follow-through.* ■ The fireball is also much larger in size than it would be if it consisted only of protons and neutrons knocking about. *The fireball is also much larger than it would be if it consisted only of protons and neutrons knocking about.* ■ Situated in Linlithgow, 15 miles west of Edinburgh, the facility is expected to be between 120,000 and 140,000 square feet in size. *Situated in Linlithgow, 15 miles west of Edinburgh, the facility is expected to be between 120,000 and 140,000 square feet.*

insofar as *as far as; as much as; so far as; so much as.* Insofar as the lead market is a reliable predictor of behavior in other markets, useful insights into appropriate target markets and product diffusion strategies are provided. *So far as the lead market is a reliable predictor of behavior in other markets, useful insights into appropriate target markets and product diffusion strategies are provided.* ■ As a historian, Mr. Chaudhuri is useful insofar as he recounts personal experience—for example, his accounts of the Bose brothers or of Hindu-Muslim riots at the time of partition. *As a historian, Mr. Chaudhuri is useful so far as he recounts personal experience—for example, his accounts of the Bose brothers or of Hindu-Muslim riots at the time of partition.*

insofar as *because; considering; for; in that; since.* Insofar as more than 98 percent of House incumbents were returned to office in the last election, it shouldn't surprise anyone that the members are turning Congress into a family business. *Since more than 98 percent of House incumbents were returned to office in the last election, it shouldn't surprise anyone that the members are turning Congress into a family business.* ■ The blended rates that are being proposed are discriminatory insofar as they do not reflect the costs of care being rendered to the subscriber. *The blended rates that are being proposed are discriminatory for they do not reflect the costs of care being rendered to the subscriber.*

insofar as … goes (is concerned) *about; as for; as to; concerning; for; in; of; on; over; regarding; respecting; to; toward; with;* delete. The president's position, insofar as negotiations are concerned, has never changed. *The president's position on negotiations has never changed.* ■ Insofar as Pakistan is concerned, it views the issue as India's internal matter and, therefore, has scrupulously refrained from involvement in it. *As to Pakistan, it views the issue as India's internal matter and, therefore, has scrupulously refrained from involvement in it.* ■ Insofar as my qualifications as a reviewer are concerned, I will be happy to defer to the judgment of my peers. *Concerning my qualifications as a reviewer, I will be happy to defer to the judgment of my peers.*

in some fashion (manner; way) *somehow; someway(s).* For most of us, the closest we ever come to a ghost is the occasional feeling that something is watching us or that a place never visited before is in some way familiar. *For most of us, the closest we ever come to a ghost is the occasional feeling that something is watching us or that a place never visited before is somehow familiar.* ■ He makes clear he does not consider it a figment of his imagination, but rather an idea that eventually will be adopted in some fashion to meet the spiraling demands on air travel. *He makes clear he does not consider it a figment of his imagination, but rather an idea that eventually will somehow be adopted to meet the spiraling demands on air travel.*

in spite of *after all; apart; aside; despite; even with; for all; with all.* In spite of his malady, he wrote music with great skill and creativity. *Even with his malady, he wrote music with great skill and creativity.* ■ In spite of Meese's legal problems, Reagan has consistently defended his attorney general's ethics. *With all Meese's legal problems, Reagan has consistently defended his attorney general's ethics.* ■ In spite of difficulties, in the long run, the rational win and the "invisible hand" continue to rule. *Difficulties aside, in the long run, the rational win and the "invisible hand" continue to rule.* ■ As always, it is the spectacle of great courage that, in spite of his failings, merits a salute. *As always, it is the spectacle of great courage that, for all his failings, merits a salute.* ■ We must operate as one Company in spite of cultural differences, and in spite of our varied professional interests, personalities, and aspirations. *We must operate as one Company despite cultural differences, and despite our varied professional interests, personalities, and aspirations.*

in spite of the fact that *although; but; even though; still; though; yet.* The poll of 926 women readers generally gives higher marks to male co-workers and bosses in spite of the fact that most respondents said they enjoyed working with other women. *The poll of 926 women readers generally gives higher marks to male co-workers and bosses though most respondents said they enjoyed working with other women.* ■ The number of deaths from asthma has doubled in the past decade in spite of the fact that treatments have improved. *The number of deaths from asthma has doubled in the past decade, yet treatments have improved.* ■ This guidance came in spite of the fact that U.S. satellites were commonly acknowledged to be better and cheaper than Japan's. *This guidance came* *although U.S. satellites were commonly acknowledged to be better and cheaper than Japan's.* ■ Some commentators claim that careful writers avoid the adverb *slow* in spite of the fact that it has over four centuries of usage behind it. *Some commentators claim that careful writers avoid the adverb slow even though it has over four centuries of usage behind it.*

instantaneous (instantaneously) *at once; instant (instantly); straightaway.* We fell in love with her instantaneously. *We fell in love with her at once.* ■ Transit time vanishes, queues can be shared, and mode of operation can shift at will between sequential and simultaneous views of documents—all because documents are available almost instantaneously. *Transit time vanishes, queues can be shared, and mode of operation can shift at will between sequential and simultaneous views of documents—all because documents are available almost instantly.* ■ This handler provides instantaneous response when you initiate one of the keyboard commands. *This handler provides instant response when you initiate one of the keyboard commands.*

institute *set up.*

institution *building; factory; hospital; institute; jail; office; place; plant; prison; school;* delete.

in such a fashion (manner; way) as to (so as to) *so as to; to.* The light fixture had to be designed in such a manner so as to provide the maximum light to the operating area. *The light fixture had to be designed to provide the maximum light to the operating area.* ■ A national choice should not be used in international relations in such a way as to cause trends and events that trigger conflicts and military confrontations. *A national choice should not be used in international relations to cause trends and events that trigger conflicts and military confrontations.* ■ Further, we do not authorize any organization to use the Association's name in such a way as to imply that such a relationship exists. *Further, we do not authorize any organization to use the Association's name so as to imply that such a relationship exists.* ■ These things organize themselves in water in such a way as to scavenge any organic material in the water and subject it to a very large intensity of ultraviolet light. *These things organize themselves in water so as to scavenge any organic material in the water and subject it to a very large intensity of ultraviolet light.*

in such a fashion (manner; way) so (so that) *so; so that.* Only meter stamped, return address labels may be used on single piece, special fourth-class rate or library rate mail, and these labels must adhere in such a manner so they will not come off in one piece. *Only meter stamped, return address labels may be used on single piece, special fourth-class rate or library rate mail, and these labels must adhere so that they will not come off in one piece.* ■ The 45-day suspension will give the department a chance to modify the regulations in such a way so that we can accommodate the needs of the shrimpers and still protect the turtles. *The 45-day suspension will give the department a chance to modify the regulations* *so that we can accommodate the needs of the shrimpers and still protect the turtles.*

in such a fashion (manner; way) that *so; so that.* If this is to occur, the development process should be organized in such a manner that the focus is firmly on international market opportunities rather than on individual markets. *If this is to occur, the development process should be organized so that the focus is firmly on international market opportunities rather than on individual markets.* ■ The first was the "store," designed in such a way that numbers could be stored in 1,000 "registers," each capable of storing 50 digits. *The first was the "store," designed so that numbers could be stored in 1,000 "registers," each capable of storing 50 digits.* ■ The foreign and international marketing efforts of a global company need to be harmonized in such as way that they are consistent with and supportive of the company's goals. *The foreign and international marketing efforts of a global company need to be harmonized so that they are consistent with and supportive of the company's goals.* ■ Export business may be structured in such a way that the buyer bears most of the risks. *Export business may be structured so that the buyer bears most of the risks.*

in such (a; the) ... fashion (manner; way) *so -(al)ly;* delete.

insufficient *dis-; il-; im-; in-; ir-; lack of; -less(ness); mis-; no; non-; not; not enough; scant; too few; too little; un-.* There is insufficient reason for joy. *There is not enough reason for joy.* ■ In the area of pricing, common problems are cost-plus export pricing, insufficient attention to the pricing environment in individual markets, and excessive overseas distributor price margins. *In the area of pricing, common problems are cost-plus export pricing, inattention to the pricing environment in individual markets, and excessive overseas distributor price margins.*

(a; the) insufficient amount (of) *not enough; too little.*

in sufficient amount *enough.* If radon gas enters your lungs in sufficient amounts, it can emit alpha particles that attack tissue and lead to lung cancer. *If enough radon gas enters your lungs, it can emit alpha particles that attack tissue and lead to lung cancer.*

(a; the) insufficient number (of) *not enough; too few.* Within two years, other American cities expect a similar gridlock of hospital beds, largely because of AIDS and an insufficient number of health-care workers. *Within two years, other American cities expect a similar gridlock of hospital beds, largely because of AIDS and too few health-care workers.*

in sufficient number *enough.* I hope you heard from people in sufficient number to alert you to the possibility of a nationwide constituency for extended incarceration of violent felons. *I hope you heard from enough people to alert you to* *the possibility of a nationwide constituency for extended incarceration of violent felons.*

in sufficient quantity *enough.* Libya doesn't have the industrial capacity to make toxic agents in sufficient quantities to conduct warfare. *Libya doesn't have the industrial capacity to make enough toxic agents to conduct warfare.*

in summary (summation) *in brief; in fine; in short; in sum.* In summary, you have printed a drawing to a file, returned to Desktop, opened up the TOPS directory, and clicked on TPRINT. *In sum, you have printed a drawing to a file, returned to Desktop, opened up the TOPS directory, and clicked on TPRINT.* ■ In summary, it is apparent that a country's comparative advantage situation will be vitally affected by the productivity of available factor inputs. *In short, it is apparent that a country's comparative advantage situation will be vitally affected by the productivity of available factor inputs.*

in support of *for; with.* Radical environmentalists are already demanding that legal and ethical protection be extended to all of nature, and a few of them have demonstrated a willingness to fight, break the law, and even die in support of this conviction. *Radical environmentalists are already demanding that legal and ethical protection be extended to all of nature, and a few of them have demonstrated a willingness to fight, break the law, and even die for this conviction.*

intellectual ability (capacity) *ability; capacity; intellect; intelligence.* Tools and other remains left by Neanderthals show no indication that these creatures possessed the intellectual capacity for symbolic thought or language. *Tools and other remains left by Neanderthals show no indication that these creatures possessed the capacity for symbolic thought or language.*

interdependency *interdependence.*

interestingly (enough) delete. Interestingly enough, in about 50 percent of the cases involved, the professional offering an opinion believed abuse had occurred; 33 percent thought there had been none. *In about 50 percent of the cases involved, the professional offering an opinion believed abuse had occurred; 33 percent thought there had been none.* ■ Interestingly, although consumers say they are very interested in one-stop shopping for financial services, they may not be persuaded yet that the major chain retailers can provide what they want. *Although consumers say they are very interested in one-stop shopping for financial services, they may not be persuaded yet that the major chain retailers can provide what they want.*

interlocutor *speaker; talker.*

in ... terms *-(al)ly;* delete. You must be able to state in specific terms what it is that you want from your present job. *You must be able to state specifically what it* *is that you want from your present job.* ■ In general terms, it is, as 36 requires, that the rates were not adequate, fair, and reasonable. *Generally, it is, as 36 requires, that the rates were not adequate, fair, and reasonable.* ■ They both spoke in optimistic terms. *They both spoke optimistically.*

in terms of *about; as; as for; as to; by; concerning; for; in; of; on; regarding; respecting; through; under; with;* delete. In terms of safety, honesty, and trust, banks consistently score higher than life insurance companies. *In safety, honesty, and trust, banks consistently score higher than life insurance companies.* ■ Changes can define each domain in terms of a target amount of CPU time, main storage, and channels. *Changes can define each domain by a target amount of CPU time, main storage, and channels.* ■ How would you say you are different in terms of your personas? *How would you say your personas are different?* ■ She's more aggressive in terms of what she wants. *She's more aggressive about what she wants.* ■ Women are looking for help in terms of PMS. *Women are looking for help with PMS.* ■ Other doctors have criticized IL-2 therapy in terms of its toxicity. *Other doctors have criticized IL-2 therapy for its toxicity.* ■ The forecast level should be judged in terms of its reasonableness. *The forecast level should be judged on its reasonableness.* ■ In terms of total financial assets, S&Ls ranked second among all types of financial institutions. *As for total financial assets, S&Ls ranked second among all types of financial institutions.* ■ A regiocentric attitude assumes that countries can be geographically grouped since they have commonalities in terms of cultures, management practices, and experiences. *A regiocentric attitude assumes that countries can be geographically grouped since they have cultures, management practices, and experiences in common.*

interpretative *interpretive.*

interpret to mean *interpret as.* Achieving a desired standard of living must be interpreted to mean finding the pattern of consumption expenditures that yields maximum satisfaction. *Achieving a desired standard of living must be interpreted as finding the pattern of consumption expenditures that yields maximum satisfaction.*

in that *because; for; since.* The case is unusual in that a Japanese company is aggressively taking legal action to seek protection under a US trade law originally designed to protect American industries and manufacturers. *The case is unusual because a Japanese company is aggressively taking legal action to seek protection under a US trade law originally designed to protect American industries and manufacturers.* ■ Their goals and expectations are different from a generation ago in that both boys and girls expect to go to college and have full-time careers. *Their goals and expectations are different from a generation ago since both boys and girls expect to go to college and have full-time careers.* ■ But males play an important part, too, in that it takes more than a good teacher for learning to take place; the student must be receptive and astute enough to respond. *But males* *play an important part, too, for it takes more than a good teacher for learning to take place; the student must be receptive and astute enough to respond.*

in that (this) case (circumstance; instance; situation) *here; now; then; there;* delete. No ampersand is required in this case because the argument will not be modified. *No ampersand is required now because the argument will not be modified.* ■ The factor that has to be evaluated by management in this situation is the cost of opening other checkout areas to provide faster service. *The factor that has to be evaluated by management here is the cost of opening other checkout areas to provide faster service.* ■ What is wanted in these circumstances is not necessarily the instinctive response of the economist—to assign every activity a shadow price and let the market do the rationing. *What is wanted here is not necessarily the instinctive response of the economist—to assign every activity a shadow price and let the market do the rationing.* ■ In that instance, all I did was apply KITA frontally; I exerted a pull instead of a push. *All I did there was apply KITA frontally; I exerted a pull instead of a push.*

in that (this) connection *about (for; in; on; to) that (this);* delete.

in that (this) day and age *in that (this) age; in that (this) day; in that (this) time; (just; right) now; nowadays; then; these (those) days; today.* In this day and age, a lot of women expect men to be bad. *Nowadays, a lot of women expect men to be bad.* ■ In this day and age of global violence, I find it interesting that the *Globe Magazine* would publish articles about two international terrorists. *In this age of global violence, I find it interesting that the* Globe Magazine *would publish articles about two international terrorists.* ■ Why should we, in this day and age, have double standards when a marriage breaks up? *Why should we, today, have double standards when a marriage breaks up?*

in that (this) direction *toward that (this).* That means any push in this direction would require guidance from officials of the new administration. *That means any push toward this would require guidance from officials of the new administration.* ■ Those who guided them in that direction have waited for someone to pull the whole thing together. *Those who guided them toward that have waited for someone to pull the whole thing together.*

in that (this) fashion (manner; way) *like this (that); so; thus.* Let me explain it in this fashion. *Let me explain it like this.* ■ What can she expect if she behaves in this manner? *What can she expect if she behaves like this?*

in that (this) general vicinity *near here (there); thereabouts (hereabouts).* There have been a lot of crimes in this general vicinity. *There have been a lot of crimes near here.*

in (on) that (this) matter *about (for; in; on; to) that (this);* delete. Rothko's views on this matter were very well known among his circle of friends. *Rothko's views on this were very well known among his circle of friends.*

in that (this) regard *about (for; in; on; to) that (this);* delete. Good luck to you in that regard. *Good luck to you.* ■ There will be no change at all in that regard. *There will be no change at all in that.* ■ The experiences of other countries are quite relevant in this regard. *The experiences of other countries are quite relevant to this.* ■ The Patrolmen's Association is right in that regard. *The Patrolmen's Association is right about that.* ■ The judge's examination of the defendant in this regard was as thorough and probing as reasonably can be required. *The judge's examination of the defendant on this was as thorough and probing as reasonably can be required.*

in that (this) respect *about (for; in; on; to) that (this);* delete.

in the absence of *having no; lacking; minus; missing; not having; short of; with no; without.* Women must realize that life can be meaningful and full and rich in the absence of having a man to love. *Women must realize that life can be meaningful and full and rich without having a man to love.* ■ In the absence of quality, employees may face an "unclean" environment, which can lead to dissatisfaction for the workforce. *Lacking quality, employees may face an "unclean" environment, which can lead to dissatisfaction for the workforce.* ■ In the absence of global competitors, the company can concentrate its marketing efforts on establishing a firm footing in the market, developing its competitive position, and building market share. *Having no global competitors, the company can concentrate its marketing efforts on establishing a firm footing in the market, developing its competitive position, and building market share.* ■ Much scholarship supporting expanded, freer trade and projecting benefits to America from a more prosperous Japan has occurred in the absence of any such aid. *Much scholarship supporting expanded, freer trade and projecting benefits to America from a more prosperous Japan has occurred with no such aid.* ■ He had another book which was selling very well, but in the absence of a contractual provision like this, we couldn't touch that other royalty account. *He had another book which was selling very well, but not having a contractual provision like this, we couldn't touch that other royalty account.*

in the act of -ing *-ing.*

in the affirmative *affirmatively; favorably; positively; yes.* Eight members having voted in the affirmative, the vote carries. *Eight members having voted yes, the vote carries.*

in the aftermath of *(just; right) after; (close) behind; ensuing; following; succeeding.* In the aftermath of the assault-rifle mass murder, Americans should remain rational and not legislate away the right to own any type of firearm. *Following the assault-rifle mass murder, Americans should remain rational and not legislate away the right to own any type of firearm.*

in the altogether *naked; nude.*

in the amount (sum) of *for; of;* delete. Enclosed is a check in the amount of $900.00. *Enclosed is a check for $900.00.* ■ Client shall pay to Licensor a fee in the amount of $1000.00 or 8% of the fee actually received by Client, whichever is greater for each sublicense of the Package. *Client shall pay to Licensor a fee of $1000.00 or 8% of the fee actually received by Client, whichever is greater for each sublicense of the Package.* ■ Commonwealth indicated that they were only requesting repayment of current credit lines with regard to Kaypro inventory and account receivables in the amount of $3.5 million. *Commonwealth indicated that they were only requesting repayment of current credit lines with regard to Kaypro inventory and account receivables of $3.5 million.*

in the area of *about; as for; as to; concerning; for; in; of; on; over; regarding; respecting; to; toward; with;* delete. The secondary gains for the phobic partner may be in the area of fulfilling nurturing needs. *The secondary gains for the phobic partner may be in fulfilling nurturing needs.* ■ We are researching the outcomes of cases in the areas of divorce, child custody and support, domestic violence, sexual assault, adult and juvenile offenders, and civil damage awards. *We are researching the outcomes of cases of divorce, child custody and support, domestic violence, sexual assault, adult and juvenile offenders, and civil damage awards.* ■ This is particularly true in the area of equity underwriting. *This is particularly true for equity underwriting.*

(something; somewhere) in the area (of) *about; around; close to; more or less; near; nearly; or so; roughly; some;* delete. The trial is expected to run in the area of nine months. *The trial is expected to run some nine months.*

in the assessment of *assert; believe; claim; consider; contend; feel; hold; judge; maintain; regard; say; think; to; view; with.*

in (within) the boundaries (limits; parameters) of *in (within).*

in the capacity of *as.*

in the company of *alongside; among; beside; during; in; with.* She arrived in the company of a hired male escort. *She arrived alongside a hired male escort.* ■ These children are here in the company of their fathers. *These children are here with their fathers.*

in the context of *in.* In the context of personal financial planning, the application of controls is even more important. *In personal financial planning, the application of controls is even more important.*

(somewhere) in the course of *during; for; in; over; throughout; when; while; with.* There were several suspects that came up in the course of our investigation, but Nancy Douglas was not one of them. *There were several suspects that came up during our investigation, but Nancy Douglas was not one of* *them.* ■ The chairman of the committee that wrote the 37,000-word, 99-page letter said the five-bishop committee had a change of heart in the course of developing the document. *The chairman of the committee that wrote the 37,000-word, 99-page letter said the five-bishop committee had a change of heart while developing the document.* ■ In the course of any business day, you jot down notes on paper, make appointments on calendars, and enter phone numbers into phone directories. *Throughout any business day, you jot down notes on paper, make appointments on calendars, and enter phone numbers into phone directories.* ■ Men do not make as many listening noises ("yeah" or "un-hunh") as women do in the course of a discussion. *Men do not make as many listening noises ("yeah" or "un-hunh") as women do in a discussion.* ■ In the course of doing these exercises, students are introduced to almost all of their word processing program's features. *When doing these exercises, students are introduced to almost all of their word processing program's features.*

in the course of events (things; time) *at length; eventually; in due time; in the end; in time; later; one day; over the months (years); over time; someday; sometime; ultimately; with time; yet.* In the course of events, the condominium market went through transition and became an association with a board of trustees who proceeded to ignore Betty H.'s notes and calls informing them of common area problems. *At length, the condominium market went through transition and became an association with a board of trustees who proceeded to ignore Betty H.'s notes and calls informing them of common area problems.* ■ Continued observation of such men indicates that this is exactly what happens in many cases, and more evidence of this may show up in the course of time. *Continued observation of such men indicates that this is exactly what happens in many cases, and more evidence of this may show up over time.*

in the days (decades; months; weeks; years) before (prior to) *before.* In the days before LANs, if you wanted a coworker to add to a report you were writing, you copied the file to a disk and delivered it by hand. *Before LANs, if you wanted a coworker to add to a report you were writing, you copied the file to a disk and delivered it by hand.*

in the direction of (toward) *at; for; in; on; through; to; toward; with.* It appears it's headed in the direction of becoming a more conventional school that focuses on finances. *It appears it's headed toward becoming a more conventional school that focuses on finances.* ■ This small, grudging concession in the direction of pluralism leaves Poland still far from freedom. *This small, grudging concession to pluralism leaves Poland still far from freedom.* ■ The governor took a step in the direction toward better driving conditions by raising the speeding fines from their unreasonably low levels. *The governor took a step for better driving conditions by raising the speeding fines from their unreasonably low levels.*

in the distant future *eventual; eventually; future; in many months (years); in time; in two (ten) months (years); later; much later; next month (year); one day; over time; someday; sometime; ultimately; with time; yet;* delete. Japan, No. 2

in trade with the United States, and Mexico have both been mentioned as possibilities for free-trade partners in the distant future. *Japan, No. 2 in trade with the
United States, and Mexico have both been mentioned as possibilities for future
free-trade partners.*

in the distant past *before; earlier; formerly; long ago; long since; many months
(years) ago; once;* delete.

in the estimation of *assert; believe; claim; consider; contend; feel; hold; judge;
maintain; regard; say; think; to; view; with.*

in the eventuality of (that; this) *if (there were); if ... should; should (there); were
(there; ... to); when;* delete. In the eventuality that someone decides not to follow a court order, what do you do? *If someone should decide not to follow a
court order, what do you do?* ■ Firm answers to this question from the candidates
will be required in the eventuality that the U.S. Supreme Court overturns Roe vs.
Wade entirely this year. *Firm answers to this question from the candidates will be
required if the U.S. Supreme Court overturns Roe vs. Wade entirely this year.* ■ In
the eventuality of a buyout, would I have to pay a sales commission to the
broker? *Were there a buyout, would I have to pay a sales commission to the
broker?*

in the extreme *extremely; highly; hugely; mightily.* All three theories seem
unlikely in the extreme. *All three theories seem highly unlikely.*

in the face of *against; before; confronted by (with); confronting; faced with; facing.* In the face of those developments, the off-farm work movement was inevitable. *Faced with those developments, the off-farm work movement was inevitable.* ■ In the face of a state deficit estimated at more than $600 million, the
administration believes it is impossible that all these programs can survive. *Facing a state deficit estimated at more than $600 million, the administration
believes it is impossible that all these programs can survive.* ■ In the face of the
prospect of annual tuitions of $3,000 to $11,000, many parents back down.
*Before the prospect of annual tuitions of $3,000 to $11,000, many parents back
down.*

in the final (last) analysis *in the end; ultimately;* delete. In the final analysis, we
are still grappling with the inherent problems of being human. *In the end, we are
still grappling with the inherent problems of being human.* ■ In the final analysis,
it will be the companies who have a successful mix of environment plus capabilities, and a quality blend of products and services, who become the suppliers
of choice. *Ultimately, it will be the companies who have a successful mix of
environment plus capabilities, and a quality blend of products and services, who
become the suppliers of choice.*

in the first place *first; first of all;* delete. In the first place, Democratic administrations are associated with increased regulations, a sure-fire lure for lawyers.
First of all, Democratic administrations are associated with increased regulations,

a sure-fire lure for lawyers. ▪ We found ourselves troubleshooting the immediate need, not addressing the larger issues that caused the problem in the first place. *We found ourselves troubleshooting the immediate need, not addressing the larger issues that first caused the problem.* ▪ In the first place, it takes courage, a quality which is not too widespread. *First, it takes courage, a quality which is not too widespread.*

in the following fashion (manner; way) *as follows.* The value of *M* can be substituted in the equation in the following manner. *The value of M can be substituted in the equation as follows.*

in the foreseeable future *before long; directly; in a month (week); next month (year); presently; quickly; shortly; soon; this month (year); tomorrow;* delete. I expect in the foreseeable future we will see them looking inward and opening up to the world. *I expect we will presently see them looking inward and opening up to the world.* ▪ She singled out a monetary union with a single Eurocurrency and a central Eurobank as two absurd and "airy-fairy" concepts of an ill-defined European union that Britain will not support in the foreseeable future. *She singled out a monetary union with a single Eurocurrency and a central Eurobank as two absurd and "airy-fairy" concepts of an ill-defined European union that Britain will not soon support.* ▪ A lot of people feel there will be a recession in the foreseeable future and consequently certain kinds of investments should be questioned. *A lot of people feel there will be a recession before long and consequently certain kinds of investments should be questioned.* ▪ But precisely because the abortion debate rages so intensely, neither these nor any other so-called abortifacient drug is likely to be legally available to American women in the foreseeable future. *But precisely because the abortion debate rages so intensely, neither these nor any other so-called abortifacient drug is likely to be legally available to American women this year.*

in the form of *as;* delete. This marketing strategy for expanding banking relationships is best illustrated in the form of a triangle, with relationships ranked from routine to lead banking. *This marketing strategy for expanding banking relationships is best illustrated as a triangle, with relationships ranked from routine to lead banking.* ▪ The outstanding aspects of each design usually lend themselves to presentations in the form of graphs that compare manufacturing costs, operational characteristics, and other data. *The outstanding aspects of each design usually lend themselves to graphical presentations that compare manufacturing costs, operational characteristics, and other data.* ▪ I offer these comments in the form of advice, not criticism. *I offer these comments as advice, not criticism.* ▪ Yield is calculated by dividing the annual return—whether in the form of dividends on stock, interest on bonds, or interest on a savings account—by the amount the particular investment will cost. *Yield is calculated by dividing the annual return—whether dividends on stock, interest on bonds, or interest on a savings account—by the amount the particular investment will cost.*

in the function of *as.*

in (into) the future *at length; before long; eventually; in a month (week); in due time; in time; later; next month (year); one day; over time; someday; sometime; ultimately; with time; yet;* delete. All indications are that these patterns of change will continue into the future. *All indications are that these patterns will continue.* ▪ Sales have begun to level off and are expected to decline in the future. *Sales have begun to level off and are expected to decline.* ▪ And it's going to get worse in the future. *And it's going to get worse in time.* ▪ If in the future OSF comes up with something the industry considers valuable, we will applaud their efforts and incorporate it into future releases of Unix. *If OSF comes up with something the industry considers valuable, we will applaud their efforts and incorporate it into future releases of Unix.* ▪ In the world as a whole, there is an installed base of nearly half a billion local telephone lines that will be replaced by new digital technology in the future. *In the world as a whole, there is an installed base of nearly half a billion local telephone lines that will someday be replaced by new digital technology.* ▪ Maybe in the future we'll buy a house. *Maybe one day we'll buy a house.*

in the immediate future *at once; before long; directly; immediately; in a month (week); momentarily; next month (year); (just; right) now; presently; quickly; shortly; soon; straightaway; this month (year); tomorrow;* delete. I don't anticipate any layoffs in the immediate future. *I don't anticipate any layoffs immediately.* ▪ Few analysts think that is likely in the immediate future. *Few analysts think that is likely now.* ▪ Because the resultant new agency is expected to grow in the immediate future, an additional dozen or so creative and account executives will be hired. *Because the resultant new agency is expected to grow soon, an additional dozen or so creative and account executives will be hired.* ▪ Analysts project this investment will impact AFP's book earnings in the immediate future. *Analysts project this investment will shortly impact AFP's book earnings.* ▪ Of course, she'll go eventually, but not in the immediate future. *Of course, she'll go eventually, but not this month.*

in the immediate past *a few months (years) ago; lately; not long ago; of late; recent; recently;* delete. Computer software consulting firms constitute a growth node that will probably continue, but alone it cannot generate the numbers of jobs that have been generated in the immediate past. *Computer software consulting firms constitute a growth node that will probably continue, but alone it cannot generate the number of jobs that have been recently generated.*

in the interest of (-ing) *for; so as to; to.* The secretary took this action in the interest of ensuring an equitable investigation. *The secretary took this action to ensure an equitable investigation.* ▪ He was acting in the interest of his client. *He was acting for his client.* ▪ Supposedly in the interest of making the analytic situation more egalitarian and less authoritarian, he bared his soul to his patients, enlisting their aid by making each of them into his psychoanalyst. *Supposedly to make the analytic situation more egalitarian and less authoritarian, he bared his soul to his patients, enlisting their aid by making each of them into his psychoanalyst.*

in the interim *meantime; meanwhile.* In the interim, the Company encourages you to pursue other opportunities that may present themselves to you with respect to the Materials provided to the Company. *Meanwhile, the Company encourages you to pursue other opportunities that may present themselves to you with respect to the Materials provided to the Company.* ■ In the interim, law enforcement agencies are bracing for the worst. *Meantime, law enforcement agencies are bracing for the worst.*

in the interval *meantime; meanwhile.*

in the judgment of *assert; believe; claim; consider; contend; feel; hold; judge; maintain; regard; say; think; to; view; with.* In the judgment of these scientists, it has hurt the effort. *These scientists believe it has hurt the effort.* ■ In the judgment of the writers, this figure includes only those state and local revenue sources that impose an involuntary tax burden mainly on residents of the states by which they are collected. *To the writers, this figure includes only those state and local revenue sources that impose an involuntary tax burden mainly on residents of the states by which they are collected.*

in the least (slightest) *at all; delete.* I don't mind in the least. *I don't mind at all.*

in (over) the long run *at length; eventually; in the end; in time; later; long-term; one day; over the months (years); over time; someday; sometime; ultimately; with time; yet.* BCH doctors said they hope the treatments will save money in the long run by preventing bouts of PCP that require expensive hospitalization. *BCH doctors said they hope the treatments will ultimately save money by preventing bouts of PCP that require expensive hospitalization.* ■ Kids who are depressed tend to medicate their bad feelings with drugs and alcohol, but since alcohol is a depressant, it tends to exacerbate the depressed feelings over the long run. *Kids who are depressed tend to medicate their bad feelings with drugs and alcohol, but since alcohol is a depressant, it tends to exacerbate the depressed feelings over time.* ■ In the long run, presumably fewer citizens would require Medicaid. *In time, presumably fewer citizens would require Medicaid.* ■ Most entrepreneurs can use all the help they can get in developing and implementing the tactics that will make them successful in the long run. *Most entrepreneurs can use all the help they can get in developing and implementing the tactics that will one day make them successful.* ■ He reported that import restrictions would not be cost effective and, in the long run, would impair national security. *He reported that import restrictions would not be cost effective and, at length, would impair national security.*

in (over) the long term *at length; eventually; in the end; in time; later; long-term; one day; over the months (years); over time; someday; sometime; ultimately; with time; yet.* There is another part—perhaps not as obvious as the abandoned mines, shrinking onetime boomtowns, and partially filled office towers, but every bit as real and, in the long term, much more significant. *There is another part—perhaps not as obvious as the abandoned mines, shrinking onetime boom-towns, and partially filled office towers, but every bit as real and, in the end, much more significant.* ■ But we have the highest theft and arson rate in the country and I think this will have an effect over the long term. *But we have the highest theft and arson rate in the country and I think this will ultimately have an effect.* ■ How will the two investments compare over the long term? *How will the two investments compare over time?*

in the main *almost all; chiefly; commonly; generally; greatly; in general; largely; mainly; most; mostly; most often; much; nearly all; normally; overall; typically; usually.* In the main, politicians have become contemptuous of voters. *Generally, politicians have become contemptuous of voters.*

in the making *brewing; developing; forming.* The teams go into action when computers at the National Weather Service foresee a disturbance in the making. *The teams go into action when computers at the National Weather Service foresee a disturbance brewing.*

in (on) the matter of *about; as for; as to; concerning; for; in; of; on; over; regarding; respecting; to; toward; with;* delete. All of these factors assume you have a choice in the matter of where you will hold your meeting, while the truth is that you may not. *All of these factors assume you have a choice in where you will hold your meeting, while the truth is that you may not.* ■ His beliefs are opposite those of the president on the matter of abortion. *His beliefs are opposite those of the president on abortion.* ■ On the matter of the ordination of women, there is not a common theological mind or agreed-on practice. *As to the ordination of women, there is not a common theological mind or agreed-on practice.*

in the meantime *meantime; meanwhile.* In the meantime, I will discuss the software potential with our people and see if we can come up with some preliminary conclusions. *Meantime, I will discuss the software potential with our people and see if we can come up with some preliminary conclusions.* ■ In the meantime, they want to assure that any modernization of the arsenal serves real needs rather than the parochial interests of the services and their suppliers. *Meanwhile, they want to assure that any modernization of the arsenal serves real needs rather than the parochial interests of the services and their suppliers.*

in the middle of *amid; among; during; in; in between; inside; through; within.* Charles said that Britain was in the middle of another building boom and the important question was "whether we can get it right this time." *Charles said that Britain was amid another building boom and the important question was "whether we can get it right this time."* ■ The industry is in the middle of a price war because it is overcapitalized. *The industry is in a price war because it is overcapitalized.*

in the middle (midst) of -ing *-ing*. We are currently in the middle of improving these signs with new panels and brighter lighting. *We are currently improving these signs with new panels and brighter lighting.* ■ He said he had first thought of leaving while in the midst of negotiating the settlement earlier this year of the insider trading and stock manipulation case. *He said he had first thought of leaving while negotiating the settlement earlier this year of the insider trading and stock manipulation case.*

in the midst of *amid; among; during; in; in between; inside; through; within*. In the midst of John Kennedy's presidency, when he had some fierce showdowns with business over matters such as price increases, printed cards made the rounds of Wall Street promoting "the Kennedy cocktail—stocks on the rocks." *During John Kennedy's presidency, when he had some fierce showdowns with business over matters such as price increases, printed cards made the rounds of Wall Street promoting "the Kennedy cocktail—stocks on the rocks."* ■ Federal and state authorities are in the midst of a criminal investigation of whether an unreported series of leaks and spills was linked to groundwater polluted by more than 55 chemicals. *Federal and state authorities are amid a criminal investigation of whether an unreported series of leaks and spills was linked to groundwater polluted by more than 55 chemicals.* ■ Their fear is that they have been in the midst of people who are not of them. *Their fear is that they have been among people who are not of them.*

in the nature of *akin to; close to; like; resembling; similar to; such as*. These days it takes something in the nature of a reception with the Queen Mother to get the Maxwells together. *These days it takes something like a reception with the Queen Mother to get the Maxwells together.*

(something; somewhere) in the nature (of) *about; around; close to; more or less; near; nearly; or so; roughly; some; delete*. The owners anticipate production to be in the nature of 3,000 gallons weekly. *The owners anticipate production to be around 3,000 gallons weekly.*

in the (very) near future *before long; directly; in a month (week); next month (year); presently; quickly; shortly; soon; this month (year); tomorrow; delete*. I will visit my mother's grave site in the near future. *I will visit my mother's grave site next week.* ■ It is still not entirely bugfree, so we can look forward to at least one more version in the near future. *It is still not entirely bugfree, so we can look forward to at least one more version shortly.* ■ I'm hoping my client will be bailed out in the near future. *I'm hoping my client will be bailed out presently.* ■ Consumers should not expect to see the computerized recorders on retailers' shelves any time in the near future. *Consumers should not expect to see the computerized recorders on retailers' shelves any time soon.* ■ In the near future, it will supply company managements with critical measures of the value, use, capabilities, and costs of information systems. *Before long, it will supply company managements with critical measures of the value, use, capabilities, and costs of information systems.* ■ We hope to make the announcement in the very near future. *We hope to make the announcement tomorrow.* ■ I look forward to hearing from you in the near future. *I look forward to hearing from you in a month.*

in the (very) near past   *a few months (years) ago; before; earlier; formerly; lately; not long ago; of late; once; recent; recently;* delete.

in (over) the near term   *at first; at present; before long; currently; directly; for now; in (over) a month (week); initially; next month (year); now; presently; short-term; this month (year);* delete. That, perhaps, best sums up what to expect from AI in the near term. *That, perhaps, best sums up what to expect from AI for now.* ■ The prospects for Mideast peace, at least in the near term, do not seem any better than they have been. *The prospects for Mideast peace, at least this year, do not seem any better than they have been.*

in the negative   *negatively; no; unfavorably.*

in the neighborhood (of)   *close by; close to; near; nearby; neighboring.* "Everything around here shook," said a young woman who works at a restaurant in the neighborhood. *"Everything around here shook," said a young woman who works at a nearby restaurant.*

(something; somewhere) in the neighborhood (of)   *about; around; close to; more or less; near; nearly; or so; roughly; some;* delete. We have somewhere in the neighborhood of 6 million illegal aliens in this country. *We have about 6 million illegal aliens in this country.* ■ The one-day record for most money won is in the neighborhood of $23,000. *The one-day record for most money won is around $23,000.* ■ The privately held company now employs about 700 people and has annual revenues in the neighborhood of $100 million. *The privately held company now employs about 700 people and has annual revenues close to $100 million.* ■ Tenneco Inc. and Texaco Inc. have the largest blocks of properties on the market, with a combined price tag that analysts say is in the neighborhood of $6 billion. *Tenneco Inc. and Texaco Inc. have the largest blocks of properties on the market, with a combined price tag that analysts say is roughly $6 billion.* ■ We're probably looking at something in the neighborhood of $100 million. *We're probably looking at some $100 million.*

in the next place   *also; and; as well; besides; beyond that (this); further; furthermore; in addition; moreover; more than that (this); next; second; still more; too; what is more.*

in the normal (ordinary; typical; usual) course of business (events; things)   *as usual; commonly; customarily; normally; ordinarily; typically; usually.* In the normal course of events, the MLI command starts finishing up by restoring the values of the X and Y registers and then by executing a JSR $BF09 instruction. *Normally, the MLI command starts finishing up by restoring the values of the X and Y registers and then by executing a JSR $BF09 instruction.* ■ In the ordinary course of events, they wouldn't go to court over something like this. *Ordinarily, they wouldn't go to court over something like this.* ■ American Policyholders Insurance Co. was not put under receivership, and all its claims will be paid in the normal course of business. *American Policyholders Insurance Co. was not put under receivership, and all its claims will be paid as usual.*

in the not-so-distant (not-too-distant) future *before long; directly; in a month (week); next month (year); presently; quickly; shortly; soon; this month (year); tomorrow;* delete. This pattern has been maintained for many years and is likely to be followed in the not-too-distant future by others. *This pattern has been maintained for many years and is likely to be soon followed by others.* ■ We'll be coming out with some new communications products in the not-too-distant future. *We'll be coming out with some new communications products shortly.* ■ He says that just as the horseless carriage re-emerged as the automobile and wireless telegraph became radio, hopefully in the not-too-distant future artificial intelligence will become something else. *He says that just as the horseless carriage re-emerged as the automobile and wireless telegraph became radio, hopefully before long artificial intelligence will become something else.* ■ Companies that are now creating corporate cultures that include minorities will be better positioned to meet the challenges of domestic and international markets in the not-too-distant future. *Companies that are now creating corporate cultures that include minorities will presently be better positioned to meet the challenges of domestic and international markets.*

in the not-so-distant (not-too-distant) past *a few months (years) ago; before; earlier; formerly; lately; not long ago; of late; once; recent; recently;* delete. In the not-so-distant past, people could have dropped out of high school and gotten a decent-paying job in manufacturing. *Not long ago, people could have dropped out of high school and gotten a decent-paying job in manufacturing.*

in the opinion of *assert; believe; claim; consider; contend; feel; hold; judge; maintain; regard; say; think; to; view; with.* The Wall Street inside-information scandal could pull in yet another circle of white-collar criminals in the opinion of criminal lawyers and securities specialists. *Criminal lawyers and securities specialists contend the Wall Street inside-information scandal could pull in yet another circle of white-collar criminals.* ■ A compromise was enacted, and the Twin Cities Metropolitan Council went on to become, in the opinion of many, the most innovative and successful effort at metropolitan governance in the nation. *A compromise was enacted, and the Twin Cities Metropolitan Council went on to become, many believe, the most innovative and successful effort at metropolitan governance in the nation.*

in the opposite direction from (of) *against.* Many bicyclists do not observe traffic signals, ride in the opposite direction of motor traffic, and fail to signal when overtaking pedestrians. *Many bicyclists do not observe traffic signals, ride against motor traffic, and fail to signal when overtaking pedestrians.*

in the overall scope (sphere) of things *overall;* delete. In the overall sphere of things, a vast majority of tax problems never reach the courts, particularly not as criminal prosecutions. *Overall, a vast majority of tax problems never reach the courts, particularly not as criminal prosecutions.*

in the past *before; earlier; formerly; once;* delete. You said, in the past, that you weren't interested in the vice presidency. *Earlier you said that you weren't interested in the vice presidency.* ■ Individuals tend to find security in the ways things have been done in the past. *Individuals tend to find security in the ways things have once been done.* ■ PSATs have been offered to students in the past, but few took them. *PSATs have been offered to students before, but few took them.* ■ In the past, main memory was rather small because it was very expensive. *Formerly, main memory was rather small because it was very expensive.* ■ The U.S. government has often placed restrictions on foreign investments in certain parts of the world in the past. *The U.S. government has often placed restrictions on foreign investments in certain parts of the world.* ■ We've witnessed promises made in the past by Vietnam that were not carried out. *We've witnessed promises made by Vietnam that were not carried out.* ■ The traditional signal for a recession in the past has been at least three consecutive monthly declines in the index. *The traditional signal for a recession has been at least three consecutive monthly declines in the index.*

in (over) the past few (several) days (decades; months; weeks; years) *lately; of late; recent; recently.* Neural networks have generated much interest, not to mention hype, in the past few years. *Neural networks have lately generated much interest, not to mention hype.*

in the position of *as.*

in the presence of *alongside; among; beside; during; in; with.* On only one occasion was I in the presence of Jack and Sam at the same time. *On only one occasion was I with Jack and Sam at the same time.* ■ In the presence of a heart attack, both skeletal and cardiac enzyme levels will be high. *During a heart attack, both skeletal and cardiac enzyme levels will be high.*

in the process of -ing *-ing.* I'm in the process of cleaning the house. *I'm cleaning the house.* ■ In the process of doing so, he threw out some good material. *In doing so, he threw out some good material.* ■ Prison guards are still in the process of removing some of the inmates. *Prison guards are still removing some of the inmates.* ■ It looks as if we are in the process of repeating the experience of more than 100 years ago. *It looks as if we are repeating the experience of more than 100 years ago.* ■ The company is in the process of changing the regulatory framework in most of its states. *The company is changing the regulatory framework in most of its states.* ■ No publication date has been set for the book, which is in the process of being written. *No publication date has been set for the book, which is being written.*

in the proximity (of) *close by; close to; near; nearby.* Cosmic gamma ray bursts appear to originate in the proximity of neutron stars, but the sources have never been pinned down. *Cosmic gamma ray bursts appear to originate near neutron stars, but the sources have never been pinned down.*

(something; somewhere) in the range from (of) ... through (to) *between ... and; from ... to; to;* delete. According to a recent study by Arthur Anderson & Co., the cost of drilling new wells is in the range of $6 to $8 a barrel. *According to a recent study by Arthur Anderson & Co., the cost of drilling new wells is between $6 and $8 a barrel.* ■ Reebok projects earnings for 1988 to be in the range of $1.40 to $1.45 a share, which suggests a net income of $159 million to $165.5 million. *Reebok projects earnings for 1988 to be from $1.40 to $1.45 a share, which suggests a net income of $159 million to $165.5 million.* ■ It said earnings would be in the range of 40 to 50 cents a share. *It said earnings would be 40 to 50 cents a share.*

(something; somewhere) in the ... range (of) *about; around; close to; more or less; near; nearly; or so; roughly; some;* delete. The price tag on the three-city shuttle was in the range of $200 million. *The price tag on the three-city shuttle was about $200 million.* ■ In the last 52 weeks, the stock has had a high of $199 and a low of $91, and currently is in the $93 range. *In the last 52 weeks, the stock has had a high of $199 and a low of $91, and currently is around $93.* ■ I don't know what the latest cost estimates are, but it's got to be in the range of $25 billion. *I don't know what the latest cost estimates are, but it's got to be close to $25 billion.* ■ The chief executive officer recently announced a record year for sales, projected to be in the range of $135 million. *The chief executive officer recently announced a record year for sales, projected to be some $135 million.*

in the realm of *about; as for; as to; concerning; for; in; of; on; over; regarding; respecting; to; toward; with;* delete. Furthermore, in the realm of strategic nuclear weapons, he has overseen not reductions but improvements. *Furthermore, in strategic nuclear weapons, he has overseen not reductions but improvements.*

(something; somewhere) in the realm (of) *about; around; close to; more or less; near; nearly; or so; roughly; some;* delete. The company expects to employ somewhere in the realm of 300 people there by 1993. *The company expects to employ around 300 people there by 1993.*

in (within) the realm of possibility *conceivable; doable; possible; thinkable.* She said having a child is still within the realm of possibility. *She said having a child is still possible.*

in (within) the recent past *a few months (years) ago; before; earlier; formerly; lately; not long ago; of late; once; recent; recently;* delete. The belief that we have an open society in which anyone can get ahead is less true than in the recent past. *The belief that we have an open society in which anyone can get ahead is less true than before.* ■ A building with clothes is better than some of the naked buildings we've built in Boston in the recent past. *A building with clothes is better than some of the naked buildings we've built in Boston recently.* ■ In the recent past, projects that supported higher education or the arts have been considered frivolous or useless by state officials. *Recent projects that supported higher education or the arts have been considered frivolous or useless by state officials.*

(something; somewhere) in the region (of) *about; around; close to; more or less; near; nearly; or so; roughly; some;* delete. That's on top of an additional estimated increase in food prices somewhere in the region of 4 percent. *That's on top of an additional estimated increase in food prices of about 4 percent.*

in the role of *as.*

in the same fashion (manner; way) (as; that) *as (be); like; the same as.* Though not necessarily displayed on the screen, hard carriage returns are much like other characters you enter in a document; therefore, you delete them in the same way you would other characters. *Though not necessarily displayed on the screen, hard carriage returns are much like other characters you enter in a document; therefore, you delete them as you would other characters.* ■ The MBNA BusinessCard can be used in the same manner as a personal credit card, but offers a host of features and benefits exclusively designed to fit your business needs. *The MBNA BusinessCard can be used like a personal credit card, but offers a host of features and benefits exclusively designed to fit your business needs.* ■ The cigarette is consumed in the same manner as current regular brands, but the heat from the element warms the tobacco and capsule, thereby delivering taste and nicotine. *The cigarette is consumed as current regular brands are, but the heat from the element warms the tobacco and capsule, thereby delivering taste and nicotine.*

in the second place *also; and; as well; besides; beyond that (this); further; furthermore; in addition; moreover; more than that (this); next; second; still more; too; what is more.*

in the sense that *because; considering; for; in that; since.* Foreign and domestic marketing are the same in the sense that the purpose is to create and manage profitable exchange relationships. *Foreign and domestic marketing are the same in that the purpose is to create and manage profitable exchange relationships.* ■ The Jewish experience in the United States is unique in the sense that, more than any other immigrant group, Jews have found their way into almost every interstice of American life, have taken just about every opportunity this nation has to offer, and have given back to America in enriching ways that are wondrous. *The Jewish experience in the United States is unique since more than any other immigrant group, Jews have found their way into almost every interstice of American life, have taken just about every opportunity this nation has to* *offer, and have given back to America in enriching ways that are won-drous.* ■ This system is anarchic in the sense that it consists of sovereign states that recognize no formal authority greater than themselves. *This system is anar-chic because it consists of sovereign states that recognize no formal authority greater than themselves.*

in the sense of *that is;* delete. He is in a peculiar—in the sense of unusual—position. *He is in a peculiar—that is, unusual—position.*

in (over) the short run *at first; at present; before long; currently; directly; for now; in (over) a month (week); initially; next month (year); now; presently; short-term; this month (year); delete.* The tax-cut proposal is the nutritional equivalent of a diet of beer: in the short run, it fills you up and gives you a buzz, but eventually it devastates the body. *The tax-cut proposal is the nutritional equivalent of a diet of beer: at first, it fills you up and gives you a buzz, but eventually it devastates the body.*

in (over) the short term *at first; at present; before long; currently; directly; for now; in (over) a month (week); initially; next month (year); now; presently; short-term; this month (year); delete.* In the short term, ecologists expect the coming cold to claim a large number of elk from the park's northern herd, which spends its winters pawing for food beneath the snow. *This season, ecologists expect the coming cold to claim a large number of elk from the park's northern herd, which spends its winters pawing for food beneath the snow.* ■ People who can with-stand fluctuations over the short term are virtually guaranteed a profit in the stock market. *People who can withstand short-term fluctuations are virtually guaran-teed a profit in the stock market.*

in the support of (-ing) *for; so as to; to.*

in the ... through (to) ... range *between ... and; from ... to; to.* Whether they will be willing to pay a base price rumored to be in the $3,000 to $6,000 range remains to be answered. *Whether they will be willing to pay a base price rumored to be between $3,000 and $6,000 remains to be answered.*

in the unexpected (unlikely) event of (that) *if (there were); if ... should; should (there); were (there; . . . to); delete.* In the unexpected event that those costs exceed $30 million, other joint owners would be obligated. *Should those costs exceed $30 million, other joint owners would be obligated.* ■ The information could be used, for example, in the unlikely event of an emergency at Seabrook Station. *The information could be used, for example, were there an emergency at Seabrook Station.* ■ The employees will have a greater voice in the conduct of Procter & Gamble's business and be in a better position to influence the outcome in the unlikely event of a takeover attempt. *The employees will have a greater voice in the conduct of Procter & Gamble's business and be in a better position to influence the outcome if there is a takeover attempt.* ■ In the unlikely event of my death, please see that my body is cremated and my ashes sent home. *Were I to die, please see that my body is cremated and my ashes sent home.*

in the vicinity (of) *close by; close to; near; nearby.* It was last seen in the vicinity of the Abbot Street Bridge. *It was last seen near the Abbot Street Bridge.* ■ I would put it on a shelf in the vicinity of Aleksandr Solzhenitsyn's *Gulag,* so compelling is its testimony and analysis. *I would put it on a shelf close to Aleksandr Solzhenitsyn's Gulag, so compelling is its testimony and analysis.* ■ I want you to stay in the vicinity. *I want you to stay nearby.*

(something; somewhere) in the vicinity (of) *about; around; close to; more or less; near; nearly; or so; roughly; some;* delete. On its best day, my corporation earned in the vicinity of $2 million. *On its best day, my corporation earned around $2 million.*

in the view of *assert; believe; claim; consider; contend; feel; hold; judge; maintain; regard; say; think; to; view; with.* In the view of many analysts, the new employment data raise the possibility that the central bank won't feel obliged to tighten credit any further at least through the November elections. *To many analysts, the new employment data raise the possibility that the central bank won't feel obliged to tighten credit any further at least through the November elections.* ■ In the view of some strategists, he may lose the election unless he can reverse his fortunes on this issue. *Some strategists think he may lose the election unless he can reverse his fortunes on this issue.*

in the wake of *(just; right) after; because of; (close) behind; due to; ensuing; following; from; owing to; succeeding.* In the wake of an office and shopping-center boom comes an employment boom in business custodians. *Following an office and shopping-center boom comes an employment boom in business custodians.* ■ The Cyprus problem arose in the wake of intercommunal clashes in 1963 that led to the dispatch of a UN peace force to the island. *The Cyprus problem arose after intercommunal clashes in 1963 that led to the dispatch of a UN peace force to the island.* ■ In the wake of these changes, several top-level sales executives have quit. *Because of these changes, several top-level sales executives have quit.*

in the way of delete. All of us enter our career fields with enthusiasm and varying expectations about what lies ahead in the way of rewards and demands on our time and talents. *All of us enter our career fields with enthusiasm and varying expectations about what rewards and demands on our time and talents lie ahead.* ■ This step requires that you research jobs to determine what they call for in the way of education, skills, and aptitudes. *This step requires that you research jobs to determine what education, skills, and aptitudes they call for.* ■ There is little motivation for long periods of foolishness, and there is much in the way of market discipline to prevent it. *There is little motivation for long periods of foolishness, and there is much market discipline to prevent it.*

in thickness *thick;* delete. In their theoretical analysis, Gaylord and Brennan consider a filter consisting of nine layers, each layer a quarter or a half of the electron wavelength in thickness. *In their theoretical analysis, Gaylord and Brennan consider a filter consisting of nine layers, each layer a quarter or a half of the electron wavelength thick.*

intimately familiar *familiar; intimate.*

in times like the present *at present; currently; (just; right) now; nowadays; presently; these days; today.* In times like the present, when the dollar's value is in decline, the offshore financial services industry finds itself in the worst of all possible worlds. *Today, when the dollar's value is in decline, the offshore financial services industry finds itself in the worst of all possible worlds.*

in (the) time(s) of *amid; during; in; over; throughout.* The substantial risk of investment in junk bonds, particularly in times of economic uncertainty, is often disregarded by small investors. *The substantial risk of investment in junk bonds, particularly amid economic uncertainty, is often disregarded by small investors.* ■ In the time of the Great Depression, it was common for people to have five, six, or more children. *During the Great Depression, it was common for people to have five, six, or more children.*

in ... tones *-(al)ly;* delete. Police officers trooped into every grammar school in the city to talk with kids, explaining in dispassionate tones the use and abuse of crack. *Police officers trooped into every grammar school in the city to talk with kids, explaining dispassionately the use and abuse of crack.*

in trade (for) *for.*

introduce (a; the) new *introduce.* In 1983, Apple introduced a new, easier-to-use computer called the Lisa. *In 1983, Apple introduced an easier-to-use computer called the Lisa.* ■ He said both today and tomorrow would be bank holidays to give time to introduce the new monetary measures. *He said both today and tomorrow would be bank holidays to give time to introduce the monetary measures.*

inure to the benefit of *inure to.* This agreement shall be binding upon and inure to the benefit of the executors, administrators, and assigns of the Author and of the Client. *This agreement shall be binding upon and inure to the executors, administrators, and assigns of the Author and of the Client.*

in (to; with) various (varying) degrees (extents) *in part; in some way; more or less; partially; partly; rather; some; somehow; someway(s); somewhat; to some degree (extent); various; variously; varying; varyingly;* delete. All foreign marketing efforts depend, to varying degrees, on the marketing resources, capabilities, and experience of the parent company. *All foreign marketing efforts varyingly depend on the marketing resources, capabilities, and experience of the* *parent company.* ▪ These minicomputer makers are all, in various degrees, struggling to come to terms with the changing demands of computer languages. *These minicomputer makers are all, in some way, struggling to come to terms with the changing demands of computer languages.*

invidious discrimination *discrimination; invidiousness.*

in view of the fact that *because; considering; for; in that; since; when.* These results are particularly interesting in view of the fact that Christian Scientists are forbidden to either smoke or drink. *These results are particularly interesting considering Christian Scientists are forbidden to either smoke or drink.* ▪ Little emphasis is placed on speaking, and almost no attention has been given to the skill of listening, strange as this may be in view of the fact that so much lecturing is done in college. *Little emphasis is placed on speaking, and almost no attention has been given to the skill of listening, strange as this may be when so much lecturing is done in college.* ▪ While this goal is ambitious, it is not beyond reach, particularly in view of the fact that the college has surpassed its annual goal funds for each of the last two years. *While this goal is ambitious, it is not beyond reach, particularly since the college has surpassed its annual goal funds for each of the last two years.*

in view of the fact that *whereas.*

invited guest *guest.*

involve *for; in; mean; of; with;* delete. Census II involves using several different types of moving averages to identify trends and outliers within a data set. *Census II uses several different types of moving averages to identify trends and outliers within a data set.* ▪ Weld will be paid more than $200,000 a year to defend cases involving white collar crime. *Weld will be paid more than $200,000 a year to defend cases of white collar crime.* ▪ Foreign marketing involves crossing national borders and thus is concerned with a unique set of issues and problems. *Foreign marketing means crossing national borders and thus is concerned with a unique set of issues and problems.* ▪ Emergency-room admissions involving cocaine abuse have nearly doubled each year since 1984. *Emergency-room admissions for cocaine abuse have nearly doubled each year since 1984.* ▪ The operation is self-sustaining and has operated with no public-sector funding involved. *The operation is self-sustaining and has operated with no public-sector funding.*

involved in *in; of; within;* delete. The costs involved in refurbishing the building are prohibitive. *The costs of refurbishing the building are prohibitive.* ▪ How many times have you been involved in a conversation and tuned out the speaker? *How many times have you been in a conversation and tuned out the speaker?* ▪ He has been involved in organizing veterans since the outset of the case. *He has been organizing veterans since the outset of the case.* ▪ We are currently involved in updating our list. *We are currently updating our list.*

in (a; the) ... way *-(al)ly;* delete. Each of these variations can be revised in a different way. *Each of these variations can be revised differently.* ▪ Computer systems differ in a significant way from stereos. *Computer systems differ significantly from stereos.* ▪ Every group that has scrutinized this product in an impartial way agrees it is safe. *Every group that has impartially scrutinized this product agrees it is safe.* ▪ They're looking for permission to behave in a human way. *They're looking for permission to behave humanly.* ▪ These people were acting in violent ways. *These people were acting violently.* ▪ She treated him in a loving way. *She treated him lovingly.* ▪ He said it in a joking way. *He said it jokingly.* ▪ A home equity credit line with VISA card access or a variable-rate CD marketed in an aggressive way would probably work better with an empty nest, planner and dealer. *A home equity credit line with VISA card access or a variable-rate CD aggressively marketed would probably work better with an empty nest, planner and dealer.*

in whatever (whichever) fashion (manner; way) *despite how; however.* In whatever way it comes, the decision will be an important one. *Despite how it comes, the decision will be an important one.* ▪ They should be allowed to make the 5-percent across-the-board cut in whatever fashion they choose. *They should be allowed to make the 5-percent across-the-board cut however they choose.*

in what (which) fashion (manner; way) *how.* In what fashion does imaging technology offer potential competitive advantage? *How does imaging technology offer potential competitive advantage?*

in what (which) regard (respect) *how.* In what respect was this investment "tax free"? *How was this investment "tax free"?*

in width *wide;* delete. In high-performance hard disks, these tracks are roughly 1 micrometer in width. *In high-performance hard disks, these tracks are roughly 1 micrometer wide.*

irregardless of *despite; no matter; regardless of.*

irrelevancy *irrelevance.*

irrespective of (what) *despite (what); no matter what; regardless of; whatever.* The product-first approach meant marketing the same product to all customers, irrespective of their profiles. *The product-first approach meant marketing the same product to all customers, regardless of their profiles.* ▪ Irrespective of the reasons, the voters simply do not want to participate in a collaborative project. *No matter what the reasons, the voters simply do not want to participate in a collaborative project.* ▪ Irrespective of the genesis of the original product, the experience and perceptions of international marketing managers and overseas customers must be taken into account prior to product modification. *Despite the genesis of the original product, the experience and perceptions of international marketing managers and overseas customers must be taken into account prior to* *product modification.* ■ It is time for all of us to do something, irrespective of the odds or risks, about what we know to be important and just. *It is time for all of us to do something, whatever the odds or risks, about what we know to be important and just.*

irrespective of how *despite how; however; no matter how; regardless of how.* The margins are retained irrespective of how many characters are printed per inch. *The margins are retained despite how many characters are printed per inch.* ■ Both have the same percentage irrespective of how much they have been reduced or enlarged if they have the same percentage rating. *Both have the same percentage no matter how much they have been reduced or enlarged if they have the same percentage rating.*

irrespective of the fact that *although; but; even though; still; though; yet.*

irrespective of when *despite when; no matter when; regardless of when; whenever.*

irrespective of where *despite where; no matter where; regardless of where; wherever.* A successful company must have the necessary skill sets to meet the needs and wants of its customers irrespective of where they may do business. *A successful company must have the necessary skill sets to meet the needs and wants of its customers wherever they may do business.* ■ A properly drawn working drawing will result in the same product time and again, irrespective of where the product is made. *A properly drawn working drawing will result in the same product time and again, despite where the product is made.*

irrespective of whether ... (or) *despite whether; no matter whether; regardless of whether; whether ... or (not).* One delegate said his parish would continue to raise money for its diocese irrespective of whether the archdiocesan assessment is met. *One delegate said his parish would continue to raise money for its diocese whether or not the archdiocesan assessment is met.*

irrespective of which *despite which; no matter which; regardless of which; whichever.*

irrespective of who *despite who; no matter who; regardless of who; whoever.*

irrespective of whom *despite whom; no matter whom; regardless of whom; whomever.*

... is ... (that; which; who; whom) delete. Batch files are files that contain commands that are executed automatically when you turn on your computer or type the batch file's name. *Batch files contain commands that are executed automatically when you turn on your computer or type the batch file's name.* ■ Domestic corporations are corporations that do business in the state in which they are chartered, and foreign corporations are corporations that do business outside their chartered state. *Domestic corporations do business in the state in which they are chartered, and foreign corporations do business outside their chartered state.*

is able to *can.* Investors are able to buy and sell any quantity of securities. *Investors can buy and sell any quantity of securities.* ■ But not all Chinese are able to do that. *But not all Chinese can do that.*

is (was) accustomed to (-ing) *will (would).* They are accustomed to talking until late into the night. *They will talk until late into the night.*

is a consequence of *arises from; results from; stems from.*

is a contribution to *contributes to.* This is a continuing contribution to a company's profitability. *This continually contributes to a company's profitability.*

is acquainted with *knows.*

is a demonstration of *demonstrates; shows; proves.*

is a description of *describes.* The attached proposal is a brief description of what I have in mind. *The attached proposal briefly describes what I have in mind.*

is a deterrent to *blocks; deters; hinders; impedes; prevents; stops; thwarts.*

is advantageous for (to) *aids; benefits; favors; helps.*

is afraid of (to) *dreads; fears; frets (about; over); stews (about; over); worries (about; over).*

is a function of *depends on; relates to.* The popularity of fixed-rate versus adjustable-rate mortgages seems to be a function of the level of interest rates. *The popularity of fixed-rate versus adjustable-rate mortgages seems to depend on the level of interest rates.*

is a hindrance to *blocks; deters; hinders; impedes; prevents; stops; thwarts.* A problem is any organizational issue that could be a hindrance to organizational success. *A problem is any organizational issue that could hinder organizational success.*

is an acquaintance of *knows.* Mr. Branch was an acquaintance of Miss Gregory. *Mr. Branch knew Miss Gregory.*

is an illustration of *illustrates*. I believe that these moves by Texaco are a perfect illustration of the precept that a clear and closer relationship between active ownership and management will increase productivity. *I believe that these moves by Texaco perfectly illustrate the precept that a clear and closer relationship between active ownership and management will increase productivity.*

is an impediment to *blocks; deters; hinders; impedes; prevents; stops; thwarts.*

is an indication (indicator) of *indicates; shows; signals; signifies; suggests.* Internal company projects to develop expert system applications are a strong indication of the nature of the opportunity for AI system vendors. *Internal company projects to develop expert system applications strongly suggest the nature of the opportunity for AI system vendors.* ■ The progress made in that short span of time is an indicator of the long-range growth of management. *The progress made in that short span of time indicates the long-range growth of management.* ■ The Roman holiday atmosphere reportedly surrounding the event may be an indicator of the level of civilized intercourse we have attained in this so-called advanced industrial nation. *The Roman holiday atmosphere reportedly surrounding the event may signify the level of civilized intercourse we have attained in this so-called advanced industrial nation.*

is an obstacle to *blocks; deters; hinders; impedes; prevents; stops; thwarts.*

is applicable in (to) *applies in (to); bears on; concerns; pertains to; relates to.* Regardless, the autocratic style is applicable in some situations. *Regardless, the autocratic style applies in some situations.* ■ Much of the information about ulcerative colitis is also applicable to other gastrointestinal disorders. *Much of the information about ulcerative colitis also bears on other gastrointestinal disorders.* ■ They also said their findings are only applicable to white populations since the Utah population is primarily white and descended from British and Northern European immigrants. *They also said their findings only pertain to white populations since the Utah population is primarily white and descended from British and Northern European immigrants.*

is appreciative of *appreciates; approves of; cherishes; enjoys; esteems; likes; prizes; treasures; understands; values; welcomes.* We are especially appreciative of the item which appeared in the paper citing our need for volunteers. *We especially appreciate the item which appeared in the paper citing our need for volunteers.* ■ Encouraging individuals to pursue the maximum of their capabilities in an environment that is appreciative of their differences, whether they be different backgrounds, cultures, experiences, sexes, age groups, races, or nationalities, is essential as the business world becomes more global. *Encouraging individuals to pursue the maximum of their capabilities in an environment that prizes their differences, whether they be different backgrounds, cultures, experiences, sexes, age groups, races, or nationalities, is essential as the business world becomes more global.*

is apprehensive of *dreads; fears; frets (about; over); stews (about; over); worries (about; over).* My parents were apprehensive of my going to Iran. *My parents dreaded my going to Iran.*

is appropriate in (to) *applies in (to); bears on; concerns; pertains to; relates to.*

is a (the) process that delete. Anxiety is a process that alerts people to possible dangers. *Anxiety alerts people to possible dangers.* ■ Health-care cost containment is a process that must be managed continuously. *Health-care cost containment must be managed continuously.*

is a reflection of (on; upon) *reflects (on).* Could it be that they felt the actions by the school would be a bad reflection on them? *Could it be that they felt the actions by the school would badly reflect on them?* ■ These rules were a reflection of the company's obsession with efficiency that, admirably, extended to plants and to food quality. *These rules reflected the company's obsession with efficiency that, admirably, extended to plants and to food quality.* ■ A dictionary is a reflection of the world in which we live. *A dictionary reflects the world in which we live.*

is a representation of *represents.*

is a result of *arises from; results from; stems from.*

is associated to (with) *correlates to (with); equates with; relates to.* The development of confidence and infusions of practical, useful applications seem to be associated with success in mathematics. *The development of confidence and infusions of practical, useful applications seem to relate to success in mathematics.*

is at loggerheads (with) *clashes with; conflicts with; contradicts; differs from; disagrees with; quarrels with; varies with.* He ran unsuccessfully for the Florida house and has frequently been at loggerheads with state and federal authorities. *He ran unsuccessfully for the Florida house and has frequently quarreled with state and federal authorities.*

is at odds over (with) *clashes with; conflicts with; contradicts; differs from; disagrees with; quarrels with; varies with.* She said the strong credit figures were at odds with a stream of government reports pointing toward a slowdown and did not reflect the health of the economy. *She said the strong credit figures contradicted a stream of government reports pointing toward a slowdown and did not reflect the health of the economy.* ■ These all demonstrate the extent to which the need to power our industrialized world can be at odds with the need to preserve the health of our planet. *These all demonstrate the extent to which the need to power our industrialized world can clash with the need to preserve the' health of our planet.*

is attentive to *attends to; heeds.*

is at variance with *clashes with; conflicts with; contradicts; differs from; disagrees with; quarrels with; varies with.* Cambridge BioScience officials said they withdrew the data because the results were sharply at variance with other studies of the Recombigen test and there was no time to sort out why. *Cambridge Bio-Science officials said they withdrew the data because the results sharply differed from other studies of the Recombigen test and there was no time to sort out why.* ■ It is language which avoids or shifts responsibility, language which is at variance with its real or its purported meaning. *It is language which avoids or shifts responsibility, language which conflicts with its real or its purported meaning.* ■ Although some of its particulars are at variance with what U.S. officials have heard, most key details tend to coincide. *Although some of its particulars clash with what U.S. officials have heard, most key details tend to coincide.* ■ The statement "Grief is a human emotion," implying that only human beings mourn, is at variance with much recent scientific work on animal behavior. *The statement "Grief is a human emotion," implying that only human beings mourn, contradicts much recent scientific work on animal behavior.*

is a variant of *departs from; deviates from; differs from; diverges from; varies from.* Endowment insurance policies are a variant of whole life in that, if the insured dies within a specified period, the insurance will be paid to a designated beneficiary. *Endowment insurance policies vary from whole life in that, if the insured dies within a specified period, the insurance will be paid to a designated beneficiary.*

is aware of (that) *comprehends; knows; realizes; recognizes; sees; understands.* If you are in the same position as most consumer borrowers, you should be aware that time is not on your side. *If you are in the same position as most consumer borrowers, you should realize that time is not on your side.* ■ I am aware of that. *I know that.*

is based on (upon) *rests on.* This policy is based upon three fundamental principles of competitive behavior. *This policy rests on three fundamental principles of competitive behavior.*

is beneficial to *aids; benefits; favors; helps.* Congress needs to make important decisions that will be beneficial to all Americans on a long-range basis. *Congress needs to make important decisions that will benefit all Americans on a long-range basis.* ■ Northwestern's Jacobs, however, said he expected the survey to be beneficial to both the school's recruiting and its reputation. *Northwestern's Jacobs, however, said he expected the survey to aid both the school's recruiting and its reputation.* ■ These programs should be beneficial to the future care of our aging population of veterans. *These programs should favor the future care of our aging population of veterans.*

is capable of -ing *can; is able to.* Obsolescence exists when a person or machine is no longer capable of performing to standards or management's expectations. *Obsolescence exists when a person or machine is no longer able to perform to standards or management's expectations.* ■ According to mythology, the oracle was capable of predicting the future of those who sought counsel. *According to mythology, the oracle was able to predict the future of those who sought counsel.* ■ Although the technique is capable of basing the measurements on time, it is also capable of handling the relationship of sales to other variables. *Although the technique can base the measurements on time, it can also handle the relationship of sales to other variables.* ■ Electronic eyes can inspect along moving lines of bottled products to sense proper fill levels and are capable of rejecting improperly filled bottles and shutting down the line for adjustments. *Electronic eyes can inspect along moving lines of bottled products to sense proper fill levels and can reject improperly filled bottles and shut down the line for adjustments.*

is characteristic of *characterizes; depicts; describes; designates; illustrates; pictures; portrays.* The protein tangles in brain tissue are characteristic of advanced Alzheimer's, and he speculates that A68 may be a precursor of the tangles. *The protein tangles in brain tissue characterize advanced Alzheimer's, and he speculates that A68 may be a precursor of the tangles.*

is cognizant of (that) *comprehends; knows; realizes; recognizes; sees; understands.*

is coherent with *agrees with; coheres with; concurs with; conforms to (with); corresponds to (with).*

is comparable to (with) *compares to (with); contrasts to (with); corresponds to (with); equates with; likens to; relates to; resembles.* This revolution in medicine is comparable in certain ways to the computer boom, but is more epochal. *This revolution in medicine corresponds in certain ways to the computer boom, but is more epochal.* ■ That doesn't mean we have to bid Compaq, but just something that is comparable to that model. *That doesn't mean we have to bid Compaq, but just something that compares with that model.* ■ AIDS dementia is comparable to other progressive neurological diseases like Huntington's and Parkinson's. *AIDS dementia resembles other progressive neurological diseases like Huntington's and Parkinson's.*

is compatible with *agrees with; coheres with; concurs with; conforms to (with); corresponds to (with).*

is competitive with *competes with.*

is complementary to *complements.* Banking is an obvious area for Nomura's diversification since it is complementary to the firm's securities business. *Banking is an obvious area for Nomura's diversification since it complements the firm's securities business.*

is composed of *comprises; consists of; contains; includes.* Discipline is composed of obedience, application, energy, behavior, and outward marks of respect between employers and employees. *Discipline includes obedience, application, energy, behavior, and outward marks of respect between employers and employees.* ■ The figure is composed of three main elements marked off by three lines on the chart. *The figure comprises three main elements marked off by three lines on the chart.* ■ The informal organization is composed of all the informal groupings of people within a formal organization. *The informal organization consists of all the informal groupings of people within a formal organization.*

is comprised of *comprises; consists of; contains; includes.* The marketing infrastructure is comprised of several elements that change as a country develops its industrial and service sectors. *The marketing infrastructure contains several elements that change as a country develops its industrial and service sectors.* ■ Many religions, including Islam, Hindu, Buddhism, Catholicism, and Protestantism, are comprised of many sects or denominations. *Many religions, including Islam, Hindu, Buddhism, Catholicism, and Protestantism, consist of many sects or denominations.* ■ A complete corporate strategy is comprised of an action plan for each of the four primary areas of corporate responsibility. *A complete corporate strategy comprises an action plan for each of the four primary areas of corporate responsibility.*

is concerned with *concerns; deals with; is about; pertains to; regards; relates to.* The first two complications are external and are concerned with the environment within which the company competes. *The first two complications are external and concern the environment within which the company competes.* ■ Industrial engineering is concerned with the design, improvement, and installation of integrated systems of men, materials, and equipment. *Industrial engineering deals with the design, improvement, and installation of integrated systems of men, materials, and equipment.*

is conditional (conditioned) on (upon) *depends on; hinges on.* The willingness of VSS to proceed with the transaction is conditioned upon such an agreement. *The willingness of VSS to proceed with the transaction depends on such an agreement.* ■ The offer by S&Y is conditioned on the continued management participation of Stocker & Yale's chief executive. *The offer by S&Y hinges on the continued management participation of Stocker & Yale's chief executive.*

is conducive to *conduces to.*

is connected to (with) *correlates to (with); equates with; relates to.*

is conscious of (that) *comprehends; knows; realizes; recognizes; sees; understands.*

is consistent with *agrees with; coheres with; concurs with; conforms to (with); corresponds to (with).* That statement to which the two witnesses would have testified is consistent with Janice's earlier statements to her daughter and sister-in-law and, if believed, shows that Janice had a motive to lie. *That statement to which the two witnesses would have testified agrees with Janice's earlier statements to her daughter and sister-in-law and, if believed, shows that Janice had a motive to lie.* ■ This rate is consistent with that for psychiatric referrals by pediatricians in general. *This rate corresponds to that for psychiatric referrals by pediatricians in general.* ■ This approach is consistent with earlier rulings requiring actual proof even where overwhelming numerical evidence allows a reasonable assumption of bias. *This approach conforms to earlier rulings requiring actual proof even where overwhelming numerical evidence allows a reasonable assumption of bias.*

is contemptuous of *despises; disdains; scorns.*

is contingent on (upon) *depends on; hinges on.* Success is contingent upon careful, continuous, global market research. *Success depends on careful, continuous, global market research.* ■ The deal is contingent on shareholder approval and a favorable ruling on the tax consequences of the transaction by the IRS. *The deal hinges on shareholder approval and a favorable ruling on the tax consequences of the transaction by the IRS.*

is conversant with *knows.* I wonder whether he knows any of the Asian languages or is conversant with the sources I consulted. *I wonder whether he knows any of the Asian languages or the sources I consulted.*

is critical of *complains about; condemns; criticizes.* It's easy to be critical of others if they don't agree with you. *It's easy to criticize others if they don't agree with you.* ■ Prosecutors concede that prison crowding is a severe problem, but they and other law enforcement officials have been critical of the home-release program. *Prosecutors concede that prison crowding is a severe problem, but they and other law enforcement officials have criticized the home-release program.* ■ The United States has long been critical of human rights abuse in Nicaragua. *The United States has long condemned human rights abuse in Nicaragua.*

is dangerous to *endangers; imperils; jeopardizes.*

is deficient in *lacks; wants.* In perhaps the most troubling of its recent reports, NAEP showed that while few adults in their early 20s are wholly illiterate, most are deficient in necessary skills. *In perhaps the most troubling of its recent reports, NAEP showed that while few adults in their early 20s are wholly illiterate, most lack necessary skills.*

is defined as *is; means.* Management is defined as the process of setting and achieving goals through the execution of five basic management functions that utilize human, financial, and material resources. *Management is the process of setting and achieving goals through the execution of five basic management* *functions that utilize human, financial, and material resources.* ■ Anxiety is defined as a feeling that arises from an ambiguous, unspecific cause. *Anxiety is a feeling that arises from an ambiguous, unspecific cause.* ■ If, however, poverty is defined as lacking sufficient income to purchase some minimum requisites of living, then as long as some people have incomes above this level, poverty can be reduced. *If, however, poverty means lacking sufficient income to purchase some minimum requisites of living, then as long as some people have incomes above this level, poverty can be reduced.*

is deleterious to *damages; harms; hurts; impairs; injures; mars; wrongs.*

is dependent on (upon) *depends on; hinges on.* You shouldn't be dependent upon anyone else for your happiness. *You shouldn't depend on anyone else for your happiness.* ■ Typically, the LDCs are much more dependent upon agriculture than the rich countries, where manufacturing and service activities are of greater significance. *Typically, the LDCs depend much more on agriculture than the rich countries, where manufacturing and service activities are of greater significance.* ■ The future of the business establishment is dependent upon attention to the long-range effects of current American business policies. *The future of the business establishment hinges on attention to the long-range effects of current American business policies.*

is descriptive of *characterizes; depicts; describes; designates; illustrates; pictures; portrays.* The model is descriptive of human behavior across all cultures that we have encountered. *The model describes human behavior across all cultures that we have encountered.*

is desirous of -ing *desires to; wants to; wishes to.* She is desirous of resolving this as soon as possible, so I respectfully request that you have your client consider the proposals. *She wants to resolve this as soon as possible, so I respectfully request that you have your client consider the proposals.*

is destructive of (to) *damages; destroys; harms; hurts; impairs; injures; mars; ruins.* It is a fact that some cats are destructive of property. *It is a fact that some cats destroy property.*

is detrimental to *damages; harms; hurts; impairs; injures; mars; wrongs.* Competitors of the state's largest insurer charged the proposed exclusive care plan would violate antitrust laws and insurance laws, and ultimately be detrimental to consumers. *Competitors of the state's largest insurer charged the proposed exclusive care plan would violate antitrust laws and insurance laws, and ultimately harm consumers.* ■ The concern of the EEC is that these powerful drugs would be detrimental to the children. *The concern of the EEC is that these powerful drugs would injure the children.* ■ The corporate world is detrimental to your mental as well as your economic health. *The corporate world damages your mental as well as your economic health.*

is different from *departs from; deviates from; differs from; diverges from; varies from*. If a phrase in the file on the disk is different from a phrase in the document on the screen, the command marks the entire phrase in the document on the screen. *If a phrase in the file on the disk differs from a phrase in the document on the screen, the command marks the entire phrase in the document on the screen.*

is disposed to *tends to*.

is disrespectful of (toward) *disrespects*.

is disruptive of *disrupts*. Chapter 774 is disruptive of any sense of community because all control over its future has been removed. *Chapter 774 disrupts any sense of community because all control over its future has been removed.*

is distinguished from *departs from; deviates from; differs from; diverges from; varies from*.

is distrustful about (of) *disbelieves; distrusts; doubts; mistrusts; questions*. Until students have assimilated these attitudes, they will be distrustful of scientific information. *Until students have assimilated these attitudes, they will distrust scientific information.*

is doubtful about (of) *disbelieves; distrusts; doubts; mistrusts; questions*. Many officials are doubtful about the effectiveness of Shultz's Mideast plan. *Many officials doubt the effectiveness of Shultz's Mideast plan.* ■ Other industry spokesmen were doubtful of the future for biopesticides, citing, among other worries, the risk of higher crop loss. *Other industry spokesmen questioned the future for biopesticides, citing, among other worries, the risk of higher crop loss.*

is dubious about (of) *disbelieves; distrusts; doubts; mistrusts; questions*. The A320 and the Concorde are the only commercial aircraft that use exclusively fly-by-wire controls, in part because U.S. aircraft companies are dubious about giving up tried-and-true cables—used since the Wright brothers flew—for an all-electrical system pretty much controlled by a computer. *The A320 and the Concorde are the only commercial aircraft that use exclusively fly-by-wire controls, in part because U.S. aircraft companies question giving up tried-and-true cables—used since the Wright brothers flew—for an all-electrical system pretty much controlled by a computer.*

is duplicative of *duplicates*. The Odyssey team's responsibilities are duplicative of the nursing team's. *The Odyssey team's responsibilities duplicate the nursing team's.*

is emblematic of *emblemizes; indicates; represents; signifies; stands for; symbolizes; typifies*. The kind of comprehensive care the Clinic can provide to its cancer patients is emblematic of the Clinic's overall approach to medicine. *The kind* *of comprehensive care the Clinic can provide to its cancer patients typifies the Clinic's overall approach to medicine.*

is (the) equal to *amounts to; duplicates; equals; is; matches; rivals.* The value of the emperor's palace in the center of Tokyo is equal to the value of the entire state of California. *The value of the emperor's palace in the center of Tokyo equals the value of the entire state of California.* ■ *n* is equal to the number of sides of the polygon. n *equals the number of sides of the polygon.* ■ In this query, the command specifies that the contents of the date field be displayed for records where the ID is equal to 101 and the amount is equal to $15. *In this query, the command specifies that the contents of the date field be displayed for records where the ID is 101 and the amount is $15.*

is equipped (furnished) with *comes with.* The server normally is equipped with a large-capacity hard disk drive that acts as the central file depository for everyone on the network. *The server normally comes with a large-capacity hard disk drive that acts as the central file depository for everyone on the network.*

is (the) equivalent of (to) *amounts to; duplicates; equals; is; matches; rivals.* Ideally, the amount of this fund should be the equivalent of at least three months' income. *Ideally, the amount of this fund should equal at least three months' income.*

is evidence of (that) *evinces; indicates; proves; reveals; shows; signifies; testifies (to).* The calls are evidence of the strong temptation in the judicial arena to seize on an array of recent findings on brain chemistry and behavior. *The calls testify to the strong temptation in the judicial arena to seize on an array of recent findings on brain chemistry and behavior.* ■ Last year's homicide statistics are evidence that drug dealers are killing each other. *Last year's homicide statistics prove that drug dealers are killing each other.*

is faced with *faces.* If further tests indicate increased survival of severely handicapped children following surfactant treatment, neonatologists will be faced with an ethical can of worms, in which they will have to deal with their feelings about the value of a handicapped life. *If further tests indicate increased survival of severely handicapped children following surfactant treatment, neonatologists will face an ethical can of worms, in which they will have to deal with their feelings about the value of a handicapped life.* ■ Dynamic high-technology strategy companies are faced with few national competitors. *Dynamic high-technology strategy companies face few national competitors.*

is familiar with *knows.* European participants in the computer industry know Europe extremely well, and they are familiar with the U.S. market. *European participants in the computer industry know Europe extremely well, and they know the U.S. market.* ■ Someone who is familiar with your medical history can help you evaluate the risks of fasting. *Someone who knows your medical history can help you evaluate the risks of fasting.*

is favorable to *aids; benefits; favors; helps*. In the five years during which the leveraged buyout has blossomed, the business environment has been particularly favorable to this type of transaction. *In the five years during which the leveraged buyout has blossomed, the business environment has particularly favored this type of transaction.*

is fearful (about; of; that) *dreads; fears; frets (about; over); stews (about; over); worries (about; over)*. These leaders tend to be fearful of external forces because they may create a middle class or threaten the existing social structure. *These leaders tend to fret about external forces because they may create a middle class or threaten the existing social structure.* ■ He said his firm had complied with the law but was fearful that the public would misunderstand its report that 56,000 pounds of acetone were released into the environment. *He said his firm had complied with the law but worried that the public would misunderstand its report that 56,000 pounds of acetone were released into the environment.* ■ West German unions, in particular, are fearful that the Single Market will mean that northern European industrialists will simply move their plants to the lower-paying areas of Greece, Spain, and Portugal. *West German unions, in particular, fear the Single Market will mean that northern European industrialists will simply move their plants to the lower-paying areas of Greece, Spain, and Portugal.*

is for certain (sure) *is certain (sure)*. One thing is for certain: they'll have to deal with the governor when all this is over. *One thing is certain: they'll have to deal with the governor when all this is over.*

is founded on (upon) *rests on*.

is going to *shall; will*. It's like they're trying to look at it and all by themselves are trying to describe what the likelihood is something (such as microbursts) is going to occur. *It's like they're trying to look at it and all by themselves are trying to describe what the likelihood is something (such as microbursts) will occur.* ■ We think that is a trend that is going to continue for several years to come. *We think that is a trend that will continue for several years to come.*

is harmful to *damages; harms; hurts; impairs; injures; mars; wrongs*. It will ultimately be harmful to the state's economy in that it will make some products more expensive than anywhere else. *It will ultimately harm the state's economy in that it will make some products more expensive than anywhere else.*

is helpful in (-ing) *aids in; assists in; helps*. Intelligent market research will be helpful in settling which product lines to offer. *Intelligent market research will help settle which product lines to offer.* ■ Coalition politics can be helpful in keeping idealistic young reformers on track once they get into the Legislature. *Coalition politics can aid in keeping idealistic young reformers on track once they get into the Legislature.*

is hopeful *expects; hopes; relies on; trusts.* I am hopeful that all will go well. *I expect that all will go well.* ■ We are hopeful that we can send a message to these teens that there are other alternatives to violence and what they've seen. *We hope that we can send a message to these teens that there are other alternatives to violence and what they've seen.* ■ While I am a bit disappointed in her grade, I am hopeful that she will do well in our next unit. *While I am a bit disappointed in her grade, I trust that she will do well in our next unit.*

is identical to (with) *amounts to; duplicates; equals; is; matches; rivals.* The objective, of course, is to ensure that directors' interests are identical with those of the company and its longer-term stockholders. *The objective, of course, is to ensure that directors' interests match those of the company and its longer-term stockholders.*

is illustrative of *characterizes; depicts; describes; designates; illustrates; pictures; portrays.* Mr. Alvarez, of the Environmental Policy Institute, says the episode is illustrative of the government's management of its nuclear weapons production program. *Mr. Alvarez, of the Environmental Policy Institute, says the episode illustrates the government's management of its nuclear weapons production program.*

is imitative of *imitates.*

is in accord (accordance) on (with) *agrees with; coincides with; complies with; concurs with; conforms to (with); corresponds to (with).* We are in accord with Blackmun's opinion that the protections provided by the federal court are necessary to fairly hear investors' claims of fraud. *We agree with Blackmun's opinion that the protections provided by the federal court are necessary to fairly hear investors' claims of fraud.* ■ We feel that the activities of our diplomats in Nicaragua were in strict accordance with normal patterns of diplomatic behavior. *We feel that the activities of our diplomats in Nicaragua strictly conformed with normal patterns of diplomatic behavior.*

is in agreement (on; with) *agrees (on; with); coincides (with); complies (with); concurs (with); conforms (to; with); corresponds (to; with).* This process should repeat itself until both parties are in agreement on the meaning of the message. *This process should repeat itself until both parties agree on the meaning of the message.* ■ V is directed in the direction of decreasing h, which is in agreement with our formulation of Darcy's equation. *V is directed in the direction of decreasing h, which corresponds to our formulation of Darcy's equation.* ■ The client should be in agreement with the goals set. *The client should concur with the goals set.*

is in attendance at *attends.* Three presidents were in attendance at the graduation ceremonies. *Three presidents attended the graduation ceremonies.*

is incapable of -ing *cannot; is unable to.* All three companies were incapable of managing their prizes and two of them, Hershey and CBS, eventually discarded their acquisitions in dismay. *All three companies were unable to manage their prizes and two of them, Hershey and CBS, eventually discarded their acquisitions in dismay.*

is in charge of *controls; directs; governs; manages.*

is inclined to *tends to.*

is inclined to believe (that) *asserts; believes; claims; contends; feels; holds; maintains; says; thinks; to.* I am inclined to believe that we will receive a lot more calls when budgets make clear what cuts and fees public schools will institute. *I believe that we will receive a lot more calls when budgets make clear what cuts and fees public schools will institute.* ■ I am inclined to believe that they amount to the same thing. *To me they amount to the same thing.*

is inclined to think (that) *asserts; believes; claims; contends; feels; holds; maintains; says; thinks; to.* I am inclined to think that intravenous drug users should be given needles. *I think intravenous drug users should be given needles.*

is in competition with *competes with.*

is in compliance with *complies with; conforms to (with).* Bank representatives must not involve themselves in moving funds out of countries that impose exchange controls unless they are in full compliance with these controls. *Bank representatives must not involve themselves in moving funds out of countries that impose exchange controls unless they fully comply with these controls.* ■ No register of deeds shall accept a deed for recording unless it is in compliance with the requirements of this section. *No register of deeds shall accept a deed for recording unless it conforms to the requirements of this section.*

is in conflict with *clashes with; conflicts with; contradicts; differs from; disagrees with; quarrels with; varies with.* The petition refers to the information services prohibition in the Modification of Final Judgment as "a cumbersome, unnecessary layer of regulation that is in irreconcilable conflict with the Communications Act." *The petition refers to the information services prohibition in the Modification of Final Judgment as "a cumbersome, unnecessary layer of regulation that irreconcilably conflicts with the Communications Act."*

is in conformance to (with) *agrees with; coincides with; complies with; concurs with; conforms to (with); corresponds to (with).*

is in conformity to (with) *agrees with; coincides with; complies with; concurs with; conforms to (with); corresponds to (with).* As long as they're in conformity with the law, they can do business with whomever they like. *As long as they conform to the law, they can do business with whomever they like.*

is in contempt of *defies.*

is in (marked; sharp) contrast to *clashes with; conflicts with; contests; contradicts; contrasts with; differs from; disagrees with; disputes; opposes.* The America-first tenor of the message was in sharp contrast to a growing tide of support for the idea of major international efforts in space exploration. *The America-first tenor of the message sharply contrasted with a growing tide of support for the idea of major international efforts in space exploration.* ■ The findings are in contrast to those of the Higher Education Research Institute, which conducts an annual national survey of freshmen. *The findings conflict with those of the Higher Education Research Institute, which conducts an annual national survey of freshmen.*

is in control of *controls; directs; governs; manages.* Risk-takers feel that they are in control of their own destiny. *Risk-takers feel that they control their own destiny.*

is in defiance of *defies.* They are in defiance of my orders. *They defy my orders.*

is indicative of *indicates; shows; signals; signifies; suggests.* Current sales figures are indicative of a management problem. *Current sales figures indicate a management problem.* ■ At Harvard, some black faculty members said Counter's decision to look elsewhere is indicative of the frustrations and obstacles blacks, women, and other groups face when they attempt to move up. *At Harvard, some black faculty members said Counter's decision to look elsewhere signifies the frustrations and obstacles blacks, women, and other groups face when they attempt to move up.* ■ Poor housekeeping and a lack of computer controls in the service-parts area may be indicative of the problems you could encounter after the purchase. *Poor housekeeping and a lack of computer controls in the service-parts area may suggest the problems you could encounter after the purchase.*

is in disagreement (about; on; with) *clashes with; conflicts with; contradicts; differs from; disagrees with; quarrels with; varies with.* In the most important and urgent political debates of recent years involving science, a major difficulty has been that scientists of equal distinction and accomplishment have been in disagreement. *In the most important and urgent political debates of recent years involving science, a major difficulty has been that scientists of equal distinction and accomplishment have disagreed.*

is in doubt about (of) *disbelieves; distrusts; doubts; mistrusts; questions.* For anyone who is in doubt about whether ministers are ordinary mortals, Mr. Wangerin makes clear that this is the case. *For anyone who doubts whether ministers are ordinary mortals, Mr. Wangerin makes clear that this is the case.*

is in error *errs.* She was in error. *She erred.*

is in excess of *exceeds.* It is expected that the average weighted maturity of the trust's portfolio under normal circumstances will be in excess of 20 years. *It is expected that the average weighted maturity of the trust's portfolio under normal circumstances will exceed 20 years.* ■ The size of the droplets produced by the unit is in excess of 8 microns. *The size of the droplets produced by the unit exceeds 8 microns.*

is in existence *exists.* More than 1,000 successful AI applications are in existence today. *More than 1,000 successful AI applications exist today.* ■ But industry observers note that these buyout funds have been in existence too few years to establish a definitive trend. *But industry observers note that these buyout funds have existed too few years to establish a definitive trend.*

is in favor of *backs; endorses; favors; prefers; supports.* Whom are you in favor of? *Whom do you endorse?* ■ We are in favor of reform, but we don't like the way it is being implemented. *We favor reform, but we don't like the way it is being implemented.* ■ The prelate said he was unable in conscience to remain a Democrat because the party is officially in favor of executing unborn babies whose only crime is that they temporarily occupy their mother's womb. *The prelate said he was unable in conscience to remain a Democrat because the party officially supports executing unborn babies whose only crime is that they temporarily occupy their mother's womb.* ■ Longtime as well as new users were overwhelmingly in favor of the familiar "Professional" name. *Longtime as well as new users overwhelmingly preferred the familiar "Professional" name.*

is in fear for (of) *dreads; fears (for); frets (about; over); stews (about; over); worries (about; over).* I was in fear for my life. *I feared for my life.*

is influential in (-ing) *affects; influences.* The problem with this generalization is that other factors can be influential in determining how many subordinates a manager has. *The problem with this generalization is that other factors can influence how many subordinates a manager has.*

is -ing *delete.* What the kids are wanting is to be loved. *What the kids want is to be loved.* ■ A person who encourages us to elaborate on a story while struggling with a knotted shoelace is contradicting the spoken message with body language. *A person who encourages us to elaborate on a story while struggling with a knotted shoelace contradicts the spoken message with body language.* ■ I would like to believe that the trading company concept is deserving of serious treatment by a magazine as exemplary as yours. *I would like to believe that the trading company concept deserves serious treatment by a magazine as exemplary as yours.* ■ The vendor is hoping to expand its base into volume sales of larger switches, and the Southwestern Bell deal appears to be a step in the right direction. *The vendor hopes to expand its base into volume sales of larger switches, and the Southwestern Bell deal appears to be a step in the right direction.* ■ We have gained a much better understanding of what providers are seeking from our networks, and we are looking forward to presenting our plan. *We have gained a* *much better understanding of what providers seek from our networks, and we look forward to presenting our plan.*

is in harmony with *agrees with; coheres with; concurs with; conforms to (with); corresponds to (with).*

is injurious to *damages; harms; hurts; impairs; injures; mars; wrongs.*

is in keeping with *agrees with; coheres with; concurs with; conforms to (with); corresponds to (with).* This is in keeping with MicroPro International's focus and marketing. *This conforms to MicroPro International's focus and marketing.* ■ Earnings for the year should be in keeping with earlier analyst projections of $5.2 million. *Earnings for the year should correspond to earlier analyst projections of $5.2 million.*

is in line with *agrees with; coheres with; concurs with; conforms to (with); corresponds to (with).* The figures are in line with recent years, when the number of taxpayers filing early in the season declined each year. *The figures conform with recent years, when the number of taxpayers filing early in the season declined each year.*

is in need of *needs.* Do you think the computer business is in need of further regulation? *Do you think the computer business needs further regulation?* ■ No animals are more in need of an improved public image than bats. *No animals need an improved public image more than bats.* ■ Thousands of people are in need of medical attention that private insurance does not offer. *Thousands of people need medical attention that private insurance does not offer.*

is in opposition to *conflicts with; contests; disagrees with; disapproves of; disputes; objects to; opposes; protests; resists.* They are in opposition to the United States. *They oppose the United States.* ■ You can assume that each of your participants may have goals that are in opposition to what you are trying to achieve. *You can assume that each of your participants may have goals that conflict with what you are trying to achieve.*

is in possession of *has; possesses.* They were in possession of a large quantity of cocaine. *They possessed a large quantity of cocaine.*

is in receipt of *receives.* We are in receipt of your proposal. *We received your proposal.* ■ I am in receipt of your impressive résumé and references. *I received your impressive résumé and references.* ■ I/We understand and agree that neither Fidelity Service Co., FBSI, nor NAFSCO will be liable for any loss, expense, or cost arising out of any telephone request for redemption or automatic settlement so long as Fidelity Service Co. transmits, and NAFSCO is in receipt of, or NAFSCO transmits, and Fidelity Service Co. is in receipt of, settlement proceeds. *I/We understand and agree that neither Fidelity Service Co., FBSI, nor NAFSCO will be liable for any loss, expense, or cost arising out of any telephone request* *for redemption or automatic settlement so long as Fidelity Service Co. transmits, and NAFSCO receives, or NAFSCO transmits, and Fidelity Service Co. receives, settlement proceeds.*

is insistent on *insists on.* If people are insistent on keeping the Electoral College, why not make it fair? *If people insist on keeping the Electoral College, why not make it fair?*

is in step with *agrees with; coheres with; concurs with; conforms to (with); corresponds to (with).*

is instrumental in (-ing) *aids in; assists in; helps.* Far from being the marginal movement they are perceived as being today, 19th-century evangelicals were instrumental in setting the political and social agenda for the century. *Far from being the marginal movement they are perceived as being today, 19th-century evangelicals helped set the political and social agenda for the century.* ■ How can IC managers, whom senior management often views as playing a supporting rather than a leading role, be instrumental in causing change to occur? *How can IC managers, whom senior management often views as playing a supporting rather than a leading role, aid in causing change to occur?*

is instrumental in helping *aids in; assists in; helps.* He was instrumental in helping them put together a financial plan. *He helped them put together a financial plan.* ■ He was one of the chief architects of last year's auto insurance bill and was instrumental in helping win its passage in the legislature. *He was one of the chief architects of last year's auto insurance bill and helped win its passage in the legislature.*

is in support of *backs; endorses; favors; prefers; supports.* In 1986 and 1987, 6.2 percent and 6.6 percent, respectively, of the voted shares were in support of our request for information about the extent of involvement in SDI. *In 1986 and 1987, 6.2 percent and 6.6 percent, respectively, of the voted shares supported our request for information about the extent of involvement in SDI.* ■ I myself am in support of women's rights. *I myself support women's rights.* ■ The Democrat has been in support of extending the steel agreements. *The Democrat has backed extending the steel agreements.*

is (was) in the habit of (-ing) *will (would).* When I was younger, I was in the habit of reading a book a week. *When I was younger, I would read a book a week.*

is in violation of *desecrates; infringes on; violates.* My job is solely to determine whether conduct is in violation of the federal criminal law. *My job is solely to determine whether conduct violates the federal criminal law.* ■ Many programs on the market may soon be found to be in violation of patents held by others. *Many programs on the market may soon be found to infringe on patents held by others.*

is in want of *wants.*

is it possible for *can.* Is it possible for you to tell us about your relationship with your child? *Can you tell us about your relationship with your child?*

is knowledgeable in (of) *comprehends; knows; understands.* We also favor choosing directors who have worked in a company's industry at some point in their careers or are knowledgeable in some collateral industry. *We also favor choosing directors who have worked in a company's industry at some point in their careers or understand some collateral industry.*

is mindful of (that) *comprehends; knows; realizes; recognizes; sees; understands.* We should be mindful of the benefits of free trade while finding ways to limit it. *We should realize the benefits of free trade while finding ways to limit it.*

is mistrustful about (of) *disbelieves; distrusts; doubts; mistrusts; questions.* The two sides are deeply mistrustful of each other after an estimated 1 million casualties. *The two sides deeply mistrust each other after an estimated 1 million casualties.*

is needful of *needs.*

is of assistance in (-ing) *aids in (-ing); assists in (-ing); helps.*

is of benefit to *aids; benefits; favors; helps.* He agrees that companies need to take caution when choosing a system, but adds that the technology can be of great benefit to a company. *He agrees that companies need to take caution when choosing a system, but adds that the technology can greatly benefit a company.*

is of concern to *bothers; concerns; disturbs; interests; upsets; worries.* Since these factors vary considerably from one country to another, they are of particular concern to the global company interested in a new foreign market. *Since these factors vary considerably from one country to another, they particularly concern the global company interested in a new foreign market.* ■ The new strike at Nowa Huta, if it takes hold, also will be of concern to the authorities. *The new strike at Nowa Huta, if it takes hold, also will worry the authorities.* ■ It's something that is of great concern to us. *It's something that greatly bothers us.*

is offensive to *insults; offends.* Halloween represents spiritist forces that are offensive to three of the world's major religions, Judaism, Christianity, and Islam. *Halloween represents spiritist forces that offend three of the world's major religions, Judaism, Christianity, and Islam.*

is of interest to *appeals to; attracts; concerns; excites; interests.*

is of the belief (that) *asserts; believes; claims; contends; feels; holds; maintains; says; thinks; to.* The vast majority of physicians are of the belief that Ritalin is a safe drug for children. *To the vast majority of physicians, Ritalin is a safe drug for children.*

is of the opinion (that) *asserts; believes; claims; contends; feels; holds; maintains; says; thinks; to.* I am of the opinion that the Celtics are far better off this year than last. *I believe the Celtics are far better off this year than last.* ■ Impartial industry observers are of the opinion that if Pennzoil suffered any damage, it was only to the extent of about 5 percent of the award. *Impartial industry observers hold that if Pennzoil suffered any damage, it was only to the extent of about 5 percent of the award.*

is of the same opinion (as) *agrees (with); concurs (with).*

is of the view (that) *asserts; believes; claims; contends; feels; holds; maintains; says; thinks; to.* He is of the view that a person between the ages of 30 and 40 is more susceptible to tuberculosis than a person between 60 and 70. *He maintains that a person between the ages of 30 and 40 is more susceptible to tuberculosis than a person between 60 and 70.*

is one (that; which; who; whom) delete. A European option is one which can be exercised only at maturity. *A European option can be exercised only at maturity.* ■ This situation is one that ought not to be forgotten. *This situation ought not to be forgotten.* ■ An oblique plane is one that is neither parallel nor perpendicular to a projection plane. *An oblique plane is neither parallel nor perpendicular to a projection plane.* ■ A model that results in a relatively steady MSE over time is one that is relatively stable. *A model that results in a relatively steady MSE over time is relatively stable.* ■ I am one who is not easily satisfied. *I am not easily satisfied.*

is on (a) par (with) *equals.* U.S. factory wages are already at least 20 percent below comparable German wages, on a dollar basis, and virtually on a par with Japanese levels. *U.S. factory wages are already at least 20 percent below comparable German wages, on a dollar basis, and virtually equal Japanese levels.*

is opposed to *conflicts with; contests; disagrees with; disapproves of; disputes; objects to; opposes; protests; resists.* We are opposed to marketing RU 486 in the U.S. or any other country because it kills unborn babies and it can injure if not possibly kill women. *We protest marketing RU 486 in the U.S. or any other country because it kills unborn babies and it can injure if not possibly kill women.* ■ It might help us to dispel the stupid myth that only fascists, racists, and anti-Semites were opposed to the communist takeover of Eastern Europe. *It might help us to dispel the stupid myth that only fascists, racists, and anti-Semites resisted the communist takeover of Eastern Europe.* ■ The case involves white employees in Alabama who are opposed to affirmative action and are trying to dissolve a final, court-approved settlement. *The case involves white employees* *in Alabama who oppose affirmative action and are trying to dissolve a final, court-approved settlement.* ■ I would not be opposed to doing that. *I would not object to doing that.*

is outrageous to *outrages.*

is persistent in *perseveres in; persists in.* Friends must be persistent in helping the griever come out of himself. *Friends must persist in helping the griever come out of himself.*

is pertinent to *applies to; bears on; concerns; pertains to; regards; relates to.*

is proof of (that) *evinces; indicates; proves; reveals; shows; signifies; testifies (to).*

is prone to *tends to.* Company managers are prone to underestimate loyalty and their employees' need for it. *Company managers tend to underestimate loyalty and their employees' need for it.*

is protective of *defends; protects; shelters; shields.* People on the right-to-life side feel that the laws of society should be protective of every member of the human family. *People on the right-to-life side feel that the laws of society should protect every member of the human family.*

is receptive to *welcomes.* While lawmakers are generally receptive to his ideas, the feeling is not mutual. *While lawmakers generally welcome his ideas, the feeling is not mutual.*

is (a; the) recipient of *receives.* He was recipient of the Rumford Medal of the American Academy of Sciences and the Copley Medal of London's Royal Society, the highest honor open to a scientist until the founding of the Nobel Prize. *He received the Rumford Medal of the American Academy of Sciences and the Copley Medal of London's Royal Society, the highest honor open to a scientist until the founding of the Nobel Prize.* ■ The University of South Florida was the recipient of a $600,000 grant from a Florida bank to endow a professorship in banking and finance. *The University of South Florida received a $600,000 grant from a Florida bank to endow a professorship in banking and finance.*

is reflective of *reflects.* In some instances, a system is designed primarily for one category of personnel but is used for all employees; obviously, it will not be reflective of performance on the other jobs. *In some instances, a system is designed primarily for one category of personnel but is used for all employees; obviously, it will not reflect performance on the other jobs.*

is regretful about (of; that) *regrets.* Now I'm regretful that I didn't work harder this week. *Now I regret I didn't work harder this week.* ■ I can't say I'm regretful about it. *I can't say I regret it.*

is related to *correlates to (with); equates with; relates to.* It is generally assumed that a species-wide tendency to favor one hand over the other is related to the development of brain hemispheres with specialized functions. *It is generally assumed that a species-wide tendency to favor one hand over the other relates to the development of brain hemispheres with specialized functions.*

is relevant to *applies to; bears on; concerns; pertains to; regards; relates to.*

is reliant on (upon) *counts on; depends on; relies on.* South Korean builders are heavily reliant upon the Mideast market. *South Korean builders rely heavily on the Mideast market.* ■ She suffers migraine headaches and is reliant upon laxatives. *She suffers migraine headaches and depends on laxatives.*

is reminiscent of *recalls.* The vertical "tipwing" fins at the end of its wings are reminiscent of a 1948 Cadillac more than a jet plane, and a black band of air sensors circles one wing. *The vertical "tipwing" fins at the end of its wings recall a 1948 Cadillac more than a jet plane, and a black band of air sensors circles one wing.* ■ The apparatus is reminiscent of some Asian musical performances emphasizing the gestures used to play instruments. *The apparatus recalls some Asian musical performances emphasizing the gestures used to play instruments.*

is representative of *emblemizes; indicates; represents; signifies; stands for; symbolizes; typifies.* For the reader to assume that this is representative of the norm is unfortunate. *For the reader to assume that this represents the norm is unfortunate.* ■ The most important issue in choosing a sample is whether the people selected for the research are representative of those who really matter to the success of the strategy being researched. *The most important issue in choosing a sample is whether the people selected for the research typify those who really matter to the success of the strategy being researched.* ■ It should be understood that one credit at Proctor is representative of approximately 40 hours of classroom time. *It should be understood that one credit at Proctor signifies approximately 40 hours of classroom time.*

is required to *has to; must.* Managers are required to be able to perform certain roles. *Managers must be able to perform certain roles.* ■ If customers are required to wait too long, they may choose to do business at another store that provides faster service. *If customers have to wait too long, they may choose to do business at another store that provides faster service.*

is resentful of *resents.*

is resistant to *contests; disagrees with; disapproves of; disputes; objects to; opposes; protests; resists.* In fact, they are resistant to measuring learning and performance in meaningful terms. *In fact, they resist measuring learning and performance in meaningful terms.* ■ The administration is resistant to the basic premise of arms control: forgoing some options to get the other side to forgo some. *The administration opposes the basic premise of arms control: forgoing some options to get the other side to forgo some.*

is respectful of (toward) *respects.* They're respectful of me, and I'm respectful of them. *They respect me, and I respect them.* ■ The two skaters are friends and respectful of each other. *The two skaters are friends and respect each other.*

is ruinous to *damages; destroys; harms; hurts; impairs; injures; mars; ruins.*

is scornful of *despises; disdains; scorns.* Many scientists are scornful of him because of his claims that fluoride causes everything from cancer to AIDS. *Many scientists scorn him because of his claims that fluoride causes everything from cancer to AIDS.*

is similar to (with) *compares to (with); corresponds to (with); equates with; relates to; resembles.* These commands are similar to English sentences, and most of them make sense to the casual reader. *These commands resemble English sentences, and most of them make sense to the casual reader.*

is skeptical about (of; that) *disbelieves; distrusts; doubts; mistrusts; questions.* We are skeptical that Drexel, Weksel, and yourself would treat Prime and its stockholders any better than you have treated your customers and/or stockholders in previous situations. *We doubt that Drexel, Weksel, and yourself would treat Prime and its stockholders any better than you have treated your customers and/or stockholders in previous situations.* ■ Immigration officials often are skeptical of businesses' claims that they didn't know a worker was illegal or that they weren't aware of the new immigration law. *Immigration officials often disbelieve businesses' claims that they didn't know a worker was illegal or that they weren't aware of the new immigration law.*

is still to be seen *do not know; is not (now; yet) known; is uncertain; is unclear; is unknown; is unsure.* They priced it like a Mercedes; whether it's engineered like a Mercedes is still to be seen. *They priced it like a Mercedes; whether it's engineered like a Mercedes is not yet known.*

issuance *issue.* Municipal bonds and municipal notes are debt obligations of states, cities, municipalities, and municipal agencies which generally have maturities, at the time of their issuance, of either one year or more or from six months to three years. *Municipal bonds and municipal notes are debt obligations of states, cities, municipalities, and municipal agencies which generally have maturities, at the time of their issue, of either one year or more or from six months to three years.*

is subject to *depends on; hinges on.* Completion of the transactions is subject to a definitive agreement and the approval of both boards. *Completion of the transactions hinges on a definitive agreement and the approval of both boards.*

(a; the) ... issue delete. The ability to produce timely reports is an equally pressing issue. *The ability to produce timely reports is equally pressing.* ■ The question of whether a firm's financing decisions affect its value remains an unresolved issue. *The question of whether a firm's financing decisions affect its value remains unresolved.* ■ That's an issue that's still very controversial. *That's still very controversial.*

is suggestive of *indicates; shows; signals; signifies; suggests.*

is suitable to *applies to; bears on; concerns; pertains to; regards; relates to.*

is supportive of *endorses; fosters; nurtures; supports; upholds.* I have a lot of girlfriends who are supportive of me. *I have a lot of girlfriends who support me.* ■ It would make it clear that the governor is supportive of basic gay rights. *It would make it clear that the governor endorses basic gay rights.* ■ Leader behavior will increase subordinates' efforts if it links satisfaction of their needs to effective performance and is supportive of their efforts to achieve goal performance. *Leader behavior will increase subordinates' efforts if it links satisfaction of their needs to effective performance and fosters their efforts to achieve goal performance.* ■ This report is supportive of our findings. *This report supports our findings.*

is symbolic (symbolical) of *emblemizes; indicates; represents; signifies; stands for; symbolizes; typifies.*

is symptomatic of *indicates; signals; signifies; symptomizes.* The small dip is symptomatic of a pause in the housing market in October, as buyers, sellers, and lenders tried to figure out what was occurring in the financial markets. *The small dip indicates a pause in the housing market in October, as buyers, sellers, and lenders tried to figure out what was occurring in the financial markets.* ■ With Mikhail Gorbachev in our midst, Walters' statement bears scrutiny because it is symptomatic of something worrisome—an epidemic of complacency. *With Mikhail Gorbachev in our midst, Walters' statement bears scrutiny because it symptomizes something worrisome—an epidemic of complacency.*

is tantamount to *amounts to; duplicates; equals; is; matches; rivals.*

is (a) testament to *affirms; attests to; certifies to; declares; testifies to; verifies.* An excellent credit card rating is a testament to your success in business. *An excellent credit card rating attests to your success in business.*

is (a) testimony to *affirms; attests to; certifies to; declares; testifies to; verifies.* The high level of business and consumer confidence is testimony to the success of this Fed policy. *The high level of business and consumer confidence testifies to the success of this Fed policy.*

is trustful of *trusts.*

is typical of *exemplifies; symbolizes; typifies.* Those who are not familiar with feminist writings may find it useful and interesting to consider a book that is typical of the harsher brand of such works. *Those who are not familiar with feminist writings may find it useful and interesting to consider a book that typifies the harsher brand of such works.* ■ This kind of comment is typical of the Democrat's campaign. *This kind of comment exemplifies the Democrat's campaign.*

is under the assumption (that) *assumes; believes; feels; supposes; thinks.* I am under the assumption that the *Globe* is trying to ameliorate the situation. *I assume the* Globe *is trying to ameliorate the situation.*

is under the impression (that) *assumes; believes; feels; supposes; thinks.* Some will object to excluding the better-off elderly from Social Security benefits because they are under the impression that Social Security is fundamentally an annuity system. *Some will object to excluding the better-off elderly from Social Security benefits because they believe Social Security is fundamentally an annuity system.* ■ It was fine the first few times, but now he's under the impression I am his grandson. *It was fine the first few times, but now he thinks I am his grandson.* ■ Officials of Mr. Reynold's company said they were under the impression that the tenants owned the three-bedroom house. *Officials of Mr. Reynold's company said they assumed the tenants owned the three-bedroom house.*

is used (for; to) delete. Straight lines are used to indicate crest and root lines. *Straight lines indicate crest and root lines.* ■ Notes are used to explain the missing features. *Notes explain the missing features.* ■ These conventional breaks are used to indicate that a part of an object has been broken away. *These conventional breaks indicate that a part of an object has been broken away.* ■ The symbol *w* is used to indicate that the quotient is an approximate value after being rounded off. *The symbol* w *indicates that the quotient is an approximate value after being rounded off.*

is what delete. While consistency is the mainstay of our program, diversity and change are what keep it exciting. *While consistency is the mainstay of our program, diversity and change keep it exciting.*

is witness to *affirms; attests to; certifies to; declares; testifies to; verifies.* Poet Kahlil Gibran's popularity in America is witness to the presence of an essential moral and artistic quality in his work. *Poet Kahlil Gibran's popularity in America testifies to the presence of an essential moral and artistic quality in his work.*

is (a) witness to *sees; witnesses.* He was a witness to the Chinese government's crackdown on students. *He witnessed the Chinese government's crackdown on students.*

it has been called to my attention *I have learned; I understand;* delete.

it has come to my attention *I have learned; I understand;* delete.

it is ... (that; who) *is; -(al)ly;* delete. It is our intent to share ideas, thoughts, and methods with GEM users. *Our intent is to share ideas, thoughts, and methods with GEM users.* ▪ It is difficult to estimate the incidence of phobias in the general population. *To estimate the incidence of phobias in the general population is difficult.* ▪ It's time for us to rethink what it is we are asking of our employees. *It's time for us to rethink what we are asking of our employees.* ▪ It was clear that a number of complex issues had to be resolved before a fund could go forward successfully. *Clearly, a number of complex issues had to be resolved before a fund could go forward successfully.* ▪ It is not uncommon that small local changes in product attributes are desirable to ensure that the good is classified in a low tax category. *Not uncommonly, small local changes in product attributes are desirable to ensure that the good is classified in a low tax category.* ▪ It is we who are to be blamed. *We are to be blamed.* ▪ The ramp, however important it is to a developer, has to fit in. *The ramp, however important to a developer, has to fit in.*

it is apparent that *apparently; clearly; evidently; manifestly; obviously; patently; plainly;* delete. It is apparent that management needs to take into account a wide range of variables when devising international product development policies. *Clearly, management needs to take into account a wide range of variables when devising international product development policies.*

it is essential that *must; should.* It is essential that we raise federal taxes. *We must raise federal taxes.* ▪ It is essential that remaining barriers to women's entrepreneurship be eliminated. *Remaining barriers to women's entrepreneurship must be eliminated.* ▪ It is essential that nurses assess family dynamics and the ability to cope with the traumatic event to ensure that interventions are specific to each family's problems. *Nurses should assess family dynamics and the ability to cope with the traumatic event to ensure that interventions are specific to each family's problems.*

it is evident that *apparently; clearly; evidently; manifestly; obviously; patently; plainly;* delete. It is evident that service industries are more exposed to protectionism in international markets than are most other industries. *Clearly, service industries are more exposed to protectionism in international markets than are most other industries.*

it is (to be) hoped *I (we) hope; let us hope.* It is to be hoped that your exposé will help prevent this kind of performance by others. *Let's hope that your exposé will help prevent this kind of performance by others.* ▪ It is hoped that you will find it worthy of support. *We hope that you will find it worthy of support.*

it is imperative that *must; should.* It is imperative that managers and researchers try to assess the value of the information before the research is undertaken. *Managers and researchers should try to assess the value of the information before* *the research is undertaken.* ■ It is imperative that an international manager from the United States understand the cultures of countries in which he or she operates. *An international manager from the United States must understand the cultures of countries in which he or she operates.*

it is important to ... that delete. It is important to emphasize that the incidence of breast cancer has been rising. *The incidence of breast cancer has been rising.*

it is important to keep in mind *keep in mind; remember;* delete. It is important to keep in mind that these applications address only today's problems. *Keep in mind that these applications address only today's problems.*

it is important to note *note;* delete. It is important to note that different stores in a chain may perform differently. *Different stores in a chain may perform differently.*

it is important to realize (recognize) *realize (recognize).* It is important to recognize that different data sources for these trends often produce significantly different data. *Recognize that different data sources for these trends often produce significantly different data.* ■ It is important to realize that many Chinese willingly remain in their country despite the violence. *Many Chinese willingly remain in their country despite the violence.*

it is important to remember *keep in mind; remember;* delete. It is important to remember that social security reserves are expected to build to about $12 trillion in the next century. *Remember that social security reserves are expected to build to about $12 trillion in the next century.*

it is important to understand *understand;* delete. It is important to understand that not all pressures are the result of marketplace changes, nor do they necessarily affect the marketing activity. *Not all pressures are the result of marketplace changes, nor do they necessarily affect the marketing activity.*

it is interesting to note *interestingly; note;* delete. It is interesting to note that an early meaning of the Spanish word *algebrista* was bonesetter or reuniter of broken bones. *Interestingly, an early meaning of the Spanish word* algebrista *was bonesetter or reuniter of broken bones.* ■ It's interesting to note that over the range of roles we have looked at, the only disagreement between this analysis and what current regulation dictates is where the arrow appears. *Over the range of roles we have looked at, the only disagreement between this analysis and what current regulation dictates is where the arrow appears.*

it is necessary (for; that; to) *must; need to.* It is necessary for this causality to be realistic for the model to be useful. *This causality must be realistic for the model to be useful.* ■ It is necessary that we improve the standard of living and the quality of our life in order to achieve other aspects of development. *We need to* *improve the standard of living and the quality of our life in order to achieve other aspects of development.*

it is significant to note *note;* delete. It is significant to note that this land is owned by the city and leased to Harvard. *This land is owned by the city and leased to Harvard.*

it is useful (worthwhile) to mention (say; state) (that) delete. It is useful to state that most of the modernization in steel production has occurred as part of a general shift toward all-electric steelmaking. *Most of the modernization in steel production has occurred as part of a general shift toward all-electric steelmaking.*

it is useful (worthwhile) to note (that) delete. It is worthwhile to note that in this outline the results specified in step III could refer to any of several results. *In this outline the results specified in step III could refer to any of several results.*

it must (should) be mentioned (said; stated) (that) delete.

it must (should) be noted *note;* delete. It should be noted that people with gastrointestinal disorders share a number of traits. *People with gastrointestinal disorders share a number of traits.* ■ It must be noted that the larger floods produce significantly greater damages for each flood. *Note that the larger floods produce significantly greater damages for each flood.*

it must (should) be pointed out (that) delete. It should be pointed out that Boston Technical students have recently received notices of acceptance from institutions such as Princeton, Tufts, Boston College, and the University of California at Berkeley. *Boston Technical students have recently received notices of acceptance from institutions such as Princeton, Tufts, Boston College, and the University of California at Berkeley.*

it must (should) be remembered *keep in mind; remember;* delete. It must be remembered that even though this course deals with an easily measurable good, money, you must make personal value judgments concerning how money is best used. *Even though this course deals with an easily measurable good, money, you must make personal value judgments concerning how money is best used.*

it must (should) be understood *understand;* delete. It must be understood that we have a very complex, interrelated economy. *We have a very complex, interrelated economy.*

it (just) so happens *by chance; luckily; unluckily.*

I (we) would appreciate it if *please.*

J

joint agreement *agreement*.

joint cooperation *cooperation*.

join together *join*. All of these can be joined together by soldering, brazing, or welding. *All of these can be joined by soldering, brazing, or welding.* ■ Strings can be joined together into longer strings by concatenation. *Strings can be joined into longer strings by concatenation.* ■ Lately, corporate growth patterns have shown a trend toward the conglomerate merger, the joining together of unrelated corporations. *Lately, corporate growth patterns have shown a trend toward the conglomerate merger, the joining of unrelated corporations.*

judge as *judge*.

just about *about; almost; nearly*.

just as (more; most) importantly *just as (more; most) important*. But perhaps most importantly, they offer trustworthiness. *But perhaps most important, they offer trustworthiness.* ■ Just as importantly, there are many ideas about the savings rate that suggest it is not nearly as low as many people think. *Just as important, there are many ideas about the savings rate that suggest it is not nearly as low as many people think.* ■ More importantly, we are working closely with the private sector through our joint ventures program to accomplish some things government alone simply can't do. *More important, we are working closely with the private sector through our joint ventures program to accomplish some things government alone simply can't do.*

just as (more; most) significantly *just as (more; most) significant*. Most significantly, the product champion must have the drive to get the work done and the decisions made. *Most significant, the product champion must have the drive to get the work done and the decisions made.* ■ More significantly, if the unemployed had health insurance, they could partake of more appropriate health care. *More significant, if the unemployed had health insurance, they could partake of more appropriate health care.*

just exactly *exactly; just*. He's just exactly what I'm looking for. *He's just what I'm looking for.* ■ I've put it just exactly the way I want to put it. *I've put it exactly the way I want to put it.*

just recently *just; recently*. We just recently went to England. *We recently went to England.* ■ He was just recently released from prison. *He was just released from prison.* ■ My boyfriend just recently left me for another woman. *My boyfriend recently left me for another woman.*

just simply *just; simply.*

just the same as *just like; the same as.* When displayed in document view, the text can be entered and edited just the same as a normal document. *When displayed in document view, the text can be entered and edited the same as a normal document.* ■ The DEL command works just the same as the ERASE command. *The DEL command works just like the ERASE command.*

K

keep in mind *remember;* delete. Keep in mind that there are two versions of the program called PRODOS. *Remember that there are two versions of the program called PRODOS.* ■ Keep in mind that few people, if any, match a job perfectly, and few employers look for a perfect fit. *Few people, if any, match a job perfectly, and few employers look for a perfect fit.*

(a; the) key ... in (of; to) *(a; the) key to.* Market segmentation is a key aspect to strategic planning at the corporate and business levels. *Market segmentation is a key to strategic planning at the corporate and business levels.* ■ This concept, known as organizational learning, is a key element in developing a sound philosophy of change. *This concept, known as organizational learning, is a key to developing a sound philosophy of change.* ■ A key factor in developing advanced computer technology will be the evolution toward ULSI technology. *A key to developing advanced computer technology will be the evolution toward ULSI technology.* ■ Our continued commitment to quality is a key component of our success. *Our continued commitment to quality is a key to our success.* ■ In contrast, individualism was the key ingredient to the rise of Greece. *In contrast, individualism was key to the rise of Greece.*

kinder (and) gentler *amiable; compassionate; gentle; humane; kind; tender; tolerant.*

kind of delete. I kind of stumbled onto the job. *I stumbled onto the job.* ■ It's kind of ironic. *It's ironic.*

know for a fact *know.* I know for a fact she was with him. *I know she was with him.* ■ The state knows for a fact that this firm is trying to swindle consumers. *The state knows that this firm is trying to swindle consumers.*

known as *called; named; termed;* delete. The three most common knowledge representations in expert system shells are known as rules, frames, and semantic networks. *The three most common knowledge representations in expert system shells are rules, frames, and semantic networks.*

L

label as *label*. The product is labeled as a cosmetic, not a medication. *The product is labeled a cosmetic, not a medication.* ▪ If we let out our feelings of anger, women are labeled as shrews or nags. *If we let out our feelings of anger, women are labeled shrews or nags.*

lackadaisical *idle; languid; lazy; listless*.

lack for *lack*.

lacking in *dis-; -il; im-; in-; ir-; lack; -less(ness); mis-; no; non-; not; un-; want; with no; without*. The defense's case was so often lacking in credibility. *The defense's case was so often incredible.* ▪ The jury is lacking in balance. *The jury is imbalanced.* ▪ Companies lacking in clear strategy are going to be squeezed out of existence in this fiercely competitive marketplace. *Companies with no clear strategy are going to be squeezed out of existence in this fiercely competitive marketplace.*

(a; the) lack of *dis-; few; -il; im-; in-; ir-; -less(ness); mis-; no; non-; not; scant; un-; with no; without*. It is only because of the intransigence of the host country and its lack of respect for international law that it has to pick up the bill of more than a million dollars. *It is only because of the intransigence of the host country and its disrespect for international law that it has to pick up the bill of more than a million dollars.* ▪ People say they are often confronted by a lack of understanding from their clients. *People say they are often confronted by misunderstanding from their clients.* ▪ Lack of understanding the law creates a fear of the system. *Not understanding the law creates a fear of the system.* ▪ This is a result of a lack of cooperation between retailers and financial institutions. *This is a result of noncooperation between retailers and financial institutions.* ▪ American General has been amply rewarded by capitalizing on the lack of competition in this area. *American General has been amply rewarded by capitalizing on the scant competition in this area.* ▪ The gay teen is forced to struggle against a double layer of prejudice involving both his sexual feelings and his presumed lack of manliness. *The gay teen is forced to struggle against a double layer of prejudice involving both his sexual feelings and his presumed unmanliness.* ▪ Many a computer programming project has failed because of a lack of careful problem analysis and poor program design techniques. *Many a computer programming project has failed because of careless problem analysis and poor program design techniques.* ▪ Jackson concerns me because of his lack of experience in foreign policy and defense. *Jackson concerns me because of his inexperience in foreign policy and defense.* ▪ This lack of regular contact leaves room for suspicion, concern, and uneven distribution of work. *This irregular contact leaves room for suspicion, concern, and uneven distribution of work.*

(a; the) large (overwhelming; sizable; vast) plurality (of) *a good (great) deal (of); a good (great) many (of); almost all (of); (nine) in (ten) (of); many (of); most (of); much (of); nearly all (of); (43) of (48) (of); ... percent (of); three-fourths (two-thirds) (of).* Large pluralities feel Mr. Bush would do about as well as Mr. Reagan. *Most feel Mr. Bush would do about as well as Mr. Reagan.*

large-size(d) *large.*

last of all *last.*

later on *later.* I will see you later on. *I will see you later.* ■ Later on today, you may find out the truth about that. *Later today, you may find out the truth about that.*

latter part of *last half of; late.*

law enforcement officers *authorities; officers; police.*

left-hand *left.* The left-hand side of the balance sheet shows the firm's assets. *The left side of the balance sheet shows the firm's assets.*

lend out *lend.*

(a; the) length of *delete.* While adults typically grew to a length of about 30 feet, the embryos measured only about 1 1/2 feet from head to tail and fit into 7-inch-long eggs. *While adults typically grew to about 30 feet, the embryos measured only about 1 1/2 feet from head to tail and fit into 7-inch-long eggs.*

lengthy *long.* Communists must go through a lengthy selection process and ideological training before being granted membership in the party. *Communists must go through a long selection process and ideological training before being granted membership in the party.* ■ Last week, the Ocean Spray measure turned up in a lengthy document reconciling the House and Senate appropriations bills. *Last week, the Ocean Spray measure turned up in a long document reconciling the House and Senate appropriations bills.*

(a; the) ... level (of) *delete.* Usage levels of the Discover card have been limited. *Usage of the Discover card has been limited.* ■ Each organization must assess its level of willingness to take risks. *Each organization must assess its willingness to take risks.* ■ These suppliers will need to dramatically increase the level of commitment they make to their customers. *These suppliers will need to dramatically increase the commitment they make to their customers.* ■ Company personnel must be well trained and adequately informed to provide the level of service required by today's discerning consumer. *Company personnel must be well trained and adequately informed to provide the service required by today's discerning consumer.* ■ A career is made up of a series of jobs that lead you to ever-increasing levels of competency, responsibilities, and income. *A career is made up of a series of jobs that lead you to ever-increasing competency, responsibilities, and income.* ■ When a relationship reaches a certain level of intensity, the church should have some way of recognizing that commitment. *When a relationship reaches a certain intensity, the church should have some way of recognizing that commitment.* ■ Random access implies that any piece of information can be read with an equal level of difficulty and delay. *Random access implies that any piece of information can be read with equal difficulty and delay.*

level to the ground *level; raze.*

lift up *lift.*

lightning (raining; snowing) outside *lightning (raining; snowing).* It's raining outside. *It's raining.* ■ Why shouldn't you take a shower if it's lightning outside? *Why shouldn't you take a shower if it's lightning?*

like ... also (as well) *like.* Like 401(k) plans, 403(b) plans also have various investment alternatives: common stocks, bonds, money-market funds, and so on. *Like 401(k) plans, 403(b) plans have various investment alternatives: common stocks, bonds, money-market funds, and so on.*

like ... and others (and so forth; and so on; and such; and the like; et al.; etc.) *and others (and so forth; and so on; and such; and the like; et al.; etc.); like.* To allow for painless growth, you must make allowances for things like organizational changes, additional users, changing information requirements, and so on. *To allow for painless growth, you must make allowances for organizational changes, additional users, changing information requirements, and so on.* ■ Sheet sizes are specified by letters like Size A, Size B, and so forth. *Sheet sizes are specified by letters like Size A and Size B.* ■ It can be printed on any printer, but it will not have formats like boldfacing, underlining, and so on. *It can be printed on any printer, but it will not have formats like boldfacing and underlining.* ■ These come from sources like the Department of Health and Human Services, Department of Housing and Urban Development, General Accounting Office, National Research Council, and others. *These come from sources like the Department of Health and Human Services, Department of Housing and Urban Development, General Accounting Office, and National Research Council.*

like ... for example (for instance) *as; for example (for instance); like; such as.* The drug is good for ailments like insomnia for example. *The drug is good for ailments like insomnia.* ■ The Soviet Union is sensitive to industries, like, for instance, Norway's Konesberg, which sold them the controller. *The Soviet Union is sensitive to industries, for instance, Norway's Konesberg, which sold them the controller.* ■ Words like "responsibility," "growth," "achievement," and "challenge," for example, have been elevated to the lyrics of the patriotic anthem for all organizations. *Words like "responsibility," "growth," "achieve-*

ment," and "challenge" have been elevated to the lyrics of the patriotic anthem for all organizations.

limitation *limit*. There is no overall limitation on the percentage of the trust's portfolio securities which may be subject to a hedge position. *There is no overall limit on the percentage of the trust's portfolio securities which may be subject to a hedge position.*

(very) limited *bare; few; little; meager; rare; scant; scanty; scarce; short; slight; small; spare; sparse.* While opportunities for broad-scale consumer advertising may be limited for a while, there are lots of opportunities for commercial communications. *While opportunities for broad-scale consumer advertising may be scarce for a while, there are lots of opportunities for commercial communications.* ▪ But telephone analysts and the companies themselves caution that demand for the phones, which cost between $400 and $500 each, will be very limited. *But telephone analysts and the companies themselves caution that demand for the phones, which cost between $400 and $500 each, will be slight.*

(a; the) limited number of *a couple; a few; eight (four); little; meager; not many; one or two (two or three); scant; scanty; (only) so many; some; spare; sparse.* A surgeon can only do a limited number of operations. *A surgeon can only do so many operations.* ▪ These specialized skills come only from concentration, and only a limited number of banks can afford it. *These specialized skills come only from concentration, and only a few banks can afford it.* ▪ Some programs allow you to enter descriptive comments about files so you don't have to rely on the limited number of characters allowed in the filename to identify them. *Some programs allow you to enter descriptive comments about files so you don't have to rely on the eight characters allowed in the filename to identify them.* ▪ There were a limited number of episodes in which it was obvious that she had been drinking too much. *There were two or three episodes in which it was obvious that she had been drinking too much.*

(a; the) limited selection (of) *a couple; a few; eight (four); little; meager; not many; one or two (two or three); scant; scanty; (only) so many; some; spare; sparse.*

linkage *link*. Particular attention needs to be given to the linkage among the various strategic levels within and across national markets. *Particular attention needs to be given to the link among the various strategic levels within and across national markets.* ▪ There's a possibility the deaths are related, but it hasn't risen to a conclusive statement that there's a linkage. *There's a possibility the deaths are related, but it hasn't risen to a conclusive statement that there's a link.*

link together *connect; link.* It's natural to link the two of them together. *It's natural to connect the two of them.* ▪ Its many parts are linked together by computers and can respond to changing needs more quickly than their aging counterparts. *Its many parts are linked by computers and can respond to changing needs more quickly than their aging counterparts.* ■ The relationship which links God, human beings, and all of the community of the living together is emphasized in the covenant which God made with Noah after the flood. *The relationship which links God, human beings, and all of the community of the living is emphasized in the covenant which God made with Noah after the flood.*

liquid refreshment *drink.*

literally delete. We have a fee maximum on literally every CPT code imaginable. *We have a fee maximum on every CPT code imaginable.* ■ My mom was living literally with a time bomb. *My mom was living with a time bomb.* ■ The operating system literally picks itself up by its own bootstraps. *The operating system picks itself up by its own bootstraps.* ■ Wilderness areas are now literally being loved to death by burgeoning numbers of backpackers, some of them ignorant of backcountry etiquette and hygiene. *Wilderness areas are now being loved to death by burgeoning numbers of backpackers, some of them ignorant of backcountry etiquette and hygiene.*

little by little *gradually; slowly.*

little (small) child *child.* How do you tell a little child that his father isn't coming home again? *How do you tell a child that his father isn't coming home again?*

little (small; tiny) iota *iota.* I don't care one little iota less than you do about homelessness in America. *I don't care one iota less than you do about homelessness in America.*

locality *area; city; district; locale; place; point; region; site; spot; state; town; zone.* The U.S. findings are based on in-person interviews with 1,569 adults, conducted in more than 300 scientifically selected localities across the nation. *The U.S. findings are based on in-person interviews with 1,569 adults, conducted in more than 300 scientifically selected towns across the nation.* ■ Today, modern water wells in some localities are more than 300 meters deep. *Today, modern water wells in some sites are more than 300 meters deep.*

located delete. The Trust's principal office is located at One World Trade Center, New York, New York 10048. *The Trust's principal office is at One World Trade Center, New York, New York 10048.* ■ The numerals indicate which page the section is located on. *The numerals indicate which page the section is on.* ■ The school, which is located in an old, poorly cared for building, further added to our misgivings. *The school, which is in an old, poorly cared for building, further added to our misgivings.* ■ Also known as the "rational expectations school," the freshwater school takes its name from the fact that it is taught in universities located on or near the shores of the Great Lakes. *Also known as the "rational expectations school," the freshwater school takes its name from the fact that it is taught in universities on or near the shores of the Great Lakes.*

logical reason *reason.*

long suit *forte.*

look to see *check; examine; see; verify.* He is now looking to see if the same adducts occur in living cells damaged by hydroxyl radicals. *He is now seeing if the same adducts occur in living cells damaged by hydroxyl radicals.*

lose out on *lose.*

lots of *many; much.*

loudly bellow (holler; howl; roar; scream; shout; shriek; yell) *bellow (holler; howl; roar; scream; shout; shriek; yell).* In the early days of VCRs, movie companies howled loudly at the advent of movie rentals and attempted blocking legislation. *In the early days of VCRs, movie companies howled at the advent of movie rentals and attempted blocking legislation.*

-(al)ly enough *-(al)ly;* delete. Ironically enough, many states have loosened their registration laws in the last decade, but turnout still declines. *Ironically, many states have loosened their registration laws in the last decade, but turnout still declines.* ■ Interestingly enough, very few Texans bought these fantasies; the buyers came from other places. *Very few Texans bought these fantasies; the buyers came from other places.*

-(al)ly speaking *-(al)ly;* delete. All four of their parents would be the same, genetically speaking. *All four of their parents would be genetically the same.* ■ Generally speaking, sunny skies will cover the nation today. *Generally, sunny skies will cover the nation today.* ■ Broadly speaking, banks' roles have been to take deposits, lend money, pool and transform risk, direct the transfer of financial assets, and provide financial advice and service to customers. *Broadly, banks' roles have been to take deposits, lend money, pool and transform risk, direct the transfer of financial assets, and provide financial advice and service to customers.* ■ Frankly speaking, I don't believe they were percussion grenades. *Frankly, I don't believe they were percussion grenades.* ■ Although there may be small differences between the jobs, they are, relatively speaking, inconsequential. *Although there may be small differences between the jobs, they are relatively inconsequential.* ■ Personally speaking, I belonged to the Howdy Doody generation. *I belonged to the Howdy Doody generation.*

M

made of delete. The only data show small vestiges of threads made of cotton. *The only data show small vestiges of cotton threads.*

made to measure *custom; customized; custom-made; tailored; tailor-made.*

made to order *custom; customized; custom-made; tailored; tailor-made.*

made up out of *made of;* delete.

magnitude *import; moment; scope; size.* Nothing is unthinkable when you try to solve a problem of this magnitude. *Nothing is unthinkable when you try to solve a problem of this size.*

major delete. If the vice president comes in third, it's a major disaster. *If the vice president comes in third, it's a disaster.* ■ Since World War II was raging at the time, this major breakthrough was unknown by anyone outside Germany. *Since World War II was raging at the time, this breakthrough was unknown by anyone outside Germany.* ■ Combining these two world-class companies represents a major milestone for the plastics industry. *Combining these two world-class companies represents a milestone for the plastics industry.* ■ It's going to take a couple of years to shake out, but it won't result in a major calamity. *It's going to take a couple of years to shake out, but it won't result in a calamity.*

(a; the) majority (of) *almost all (of); (nine) in (ten) (of); many (of); more (of); most (of); nearly all (of); (43) of (48) (of); ... percent (of); three-fourths (two-thirds) (of).* The majority of people do not expect to experience a trauma like this. *Most people do not expect to experience a trauma like this.* ■ The majority of the uninsured and underinsured are working people whose employers do not offer health benefits. *Nearly all the uninsured and underinsured are working people whose employers do not offer health benefits.* ■ Surveys reveal that the majority of chronic fatigue syndrome victims are between 22 and 45. *Surveys reveal that 60 percent of chronic fatigue syndrome victims are between 22 and 45.* ■ The majority of successful women are found in industries that have a history of being more receptive to women. *Eight in ten successful women are found in industries that have a history of being more receptive to women.*

(a; the) major part (percentage; portion; proportion) (of) *a good (great) deal (of); a good (great) many (of); almost all (of); (nine) in (ten) (of); many (of); more (of); most (of); nearly all (of); (43) of (48) (of); ... percent (of); three-fourths (two-thirds) (of).* Murdoch could borrow a major portion of the purchase price using Triangle's assets as collateral. *Murdoch could borrow most of the purchase price using Triangle's assets as collateral.*

make ... (a; the) ... (about; of; to) delete. We made the incorrect assumption that every junior investment officer would see a loan opportunity in the sale of an entrepreneur's business. *We incorrectly assumed that every junior investment officer would see a loan opportunity in the sale of an entrepreneur's business.* ■ Dr. Koop made reference to the intravenous use of drugs and how this can cause AIDS. *Dr. Koop referred to the intravenous use of drugs and how this* *can cause AIDS.* ■ Two major issues should be considered when making a choice. *Two major issues should be considered when choosing.* ■ We made an agreement that she would keep the stereo for me. *We agreed that she would keep the stereo for me.* ■ Why make that admission to them? *Why admit that to them?* ■ The company's management may not see any reason for making a shift from their current approach. *The company's management may not see any reason for shifting from their current approach.* ■ By making adjustments to the price, promotion, or distribution elements of the marketing mix, the risks and costs associated with product innovation are minimized. *By adjusting the price, promotion, or distribution elements of the marketing mix, the risks and costs associated with product innovation are minimized.* ■ They may also make use of telex machines and other, more exclusive, communication devices. *They may also use telex machines and other, more exclusive, communication devices.* ■ Once we make that assessment, we'll make a decision. *Once we assess that, we'll decide.*

make ... acquaintance *meet.* I was very pleased to make your acquaintance. *I was very pleased to meet you.*

make allowance for *allow for; arrange for; consider; prepare for; provide for.*

make an appearance *appear; arrive; come; show up.*

make an attempt (effort; endeavor) *try.* Triton has obviously made an attempt to bring in qualified, high-potential women but has paid no attention to integrating them into the old-boy network. *Triton has obviously tried to bring in qualified, high-potential women but has paid no attention to integrating them into the old-boy network.* ■ For any question you answer incorrectly, make an effort to understand why the answer given is the correct one. *For any question you answer incorrectly, try to understand why the answer given is the correct one.* ■ We are going to make an effort to hold prices or even reduce them. *We are going to try to hold prices or even reduce them.*

make available *afford; furnish; provide; supply.* Paralleling a business school course of study, our curriculum makes available a stable, inclusive, and continuing transmittal of practices and perspectives to those working managers who want to continue their education in management. *Paralleling a business school course of study, our curriculum affords a stable, inclusive, and continuing transmittal of practices and perspectives to those working managers who want to continue their education in management.*

make believe *feign; pretend.*

make concession for *allow for; arrange for; consider; prepare for; provide for.*

make contact (with) *call; contact; discover; encounter; find; locate; meet (with); phone; reach; speak (to); talk (to); visit; write.* In Sturgis, we made contact with the Sons of Silence. *In Sturgis, we encountered the Sons of Silence.*

make (a; the) decision (determination) *conclude; decide; determine; resolve.* I made the decision to keep on good terms with all the candidates. *I decided to keep on good terms with all the candidates.* ■ I made the determination never to return to work. *I resolved never to return to work.* ■ It's premature to make that determination. *It's premature to conclude that.* ■ Who makes that determination? *Who determines that?* ■ The federal government has made a determination that if you're poor you'll be treated poorly. *The federal government has determined that if you're poor you'll be treated poorly.*

make (a; the) determined decision *conclude; decide; determine; resolve.* She made a determined decision to overcome her drug dependency. *She resolved to overcome her drug dependency.*

make (a; the) distinction *distinguish.* For some years, economists have enjoyed making a distinction between "salt water" and "fresh water" approaches to economics. *For some years, economists have enjoyed distinguishing between "salt water" and "fresh water" approaches to economics.*

make false statements *lie.* He did this by using a false Social Security number and making false statements on his application. *He did this by using a false Social Security number and lying on his application.*

(to) make matters worse *what is worse; worse still; worse yet.* To make matters worse, many bankers did not receive their Fed advisories, or comparable information, from professional banking organizations until late July or August. *Worse still, many bankers did not receive their Fed advisories, or comparable information, from professional banking organizations until late July or August.* ■ To make matters worse, companies kept retail prices artificially inflated to make the planned "sales" affordable; consumer savings were largely imaginary. *What's worse, companies kept retail prices artificially inflated to make the planned "sales" affordable; consumer savings were largely imaginary.* ■ Making matters worse, a boom in the herring export market has turned to bust. *Worse yet, a boom in the herring export market has turned to bust.*

make mention of *mention.* You made mention of the fact that S&Ls insure you only up to $100,000. *You mentioned the fact that S&Ls insure you only up to $100,000.* ■ A joint communiqué issued at the close of a two-day summit made no mention of human rights issues. *A joint communiqué issued at the close of a two-day summit mentioned no human rights issues.* ■ Someone made mention of the term old maid, which I think is no longer relevant in today's society. *Someone mentioned the term old maid, which I think is no longer relevant in today's society.*

make provision for *allow for; arrange for; consider; prepare for; provide for.* No family can attempt to establish a budget without making provision for these "unexpected" but forever recurring expenses. *No family can attempt to establish a budget without allowing for these "unexpected" but forever recurring expenses.*

make (a; the) statement saying (stating) *comment; remark; say; state.* A well-known equipment dealer made a statement saying that he felt sorry for the Amish farmers because the time would come when they couldn't make a living on their small farms. *A well-known equipment dealer said that he felt sorry for the Amish farmers because the time would come when they couldn't make a living on their small farms.* ■ I think it's important for us to make a statement saying that this veto should be overridden. *I think it's important for us to state that this veto should be overridden.*

make up (my) mind *decide.* King said he will make up his mind by mid-September on whether to seek the GOP nomination for governor. *King said he will decide by mid-September on whether to seek the GOP nomination for governor.*

make (my) way *driving; proceeding; running; walking.* The vice president is now making his way to the platform. *The vice president is now walking to the platform.*

many hundreds (thousands) *hundreds (thousands).* The abacus shown here has been used in China for many hundreds of years. *The abacus shown here has been used in China for hundreds of years.*

many times over *frequently; often; recurrently; regularly; repeatedly.*

marginal *little; narrow; slender; slight; slim; small; tiny.*

mass exodus *exodus.* The mass exodus to Penturbia is the result of a declining quality of life. *The exodus to Penturbia is the result of a declining quality of life.* ■ She saw no evidence of a conspiracy at the time of the mass exodus of doctors from Blue Shield. *She saw no evidence of a conspiracy at the time of the exodus of doctors from Blue Shield.*

mass extinction *extinction.* A comet striking Earth with the power of 300 million Hiroshima-sized atomic bombs may be the cause of mass extinction 11 million years ago. *A comet striking Earth with the power of 300 million Hiroshima-sized atomic bombs may be the cause of extinction 11 million years ago.*

match exactly *duplicate; match.* To find strings that match your case exactly, enter the appropriate characters in uppercase when specifying the string to be searched for. *To find strings that match your case, enter the appropriate characters in uppercase when specifying the string to be searched for.*

match perfectly *duplicate; match.* The fluctuations of the one variable match perfectly the fluctuations of the other variable. *The fluctuations of the one variable duplicate the fluctuations of the other variable.*

match up *match.*

materialize *develop; evolve; form; happen; occur; result; take place.*

matter-of-course *common; customary; habitual; natural; normal; ordinary; regular; routine; typical; usual.*

matter-of-fact *businesslike; factual; literal; plain; prosaic; straightforward; unfeeling.*

maximal *biggest; greatest; highest; largest; longest; most; top.*

maximize *add to; broaden; enlarge; greaten; increase; raise.*

(a; the) maximum ... of *biggest; greatest; highest; largest; longest; most; top.* It is necessary to get the maximum mileage out of existing and new products as rapidly as possible. *It is necessary to get the most mileage out of existing and new products as rapidly as possible.*

(a; the) maximum amount (of) *biggest; greatest; highest; largest; longest; most; top.*

(a; the) maximum number (of) *biggest; greatest; highest; largest; longest; most; top.* Set up your fields for the maximum number of lines. *Set up your fields for the most lines.*

may or may not *may; may not.* Your assessment of Houston's nascent ascent from the urban graveyard may or may not prove to be on the mark, but your classification of its metropolitan area as the nation's fourth largest was not. *Your assessment of Houston's nascent ascent from the urban graveyard may prove to be on the mark, but your classification of its metropolitan area as the nation's fourth largest was not.*

may (might) perhaps *may (might).*

may (might) possibly *may (might).* She said Concord Academy might possibly be too difficult. *She said Concord Academy might be too difficult.* ■ This may possibly be TV's last great miniseries. *This may be TV's last great miniseries.*

meaningful *delete.* This slope can represent miles per hour, weight versus length, or a number of other meaningful rates that are important to the analysis of data. *This slope can represent miles per hour, weight versus length, or a number of other rates that are important to the analysis of data.*

meaningful importance (significance) *importance (significance); meaning.*

meaningless gibberish *gibberish.*

measured against *against; alongside; beside; compared to (with); -(i)er than; less; less than; more; more than; next to; over; than; to; versus; vis-à-vis.* Tariffs on most consumer goods dropped by only one-tenth, a figure that looks minuscule measured against the 12-percent federal sales tax the Canadian government still slaps on everything coming into the country. *Tariffs on most consumer goods dropped by only one-tenth, a figure that looks minuscule alongside the 12-percent federal sales tax the Canadian government still slaps on everything coming into the country.* ■ Retrieving data from disks is slow measured against the speed of processing the records once they are in memory. *Retrieving data from disks is slower than the speed of processing the records once they are in memory.*

measure up to *meet.* Because many teachers expect children from the same family to behave in the same manner, it can be particularly difficult for temperamentally different siblings to measure up to their expectations. *Because many teachers expect children from the same family to behave in the same manner, it can be particularly difficult for temperamentally different siblings to meet their expectations.*

mechanical mechanism *mechanical; mechanism.* The final result was the Pascaline, a polished brass box containing a sophisticated, mechanical calculating mechanism composed of gears. *The final result was the Pascaline, a polished brass box containing a sophisticated calculating mechanism composed of gears.*

meet together *meet.*

memorandum *memo; note.* This memorandum is for informative purposes only. *This memo is for informative purposes only.*

mental ability (capacity) *ability (capacity).*

mental telepathy *telepathy.*

(a; the) -ment of *-ing.* The assignment of retirement assets to a money manager may entail a lengthy process of evaluation by the corporate client. *Assigning retirement assets to a money manager may entail a lengthy process of evaluation by the corporate client.* ■ The second step in an expansion program is the establishment of credibility in the new markets. *The second step in an expansion program is establishing credibility in the new markets.* ■ We project line widths will fall to the 1-micron level by 1990 by the development and employment of nontraditional, lithographic processes. *We project line widths will fall to the 1-micron level by 1990 by developing and employing nontraditional, lithographic processes.* ■ They are responsible for the management of their specific work groups and for the accomplishment of the actual work of the organization. *They are responsible for managing their specific work groups and for accomplishing the actual work of the organization.* ■ Meetings do not contribute to the attainment of individual objectives. *Meetings do not contribute to attaining individual objectives.* ■ The treatment of these items as expenses results in lower rents and more available apartments. *Treating these items as expenses results in lower rents and more available apartments.*

merge into one (company) *merge.* The two departments are being merged into one. *The two departments are being merged.* ■ Officials of the Farm Credit System say nine of the system's banks for cooperatives will be merged into one bank. *Officials of the Farm Credit System say nine of the system's banks for cooperatives will be merged.* ■ The Federal Home Loan Bank Board announced that eight troubled Texas savings and loan associations were being merged into one in a record $2.5 billion transaction. *The Federal Home Loan Bank Board announced that eight troubled Texas savings and loan associations were being merged in a record $2.5 billion transaction.*

merge together *merge.* First, create the files to be merged together. *First, create the files to be merged.* ■ The strategy shifts from one of consolidation to one of integration; that is, the international and domestic activities are merged together. *The strategy shifts from one of consolidation to one of integration; that is, the international and domestic activities are merged.*

mesh together *mesh.* Gears are toothed wheels that mesh together to transmit force and motion from one gear to the next. *Gears are toothed wheels that mesh to transmit force and motion from one gear to the next.* ■ The governor's press secretary said the trip meshed together local concerns with campaign themes. *The governor's press secretary said the trip meshed local concerns with campaign themes.*

metaphorically speaking *as it were; in a sense; in a way; so to speak.*

methodology *method.* The approaches used to gain this understanding draw on the methodologies developed by such social sciences as anthropology, linguistics, and sociology. *The approaches used to gain this understanding draw on the methods developed by such social sciences as anthropology, linguistics, and sociology.* ■ When developing estimates of market size, data extrapolation methodologies may be useful. *When developing estimates of market size, data extrapolation methods may be useful.*

metropolis *city.*

(with) might and main *force; power; strength.*

might or might not *might; might not.*

mingle together *mingle.* An invitation-only crowd of some 40 people met at Kate's Mystery Books, though many in the crowd apparently did not want to mingle together. *An invitation-only crowd of some 40 people met at Kate's Mystery Books, though many in the crowd apparently did not want to mingle.*

minimal *brief; least; lowest; minor; not much; scant; short; slight; smallest.* At this point, you will want to be able to type the minimal number of keys to execute commands. *At this point, you will want to be able to type the least number of keys to execute commands.* ■ The child receives much disapproval and punishment for incorrect behavior and minimal approval for correct behavior. *The child receives much disapproval and punishment for incorrect behavior and not much approval for correct behavior.* ■ We're hoping the damage to computers is minimal. *We're hoping the damage to computers is slight.* ■ We expect the delay will be minimal. *We expect the delay will be brief.*

(a; the) minimal number (of) *a couple (of); a few (of); a handful (of); fewer than half (of); hardly any (of); (one) in (ten) (of); less than half (of); not many (of); (9) of (48) (of); one or two (two or three) (of); one-third (one-fifteenth) (of); ... percent (of); scarcely any (of).* Smith said a minimal number of people have irreconcilable differences with the roommate they selected. *Smith said hardly any people have irreconcilable differences with the roommate they selected.*

minimize *decrease; lower; reduce.*

(a; the) minimum (of) *at least; (the) least; little; lowest; minimum; scant; shortest; slightest; smallest; tiniest.* Most oxyacetylene welding is done manually with a minimum of equipment. *Most oxyacetylene welding is done manually with minimum equipment.* ■ It takes a minimum of $100,000 and a year and a half to develop a good standalone piece of software. *It takes at least $100,000 and a year and a half to develop a good standalone piece of software.* ■ A doctrine of belief in the people assumes that individuals find ways of doing good over a lifetime with a minimum of state interference. *A doctrine of belief in the people assumes that individuals find ways of doing good over a lifetime with the least state interference.*

(a; the) minority (of) *a couple (of); a few (of); a handful (of); fewer than half (of); hardly any (of); (one) in (ten) (of); less than half (of); not many (of); (9) of (48) (of); one or two (two or three) (of); one-third (one-fifteenth) (of); ... percent (of); scarcely any (of).* Despite growing political attention to the issue of financing long-term care for the elderly, the figures underscore that a minority of all elderly people actually wind up in nursing homes. *Despite growing political attention to the issue of financing long-term care for the elderly, the figures underscore that fewer than half of all elderly people actually wind up in nursing homes.* ■ A minority of those who are comfortable financially are good givers, but some of the country's wealthiest give dramatically large sums. *Few who are comfortable financially are good givers, but some of the country's wealthiest give dramatically large sums.* ■ The transgressions of a minority of institutions is no reason to call for the dismantling of our business and to pronounce that it has outlived its usefulness. *The transgressions of a few institutions is no reason to call for the dismantling of our business and to pronounce that it has outlived its usefulness.*

minutely detail *detail.* Given a problem, engineers and computer scientists, accustomed to working with mathematical procedures, would write a program—a list of minutely detailed instructions logically guiding the computer step by step through its assigned task. *Given a problem, engineers and computer scientists, accustomed to working with mathematical procedures, would write a program—a list of detailed instructions logically guiding the computer step by step through its assigned task.*

mix and mingle *mingle; mix.*

mix together *mix.* The capability to mix text and graphics together in the same document makes it easy to produce newsletters, instructional materials, and other documents where figures, logos, and/or pictures are needed. *The capability to mix text and graphics in the same document makes it easy to produce newsletters, instructional materials, and other documents where figures, logos, and/or pictures are needed.*

modern, state-of-the-art *modern; state-of-the-art.* Today, with modern, state-of-the-art technologies, breast cancer can be detected at very early stages of development. *Today, with modern technologies, breast cancer can be detected at very early stages of development.*

(a; the) modicum of *few; little; some; tiny; trifle.*

months of age *months.* At 14 months of age, these children showed fear and shyness when taken into a room with strangers. *At 14 months, these children showed fear and shyness when taken into a room with strangers.*

more -(i)er *-(i)er; more.* Watching television is more easier than reading. *Watching television is easier than reading.* ■ She's more lovelier than I ever imagined. *She's more lovely than I ever imagined.* ■ He did it more better. *He did it better.*

more extended (lengthy; prolonged; protracted) *longer.* Even the IRS has been testing itself over a more prolonged period. *Even the IRS has been testing itself over a longer period.*

more improved *improved.*

more inferior *inferior.*

more often than not *almost always; commonly; customarily; generally; most often; nearly always; normally; typically; usually.*

(the) more ... of the two *(the) -(i)er; (the) more.* Objectivity is certainly the more difficult of the two to sustain. *Objectivity is certainly the more difficult to sustain.* ▪ From the viewpoint of cost, the secured loan is the more advantageous of the two. *From the viewpoint of cost, the secured loan is the more advantageous.*

more preferable *preferable.* We have never said any one group is more preferable to another. *We have never said any one group is preferable to another.*

more superior *superior.*

more than exceeded (surpassed) *exceeded (surpassed).* From all sides, there is little disagreement that while business more than exceeded its component goals, the schools fell short of theirs. *From all sides, there is little disagreement that while business exceeded its component goals, the schools fell short of theirs.*

most but not all *almost all; (nine) in (ten); many; most; nearly all; (43) of (48); ... percent; three-fourths (two-thirds).* Most, but not all, accounting programs store the data you enter in a database. *Almost all accounting programs store the data you enter in a database.* ▪ The business community supports the utility's position; so do most, but not all, politicians. *The business community supports the utility's position; so do most politicians.* ▪ DOSCMD can execute most, but not all, BASIC.SYSTEM disk commands. *DOSCMD can execute nearly all BASIC.SYSTEM disk commands.*

most -(i)est *-(i)est; most.* You missed two of the most simplest questions. *You missed two of the simplest questions.*

most favorite *favorite; most favored.*

most important *above all.* Most important, the system that files are designated by should be consistent and understood by everyone. *Above all, the system that files are designated by should be consistent and understood by everyone.*

most important *central; chief; critical; crucial; foremost; key; leading; main; major; pivotal; principal; seminal.* The Medical Society's central point was that access, not the number of physicians licensed, is the most important issue facing the delivery of medical services. *The Medical Society's central point was that access, not the number of physicians licensed, is the main issue facing the delivery of medical services.* ▪ The company's most important product, Mechanical Advantage, began shipping in early 1987. *The company's leading product, Mechanical Advantage, began shipping in early 1987.* ▪ Recent studies have shown that for most investors, retiring comfortably is their most important financial goal. *Recent studies have shown that for most investors, retiring comfortably is their foremost financial goal.* ▪ The most important factor in determining the amount of pension plan income you receive is your longevity with one company. *The key factor in determining the amount of pension plan income you receive is your longevity with one company.*

most ... one *most*. It's fairly obvious that the third approach will get the best results, but it is also the most difficult one to employ. *It's fairly obvious that the third approach will get the best results, but it is also the most difficult to employ.*

most (of the) time(s) *almost always; commonly; generally; most often; nearly always; normally; typically; usually*.

motion picture *film; movie*.

motivating force *drive; energy; force; impetus; motivation; power*. The primary motivating force behind their behavior is the need to shock others. *The primary motivation behind their behavior is the need to shock others.* ■ A place for the governor to demonstrate that he has not forgotten the central motivating force in his early political career is the lobby of 75 State Street. *A place for the governor to demonstrate that he has not forgotten the central force in his early political career is the lobby of 75 State Street.*

motivation *motive*. There is doubt about the ethical standards of life insurance companies as well as the motivations and practices of the agents selling their products. *There is doubt about the ethical standards of life insurance companies as well as the motives and practices of the agents selling their products.*

move forward *advance; go on; move on; proceed; progress*. We urge all involved to move forward with whatever plans make the most sense for both the city and the college. *We urge all involved to proceed with whatever plans make the most sense for both the city and the college.*

multiple *many; several*. You are taking in data on multiple levels. *You are taking in data on many levels.*

(a; the) multiplicity of *a good (great) many; countless; endless; infinite; many; millions (of); numberless; numerous; thousands (of); untold*. She suffers from a multiplicity of moods and personalities. *She suffers from many moods and personalities.*

(a; the) multitude of *a good (great) many; countless; endless; infinite; many; millions (of); numberless; numerous; thousands (of); untold*. How do our customers and prospects view us given the multitude of changes in customers' needs and behaviors? *How do our customers and prospects view us given the many changes in customers' needs and behaviors?*

multitudinous *a good (great) many; countless; endless; infinite; many; millions (of); numberless; numerous; thousands (of); untold*.

must necessarily (of necessity) *inevitably; must; necessarily; of necessity; unavoidably*. Texts organized around specific topics must of necessity limit their discussion to the features contained in those programs. *Texts organized around* *specific topics must limit their discussion to the features contained in those pro-grams.* ■ Such people must of necessity feel accountable to the public they serve, rather than to a structure that could become bureaucratic as easily as any other. *Such people must feel accountable to the public they serve, rather than to a structure that could become bureaucratic as easily as any other.*

mutual agreement (mutually agree) *agreement (agree).* The NATO leaders pro-claimed mutual agreement about reducing the missile systems. *The NATO lead-ers proclaimed agreement about reducing the missile systems.* ■ They have mutually agreed that it would be in the best interest of both parties to amend the terms of the management and operating contract. *They have agreed that it would be in the best interest of both parties to amend the terms of the management and operating contract.*

mutual ... and (between ... and; both; each other; one another; two) *and (be-tween ... and; both; each other; one another; two).* I think all three news direc-tors in town have a mutual respect for one another. *I think all three news direc-tors in town have a respect for one another.* ■ Understanding exists when both parties involved in the communication mutually agree not only on the informa-tion but also on the meaning of the information. *Understanding exists when both parties involved in the communication agree not only on the information but also on the meaning of the information.* ■ Both Herzberg's research and the Tarry-town experiment tell us that job enrichment must take place in an atmosphere of mutual trust between labor and management. *Both Herzberg's research and the Tarrytown experiment tell us that job enrichment must take place in an atmos-phere of trust between labor and management.*

mutual communication *communication.* In this way, mutual communication is established, and some type of agreement becomes much more possible. *In this way, communication is established, and some type of agreement becomes much more possible.*

mutual cooperation *cooperation.*

mutual friendship *friendship.*

my feeling (thinking) is *I assert; I believe; I claim; I contend; I feel; I hold; I judge; I maintain; I say; I think; I view; to me;* delete. My feeling is we're not talking about McCarthyism, we're talking about a crippled attorney general. *We're not talking about McCarthyism, we're talking about a crippled attorney general.*

(a) myriad of *a good (great) many; countless; endless; infinite; many; millions (of); numberless; numerous; thousands (of); untold.*

N

name as *name.*

... nature delete. The heinous nature of the crime staggers the imagination. *The heinousness of the crime staggers the imagination.* ■ A stubborn democrat, Snow was troubled by the authoritarian nature of the Communist movement, but saw it as a lesser evil than the inadequacies of the Chiang Kai-shek Government. *A stubborn democrat, Snow was troubled by the authoritarianism of the Communist movement, but saw it as a lesser evil than the inadequacies of the Chiang Kai-shek Government.* ■ The possibly blasphemous nature of this comment aside, a couple of thoughts come to mind. *The possible blasphemy of this comment aside, a couple of thoughts come to mind.* ■ The ashes are a reminder of the transitory nature of life. *The ashes are a reminder of the transitoriness of life.*

neat and tidy *neat; tidy.*

necessarily have to *have to.* It doesn't necessarily have to be a bad place to go. *It doesn't have to be a bad place to go.*

necessary *needed; needful; pressing; urgent; vital.* The symbol is often in a more simple form when all the specifications are not necessary. *The symbol is often in a more simple form when all the specifications are not needed.*

necessary essential *essential; necessary.*

necessary prerequisite *necessary; prerequisite.*

necessary requirement *necessary; requirement.* Naturally, we are complying with any necessary reporting requirements. *Naturally, we are complying with any reporting requirements.* ■ "As consistent with school policies" refers to the student satisfying necessary requirements for leaving campus on a weekend. *"As consistent with school policies" refers to the student satisfying requirements for leaving campus on a weekend.*

necessary requisite *necessary; requisite.*

necessitate *demand; exact; must; need; require.* This is expensive and time-consuming and necessitates the establishment of an explicit export infrastructure within the firm. *This is expensive and time-consuming and requires the establishment of an explicit export infrastructure within the firm.* ■ Your husband's job necessitates a great deal of independence and a lot of latitude in his hours. *Your husband's job demands a great deal of independence and a lot of latitude in his hours.*

necessity *need.* The emphasis on technical expertise is being balanced by a necessity for good interpersonal skills. *The emphasis on technical expertise is being balanced by a need for good interpersonal skills.*

needless to say *clearly; naturally; obviously; of course; plainly;* delete.

need not necessarily (of necessity) *need not.* This need not necessarily mean that the regime must fall before it can be studied. *This need not mean that the regime must fall before it can be studied.* ▪ This need not of necessity be conservative, for the status quo may as readily lead to civil strife as indoctrination by radical parties. *This need not be conservative, for the status quo may as readily lead to civil strife as indoctrination by radical parties.*

needs hardly be said *clearly; naturally; obviously; of course; plainly;* delete.

need to have *need.* We felt in order to support the nugget we needed to have an overall precious metals plan. *We felt in order to support the nugget we needed an overall precious metals plan.* ▪ Managers need to have technical, human, and conceptual skills. *Managers need technical, human, and conceptual skills.*

negative feelings *anger; annoyance; disfavor; dislike; displeasure; disregard; distaste; hate; hatred; indifference; resentment.* I have nothing but negative feelings for her. *I have nothing but hatred for her.*

neither here nor there *immaterial; inapt; irrelevant; not pertinent.*

neither one *neither.* He was promised immunity from prosecution and a meeting with the mayor, but he got neither one. *He was promised immunity from prosecution and a meeting with the mayor, but he got neither.* ▪ Neither one of us wanted to admit it. *Neither of us wanted to admit it.*

never at any time *never; not ever; not once.*

never ever *never; not ever; not once.* You never ever make concessions to terrorists. *You never make concessions to terrorists.*

nevertheless *anyhow; even so; still; yet.* There are nagging questions, nevertheless. *Still, there are nagging questions.*

new and innovative *innovative; new.* The health care industry is marketing many new and innovative products. *The health care industry is marketing many innovative products.* ▪ We must continue to develop a range of new and innovative network products and services for both the office and the home. *We must continue to develop a range of new network products and services for both the office and the home.*

(brand) new baby *baby.*

new beginning *beginning.*

new construction *construction.* Both firms predict the vacancy rate will fall, if only because of a lack of new construction. *Both firms predict the vacancy rate will fall, if only because of a lack of construction.*

new creation *creation.*

new departure *departure.* The environmental community is hopeful that Bush will represent a new departure in environmental protection. *The environmental community is hopeful that Bush will represent a departure in environmental protection.*

new innovation *innovation.* There is now ample evidence that the United States is lagging behind Japan in new innovations. *There is now ample evidence that the United States is lagging behind Japan in innovations.*

new introduction *introduction.*

new (high) record *record.* This computer, introduced in 1981, set a new record for sales and quickly became the standard around which most other manufacturers designed their machines. *This computer, introduced in 1981, set a record for sales and quickly became the standard around which most other manufacturers designed their machines.* ■ The New England Power Pool said a new record for the six-state region was set yesterday at noon as a reading of 19,383 megawatts was registered. *The New England Power Pool said a record for the six-state region was set yesterday at noon as a reading of 19,383 megawatts was registered.*

new recruit *recruit.*

next of all *also; and; as well; besides; further; furthermore; moreover; next; second; still more; too.*

no basis in fact *baseless; groundless; unfounded.*

no better (than) *best.* This last point is perhaps no better illustrated than by the recent acquisition of Applied Data Research by Computer Associates. *This last point is perhaps best illustrated by the recent acquisition of Applied Data Research by Computer Associates.*

no longer in existence *dead; defunct; extinct.*

no longer with us *dead; fired.*

no matter (what) *despite (what); whatever.* No matter what the period to maturity, they are accepted for payment of taxes due at face or par value. *Whatever* *the period to maturity, they are accepted for payment of taxes due at face or par value.* ■ No matter what form your writing takes, after just one day at our workshop you'll be better equipped to write your ideas in a clear, logical and persuasive style. *Despite what form your writing takes, after just one day at our workshop you'll be better equipped to write your ideas in a clear, logical and persuasive style.*

no matter how *despite how; however.* She was determined, no matter how long it took, to find out the truth. *She was determined, despite how long it took, to find out the truth.* ■ Americans should rejoice in the knowledge that a nation that has had so little use for aesthetic endeavor has developed sufficient maturity to honor genuine artists, no matter how imperfect their achievements. *Americans should rejoice in the knowledge that a nation that has had so little use for aesthetic endeavor has developed sufficient maturity to honor genuine artists, however imperfect their achievements.* ■ In the current Washington climate, it would be next to impossible to introduce any revenue-losing measure no matter how justified and no matter how favorable the effect on our national saving rate. *In the current Washington climate, it would be next to impossible to introduce any revenue-losing measure however justified and however favorable the effect on our national saving rate.*

no matter when *despite when; whenever.* No matter when you use them, voice-mail messages are usually a lot briefer and more efficient than the give-and-take of ordinary conversation. *Despite when you use them, voice-mail messages are usually a lot briefer and more efficient than the give-and-take of ordinary conversation.*

no matter where *despite where; wherever.* From the state's point of view, the collider will be a boon no matter where it is located. *From the state's point of view, the collider will be a boon wherever it is located.* ■ Being an adolescent today is tough no matter where you come from. *Being an adolescent today is tough wherever you come from.* ■ Using the new, more powerful accelerator, doctors expect to be able to treat virtually any tumor no matter where it is in the body. *Using the new, more powerful accelerator, doctors expect to be able to treat virtually any tumor despite where it is in the body.*

no matter whether ... (or) *despite whether; whether ... or (not).*

no matter which *despite which; whichever.* After it has been started, CUBIT functions in exactly the same manner no matter which load method is used. *After it has been started, CUBIT functions in exactly the same manner despite which load method is used.* ■ No matter which way I decide, I will be blamed for making the wrong decision. *Whichever way I decide, I will be blamed for making the wrong decision.*

no matter who *despite who; whoever.* It is still a good idea and should be adopted, no matter who wins the presidency. *It is still a good idea and should be* *adopted, whoever wins the presidency.* ■ When you look at two of the primary markets NYNEX serves—large business customers and the financial marketplace—you'll see that we get consistently high marks in identification and recognition—no matter who does the measuring. *When you look at two of the primary markets NYNEX serves—large business customers and the financial marketplace—you'll see that we get consistently high marks in identification and recognition—despite who does the measuring.* ■ We expect that *The Book Review* is committed to reviewing books it finds intriguing, no matter who the publisher. *We expect that* The Book Review *is committed to reviewing books it finds intriguing, whoever the publisher.*

no matter whom *despite whom; whomever.* No matter whom the voters choose, investors will be contemplating the first change of presidents since 1980, with all the questions about future policies that implies. *Whomever the voters choose, investors will be contemplating the first change of presidents since 1980, with all the questions about future policies that implies.*

no more (and) no less *exactly; just; precisely.*

no more than *but; merely; only.*

nonetheless *anyhow; even so; still; yet.*

noontime *noon.* The meeting on the 29th will be held at noontime in room 901. *The meeting on the 29th will be held at noon in room 901.* ■ The 23-year-old began releasing his prisoners around noontime. *The 23-year-old began releasing his prisoners around noon.*

no question (about it) *yes.*

not anything *nothing.* There's not anything wrong with this housing code. *There's nothing wrong with this housing code.*

not anywhere *nowhere.* But this total is not anywhere near the level of demand. *But this total is nowhere near the level of demand.*

not a one *none; no one.*

not ... at any time *never; not ever; not once.* My mother was not in a coma at any time; her last few weeks were the only period of very serious pain. *My mother was never in a coma; her last few weeks were the only period of very serious pain.*

notation *memo; note.* Read the entire chapter carefully and methodically, underlining key points and making marginal notations as you go. *Read the entire chapter carefully and methodically, underlining key points and making marginal notes as you go.*

note how (that) delete. Note that character and integer expressions can be free-ly intermixed in output operations. *Character and integer expressions can be freely intermixed in output operations.* ■ Note how in this case, the pathname is not preceded by a slash. *In this case, the pathname is not preceded by a slash.*

not ever *never.*

not hardly (scarcely) *hardly (scarcely).*

notice how (that) delete. Notice how the message line indicates how many characters were saved on the disk. *The message line indicates how many characters were saved on the disk.* ■ Notice that the subscript values dictate which weight is assigned to which observed historical admissions level. *The subscript values dictate which weight is assigned to which observed historical admissions level.*

not in favor of *disagree (with); oppose.*

not in the least *not at all.*

notwithstanding *after all; apart; aside; despite; even with; for all; with all.* Not-withstanding the foregoing, you will retain any rights you may have in the Mate-rials under applicable patent or copyright laws. *Despite the foregoing, you will retain any rights you may have in the Materials under applicable patent or copy-right laws.* ■ These misfortunes notwithstanding, the numbers of gorillas are believed to be growing. *These misfortunes aside, the numbers of gorillas are believed to be growing.* ■ The product's performance notwithstanding, analysts are hesitant to predict how it will fare in the marketplace. *For all the product's performance, analysts are hesitant to predict how it will fare in the market-place.*

notwithstanding the fact that *although; but; even though; still; though; yet.* Of what relevance to usage (notwithstanding the fact that the topic is interesting) is an entry on eponyms? *Of what relevance to usage (even though the topic is interesting) is an entry on eponyms?*

null and void *invalid; not binding; null; void; worthless.*

number-one *central; chief; foremost; key; leading; main; major.* That slow start-up is often the number-one reason why many financial analysts consider bio-technology companies to be a gamble. *That slow start-up is often the main rea-son why many financial analysts consider biotechnology companies to be a gamble.*

numeral *number.* Each end of the cutting plane can be labeled with a letter and a numeral. *Each end of the cutting plane can be labeled with a letter and a number.*

numerical *numeric.*

numerous *countless; endless; many; untold.* There were numerous women in his life. *There were untold women in his life.* ■ I have been in numerous gatherings at which someone excused a momentary lapse of memory with just such a reference to Alzheimer's. *I have been in many gatherings at which someone excused a momentary lapse of memory with just such a reference to Alzheimer's.* ■ Unleashing market forces would bring numerous benefits to Brazil and other troubled debtor countries. *Unleashing market forces would bring countless benefits to Brazil and other troubled debtor countries.*

O

observe *see.*

observe to see *check; examine; see; verify* When the trainee is performing the task, the manager is on the scene, observing to see if any deviations from the intended processes take place. *When the trainee is performing the task, the manager is on the scene, checking if any deviations from the intended processes take place.*

obtain (a; the) ... (for; of; to) delete. Using the first number less than 3.257 and the first number greater than 3.257, it is possible to obtain an approximation for log 3.257 by using linear interpolation. *Using the first number less than 3.257 and the first number greater than 3.257, it is possible to approximate log 3.257 by using linear interpolation.*

obviate the necessity (need) for (of; to) *obviate (-ing).* In an era of extreme sensitivity to health-care costs, they claim their treatments can actually save money, in many cases obviating the need for expensive medical procedures. *In an era of extreme sensitivity to health-care costs, they claim their treatments can actually save money, in many cases obviating expensive medical procedures.* ■ Of course, an awareness of this uncertainty doesn't obviate the need to make decisions based on your best guess about what the future holds. *Of course, an awareness of this uncertainty doesn't obviate making decisions based on your best guess about what the future holds.*

occasion *time.* There are also occasions when you must make extensive revisions to long documents. *There are also times when you must make extensive revisions to long documents.*

occasionally *at times; now and again; now and then; sometimes.* Getting to the actual command you want to execute occasionally means you must select a series of commands from the displayed submenus. *Getting to the actual command you want to execute sometimes means you must select a series of commands from the displayed submenus.*

occur again *recur.* It will never occur again. *It will never recur.* ▪ Key elements of the measure include $20,000 in tax-free compensation to each of the 60,000 internees still living and an education trust fund of $1.3 million to help insure that similar civil-rights violations never occur again. *Key elements of the measure include $20,000 in tax-free compensation to each of the 60,000 internees still living and an education trust fund of $1.3 million to help insure that similar civil-rights violations never recur.*

of (a; the) ... delete. I'd like to ask a question of the senator. *I'd like to ask the senator a question.* ▪ The article failed to mention that a two-year-old investigation by the VA concluded that any irregularities were minor and of no significance. *The article failed to mention that a two-year-old investigation by the VA concluded that any irregularities were minor and insignificant.* ▪ You would adjust columns as needed to print on labels of a different size. *You would adjust columns as needed to print on different-size labels.*

(a; the) ... of *-ing.* For most American families, this means an analysis of the costs of operating and financing their automobiles. *For most American families, this means analyzing the costs of operating and financing their automobiles.* ▪ Even more important is a knowledge of the costs of consumption in terms of the alternative consumption opportunities that are given up because of the particular choices made. *Even more important is knowing the costs of consumption in terms of the alternative consumption opportunities that are given up because of the particular choices made.*

of all delete. An executive information system must be easy to learn, easy to use, and most important of all, consistent with the executive's work style. *An executive information system must be easy to learn, easy to use, and most important, consistent with the executive's work style.* ▪ A cyclical pattern is the most difficult of all to predict. *A cyclical pattern is the most difficult to predict.* ▪ First of all, he has to be Korean. *First, he has to be Korean.*

of between ... and *between ... and; of ... to.* The benefit is phased out for investors with incomes of between $200,000 and $250,000. *The benefit is phased out for investors with incomes between $200,000 and $250,000.*

of (a; the) ... character delete. A license may be revoked if a meter is used in operating any scheme or enterprise of an unlawful character, for nonuse during any consecutive 12 months, or for any failure of the licensee to comply with the regulations governing the use of postage meters. *A license may be revoked if a meter is used in operating any scheme or unlawful enterprise, for nonuse during any consecutive 12 months, or for any failure of the licensee to comply with the regulations governing the use of postage meters.*

of (a) different opinion *at odds.*

of ... dimensions (magnitude; proportions; size) delete. It was a success of monumental dimensions. *It was a monumental success.* ▪ Trying to balance family life and modern corporate life is a problem of increasingly large proportions. *Trying to balance family life and modern corporate life is an increasingly large problem.* ■ Massachusetts is now facing a public health crisis of serious proportions. *Massachusetts is now facing a serious public health crisis.* ■ This is a tragedy of immense magnitude. *This is an immense tragedy.*

offer (a; the) ... (at; of; to) delete. In this column, we offer a brief look at five organizations that have found methods of reducing the burden. *In this column, we briefly look at five organizations that have found methods of reducing the burden.* ■ Table 6-12 offers an evaluation of the nursing care of a client with cancer. *Table 6-12 evaluates the nursing care of a client with cancer.* ■ This author offers an examination of the research findings on age and performance, and also supports those findings with his own field experience in companies in various parts of the country. *This author examines the research findings on age and performance, and also supports those findings with his own field experience in companies in various parts of the country.*

official business *business.*

off of *from; off.* She lived one block off of campus. *She lived one block off campus.* ■ They're making a lot of money off of cocaine trafficking. *They're making a lot of money from cocaine trafficking.* ■ The sale price of an IBM PS/2 Model 60 is $2995, which is 25 percent off of the regular price. *The sale price of an IBM PS/2 Model 60 is $2995, which is 25 percent off the regular price.*

of from ... to *from ... to; of ... to.*

of (a; the) ... importance (that; to) *important; -(al)ly important;* delete. I believe it is of critical importance that I set the record straight to clear the names of those who have been compromised by this attack. *I believe it is critical that I set the record straight to clear the names of those who have been compromised by this attack.* ■ They also stated that their innovation was of importance to their superiors' evaluation of their work. *They also stated that their innovation was important to their superiors' evaluation of their work.* ■ Since increased involvement is generally associated with increased management and financial costs, not all foreign markets are of equal importance. *Since increased involvement is generally associated with increased management and financial costs, not all foreign markets are equally important.* ■ Information service issues are of vital importance to the telecommunications industry as well as to the general public. *Information service issues are vital to the telecommunications industry as well as to the general public.*

of (a; the) ... nature delete. The collateral often includes such assets as unlisted shares, works of art, blood stock, antiques, and real estate of an unusual nature. *The collateral often includes such assets as unlisted shares, works of art, blood stock, antiques, and unusual real estate.* ■ First-level management deals with day-to-day operations of a repetitive nature. *First-level management deals with repetitive day-to-day operations.* ■ United Kingdom respondents tend to be more reluctant to answer questions of a personal nature than U.S. respondents. *United Kingdom respondents tend to be more reluctant to answer personal questions than U.S. respondents.* ■ The new test will help tell how early math anxiety of a severe nature is appearing. *The new test will help tell how early severe math anxiety is appearing.* ■ This type of analysis is of recent origin and is primarily of a conceptual rather than analytical nature. *This type of analysis is of recent origin and is primarily conceptual rather than analytical.*

of (to) no avail *unsuccessful.*

of one form (kind; sort; type) or another *in some way; some form (kind; sort; type) of; somehow; someway(s);* delete. About 15 percent of all U.S. and Soviet missions involving nuclear reactors have suffered failures of one sort or another. *About 15 percent of all U.S. and Soviet missions involving nuclear reactors have suffered some sort of failure.* ■ Too many members of Congress are engaging in "sexcapades" of one form or another. *Too many members of Congress are engaging in some form of "sexcapades."*

of ... own accord (free will) *gladly; readily; willingly.*

of (a; the) ... persuasion delete. A physician of liberal persuasion agonized over the senator's fall from grace. *A liberal physician agonized over the senator's fall from grace.*

of such *so.* The personal balance sheet is of such simplicity that anyone who can add and subtract can also develop the entries. *The personal balance sheet is so simple that anyone who can add and subtract can also develop the entries.*

oftentimes (ofttimes) *often.* Oftentimes, they're their own worst enemies. *Often, they're their own worst enemies.* ■ Oftentimes, bacteria is present in food when you buy it. *Bacteria is often present in food when you buy it.*

of that (this) kind (sort; type) *like that (this).* For an accident of this kind, you can't help blaming yourself. *For an accident like this, you can't help blaming yourself.*

of that (this) nature *like that (this).* The Boston Juvenile Court deals with cases of this nature. *The Boston Juvenile Court deals with cases like this.* ■ But something of that nature may be necessary as competition heats up. *But something like that may be necessary as competition heats up.*

of that (this) year *(1992);* delete. Pioneer says that between December 1974 and August 31 of this year, a bank deposit would have grown to just $21,760. *Pioneer says that between December 1974 and August 31, 1990, a bank deposit would have grown to just $21,760.* ■ In July of this year, the three-month Treasury stood at 6.73 percent. *In July, the three-month Treasury stood at 6.73 percent.*

of the (them; these) delete. Each of the binomial random variables tends toward
v. Each binomial random variable tends toward v. ■ Each of them looks different. *Each looks different.* ■ There were life insurance companies in the United
States in the late 1700s but only a handful of them. *There were life insurance
companies in the United States in the late 1700s but only a handful.* ■ One of the
reasons I left her is she's unkind. *One reason I left her is she's unkind.*

of the first (highest) magnitude *best; central; chief; finest; first-class; foremost;
great; key; leading; main; major; most important; principal; superior.*

of the first (highest) order *best; central; chief; finest; first-class; foremost; great;
key; leading; main; major; most important; principal; superior.* She called it a
tragedy of the first order. *She called it a major tragedy.* ■ They join the *Letters* and
Diaries of Virginia Woolf as literary achievements of the highest order. *They join
the* Letters *and* Diaries *of Virginia Woolf as superior literary achievements.*

of the same opinion *at one.*

of (a; the) ... variety delete. The condos will be of the luxury variety, with a size
range of 850 to 2,500 square feet. *The condos will be luxurious, with a size range
of 850 to 2,500 square feet.* ■ Snow of the heavy variety is now falling. *Heavy
snow is now falling.*

(a; the) ... of which *whose.* It is one of the few gifts the value of which can be
juggled successfully to get greater leverage. *It is one of the few gifts whose value
can be juggled successfully to get greater leverage.*

old adage *adage.* As the old adage says, "Patriotism is the last refuge of a scoundrel." *As the adage says, "Patriotism is the last refuge of a scoundrel."* ■ British
children, according to the old adage, are to be seen, not heard. *British children,
according to the adage, are to be seen, not heard.*

old cliché *cliché.* Must you always rely on such old clichés? *Must you always
rely on such clichés?*

old maxim *maxim.* Your analysis of that proposal vividly demonstrates an old
maxim: For every complex problem, there is an answer that is absolutely obvious, absolutely simple, and absolutely wrong. *Your analysis of that proposal
vividly demonstrates a maxim: For every complex problem, there is an answer
that is absolutely obvious, absolutely simple, and absolutely wrong.*

old proverb *proverb.*

old relic *relic.*

old saw *saw.* The essence of marginal utility boils down to the old saw that pearls don't cost a lot because men have to dive for them, but rather men dive for them because they command a high price. *The essence of marginal utility boils down to the saw that pearls don't cost a lot because men have to dive for them, but rather men dive for them because they command a high price.*

old saying *saying.* The old saying "a picture is worth a thousand words" appropriately applies to computer graphics. *The saying "a picture is worth a thousand words" appropriately applies to computer graphics.*

on a (the) ... basis *-(al)ly;* delete. The exercises must be done for 20 to 25 minutes on a continuous basis. *The exercises must be done continuously for 20 to 25 minutes.* ■ Every exchange has a clearinghouse that transfers funds from losers to winners on a daily basis. *Every exchange has a clearinghouse that transfers funds daily from losers to winners.* ■ Our sole interest in the report is to be sure that each application is evaluated on a fair basis. *Our sole interest in the report is to be sure that each application is evaluated fairly.* ■ Does it mean we should all start taking aspirin on a regular basis? *Does it mean we should all start taking aspirin regularly?* ■ You should take the medication on an as-needed basis. *You should take the medication as needed.* ■ They are on equal footing and can get to know each other on a personal basis. *They are on equal footing and can get to know each other personally.* ■ To provide this environment, all employees must be dealt with on an individual basis. *To provide this environment, all employees must be dealt with individually.* ■ We have no intention of discussing Bernknopf's model on a point-by-point basis. *We have no intention of discussing Bernknopf's model point by point.* ■ If it happens on a frequent basis, see a doctor. *If it happens frequently, see a doctor.* ■ A lot of tax assistors are hired on a part-time basis. *A lot of tax assistors are hired part time.*

on account of *after; because of; by; due to; following; for; from; in; out of; owing to; through; with.* There are millions of women in this country who have been discriminated against on account of their sex. *There are millions of women in this country who have been discriminated against because of their sex.* ■ Neither party shall be liable for any incidental, special, or consequential damages on account of this Agreement. *Neither party shall be liable for any incidental, special, or consequential damages through this Agreement.*

on account of the fact that *because; considering; for; in that; since.*

on a couple of (a few) occasions *a few times; once or twice; twice; two or three times.* On a couple of occasions, the entire system shut down. *Once or twice, the entire system shut down.* ■ He said he briefed Quayle on a couple of occasions after the trip, during which he visited Costa Rica, Nicaragua, El Salvador, and Honduras. *He said he briefed Quayle twice after the trip, during which he visited Costa Rica, Nicaragua, El Salvador, and Honduras.*

on a (the) ... note *-(al)ly;* delete. On a disconcerting note, 18 percent of the children surveyed said they had been approached to buy or use drugs. *Discon-*

certingly, 18 percent of the children surveyed said they had been approached to buy or use drugs. ▪ On a personal note, I am today announcing my resignation. *I am today announcing my resignation.* ▪ The market began the week on a cautious note. *The market began the week cautiously.*

on a number of (any number of; frequent; many; numerous; several) occasions frequently; many times; numerous times; often; regularly; repeatedly; several times. *They have done that on a number of occasions. They have often done that.* ▪ This has happened on numerous occasions. *This has happened frequently.* ▪ I met her, the woman who stole my husband, on several occasions. *I met her, the woman who stole my husband, several times.* ▪ Quaker Oats had to close down its rolled oats operations on many occasions while it sought relief from the prohibition. *Quaker Oats had to close down its rolled oats operations repeatedly while it sought relief from the prohibition.* ▪ The ACLU has defended American Nazis on numerous occasions. *The ACLU has regularly defended American Nazis.*

on a (the) ... scale (scope) *-(al)ly;* delete. Banks like Citibank, Chase, and the big Swiss banks have pursued business on an international scale since the mid-1960s. *Banks like Citibank, Chase, and the big Swiss banks have pursued international business since the mid-1960s.* ▪ We can do projects on a much larger scale today. *We can do much larger projects today.* ▪ The inescapable conclusion is that survival on the planet will require social planning on an increasing scale. *The inescapable conclusion is that survival on the planet will increasingly require social planning.* ▪ American business cannot expect to compete on a global scale if it must act as a substitute educational system. *American business cannot expect to compete globally if it must act as a substitute educational system.*

on a (the) ... scene *-(al)ly;* delete. On the national scene, here's what's happening. *Here's what's happening nationally.*

on (an; the) average *commonly; customarily; generally; normally; often; ordinarily; typically.*

on ... behalf (of) *for.* CUFT maintains the most active patent licensing office in the U.S. government and handles the patent licensing on behalf of many cooperating federal agencies. *CUFT maintains the most active patent licensing office in the U.S. government and handles the patent licensing for many cooperating federal agencies.* ▪ Nobody is authorized to speak on my behalf. *Nobody is authorized to speak for me.* ▪ All statements made by the Insured or on his behalf shall, in the absence of fraud, be deemed representations and not warranties. *All statements made by or for the Insured shall, in the absence of fraud, be deemed representations and not warranties.*

once (and) for all *conclusively; decisively; finally;* delete. Now, in the sexually rational 1980s, men and women, it seems, trust only scientists to settle once and for all what makes men men and women women. *Now, in the sexually rational*

1980s, men and women, it seems, trust only scientists to settle decisively what makes men men and women women. ■ Analysts expect their questions about Raytheon's nondefense subsidiaries to be answered once and for all when Phillips' successor makes known his intentions. *Analysts expect their questions about Raytheon's nondefense subsidiaries to be finally answered when Phillips' successor makes known his intentions.*

once in a (great) while *at times; now and again; now and then; on occasion; sometimes.*

on certain (some) occasions *at times; now and again; now and then; occasionally; sometimes.* On some occasions, the treatment may retard progression of the disease. *Sometimes, the treatment may retard progression of the disease.*

once ... then *once.* Once this analysis is done, then special attention may be paid to various short pieces of code that consume the most time. *Once this analysis is done, special attention may be paid to various short pieces of code that consume the most time.* ■ Once subglobal market groups have been delineated, the firm then develops uniform product programs for each market cluster it chooses to service. *Once subglobal market groups have been delineated, the firm develops uniform product programs for each market cluster it chooses to service.*

on (the) condition (of; that) *as long as; if; provided; so long as.* The Baker strategy offered limited new funds for debt-strapped nations but only on the condition that the debtors pay full interest, at market rates, on everything they owe. *The Baker strategy offered limited new funds for debt-strapped nations but only if the debtors pay full interest, at market rates, on everything they owe.* ■ The Maynard computer maker will offer a generous financial-support package to 700 employees on condition that they agree to leave the company. *The Maynard computer maker will offer a generous financial-support package to 700 employees provided that they agree to leave the company.* ■ "It will mean renewed persecution," said a woman who spoke only on the condition that her name not be used. *"It will mean renewed persecution," said a woman who spoke only so long as her name not be used.*

on -day *-day.* All that the police know is the bank was robbed sometime on Monday morning. *All that the police know is the bank was robbed sometime Monday morning.* ■ It's usually habit that makes us turn on the television set, eat out on Wednesdays, and drive to work the same way. *It's usually habit that makes us turn on the television set, eat out Wednesdays, and drive to work the same way.* ■ I started work on Friday, September 12. *I started work Friday, September 12.*

on each (every) occasion *all; always; consistently; constantly; each; each time; for (in) each; for (in) every; every time; invariably; unfailingly;* delete.

one and all *all; everyone.*

one and only *one; only; sole.* Is that the one and only time you have engaged in group counseling? *Is that the only time you have engaged in group counseling?*

one and the same *identical; one; the same.* Anyone who has visited countries of the world where the military and the law enforcement agencies are one and the same can appreciate the wisdom of separating these arms of the government. *Anyone who has visited countries of the world where the military and the law enforcement agencies are one can appreciate the wisdom of separating these arms of the government.* ■ We do not believe that computers and communications are going to converge and become one and the same business. *We do not believe that computers and communications are going to converge and become the same business.* ■ Calculations have revealed not only that the newly found object and HAPAG are one and the same, but also that HAPAG appears on several photographic plates taken in the 1950s and 1980s. *Calculations have revealed not only that the newly found object and HAPAG are identical, but also that HAPAG appears on several photographic plates taken in the 1950s and 1980s.*

on earlier (former; previous; prior) occasions *before; earlier; formerly; previously.* I asked Governor Cuomo for his support, as I have on prior occasions. *I asked Governor Cuomo for his support, as I have before.*

one best (most) *best (most).* Each alternative needs to be evaluated to determine which one best achieves the objective. *Each alternative needs to be evaluated to determine which best achieves the objective.*

one-half (one-third) *half (third).* The data is derived from the first one-third of the observations. *The data is derived from the first third of the observations.* ■ Its transmitter reaches only one-half of the homes in the Chicago area. *Its transmitter reaches only half of the homes in the Chicago area.*

one-half (seven-eighths) of an inch *one-half (seven-eighths) inch.* Alternate pages are offset from the left margin by an additional one-half of an inch. *Alternate pages are offset from the left margin by an additional one-half inch.*

one more time *again; once more; re-.* If you position the highlight over the first or last choice on the menu and then press the arrow key one more time, the highlight wraps around to the other end of the menu. *If you position the highlight over the first or last choice on the menu and then press the arrow key again, the highlight wraps around to the other end of the menu.*

one of delete. The second issue is one of market entry. *The second issue is market entry.* ■ In the United States, such a gesture is merely one of politeness. *In the*

United States, such a gesture is merely politeness. ■ The strategy then shifts from one of consolidation to one of integration. *The strategy then shifts from consolidation to integration.*

one-of-a-kind *matchless; novel; peerless; singular; special; unequaled; unique; unmatched; unrivaled.* "Learn C Now" is a one-of-a-kind course that's designed to make beginning programmers productive quickly. *"Learn C Now" is a unique course that's designed to make beginning programmers productive quickly.*

one single *one; (a) single.* Not one single college president has ever attempted to lay off a single high-paid administrator. *Not one college president has ever attempted to lay off a single high-paid administrator.*

one (two) time(s) *once (twice).* We visited them two times in two days. *We visited them twice in two days.* ■ Two times homeless herself, she says that without the state's Employment and Training program, she would still be on welfare. *Twice homeless herself, she says that without the state's Employment and Training program, she would still be on welfare.*

(in) one way or another *anyhow; anyway; by some means; however; in any way; in some way; in whatever way; somehow; somehow or another; someway(s).* He seemed deranged in one way or another. *He seemed deranged somehow.* ■ McDonald's has developed a senior sensitivity workshop for managers, and all the companies, in one way or another, have adopted attractive perks, with flexible working hours. *McDonald's has developed a senior sensitivity workshop for managers, and all the companies, in some way, have adopted attractive perks, with flexible working hours.*

(in) one way or the other *at all; either way; in the least; in the slightest;* delete. It didn't change my religious beliefs one way or the other. *It didn't change my religious beliefs in the least.* ■ The source said the firm's board of directors never decided one way or the other to accept the government's earlier demands. *The source said the firm's board of directors never decided to accept the government's earlier demands.* ■ I knew that the absence of erotic material in these letters could offer no conclusive demonstration one way or the other. *I knew that the absence of erotic material in these letters could offer no conclusive demonstration either way.*

on (the) grounds that *because; considering; for; in that; since.* The decision not to cooperate with this manufacturer was made primarily on the grounds that it made little sense to McDonnell Douglas. *The decision not to cooperate with this manufacturer was made primarily because it made little sense to McDonnell Douglas.* ■ Democratic leaders oppose the tax cut on grounds that it benefits mainly the rich. *Democratic leaders oppose the tax cut since it benefits mainly the rich.*

on ... grounds *about; -(al)ly; on;* delete. If business is not based on ethical grounds, it is of no benefit to society, and it will pass into oblivion. *If business is* *not based on ethics, it is of no benefit to society, and it will pass into oblivion.* ■ The proposed increase in rapid transit fares may be justified on economic grounds. *The proposed increase in rapid transit fares may be economically justified.*

on its (the) face (of it; of things) *apparently; appear (to); outwardly; seem (to); seemingly; superficially.* On the face of it, no term fits the Parisian beau monde of the late 18th century better than the one invented 200 years later by Tom Wolfe. *No term seems to fit the Parisian beau monde of the late 18th century better than the one invented 200 years later by Tom Wolfe.*

on its (the) face (of it; of things) ... appear (seem) *appear (seem).* On the face of it, this would appear to be a simple evaluation to make. *This would appear to be a simple evaluation to make.* ■ On its face, it seems that desegregation has created even more of an imbalance within the school system. *It seems that desegregation has created even more of an imbalance within the school system.*

on (a; the) ... level *-(al)ly;* delete. On a personal level, I cannot stand how he behaves. *Personally, I cannot stand how he behaves.* ■ It will allow you to deal with life on a calmer level. *It will allow you to deal with life more calmly.* ■ I feel it's not possible to have a relationship with a man on a spiritual and emotional level. *I feel it's not possible to have a spiritual and emotional relationship with a man.* ■ In the past year, the media has gotten to know her, at least on a superficial level. *In the past year, the media has gotten to know her, at least superficially.* ■ It has only been 15 years that women have been participating in business on a serious level. *It has only been 15 years that women have been seriously participating in business.* ■ On a less obvious level, they will be able to support very sophisticated layout and composition functions. *Less obviously, they will be able to support very sophisticated layout and composition functions.*

on more than one occasion *a few times; frequently; many times; more than once; often; several times.* I've been asked that question on more than one occasion. *I've been asked that question more than once.* ■ This was a source of irritation to them on more than one occasion during the next few weeks. *This was a source of irritation to them several times during the next few weeks.* ■ On more than one occasion, they would not take the one credit card that I had. *They often would not take the one credit card that I had.* ■ I have told you that on more than one occasion. *I have told you that frequently.*

on no consideration *never; not ever; not once.*

on no occasion *never; not ever; not once.*

on (the) one hand ... on the other (hand) delete. Another way of looking at the basic strategic tradeoffs that Bell Operating Companies are facing is to look at the relationship between their competitiveness on one hand and the need to avoid conflict with various players on the other. *Another way of looking at the basic* *strategic tradeoffs that Bell Operating Companies are facing is to look at the relationship between their competitiveness and the need to avoid conflict with various players.*

on one (two; three) occasion(s) *a few times; once; once or twice; one time; several times; three times; twice; two times.* On only one occasion in the three years of our negotiations were the Angels and Dick unable to come to a satisfactory agreement. *Only once in the three years of our negotiations were the Angels and Dick unable to come to a satisfactory agreement.* ■ Sources familiar with the inquiry inside the Justice Department said Meese was interviewed by FBI agents on two occasions in April. *Sources familiar with the inquiry inside the Justice Department said Meese was twice interviewed by FBI agents in April.*

on ... part *among; by; for; from; of; -'s;* delete. To beat the Soviets will take a great effort on our part. *To beat the Soviets will take a great effort by us.* ■ I think it's foolhardy on your part. *I think it's foolhardy of you.* ■ The shorter work hours logged by women had more to do with their heavy concentration in retail trade and service-oriented industries than a reluctance on their part to work longer hours. *The shorter work hours logged by women had more to do with their heavy concentration in retail trade and service-oriented industries than their reluctance to work longer hours.* ■ It was the first time I felt a real commitment on his part. *It was the first time I felt a real commitment from him.* ■ They think it's a weakness on their part. *They think it's their weakness.* ■ It was a voluntary decision on Steve's part; he resigned to pursue other interests. *It was a voluntary decision of Steve's; he resigned to pursue other interests.*

on ... terms delete. We are no longer on speaking terms with each other. *We are no longer speaking with each other.* ■ We are on cordial terms now. *We are cordial now.*

on that (this) (particular) occasion *at present; at that (this) time; currently; (just; right) now; presently; then; today; (just) yet;* delete.

on the basis of *after; based on; because of; by; for; from; in; on; through; with;* delete. The Money Study segmented the U.S. adult population into five groups on the basis of financial attitudes. *The Money Study segmented, by financial attitudes, the U.S. adult population into five groups.* ■ What one would predict on the basis of these monkey studies is that if the drug is well tolerated in humans, there is every reason to hope that patients should live significantly longer and feel significantly better. *What one would predict from these monkey studies is that if the drug is well tolerated in humans, there is every reason to hope that patients should live significantly longer and feel significantly better.* ■ Employees do not act on the basis of what management thinks, or what management thinks they think; they act on their own opinions. *Employees do not act on what management thinks, or what management thinks they think; they act on their own opinions.* ■ Its managers should be selected on the basis of their ability to further the company's goals and maximize its earnings. *Its managers should be* *selected for their ability to further the company's goals and maximize its earnings.*

on the basis of the fact that *because; considering; for; in that; since.*

on the bottom of *below; beneath; under; underneath.*

on the contrary *but; conversely; however; instead; not so; rather; still; whereas; yet.*

on the decline *abating; declining; decreasing; waning.*

on the decrease *abating; declining; decreasing; waning.*

on the increase *booming; flourishing; growing; increasing; rising.* The Department of Revenue recently released a report on the state's economic indicators that showed personal savings are on the increase. *The Department of Revenue recently released a report on the state's economic indicators that showed personal savings are increasing.*

on the inside of *inside.* An undercut could also be a recessed neck on the inside of a cylindrical hole. *An undercut could also be a recessed neck inside a cylindrical hole.*

on (upon) the heels of *(just; right) after; (close) behind; ensuing; following; succeeding.* On the heels of an FBI investigation, a federal grand jury has indicted five people on charges they defrauded ComFed Savings Bank. *Following an FBI investigation, a federal grand jury has indicted five people on charges they defrauded ComFed Savings Bank.*

on the occasion of *if (there were); if ... should; should (there); were (there; to); when;* delete. On the occasion of a positive test result, a second test would be conducted to verify the results of the first. *Were there a positive test result, a second test would be conducted to verify the results of the first.* ■ The machinists' union has agreements that members of other unions will not do their work on the occasion of a strike. *The machinists' union has agreements that members of other unions will not do their work if there were a strike.*

(something; somewhere) on the order (of) *about; around; close to; more or less; near; nearly; or so; roughly; some;* delete. The company is probably worth something on the order of $30 or $35 a share. *The company is probably worth close to $30 or $35 a share.* ■ Type I are diaphanous sheets containing small particles with a diameter on the order of 1 micron, or one-millionth of a meter. *Type I are diaphanous sheets containing small particles with a diameter around 1 micron, or one-millionth of a meter.* ■ The fare increases are on the order of 3 or 4 percent. *The fare increases are about 3 or 4 percent.* ■ Typically, the ratio of injury to mortality is something on the order of three or four to one. *Typically, the* *ratio of injury to mortality is some three or four to one.* ■ I counted something on the order of 50 interruptions for applause. *I counted 50 or so interruptions for applause.*

on the other hand *but; by (in) contrast; conversely; however; whereas; yet.* A parallel device, on the other hand, sends or receives information in packets all at once over many data lines. *A parallel device, in contrast, sends or receives information in packets all at once over many data lines.* ■ Throughout most of Western Europe, Brazil, and the United States, a raised thumb is used as a signal of approval; in Greece, on the other hand, this hand sign is a gross insult. *Throughout most of Western Europe, Brazil, and the United States, a raised thumb is used as a signal of approval, but in Greece, this hand sign is a gross insult.*

on the outside of *outside.* The fan blades are on the outside of the engine like a propeller, and all the air that passes inside the engine goes through the combustion chamber as in the earliest jets. *The fan blades are outside the engine like a propeller, and all the air that passes inside the engine goes through the combustion chamber as in the earliest jets.*

on the part of *among; by; for; from; of; -'s; delete.* Though deliberate discrimination on the part of the Japanese is often charged, it isn't necessary to prove a discriminatory intent. *Though deliberate discrimination by the Japanese is often charged, it isn't necessary to prove a discriminatory intent.* ■ It was an inspiration on the part of the producers. *It was an inspiration of the producers.* ■ A willingness on the part of foreigners to increase long- and short-term U.S. investment holdings and to lower U.S. overseas investment have financed the current account deficit. *A willingness among foreigners to increase long- and short-term U.S. investment holdings and to lower U.S. overseas investment have financed the current account deficit.* ■ There's a reluctance on the part of the passengers to move. *The passengers are reluctant to move.* ■ Careful attention will be paid to long-term global trends, balanced by constant reminders on the part of senior management that trees do not grow to the sky. *Careful attention will be paid to long-term global trends, balanced by senior management's constant reminders that trees do not grow to the sky.* ■ The effective teaching of language arts requires a commitment to excellence on the part of the classroom teacher. *The effective teaching of language arts requires a commitment to excellence from the classroom teacher.* ■ His apt observations point out the need for greater awareness on the part of the public of the architecture that surrounds them. *His apt observations point out the need for greater public awareness of the architecture that surrounds them.*

on the rise *booming; flourishing; growing; increasing; rising.*

on the side of *for; with.* The second factor working on the side of savings is the president and his wife. *The second factor working for savings is the president and his wife.*

on the ... side *among; in; -(al)ly;* delete. I think it's going to be a four-way tie on the Democratic side. *I think it's going to be a four-way tie among the Democrats.* ■ On the Republican side, 15 percent of the voters remain undecided. *Fifteen percent of the Republican voters remain undecided.* ■ How would you assess the progress that she has made on the artistic side? *How would you assess the artistic progress that she has made?* ■ On the offensive side, the Army is preparing to spend $286.5 million in fiscal 1990 to destroy aging stocks of chemical weapons stored at eight different locations. *Offensively, the Army is preparing to spend $286.5 million in fiscal 1990 to destroy aging stocks of chemical weapons stored at eight different locations.* ■ There will be some job losses on the manufacturing side, but some employees will be transferred. *There will be some job losses in manufacturing, but some employees will be transferred.*

on the surface (of it; of things) *apparently; appear (to); outwardly; seem (to); seemingly; superficially.*

on the surface (of it; of things) ... appear (seem) *appear (seem).* On the surface, a firm may appear to be sound—its balance sheet contains an impressive amount of current assets. *A firm may appear to be sound—its balance sheet contains an impressive amount of current assets.* ■ On the surface, Angell Memorial Animal Hospital's recent blood drive for animals seems admirable, but let's look at a few facts. *Angell Memorial Animal Hospital's recent blood drive for animals seems admirable, but let's look at a few facts.*

on the surface of *on.*

on the threshold of *about to; approaching; close to; near; nearly; verging on.* After decades of painstaking and expensive work, several groups are on the threshold of achieving the necessary conditions for "breakeven"—a reaction that yields as much energy as it uses. *After decades of painstaking and expensive work, several groups are about to achieve the necessary conditions for "breakeven"—a reaction that yields as much energy as it uses.* ■ We are on the threshold of real educational quality and achievement. *We are verging on real educational quality and achievement.*

on the verge of *about to; approaching; close to; near; nearly; verging on.* The United States is on the verge of a diplomatic triumph after brokering a withdrawal of foreign troops from Angola. *The United States is near a diplomatic triumph after brokering a withdrawal of foreign troops from Angola.* ■ Is he or is he not on the verge of producing chemical weapons? *Is he or is he not about to produce chemical weapons?* ■ I look for undervalued securities as well as industries that are depressed and that I have some reason to believe are on the verge of recovery. *I look for undervalued securities as well as industries that are depressed and that I have some reason to believe are close to recovery.* ■ The General Accounting Office criticized the Fish and Wildlife Service's practice of concentrating on high-profile species, such as the bald eagle, over those on the verge of extinction. *The General Accounting Office criticized the Fish and Wildlife Service's* *practice of concentrating on high-profile species, such as the bald eagle, over those verging on extinction.*

on the whole *all told; in all; overall.*

on (upon) the whole *almost all; chiefly; commonly; generally; greatly; in general; largely; mainly; most; mostly; most often; much; nearly all; normally; overall; typically; usually.* On the whole, Boston's nurses were more likely to describe themselves as satisfied with their earnings than their counterparts in other cities. *Overall, Boston's nurses were more likely to describe themselves as satisfied with their earnings than their counterparts in other cities.*

on top of (that; this) *also; and; as well; besides; beyond that (this); even; further; furthermore; moreover; more than that (this); still more; then; too; what is more.* On top of that, interest rates went up to 18 percent or more. *What's more, interest rates went up to 18 percent or more.* ■ On top of the low prices, Sears is making a lowest-price pledge for the first time. *Besides the low prices, Sears is making a lowest-price pledge for the first time.*

on (the) understanding (of; that) *as long as; if; provided; so long as.*

open to doubt *arguable; debatable; disputable; doubtful; dubious; in doubt; in question; moot; questionable.*

open to question *arguable; debatable; disputable; doubtful; dubious; in doubt; in question; moot; questionable.* His clout on Capitol Hill remains open to question. *His clout on Capitol Hill remains in doubt.*

open up *open.* When you use the Note command, a window opens up. *When you use the Note command, a window opens.*

(a; the) ... operation *delete.* With the measurement of quality and quantity, process control is a fairly automatic operation. *With the measurement of quality and quantity, process control is fairly automatic.* ■ The opportunities for price discrimination are likely to be greatest for intangible products that do not lend themselves to arbitrage operations. *The opportunities for price discrimination are likely to be greatest for intangible products that do not lend themselves to arbitrage.*

operational *active; live; running; working.*

operative *active; at work; effective; in action; in effect; in force; in play; working.*

optimal (optimum) *best.* As organizations begin to move their R&D back and forth to various countries, it will be the responsibility of the company's tax advisors to provide counseling on the optimal tax structure for a variety of arrange-ments. *As organizations begin to move their R&D back and forth to various countries, it will be the responsibility of the company's tax advisors to provide counseling on the best tax structure for a variety of arrangements.*

or anything delete.

or else *or.* Two pathnames must be specified, or else the first letter parameter will be incorrectly interpreted as a pathname. *Two pathnames must be specified, or the first letter parameter will be incorrectly interpreted as a pathname.*

orientate *orient.*

... oriented delete. Some depressed people become more activity oriented. *Some depressed people become more active.*

original coiner (originally coined) *coiner (coined).* Usually the identity of the original coiner of a new word is lost in the mists of history. *Usually the identity of the coiner of a new word is lost in the mists of history.* ■ The term *brainstorming* was originally coined by advertising genius Alex F. Osborne in the late 1930s. *The term* brainstorming *was coined by advertising genius Alex F. Osborne in the late 1930s.*

original creator (originally created) *creator (created).* An impressive number of neologisms can be traced to their original creators. *An impressive number of neologisms can be traced to their creators.*

original founder (originally founded) *founder (founded).*

original inventor (originally invented) *inventor (invented).* The courts deter-mined the patents were invalid on the grounds that Atanasoff was the original inventor. *The courts determined the patents were invalid on the grounds that Atanasoff was the inventor.*

original source *source.*

originate *arise; begin; start.*

originate from *come from; date from.*

or something delete.

or thereabouts *or so.*

or whatever delete.

other people (persons) *others.* Elizabeth Taylor, among other people, has written about this topic. *Elizabeth Taylor, among others, has written about this topic.*

other similar *similar.* In addition, the order permits the companies to provide electronic mail, voice messaging, and other similar services. *In addition, the order permits the companies to provide electronic mail, voice messaging, and similar services.*

other than *besides.*

other than ... also (as well) *besides; beyond; other than.*

other than to *but to.*

otherwise *not; other.* In many competitions, athletic and otherwise, the Finns and Swedes excel. *In many competitions, athletic and other, the Finns and Swedes excel.* ■ The perception would be strong that a Massachusetts-based law firm could get things done faster and more efficiently with an administration with which it had a relationship, presumed or otherwise. *The perception would be strong that a Massachusetts-based law firm could get things done faster and more efficiently with an administration with which it had a relationship, presumed or not.*

out in *in.* I have several relatives out in the Springfield area. *I have several relatives in the Springfield area.*

out loud *aloud.*

out of *of.* He's only one out of many who are being considered for the position. *He's only one of many who are being considered for the position.* ■ Three out of every four parents never visit their child's school. *Three of every four parents never visit their child's school.*

out of control *unruly; wild.*

(just) out of curiosity *delete.* Just out of curiosity, is Alexander Haig on the Minnesota ballot? *Is Alexander Haig on the Minnesota ballot?*

out of favor *deprecated; disapproved; disfavored; disliked; disparaged.* But he goes on to say, the time to buy them is when they are out of favor. *But he goes on to say, the time to buy them is when they are disfavored.*

out of fear (of; that) ... can (could; may; might; shall; should; will; would) *lest.* No one would be so foolish as to sell one's house out of fear that it might someday burn to the ground. *No one would be so foolish as to sell one's house lest it someday burn to the ground.* ■ The seven Baby Bells have been barred from generating information services, including cable TV programming, out of fear they could use their vast financial resources to compete unfairly. *The seven Baby Bells have been barred from generating information services, including cable TV programming, lest they use their vast financial resources to compete unfairly.*

out of focus *blurred; indistinct.*

out of the ordinary *curious; different; exceptional; extraordinary; irregular; novel; odd; rare; singular; strange; uncommon; unusual.* Will you give me a call if anything out of the ordinary happens? *Will you give me a call if anything curious happens?* ■ Where necessary, brief but not cryptic explanations are provided of any information that might seem to be out of the ordinary. *Where necessary, brief but not cryptic explanations are provided of any information that might seem to be uncommon.*

out of the question *impossible; inconceivable; undoable; unthinkable.* Returning to college was out of the question, so with nothing to do, she signed up for oil painting lessons. *Returning to college was unthinkable, so with nothing to do, she signed up for oil painting lessons.*

out of the realm of possibility *impossible; inconceivable; undoable; unthinkable.* It is not out of the realm of possibility that Exxon could be facing a billion dollars or more in punitive damages. *It is not impossible that Exxon could be facing a billion dollars or more in punitive damages.*

outside of *outside.* My daughters don't know many families where the mother doesn't work outside of the home. *My daughters don't know many families where the mother doesn't work outside the home.* ■ Chase Manhattan and Bank of America are following a similar strategy, with less emphasis on domestic markets outside of the United States. *Chase Manhattan and Bank of America are following a similar strategy, with less emphasis on domestic markets outside the United States.*

over again *again; afresh; anew; once more; re-.* I think his idea is a nutty one; however, if he or Uncle Sam would like to write me a check for the amount of money my company and I put in over the last 21 years, I will think it over again. *I think his idea is a nutty one; however, if he or Uncle Sam would like to write me a check for the amount of money my company and I put in over the last 21 years, I will rethink it.*

overall look (view) *overview.* The introduction gives the readers an overall view of your business and what you want to achieve. *The introduction gives the readers an overview of your business and what you want to achieve.*

over and above *besides; beyond; more than; over.* Anesthesia doesn't add to the risk over and above that of the surgery itself and the extent of the medical problem the patient already has. *Anesthesia doesn't add to the risk more than that of the surgery itself and the extent of the medical problem the patient already has.*

over and done with *complete; done; ended; finished; over; past.* I just want this to be over and done with. *I just want this to be over.*

over and over (again) *frequently; often; recurrently; regularly; repeatedly.* Professor Sommers refers over and over to a "bag of virtues." *Professor Sommers refers often to a "bag of virtues."* ■ This saves you time when you use the same commands over and over again. *This saves you time when you use the same commands repeatedly.*

overly *over-.* We thought he was overly enthusiastic about winning. *We thought he was overenthusiastic about winning.* ■ Men say women are overly emotional. *Men say women are overemotional.* ■ Employers are not overly discriminating, but they are trying to minimize their risk. *Employers are not overdiscriminating, but they are trying to minimize their risk.* ■ Rather than taxing what some overly moralistic legislator feels may be "sinful," how about concentrating on those areas that have caused our debt problem? *Rather than taxing what some over-moralistic legislator feels may be "sinful," how about concentrating on those areas that have caused our debt problem?*

over the course (duration; length) of *during; for; in; over; throughout; when; while; with.* Over the course of a single day, he transformed his appearance from a gum-chewing convict to a respectable citizen. *In a single day, he transformed his appearance from a gum-chewing convict to a respectable citizen.* ■ Tropical downpours are what we have to look forward to over the course of the next couple of days. *Tropical downpours are what we have to look forward to over the next couple of days.* ■ Over the duration of the project, we expect there will be some disruption due to noise, dirt, and dust. *During the project, we expect there will be some disruption due to noise, dirt, and dust.*

over the fact that *because; for; in that; since; that;* delete. I am concerned over the fact that they made us work so hard. *I am concerned that they made us work so hard.* ■ He is angry over the fact that Mr. Kennedy did not immediately call the police. *He is angry because Mr. Kennedy did not immediately call the police.*

over the long haul *at length; eventually; in the end; in time; later; long-term; one day; over the months (years); over time; someday; sometime; ultimately; with time; yet.* These companies suffer the historically high price exacted for the thrill of this breeze—the death of their full-price, full-margin business over the long haul. *These companies suffer the historically high price exacted for the thrill of this breeze—the death of their full-price, full-margin business over time.* ■ Over the long haul, I still believe that housing is a good investment. *I still believe that housing is a good long-term investment.*

over the short haul *at first; at present; before long; currently; directly; for now; in (over) a month (week); initially; next month (year); (just; right) now; presently; quickly; shortly; short-term; soon; straightaway; this month (year); tomorrow;* delete. We approached it not as a revenue-raising proposal but as an environmental proposal, and over the short haul, it would raise substantial amounts of revenue. *We approached it not as a revenue-raising proposal but as an environmental proposal, and before long, it would raise substantial amounts of revenue.* ■ Industry analysts say they expect the new rules to have little impact, at least over the short haul. *Industry analysts say they expect the new rules to have little impact, at least initially.*

(a; the) overwhelming (vast) consensus (of opinion) *consensus.*

(a; the) overwhelming (vast) preponderance (of) *a good (great) deal (of); a good (great) many (of); almost all (of); (nine) in (ten) (of); many (of); most (of); much (of); nearly all (of); (43) of (48); ... percent (of); three-fourths (two-thirds) (of);* delete. The overwhelming preponderance of opinion favors the conclusion that *P* is a proper subset of *NP*. *Opinion favors the conclusion that P is a proper subset of NP.* ■ A recent poll showed that a vast preponderance of city councilors oppose the relocation. *A recent poll showed that almost all city councilors oppose the relocation.*

over with *complete; done; ended; finished; over; past.*

owing to the fact that *because; considering; for; in that; since.* However, owing to the fact that NRDC is a well-thought-of organization, capable of good quality research, we're clearly going to go through their report carefully. *However, since NRDC is a well-thought-of organization, capable of good quality research, we're clearly going to go through their report carefully.*

P

pack together *pack.* Stars in a globular cluster are packed so tightly together that ordinary optical telescopes have trouble resolving individual stars. *Stars in a globular cluster are packed so tightly that ordinary optical telescopes have trouble resolving individual stars.* ■ Recent advances have made it possible to pack thousands, even millions, of transistors together on a single silicon chip. *Recent advances have made it possible to pack thousands, even millions, of transistors on a single silicon chip.*

pair of twins *twins.*

parameter *boundary; limit.*

par for the course *normal; typical; usual.*

part and parcel *part.* This generalized tendency to place conflicts in the outside world is part and parcel of a well-known mechanism of the mind called projection. *This generalized tendency to place conflicts in the outside world is part of a well-known mechanism of the mind called projection.*

partially *partly.* My difficulty with her is partially due to a clash of personalities. *My difficulty with her is partly due to a clash of personalities.* ■ Housing sales are, at least partially, caused by interest rates. *Housing sales are, at least partly, caused by interest rates.*

particular delete. We would hope that you have already found a new church home that you can serve and that can meet your needs at this particular time in your life. *We would hope that you have already found a new church home that you can serve and that can meet your needs at this time in your life.* ■ The failure by upper management to recognize this particular aspect of computer security as significant will continue to result in flawed security policy. *The failure by upper management to recognize this aspect of computer security as significant will continue to result in flawed security policy.*

pass away (on) *die.*

passing craze (fad; fancy) *craze (fad; fancy).*

passing phase *phase.*

pass judgment (sentence) on (upon) *judge (sentence).* Passing judgment on one's potential earnings is even more painful than passing judgment on a former colleague. *Judging one's potential earnings is even more painful than judging a former colleague.*

past (previous; prior) accomplishment *accomplishment.* It is startling that he supposes some imagined past accomplishment of his should exempt him from paying rent. *It is startling that he supposes some imagined accomplishment of his should exempt him from paying rent.*

past (previous; prior) achievement *achievement.*

past (previous; prior) experience *experience.* A shortage of workers for jobs requiring little skill is forcing some employers to hire people without considering their references, previous experience, or education. *A shortage of workers for jobs requiring little skill is forcing some employers to hire people without considering their references, experience, or education.* ■ This may not be reasonable in light of our past experiences with competitors. *This may not be reasonable in light of our experiences with competitors.* ■ In describing Hispanics as "foreign consumers," I refer to the fact that knowledge and usage of some brands by foreign-born Hispanics is influenced by their prior experiences as consumers in Latin America. *In describing Hispanics as "foreign consumers," I refer to the fact* *that knowledge and usage of some brands by foreign-born Hispanics is influenced by their experiences as consumers in Latin America.*

past (previous; prior) history *history.* Even though forecasts deal with the future, past history is not irrelevant. *Even though forecasts deal with the future, history is not irrelevant.* ■ Manufacturers aware of operators with a previous history of producing rejected units, may want to inspect the output of certain machines or people closely. *Manufacturers aware of operators with a history of producing rejected units, may want to inspect the output of certain machines or people closely.*

past (previous; prior) performance *performance.* Normally, one judges the ability to succeed based on past performance. *Normally, one judges the ability to succeed based on performance.*

past (previous; prior) practice *practice.* But in keeping with past practice for such flights, the Pentagon is expected to announce a three-hour launch-window early this week. *But in keeping with practice for such flights, the Pentagon is expected to announce a three-hour launch-window early this week.*

past (previous; prior) precedent *precedent.* Based on past precedent, Mr. Indelicato would likely serve 12 to 18 months in prison. *Based on precedent, Mr. Indelicato would likely serve 12 to 18 months in prison.*

past (previous; prior) record *record.* I think the endorsement of Willie Horton says more about the merits of the governor's past record and his campaign promises. *I think the endorsement of Willie Horton says more about the merits of the governor's record and his campaign promises.* ■ Both the summer's drought and the fire's extent surpassed all previous records in the park. *Both the summer's drought and the fire's extent surpassed all records in the park.* ■ Because of the region's prior record and the limited length of nearby faults, the December 7 jolt was probably the largest earthquake this area could produce. *Because of the region's record and the limited length of nearby faults, the December 7 jolt was probably the largest earthquake this area could produce.*

patchwork quilt *patchquilt; patchwork.* The question then becomes how to organize this patchwork quilt of topics. *The question then becomes how to organize this patchwork of topics.*

patently evident (obvious; plain) *evident (obvious; plain); patent.* It would have been patently obvious that their cost of money could change. *It would have been patent that their cost of money could change.*

pathetical *pathetic.*

pathological *pathologic.* Even though this response is accompanied by redness, warmth, and pain, it is not naturally a pathological process. *Even though this* *response is accompanied by redness, warmth, and pain, it is not naturally a pathologic process.*

pay attention to *attend to; consider; hearken to; heed; listen to; mind; note; notice; observe; regard; see; tend to; watch; witness.* The Amishman's fields flourish because he pays close attention to them, because he is sensitive to the earth, because he lets it guide him. *The Amishman's fields flourish because he attends to them closely, because he is sensitive to the earth, because he lets it guide him.* ■ We need to pay attention to the image we're projecting. *We need to consider the image we're projecting.* ■ He focused resources toward building some of the other businesses, many of which worked out well, but he neglected to pay attention to the core business. *He focused resources toward building some of the other businesses, many of which worked out well, but he neglected to mind the core business.* ■ Business needs to pay attention to housing not out of a sense of do-goodism or civic pride but out of concern for their own bottom line. *Business needs to tend to housing not out of a sense of do-goodism or civic pride but out of concern for their own bottom line.*

pay heed to *attend to; consider; hearken to; heed; listen to; mind; note; notice; observe; regard; see; tend to; watch; witness.* I suggest you pay heed to what she says. *I suggest you note what she says.* ■ Many Americans have paid heed to the results of research and changed their ways of living remarkably. *Many Americans have heeded the results of research and changed their ways of living remarkably.*

peace and quiet *peace; quiet.* South Korea's four major parties declared a one-month political truce yesterday to assure peace and quiet during this month's Summer Olympics. *South Korea's four major parties declared a one-month political truce yesterday to assure peace during this month's Summer Olympics.* ■ It is annoying not to have peace and quiet in one's own home. *It is annoying not to have quiet in one's own home.*

penetrate into *penetrate.*

per *a.* According to this study, the average executive spends 11 weeks per year reading memos. *According to this study, the average executive spends 11 weeks a year reading memos.*

percentage point (unit) *percent; point (unit).* The notes, sold in denominations of $1,000, were priced to yield 8.826 percent, or a slim 38-hundredths of a percentage point more than Treasury securities with a similar maturity. *The notes, sold in denominations of $1,000, were priced to yield 8.826 percent, or a slim 38-hundredths of a percent more than Treasury securities with a similar maturity.* ■ The Labor Department reported that the September unemployment rate fell 0.2 percentage points, to 5.4 percent. *The Labor Department reported that the September unemployment rate fell 0.2 points, to 5.4 percent.*

perfect (perfectly) match *duplicate; exact; identical; match; (the) same.* Spreadsheets and television may seem unlikely partners, but if what's going on at the Tulsa, Oklahoma, offices of United Video is anything to go by, they are a perfect match. *Spreadsheets and television may seem unlikely partners, but if what's going on at the Tulsa, Oklahoma, offices of United Video is anything to go by, they are a match.*

perform *do;* delete. He performed an extensive analysis of the financing patterns of U.S. corporations. *He extensively analyzed the financing patterns of U.S. corporations.* ▪ He described a study performed at the University of British Columbia that showed a combination of graphs and tables outperformed either of them alone. *He described a study done at the University of British Columbia that showed a combination of graphs and tables outperformed either of them alone.*

perhaps may (might) *may (might).*

periodical *periodic.*

(a; the) period (time) of delete. Crop plants especially might be better equipped in a carbon dioxide-rich environment to compete with weeds for growing space, ward off destructive insects, and survive periods of drought. *Crop plants especially might be better equipped in a carbon dioxide-rich environment to compete with weeds for growing space, ward off destructive insects, and survive droughts.* ▪ After the shock comes a period of doubt and resignation. *After the shock comes doubt and resignation.*

permit ... to *let.*

(a; the) ... person delete. If you believe your husband is a competent person, you don't mind his doing it. *If you believe your husband is competent, you don't mind his doing it.* ▪ You do not need to be a gourmet cook or model housecleaner to be a worthwhile person. *You do not need to be a gourmet cook or model housecleaner to be worthwhile.*

personal belief (opinion; point of view; view; viewpoint) *belief (opinion; point of view; view; viewpoint).* My personal opinion is that he should be publicly scolded for his actions. *My opinion is that he should be publicly scolded for his actions.*

personal bias *bias.* Some experts do inject personal bias into the process. *Some experts do inject bias into the process.* ▪ A person who has a personally biased interpretation of reality is guilty of selective perception. *A person who has a biased interpretation of reality is guilty of selective perception.*

personal charm *charm.*

personal feeling *feeling.* What are your personal feelings about this? *What are your feelings about this?*

personal friend (friendship) *friend (friendship).* She is a personal friend of mine. *She is a friend of mine.*

personal rapport *rapport.* Account managers are advised to develop a personal rapport with their clients. *Account managers are advised to develop a rapport with their clients.*

pertain (pertaining) to *about; as for; as to; concerning; for; in; of; on; over; regarding; to; toward; with.* An assets management system can answer these what-if budget questions pertaining to equipment. *An assets management system can answer these what-if budget questions about equipment.* ■ For information pertaining to this policy, the Insured or, in event of his death, the beneficiary, should communicate with one of the following places. *For information concerning this policy, the Insured or, in event of his death, the beneficiary, should communicate with one of the following places.*

pharmacological *pharmacologic.*

phone up *phone.*

physiological *physiologic.* It is believed that anxiety is expressed through physiological processes rather than symbolically through coping mechanisms. *It is believed that anxiety is expressed through physiologic processes rather than symbolically through coping mechanisms.*

pick and choose *choose; cull; pick; select.* Its organization into independent topics that you can pick and choose from allows you to use it in a one-semester course. *Its organization into independent topics that you can pick from allows you to use it in a one-semester course.* ■ To leave it up to one person to pick and choose when to reveal autopsy information leads to the ability to shield from the public corruption and cover-ups in the medical examiner's office of cases of police brutality. *To leave it up to one person to choose when to reveal autopsy information leads to the ability to shield from the public corruption and cover-ups in the medical examiner's office of cases of police brutality.*

pick up the phone (telephone) and call *call; phone.* Buying or selling ownership in a corporation is simply a matter of picking up the phone and calling a stockbroker, who can, within minutes, buy or sell stock listed on a stock exchange. *Buying or selling ownership in a corporation is simply a matter of calling a stockbroker, who can, within minutes, buy or sell stock listed on a stock exchange.*

place (put) (a) ... (in; into; on; under; upon) delete. In determining the relative quality of municipal securities, many investors place great reliance on the rating provided by the two major rating agencies. *In determining the relative quality of* *municipal securities, many investors greatly rely on the rating provided by the two major rating agencies.* ■ But at the same time that Washington puts pressure on European governments and companies, the administration ought to examine the inconsistencies in U.S. policy that confuse, and sometimes alarm, our allies. *But at the same time that Washington pressures European governments and companies, the administration ought to examine the inconsistencies in U.S. policy that confuse, and sometimes alarm, our allies.* ■ The Act only covers the actual cost of cleaning up pollution damage, and does not put a limit on compensation claims from third parties. *The Act only covers the actual cost of cleaning up pollution damage, and does not limit compensation claims from third parties.* ■ The strategy placed strong emphasis on the triangle of concerns that determines the marketing strategies of all highly profitable financial institutions. *The strategy strongly emphasized the triangle of concerns that determines the marketing strategies of all highly profitable financial institutions.* ■ He was placed under arrest at 4 a.m. Thursday. *He was arrested at 4 a.m. Thursday.*

place (put) a burden on (upon) *burden; encumber; hamper; hinder; oppress; overtax; strain; tax; weigh down.* The result can be the gradual accumulation of policies and practices that, like a bad diet, overload the organs and place burdens on the members struggling to keep it alive. *The result can be the gradual accumulation of policies and practices that, like a bad diet, overload the organs and burden the members struggling to keep it alive.* ■ As with other Sun Belt states, population growth has placed a great burden on the area's infrastructure. *As with other Sun Belt states, population growth has greatly taxed the area's infrastructure.*

place (put) a premium on (upon) *appreciate; cherish; esteem; prize; respect; treasure; value.* Employees who are not trained for advancement invariably head for the larger companies that place a premium on training programs. *Employees who are not trained for advancement invariably head for the larger companies that appreciate training programs.* ■ Like our staff members, who place a premium on their intellectual and professional independence, our clients made it clear that they consider it essential to be able to work with us without concern about any conflicting interests. *Like our staff members, who prize their intellectual and professional independence, our clients made it clear that they consider it essential to be able to work with us without concern about any conflicting interests.*

place (put) a priority on (upon) *esteem; favor; prefer; prize; treasure; value.*

place (put) a strain on (upon) *burden; encumber; hamper; hinder; oppress; overtax; strain; tax; weigh down.* Hot weather puts a strain on the heart and can lead to exhaustion, heart failure, and stroke. *Hot weather overtaxes the heart and can lead to exhaustion, heart failure, and stroke.*

place (put) a value on (upon) *appreciate; cherish; esteem; prize; respect; treasure; value.*

place (put) credence in *accept; believe; credit.* You might never have guessed some of these achievements if you placed credence in the threats, warnings, caveats, criticisms, advisories and the like that accompanied daily, weekly and monthly analyses from research departments. *You might never have guessed some of these achievements if you believed the threats, warnings, caveats, criticisms, advisories and the like that accompanied daily, weekly and monthly analyses from research departments.* ■ A physical model of health and illness was emphasized that didn't place credence in the idea that our thinking and health were related. *A physical model of health and illness was emphasized that didn't accept the idea that our thinking and health were related.*

place (put) ... in danger *endanger; imperil; jeopardize.*

place (put) ... in jeopardy *endanger; imperil; jeopardize.* Over time, the defense bill that I have just vetoed would have placed in jeopardy all these diplomatic and strategic advances. *Over time, the defense bill that I have just vetoed would have jeopardized all these diplomatic and strategic advances.* ■ The scientific quest for truth is placed in jeopardy when it is commingled with the prospect of personal profit. *The scientific quest for truth is imperiled when it is commingled with the prospect of personal profit.* ■ The opposition Liberal Party, two weeks away from a crucial general election, has strengthened its position among voters and placed the U.S.–Canada trade agreement in serious jeopardy. *The opposition Liberal Party, two weeks away from a crucial general election, has strengthened its position among voters and seriously endangered the U.S.–Canada trade agreement.*

place (put) ... in (into) peril *endanger; imperil; jeopardize.* The uncertainties about sales and service are putting into peril the very reason for the Chapter 11 bankruptcy filing: to allow Yugo America to reorganize and keep selling cars in the United States. *The uncertainties about sales and service are endangering the very reason for the Chapter 11 bankruptcy filing: to allow Yugo America to reorganize and keep selling cars in the United States.* ■ To do otherwise would invite serious trouble and even place our nation in great peril. *To do otherwise would invite serious trouble and even greatly imperil our nation.*

place (put) into question *challenge; contradict; dispute; doubt; question.*

place of employment *business; company; firm; job; office; work; workplace.* After the Commonwealth rested its case, the defendant indicated that he intended to call two witnesses to testify to having overheard Janice yelling at the defendant at his place of employment, a restaurant where the witnesses also worked. *After the Commonwealth rested its case, the defendant indicated that he intended to call two witnesses to testify to having overheard Janice yelling at the defendant at his workplace, a restaurant where the witnesses also worked.*

place (put) restrictions on (upon) *bind; compel; force; obligate; restrict.*

place (put) stress on (upon) *strain; stress.* Fasting places great stress on your body. *Fasting greatly stresses your body.* ▪ If people can't support themselves in their retirement years, it places undue stress on the nation's social services, and taxes must go up. *If people can't support themselves in their retirement years, it unduly strains the nation's social services, and taxes must go up.*

place (put) under obligation *bind; compel; force; obligate; restrict.*

plain and simple *clear; obvious; plain; simple.* Associating tobacco with the pastoral joy of watching a baseball game or a golf or tennis tournament is plainly and simply false advertising. *Associating tobacco with the pastoral joy of watching a baseball game or a golf or tennis tournament is clearly false advertising.* ▪ The decision of the School Committee was plain and simple in its message. *The decision of the School Committee was plain in its message.*

plan ahead *plan.* If people would plan ahead, they wouldn't be confronted by these crisis situations. *If people would plan, they wouldn't be confronted by these crisis situations.* ▪ When you first create a data file, you should plan ahead so that the data are effectively organized. *When you first create a data file, you should plan so that the data are effectively organized.*

plan of action (attack; battle) *action; course; direction; intention; method; move; plan; policy; procedure; route; scheme; strategy.* If Polaroid rejects your offer and expresses no interest in talking with you, what's your next plan of action? *If Polaroid rejects your offer and expresses no interest in talking with you, what's your next move?* ▪ Environmentalists say their failure to agree on a plan of battle raises doubts about whether they are up to the challenge. *Environmentalists say their failure to agree on a strategy raises doubts about whether they are up to the challenge.*

plan out *plan.* It pays in the long run to plan out your career. *It pays in the long run to plan your career.*

plans and specifications *plans; specifications.*

plummet down *down; plummet.* I can provide a litany of cases where competition has brought prices plummeting down. *I can provide a litany of cases where competition has brought prices plummeting.*

plunge down *down; plunge.*

(a; the) plurality (of) *almost all (of); (nine) in (ten) (of); many (of); more (of); most (of); nearly all (of); (43) of (48) (of); ... percent (of); three-fourths (two-thirds) (of).* The poll also found that 89 percent of Americans would not want to be president, and a plurality would not want their children to be. *The poll also found that 89 percent of Americans would not want to be president, and 60* *percent would not want their children to be.* ■ A plurality of the 1,084 adults surveyed primarily faulted society rather than the homeless for homelessness. *Almost all the 1,084 adults surveyed primarily faulted society rather than the homeless for homelessness.* ■ In a national poll, a plurality of young women described their female colleagues as "competitive in a sneaky, backstabbing way." *In a national poll, five in seven young women described their female colleagues as "competitive in a sneaky, backstabbing way."*

(3:00) p.m. ... afternoon (evening) *afternoon (evening); (3:00) p.m.* It was 2 p.m. in the afternoon before we saw her. *It was 2 p.m. before we saw her.*

point of departure *starting point.*

point of view *attitude; belief; opinion; position; posture; stand; standpoint; vantage; view; viewpoint.* In the United States, there is an increase in sympathy for the Palestinian point of view. *In the United States, there is an increase in sympathy for the Palestinian viewpoint.* ■ It is quite natural for two countries with different points of view to have some differences. *It is quite natural for two countries with different standpoints to have some differences.* ■ Could it be that the point of view of his organization is that protectionism is bad when designed to help working people or their communities and good only when it benefits corporations? *Could it be that the attitude of his organization is that protectionism is bad when designed to help working people or their communities and good only when it benefits corporations?*

point to the conclusion *indicate; show; signal; signify; suggest.*

polish up *polish.*

polite euphemism *euphemism.* Even its fans call it "difficult" and "uningratiating," polite euphemisms for off the wall, a very appropriate pun to describe this museum-proof collection of dirt piles, rusted girders and "conceptual" creations. *Even its fans call it "difficult" and "uningratiating," euphemisms for off the wall, a very appropriate pun to describe this museum-proof collection of dirt piles, rusted girders and "conceptual" creations.*

popular consensus *consensus.* The opportunity to conduct a rigorous drug trial can only come early in a drug's life, before a popular consensus develops. *The opportunity to conduct a rigorous drug trial can only come early in a drug's life, before a consensus develops.*

position *job.*

(a; the) ... position *delete.* In the mid-1980s, they began a succession of investments in Telerate, which had a monopoly position in the distribution of quotations on U.S. government securities. *In the mid-1980s, they began a succession* *of investments in Telerate, which had a monopoly in the distribution of quotations on U.S. government securities.*

positive assurance *assurance.* Through the end of last week, we received positive assurances the vote would go through, which makes this doubly frustrating. *Through the end of last week, we received assurances the vote would go through, which makes this doubly frustrating.*

positive feelings *affection; attraction; confidence; esteem; faith; favor; fondness; hope; interest; liking; love; regard; tenderness; trust.* I'm anticipating this launch with positive feelings. *I'm anticipating this launch with confidence.*

possess (a; the) ... (about; for; of; on; over) *have; own;* delete. If teachers do not possess a firm understanding of both science content and science curriculum goals, even the best of assessments will not be sufficient to guide their classroom instruction. *If teachers do not firmly understand both science content and science curriculum goals, even the best of assessments will not be sufficient to guide their classroom instruction.* ■ Most materials called aluminum are actually aluminum alloys, which possess greater strength than the pure metal. *Most materials called aluminum are actually aluminum alloys, which have greater strength than the pure metal.* ■ Thomas A. Edison had little formal education, but he possessed an exceptional ability to design and perfect some of the world's most significant inventions. *Thomas A. Edison had little formal education, but he had an exceptional ability to design and perfect some of the world's most significant inventions.*

possibility *chance; likelihood; prospect.*

possibly may (might) *may (might).* Swaggart possibly may decide to start his own church. *Swaggart may decide to start his own church.* ■ For the really scary story could be that the boom just possibly might happen here again. *For the really scary story could be that the boom just might happen here again.*

posterior to *after; behind; following; later.*

potentiality *potential.* All these tools have the same power sources, materials, and styling, and most important, each has identical market potentiality. *All these tools have the same power sources, materials, and styling, and most important, each has identical market potential.*

pouring (down) rain *pouring.* It will probably be pouring down rain at the lake. *It will probably be pouring at the lake.*

practically *almost; nearly.*

predicate on (upon) *base on.*

predict ahead of time (beforehand; in advance) *predict.* I'm not privy to the secret of how to predict ahead of time who will succeed. *I'm not privy to the secret of how to predict who will succeed.* ■ Could epidemiologists have predicted some of these outbreaks in advance? *Could epidemiologists have predicted some of these outbreaks?*

predict ... future *forecast; foretell; predict.* No one, not the fund manager, not the investor, can predict the future course of financial markets. *No one, not the fund manager, not the investor, can predict the course of financial markets.* ■ Thus predictions of future performance will be important criteria in performance appraisal. *Thus predictions of performance will be important criteria in performance appraisal.*

predominant (predominantly) *almost all; chief; chiefly; generally; in general; largely; main; mainly; most; mostly; most often; nearly all.* The social structure of this country is predominantly white. *The social structure of this country is largely white.* ■ Simple lack of balanced expense control is the predominant cause of personal financial disaster. *Simple lack of balanced expense control is the main cause of personal financial disaster.*

prefer ... as opposed to (instead of; rather than) *prefer ... over; prefer ... to.* The Regional Bell Operating Companies would prefer having the ability to program advanced features into a network themselves as opposed to having the switch vendor do it. *The Regional Bell Operating Companies would prefer having the ability to program advanced features into a network themselves to having the switch vendor do it.* ■ Nurses who prefer listening and comprehension as opposed to verbalization generally experience the most productive and satisfying interactions. *Nurses who prefer listening and comprehension over verbalization generally experience the most productive and satisfying interactions.*

prejudicial opinion *bias; prejudice.* Contrary to the prejudicial opinion of most women libbers, physical attractiveness has been and will always be a definite asset. *Contrary to the prejudice of most women libbers, physical attractiveness has been and will always be a definite asset.*

preliminary draft *draft.* He gave me the preliminary draft of their report to review. *He gave me the draft of their report to review.*

preliminary to *before.*

premises *building; house; office; store.*

preparation (prepare) ... before *preparation (prepare) ... for.* In some ways, it is no different from the preparation people are asked to do before any meeting. *In some ways, it is no different from the preparation people are asked to do for any meeting.*

preparatory to *before.*

prepare for in advance *prepare for.* Try to anticipate problems and prepare for them in advance. *Try to anticipate problems and prepare for them.*

preplan *plan.* In short programs, much of the cognitive input or preplanning takes place on the trainees' own time, thus keeping the seminar to the shortest possible number of hours. *In short programs, much of the cognitive input or planning takes place on the trainees' own time, thus keeping the seminar to the shortest possible number of hours.*

present (a; the) ... (of; on; to) *(v)* delete. Exhibit 2-2 presents a plot of the same data. *Exhibit 2-2 plots the same data.* ■ The analysis of sales cycles presents little added difficulty to the material we have covered. *The analysis of sales cycles adds little difficulty to the material we have covered.* ■ We present a summary of the key trends that are important to monitor in the future. *We summarize the key trends that are important to monitor in the future.* ■ Increased competition, shrinking profit margins, and escalating costs are presenting challenges to management. *Increased competition, shrinking profit margins, and escalating costs are challenging management.* ■ In Chapter 1, we presented a definition of global marketing and its elements. *In Chapter 1, we defined global marketing and its elements.*

present everywhere *all over; everywhere; omnipresent; ubiquitous; widespread.* Talk about sex is present everywhere. *Talk about sex is ubiquitous.*

present incumbent *incumbent.*

presently *quickly; shortly; soon.*

presently *(just; right) now; today; (just) yet;* delete. The computer industry is presently changing from fourth- to fifth-generation computer systems. *The computer industry is now changing from fourth- to fifth-generation computer systems.* ■ Each of these phases presently exists to some extent in American business. *Each of these phases exists to some extent in American business.* ■ The town presently practices a minimum salt program on its roadways within the watershed area. *Today, the town practices a minimum salt program on its roadways within the watershed area.* ■ No one is presently available to answer your call. *No one is available just yet to answer your call.*

present with *give.* The disabled people met with James O'Leary, MBTA general manager, and presented him with a list of 19 demands. *The disabled people met with James O'Leary, MBTA general manager, and gave him a list of 19 demands.*

pressurize *pressure.*

pretty delete. It's pretty awesome to think of a single gene abnormality that can accelerate the age for a heart attack by 50 years. *It's awesome to think of a single gene abnormality that can accelerate the age for a heart attack by 50 years.*

preventative *preventive.* The idea of preventative training seems to be a necessity in any educational program. *The idea of preventive training seems to be a necessity in any educational program.* ■ Widespread inoculation of children has been one of the greatest examples of preventative medicine in this century. *Widespread inoculation of children has been one of the greatest examples of preventive medicine in this century.*

previous (previously) *ago; before; earlier;* delete. We are no closer to resolution than we were three years previously. *We are no closer to resolution than we were three years ago.* ■ Bonnie beat her competitor, as she had the previous day. *Bonnie beat her competitor, as she had the day before.* ■ Two years previous, I was going through a period of emotional stress. *Two years ago, I was going through a period of emotional stress.*

previous to *before.* The Angels have played 16 extra-inning games previous to today. *The Angels have played 16 extra-inning games before today.*

primary (primarily) *almost all; chief; chiefly; largely; main; mainly; most; mostly; most often; nearly all.* The assumption is that foreign customers are primarily interested in product availability. *The assumption is that foreign customers are mainly interested in product availability.*

principal (principally) *almost all; chief; chiefly; largely; main; mainly; most; mostly; most often; nearly all.*

prior approval (consent) *approval (consent).* This Software is licensed only to you, the Licensee, and may not be transferred to anyone without the prior written consent of Microsoft. *This Software is licensed only to you, the Licensee, and may not be transferred to anyone without the written consent of Microsoft.* ■ He deeply resents that institution's issuance of a press release concerning him without his knowledge and prior consent or approval. *He deeply resents that institution's issuance of a press release concerning him without his knowledge and consent or approval.*

prioritize *arrange; list; order; rank; rate.* By prioritizing your objectives, devising your plan, and controlling your expenditures, you should be able to build your net worth over the course of your career. *By ranking your objectives, devising your plan, and controlling your expenditures, you should be able to build your net worth over the course of your career.*

prior to *before.* The gas velocity profiles prior to and after the head-on collision are seen here. *The gas velocity profiles before and after the head-on collision are seen here.* ■ Prior to the sixteenth century, unknown quantities were represented by words. *Before the sixteenth century, unknown quantities were represented by words.*

prior to that (the; this) time (of) *before; before now (then).* We will not pay for transportation expenses incurred prior to that time. *We will not pay for transportation expenses incurred before then.* ■ Prior to the time of the killing, he was under investigation for two or three robberies. *Before the killing, he was under investigation for two or three robberies.*

probability *chance; likelihood; prospect.* Others may be less familiar with the model or unfamiliar with the program, thus increasing the probability of mistakes. *Others may be less familiar with the model or unfamiliar with the program, thus increasing the likelihood of mistakes.*

problematical *problematic.* Since the U.K. banking industry was both mature and increasingly competitive, the clear differentiation of services was becoming problematical. *Since the U.K. banking industry was both mature and increasingly competitive, the clear differentiation of services was becoming problematic.*

(a; the) ... procedure delete. Autocorrelation analysis is a useful procedure for identifying the existence and shape of a trend. *Autocorrelation analysis is useful for identifying the existence and shape of a trend.*

proceed *go; move; run; walk.*

(then) ... proceed (to) *later; next; then;* delete. They tied me to a cross and proceeded to light the fire. *They tied me to a cross and then lit the fire.* ■ He took my number, which he proceeded to lose. *He took my number, which he later lost.* ■ When you are ill, you don't read the medical encyclopedia, diagnose your case, and then proceed to doctor yourself. *When you are ill, you don't read the medical encyclopedia, diagnose your case, and then doctor yourself.*

proceed ahead (forward; on; onward) *advance; go on; move on; proceed; progress.* We ran into a brick wall on getting the kind of commitment from a big player that we felt was necessary to proceed ahead. *We ran into a brick wall on getting the kind of commitment from a big player that we felt was necessary to proceed.*

(a; the) ... process delete. It's been a gradual process. *It's been gradual.* ■ The assessment process involves rigorously examining the methods used. *Assessment involves rigorously examining the methods used.* ■ Defining a database—often a laborious and time-consuming process—is simplified with the menu-driven definition scheme. *Defining a database—often laborious and time consuming—is simplified with the menu-driven definition scheme.* ■ Getting into the honesty business, in short, can be an expensive and arduous process. *Getting into the honesty business, in short, can be expensive and arduous.* ■ If there is any shortcoming, it's that no patients are included in the decision-making process. *If there* *is any shortcoming, it's that no patients are included in the decision mak-ing.* ■ Doctors should not dismiss complaints of incontinence as an inevitable part of the aging process. *Doctors should not dismiss complaints of incontinence as an inevitable part of aging.*

procure *get.*

produce (a; the) ... (of; to) delete. The model is an analytic framework that produces estimates of future sales. *The model is an analytic framework that estimates future sales.* ■ The researcher will produce a written report not to exceed 25 pages in length, including an executive summary. *The researcher will write a report not to exceed 25 pages in length, including an executive summary.*

proffer *give; offer.* Another way of observing a culture is to note the manner and method of proffering praise for superior performance and accomplishment. *Another way of observing a culture is to note the manner and method of giving praise for superior performance and accomplishment.* ■ An interesting response to the pricing dilemma has been proffered by several traditional broker-distrib-uted fund sponsors. *An interesting response to the pricing dilemma has been offered by several traditional broker-distributed fund sponsors.*

profitability (profitableness) *profits.* The strategy for achieving higher profitabil-ity was simple: organize our businesses around the customer, not the product. *The strategy for achieving higher profits was simple: organize our businesses around the customer, not the product.*

progress ahead (forward; on; onward) *advance; go on; move on; proceed; progress.*

proliferate *spread.*

protestation *protest.* Despite Solomon's protestation, the five-member board is expected to consider changing its rules, which also prohibit CPAs from taking commissions. *Despite Solomon's protest, the five-member board is expected to consider changing its rules, which also prohibit CPAs from taking commis-sions.*

protrude out *protrude.*

proven *(v) proved.* The exact number of data points has not yet been proven. *The exact number of data points has not yet been proved.* ■ The nondegree program, once ridiculed in academic circles, has proven critics wrong. *The nondegree program, once ridiculed in academic circles, has proved critics wrong.*

proven fact *fact; proof.* That's a proven fact. *That's a fact.*

prove of benefit to *benefit.*

provide (a; the) ... (for; of; to) delete. This book provides a review of those techniques. *This book reviews those techniques.* ■ The costs of bankruptcies are trivial and do not provide a significant limitation to the use of debt financing. *The costs of bankruptcies are trivial and do not significantly limit the use of debt financing.* ■ In this chapter we provide an introduction to data processing. *In this chapter we introduce data processing.* ■ The size of the resulting MSE provides an indication of whether additional information is needed. *The size of the resulting MSE indicates whether additional information is needed.* ■ Only the firm's internal balance data provided an accurate estimate of the magnitude of the effect of service dissatisfaction in terms of lost revenues and profits. *Only the firm's internal balance data accurately estimated the magnitude of the effect of service dissatisfaction in terms of lost revenues and profits.* ■ Nurses check with other members of the health team when they are unable to provide answers to questions. *Nurses check with other members of the health team when they are unable to answer questions.*

provided (providing) (that) *if.* You can use the same filename more than once provided that the files are stored in different directories. *You can use the same filename more than once if the files are stored in different directories.*

provide ... with *give.* It provides us with a starting point for our analysis. *It gives us a starting point for our analysis.* ■ The Dubuque provided them with several hundred pounds of food and water and navigational aids but did not take them aboard. *The Dubuque gave them several hundred pounds of food and water and navigational aids but did not take them aboard.*

proximity *closeness; nearness.* Its proximity to the edge of the street and the limits of one's field of vision restrict how much of it one can see. *Its nearness to the edge of the street and the limits of one's field of vision restrict how much of it one can see.* ■ In the search for techniques to establish distance between ourselves and others we find that praise is one of the most effective, simply because, when we evaluate people, we are not likely to gain emotional proximity to them. *In the search for techniques to establish distance between ourselves and others we find that praise is one of the most effective, simply because, when we evaluate people, we are not likely to gain emotional closeness to them.*

psychiatrical *psychiatric.*

psychical *psychic.*

psychoanalytical *psychoanalytic.*

psychobiological *psychobiologic.*

psychometrical *psychometric.*

psychopathological *psychopathologic.*

psychophysiological *psychophysiologic.*

purchase *buy.* Why would a sensitive, intelligent woman purchase a handgun? *Why would a sensitive, intelligent woman buy a handgun?* ■ If you act before April 30, you can purchase the *Compact Supplement* for just $60. *If you act before April 30, you can buy the* Compact Supplement *for just $60.*

pure and simple *pure; simple.*

pure (and) unadulterated *pure; simple; unadulterated.* This movie is pure, unadulterated blasphemy. *This movie is pure blasphemy.*

pursuant to *by; following; under.* Licenses issued pursuant to this Article shall be issued for terms not exceeding one year. *Licenses issued under this Article shall be issued for terms not exceeding one year.*

put a halt to *cease; close; complete; conclude; end; finish; halt; settle; stop.* Before things get out of hand again this year, let's try to put a halt to it now. *Before things get out of hand again this year, let's try to halt it now.*

put an end to *cease; close; complete; conclude; end; finish; halt; settle; stop.* In the last century, liberals fought to put an end to the cruel traffic in human flesh known as slavery. *In the last century, liberals fought to end the cruel traffic in human flesh known as slavery.*

(to) put (it) another way *namely; that is; to wit.*

put a stop to *cease; close; complete; conclude; end; finish; halt; settle; stop.* I want you to put a stop to all of this nonsense. *I want you to stop all of this nonsense.*

put ... finger on (upon) *identify.*

put forth *advance; exert; give; offer; present; propose; submit; suggest.* Their employees, free to put forth their best efforts, thrive in this environment. *Their employees, free to give their best efforts, thrive in this environment.*

put forward *advance; give; offer; present; propose; submit; suggest.*

put in alphabetical order *alphabetize.* Suppose we have a list of words that we want to put in alphabetical order. *Suppose we have a list of words that we want to alphabetize.*

put in an appearance *appear; arrive; come; show up.*

put into effect *effect; make; perform; produce.* Quaker Fabrics Corp. said it would put into effect cost-cutting measures that specifically exclude personnel reductions. *Quaker Fabrics Corp. said it would effect cost-cutting measures that specifically exclude personnel reductions.*

put on an act *feign; pretend.*

put together *assemble; build; construct; create; devise; fashion; form; mold; set up; shape.* Thus far, KKR has put together four of the largest leveraged buyouts in history. *Thus far, KKR has fashioned four of the largest leveraged buyouts in history.*

put to sleep *destroy; kill.*

put two and two together *conclude; deduce; draw; infer; reason.*

put up with *abide; bear; endure; stand; suffer; tolerate.*

puzzlement *puzzle.*

Q

qualified expert *expert.*

quality *(adj) fine; good.* Cuddle Care offers quality care for all children of working parents. *Cuddle Care offers fine care for all children of working parents.*

question mark *enigma; mystery; puzzle; question; unknown.* For scientists trying to forecast how the world will react to the burgeoning burden of greenhouse gases, clouds pose a vexing question mark. *For scientists trying to forecast how the world will react to the burgeoning burden of greenhouse gases, clouds pose a vexing question.* ■ At present, the oceans constitute the biggest question mark in the future of the world's climate. *At present, the oceans constitute the biggest unknown in the future of the world's climate.*

(a; the) question to answer *question.* That remains a question to be answered. *That remains a question.* ■ The question to answer is what value should be used for the beginning periods in the series. *The question is what value should be used for the beginning periods in the series.*

quickly expedite *expedite.*

quite *delete.* The Microsoft Project period demand report does quite an excellent job of profiling resource workloads. *The Microsoft Project period demand report does an excellent job of profiling resource workloads.*

quixotical *quixotic.*

R

radiate out *radiate.* Tracks run in concentric circles around the disk, and sectors radiate out from the center in pie-shaped wedges. *Tracks run in concentric circles around the disk, and sectors radiate from the center in pie-shaped wedges.*

raise doubts about (on) *challenge; contradict; dispute; doubt; question.*

raise objections about (on; to) *challenge; complain about; criticize; demur; deprecate; differ in; disagree with; disapprove of; dispute; find fault with; object to; oppose; protest; question; resent.* Government employees raised objections to the bill, saying they were worried about getting jobs after leaving government. *Government employees objected to the bill, saying they were worried about getting jobs after leaving government.*

raise opposition about (on; to) *challenge; complain about; criticize; demur; deprecate; differ in; disagree with; disapprove of; dispute; find fault with; object to; oppose; protest; question; resent.* One longs to get a wider view of the times and the people she presents, particularly the women of the period who were raising strong opposition to male authority. *One longs to get a wider view of the times and the people she presents, particularly the women of the period who were strongly deprecating male authority.*

raise questions about (on) *challenge; contradict; dispute; doubt; question.* Congressional critics have raised questions about the plane's future, particularly as cost estimates have increased. *Congressional critics have questioned the plane's future, particularly as cost estimates have increased.* ■ Critics for several years have raised questions about the safety provided by the lap belts alone. *Critics for several years have disputed the safety provided by the lap belts alone.* ■ But while this helps develop the executive, it restricts the outside board members' willingness to raise questions about top management's proposals and performance. *But while this helps develop the executive, it restricts the outside board members' willingness to challenge top management's proposals and performance.*

raise up *raise.*

range anywhere (somewhere) from ... to *range from ... to.* Estimates of sales growth in the industry this year range anywhere from 12 to 50 percent. *Estimates of sales growth in the industry this year range from 12 to 50 percent.*

range from ... all the way to (all the way up to; up to) *range from ... to.* The cost ranges from $500 up to $10,000. *The cost ranges from $500 to $10,000.*

range from a low of ... to a high of *range from ... to.* The 1987 rates range from a low of 14.8 percent at St. Vincent's Hospital to a high of 35.8 percent at St. Joseph's Hospital. *The 1987 rates range from 14.8 percent at St. Vincent's Hospital to 35.8 percent at St. Joseph's Hospital.*

rant and rave *rant; rave.*

rapidity *quickness; speed.*

rarely (seldom) ever *rarely (seldom).*

rather delete. I thought this idea was rather astonishing. *I thought this idea was astonishing.*

rationale *reason; thinking.* The primary rationale is that it is a necessary condition for an otherwise attractive business deal. *The primary reason is that it is a necessary condition for an otherwise attractive business deal.*

rational reason *reason.* There's no rational reason for astrology to work. *There's no reason for astrology to work.*

raze to the ground *level; raze.*

reach (a; the) ... (of) delete. The dividends question is part of the union's proxy fight with the company that is expected to reach a culmination at next week's annual meeting. *The dividends question is part of the union's proxy fight with the company that is expected to culminate at next week's annual meeting.* ■ We tried to reach an accommodation with both parties. *We tried to accommodate both parties.*

reach (an; the) accord *agree; compromise; concur; decide; resolve; settle.* An attorney representing Eastern said the airline wants to reach an accord with the American Society of Travel Agents. *An attorney representing Eastern said the airline wants to settle with the American Society of Travel Agents.*

reach (an; the) agreement *agree; compromise; concur; decide; resolve; settle.* Both he and Chandler said the two sides had reached a tentative agreement on an educational trust fund demanded by the union. *Both he and Chandler said the two sides had tentatively agreed on an educational trust fund demanded by the union.* ■ There can be no assurance that the two parties will be able to reach agreement on any transaction. *There can be no assurance that the two parties will be able to decide on any transaction.* ■ Reportedly, the two sides have reached agreement on a number of issues. *Reportedly, the two sides have resolved a number of issues.*

reach (a; the) compromise *agree; compromise; concur; decide; resolve; settle.*

reach (a; the) conclusion *conclude; decide; deduce; determine; infer; judge; reason; resolve; settle.* Having reached this conclusion, we overturn the defendant's conviction for armed assault within a dwelling with the intent to commit a felony and assault and battery by means of a dangerous weapon. *Having concluded this, we overturn the defendant's conviction for armed assault within a dwelling with the intent to commit a felony and assault and battery by means of a dangerous weapon.* ■ The Japanese did not reach that conclusion by engaging in abstract reasoning but by observing England's industrial relations. *The Japanese did not deduce that by engaging in abstract reasoning but by observing England's industrial relations.*

reach (a; the) decision (on; upon) *conclude; decide; deduce; determine; infer; judge; reason; resolve; settle.* He said the committee also is weighing the issue of who was responsible for the overstatement and probably will reach a decision within a few weeks. *He said the committee also is weighing the issue of who was responsible for the overstatement and probably will decide within a few weeks.*

reach (a; the) determination (on; upon) *conclude; decide; deduce; determine; infer; judge; reason; resolve; settle.*

reach (an; the) estimate (estimation) (of) *approximate; assess; estimate; evaluate; rate.*

reach (an; the) opinion *conclude; decide; deduce; determine; infer; judge; reason; resolve; settle.*

reach (a; the) resolution (about; on); *agree; conclude; decide; determine; resolve; settle.*

reach (a; the) settlement *agree; conclude; decide; resolve; settle.* One union source said that the Justice Department and the union leadership were not likely to reach an out-of-court settlement before the start of the racketeering trial. *One union source said that the Justice Department and the union leadership were not likely to settle out of court before the start of the racketeering trial.*

reach (an; the) understanding *agree; compromise; concur; decide; resolve; settle.*

read where *read (that).*

real (really) delete. The legislature made a real major effort to pass the bill. *The legislature made a major effort to pass the bill.* ■ We know the governor has really serious budget problems this year. *We know the governor has serious budget problems this year.* ■ The equations may look more complicated than they really are. *The equations may look more complicated than they are.*

(a; the) real fact *fact; truth.*

real live delete. This appears to be a real live medical problem. *This appears to be a medical problem.*

really (and) truly *actually; indeed; in fact; in faith; in reality; in truth; really; truly;* delete. They really truly did have a unique product. *They truly did have a unique product.* ■ Managing the house often kept him from what he was really, truly cut out to do. *Managing the house often kept him from what he was cut out to do.*

reason being is *reason is.*

reason (why) … is because *because; reason is (that).* The reason the business failed was because it was undercapitalized. *The business failed because it was undercapitalized.* ■ Another reason why the example fails as a good strategic goal is because it violates the rule of accountability. *Another reason the example fails as a good strategic goal is it violates the rule of accountability.* ■ The reason I say that is because he was the only lawyer who charged me for interviewing him. *I say that because he was the only lawyer who charged me for interviewing him.* ■ One reason Magellan is so successful is because the fund doesn't pull in and out of the stock market. *One reason Magellan is so successful is that the fund doesn't pull in and out of the stock market.*

reason (why) … is due to (the fact that) *because of; due to; reason is (that).* The reason the flooding is so bad this year is due to torrential rains and soil erosion. *The flooding is so bad this year because of torrential rains and soil erosion.* ■ One of the reasons the big, comfortable, rear-wheel-drive sedan has remained popular is due to the increased affluence and mobility of our senior generation. *One of the reasons the big, comfortable, rear-wheel-drive sedan has remained popular is the increased affluence and mobility of our senior generation.*

reason (why) … is that *because.* The reason why it's more complicated is that we have more leaders today. *It's more complicated because we have more leaders today.* ■ The reason we're so successful is that the projects we work with are good ones and we're good at working with community groups. *We're so successful because the projects we work with are good ones and we're good at working with community groups.*

reason why *reason.* It's one of the reasons why we have so much misconduct, so much scandal, in government. *It's one of the reasons we have so much misconduct, so much scandal, in government.* ■ You have to give the American people a reason why. *You have to give the American people a reason.* ■ Benefits such as these were the reasons why a large number of U.S. companies originally entered Europe in the 1950s and 1960s via joint ventures. *Benefits such as these were the* *reasons a large number of U.S. companies originally entered Europe in the 1950s and 1960s via joint ventures.*

recall back *recall.*

receive back *receive.* People express doubt that they will receive back as much in benefits as they paid in Social Security taxes. *People express doubt that they will receive as much in benefits as they paid in Social Security taxes.*

recoil back *recoil.*

reconvert *convert.* The company is no newcomer to reconverting abandoned mills to office and research and development space. *The company is no new-comer to converting abandoned mills to office and research and development space.*

record-breaking (high) *record.* The Cape is burdened with a record-breaking number of houses for sale. *The Cape is burdened with a record number of houses for sale.* ■ As record-breaking temperatures continue to assault the nation, people may find themselves snarling where they used to smile and being grouchy when they used to grin. *As record temperatures continue to assault the nation, people may find themselves snarling where they used to smile and being grouchy when they used to grin.*

record high *record.* Young adults are returning home to live with their parents in record-high numbers. *Young adults are returning home to live with their parents in record numbers.* ■ The number of women in Congress has inched to a record high of 27, with careful targeting, smart politics, and luck all playing a part. *The number of women in Congress has inched to a record of 27, with careful targeting, smart politics, and luck all playing a part.*

record-setting *record.* That should mean a blessed end to record-setting heat and a host of problems that arose from or probably interacted with it. *That should mean a blessed end to record heat and a host of problems that arose from or probably interacted with it.*

record-size *record.* It appears we've had a record-size turnout at the polls. *It appears we've had a record turnout at the polls.*

rectify *correct; fix; improve.* Why can't they rectify the conditions at Danvers State Hospital? *Why can't they improve the conditions at Danvers State Hospital?*

recur again (and again) *recur.* The lapse has already been corrected within our systems to insure that the problem will not recur again. *The lapse has already been corrected within our systems to insure that the problem will not recur.* ■ I didn't realize that depression can recur again and again. *I didn't realize that depression can recur.*

reduce by (to) half *halve.*

reduce down *reduce.* Reduce the number of paid sick days from 20 down to some lower number. *Reduce the number of paid sick days from 20 to some lower number.*

refer back *refer.* He constantly refers back to the incident. *He constantly refers to the incident.* ■ With this change of emphasis, the general case allows the process to be repeated again from the beginning by referring back to the original procedure. *With this change of emphasis, the general case allows the process to be repeated again from the beginning by referring to the original procedure.* ■ The reader may find it helpful to refer back to this diagram after we have completed our discussion. *The reader may find it helpful to refer to this diagram after we have completed our discussion.*

refer to *see.* For a detailed description of this form, refer to Chapter 4 of *Inside the Apple IIe.* For a detailed description of this form, *see Chapter 4 of* Inside the Apple IIe.

refer to as *call; name; term;* delete. Unconscious attempts to manage anxiety are referred to as defense mechanisms. *Unconscious attempts to manage anxiety are termed defense mechanisms.* ■ Multiview drawings are often referred to as mechanical drawings. *Multiview drawings are often called mechanical drawings.* ■ The circle is referred to as the bolt circle, or circle of centers. *The circle is the bolt circle, or circle of centers.*

reflect back *reflect.* "It really was one of the smartest decisions I had ever made," she says, reflecting back on those days. *"It really was one of the smartest decisions I had ever made," she says, reflecting on those days.* ■ Reflecting back on my years at BB&N, I tried to understand why neither the school nor the parents were willing to give this case the publicity it deserved. *Reflecting on my years at BB&N, I tried to understand why neither the school nor the parents were willing to give this case the publicity it deserved.*

regard (regarding) *about; as for; as to; for; in; of; on; over; to; toward; with.* New Jersey has no law regarding traffic circles. *New Jersey has no law on traffic circles.* ■ Women do have some leeway regarding what we give up at various points in our lives. *Women do have some leeway in what we give up at various points in our lives.* ■ Although we try to contact you regarding any significant medical treatment, it is not always possible. *Although we try to contact you about any significant medical treatment, it is not always possible.*

regard as being *regard as.*

regardless of (what) *despite (what); no matter what; whatever.* Regardless of a firm's individual situation, standardization possibilities, particularly in the context of product and advertising policy, should be carefully evaluated. *Whatever a firm's individual situation, standardization possibilities, particularly in the con-*

text of product and advertising policy, should be carefully evaluated. ■ Regard-less of the answers to these questions, some officials in the Pentagon and on Capitol Hill are already noting three lessons from the downing of the airliner. *Despite the answers to these questions, some officials in the Pentagon and on Capitol Hill are already noting three lessons from the downing of the airlin-er.* ■ Regardless of what women may accomplish one on one, the most effective agent for change is the company itself. *No matter what women may accomplish one on one, the most effective agent for change is the company itself.*

regardless of how *despite how; however; no matter how.* Regardless of how you get there, once the document screen appears, you are ready to enter text. *No matter how you get there, once the document screen appears, you are ready to enter text.* ■ Regardless of how one estimates the enhanced services business, it is extremely important and clearly will become more so over the next decade. *However one estimates the enhanced services business, it is extremely important and clearly will become more so over the next decade.* ■ All lines and lettering must be absolutely black regardless of how fine the lines may be. *All lines and lettering must be absolutely black despite how fine the lines may be.*

regardless of the fact that *although; but; even though; still; though; yet.* Because the aquarium is a private enterprise—regardless of the fact that it is nonprofit—such a transfer is not supposed to take place. *Because the aquarium is a private enterprise—even though it is nonprofit—such a transfer is not supposed to take place.*

regardless of when *despite when; no matter when; whenever.* Both proposals would cover all capital assets regardless of when taxpayers bought them. *Both proposals would cover all capital assets despite when taxpayers bought them.*

regardless of where *despite where; no matter where; wherever.* Visible soft hyphens appear on the screen and print out regardless of where they fall in the document. *Visible soft hyphens appear on the screen and print out wherever they fall in the document.* ■ Regardless of where he lived or went to school, he still might have committed this tragedy. *No matter where he lived or went to school, he still might have committed this tragedy.*

regardless of whether ... (or) *despite whether; no matter whether; whether ... or (not).* Men's masculinity, looks, and concern about their appearance were rated the same regardless of whether lunch was a salad and coffee or a five-course extravaganza. *Men's masculinity, looks, and concern about their appearance were rated the same whether lunch was a salad and coffee or a five-course extravaganza.* ■ Regardless of whether the reason is internal or external, it has an important bearing on the market-presence alternatives investigated. *Whether the reason is internal or external, it has an important bearing on the market-presence alternatives investigated.* ■ He would carry one crumpled tie around in his brief-case and pull it out for debates, regardless of whether it matched the rest of his wardrobe. *He would carry one crumpled tie around in his briefcase and pull it* *out for debates, whether or not it matched the rest of his wardrobe.* ■ If a point is to be located at the midpoint of a line, it will be at the line's midpoint regardless of whether the line appears true length or foreshortened. *If a point is to be located at the midpoint of a line, it will be at the line's midpoint whether the line appears true length or foreshortened.*

regardless of which *despite which; no matter which; whichever.* The relative references to cell B8 in the original formula always refer to sales in the column to its left regardless of which cell it was copied to on the same row. *The relative references to cell B8 in the original formula always refer to sales in the column to its left despite which cell it was copied to on the same row.* ■ Regardless of which happens, you can change the result. *Whichever happens, you can change the result.*

regardless of who *despite who; no matter who; whoever.* Regardless of who we may be, we all have the right to economic opportunity. *Whoever we may be, we all have the right to economic opportunity.* ■ Regardless of who decides, graphics is a primary means of presenting the proposed designs for a decision. *No matter who decides, graphics is a primary means of presenting the proposed designs for a decision.* ■ Regardless of who lives in the house and whether any of the exceptions apply, the state cannot force a sale of the house while the institutionalized person is alive. *Despite who lives in the house and whether any of the exceptions apply, the state cannot force a sale of the house while the institutionalized person is alive.*

regardless of whom *despite whom; no matter whom; whomever.* Regardless of whom these books are meant for, I think they should be designed and developed to look and feel more accessible. *Whomever these books are meant for, I think they should be designed and developed to look and feel more accessible.*

regular -(al)ly *-(al)ly.* We attend the regular monthly meeting of the BCS. *We attend the monthly meeting of the BCS.* ■ Bond prices advanced yesterday as the government began its regular quarterly sale of new securities by auctioning $9.76 billion in new three-year notes. *Bond prices advanced yesterday as the government began its quarterly sale of new securities by auctioning $9.76 billion in new three-year notes.*

regular routine *routine.* Hiring, training, and record-keeping are part of the regular routine for running any business. *Hiring, training, and record-keeping are part of the routine for running any business.*

reiterate *iterate; repeat.* Baker also reiterated his insistence that Bush would not debate before September 22. *Baker also repeated his insistence that Bush would not debate before September 22.*

reiterate again (and again) *iterate; reiterate; repeat.*

reject as untrue *disbelieve.*

relate *say; tell.*

relate back *relate.*

-related delete. Peter English, CEO of American Consulting Corp., foresees an explosion of education-related products, such as books and magazines. *Peter English, CEO of American Consulting Corp., foresees an explosion of educational products, such as books and magazines.* ■ This division provides telemarketing-related and other direct marketing services for clients in four areas. *This division provides telemarketing and other direct marketing services for clients in four areas.* ■ The main reason was that NYNEX would be selling a full and varied line of computer-related products and services. *The main reason was that NYNEX would be selling a full and varied line of computer products and services.* ■ Fewer than 15 percent of visits to the clinic are for sexuality-related issues. *Fewer than 15 percent of visits to the clinic are for sexual issues.*

relate (relating) to *about; as for; as to; concerning; for; in; of; on; over; regarding; to; toward; with.* We may add to the basic rental price any taxes or other governmental assessments relating to the use or operation of the postage meter or scale. *We may add to the basic rental price any taxes or other governmental assessments on the use or operation of the postage meter or scale.* ■ The last complaint related to the market performance of Lotus' Jazz software and technical problems with Lotus' Symphony product. *The last complaint concerned the market performance of Lotus' Jazz software and technical problems with Lotus' Symphony product.* ■ Morgan, who attributed the malaise in part to uncertainty related to the presidential election, predicted that the fourth-quarter median price could dip below the third-quarter benchmark of $184,100. *Morgan, who attributed the malaise in part to uncertainty over the presidential election, predicted that the fourth-quarter median price could dip below the third-quarter benchmark of $184,100.*

relationship *bond; connection; link; relation; tie.* The photograph had no relationship to any of the elements of the story. *The photograph had no relation to any of the elements of the story.* ■ They found a relationship between age and risk-taking and also between age and the value placed on risk. *They found a link between age and risk-taking and also between age and the value placed on risk.*

relatively *-(i)er; less; more.* Lawyer Dukakis repeatedly has expressed disdain for the merger and acquisition business; oil man Bush seems to harbor relatively few such concerns. *Lawyer Dukakis repeatedly has expressed disdain for the merger and acquisition business; oil man Bush seems to harbor fewer such concerns.*

relatively ... as compared to (with) *compared to (with).*

relatively ... compared (contrasted) to (with) *compared (contrasted) to (with).* Shrinkage remains relatively low, compared to mass retailing standards. *Shrinkage remains low compared to mass retailing standards.*

relatively -(i)er than (less than; more than) *-(i)er than (less than; more than);* delete. This country is in relatively better shape than other major industrialized nations. *This country is in better shape than other major industrialized nations.* ■ Its real-estate portfolio grew relatively faster than anybody else's. *Its real-estate portfolio grew faster than anybody else's.* ■ Despite some changes over the years, the index places relatively more emphasis on manufacturing than on services. *Despite some changes over the years, the index places more emphasis on manufacturing than on services.*

relatively ... in comparison (in contrast) to (with) *compared (contrasted) to (with).* Solving the legal problems of partnerships is relatively simple in comparison to solving the problems of other types of ownership. *Solving the legal problems of partnerships is simple compared to solving the problems of other types of ownership.*

relative to *about; concerning; for; on; regarding.* She asked me questions relative to my feelings about administering heroin to relieve the excruciating pain of a terminal cancer victim. *She asked me questions on my feelings about administering heroin to relieve the excruciating pain of a terminal cancer victim.* ■ Much has been said relative to the issuance of a standard employment contract to the executive director of the GLSD. *Much has been said about the issuance of a standard employment contract to the executive director of the GLSD.*

relative to *against; alongside; beside; compared to (with); -(i)er than; less; less than; more; more than; next to; over; than; to; versus; vis-à-vis.* Relative to other societies, Brazil and the United States place considerable emphasis on youth. *Brazil and the United States place considerably more emphasis on youth than other societies.* ■ Relative to other drugs, it's much less harmful. *It's much less harmful than other drugs.* ■ Although Siemens' digital exchange reached the worldwide market late relative to most other suppliers' digital switches, the company had begun ISDN R&D efforts early at the request of the West German Bundespost. *Although Siemens' digital exchange reached the worldwide market later than most other suppliers' digital switches, the company had begun ISDN R&D efforts early at the request of the West German Bundespost.* ■ During 1988, the stock market generated superior returns relative to bonds and cash equivalents. *During 1988, the stock market generated returns superior to bonds and cash equivalents.*

relic of the past *relic.* But for most people today, CP/M is an all-but-forgotten relic of the past which is just a few years old. *But for most people today, CP/M is an all-but-forgotten relic which is just a few years old.* ■ Expensive data storage, sluggish retrieval, and complex systems that overwhelm their would-be users are all relics of the past. *Expensive data storage, sluggish retrieval, and complex systems that overwhelm their would-be users are all relics.*

remainder *remains; rest.* No economic indicators are due for the remainder of the week. *No economic indicators are due for the rest of the week.*

remains to be seen *do not know; is not (now; yet) known; is uncertain; is unclear; is unknown; is unsure.* But it remains to be seen whether the improved immune status will translate into significantly longer survival times. *But whether the improved immune status will translate into significantly longer survival times is unclear.* ■ It remains to be seen if he can sustain a housing partnership. *It's not yet known if he can sustain a housing partnership.*

remand back *remand.*

reminisce about the past *reminisce.*

remit back *remit.*

remittance *cash; fee; money; pay; payment; wage.*

remunerate *pay.*

remuneration *cash; fee; money; pay; payment; reward; wage.*

render *act; do; give; make.* The biggest question remaining about the use of phenethanolamines is whether the drugs will contaminate meat and render it unsafe for human consumption. *The biggest question remaining about the use of phenethanolamines is whether the drugs will contaminate meat and make it unsafe for human consumption.*

render assistance to *help.*

reoccur (reoccurrence) *recur (recurrence).* This behavior tends to reoccur every year. *This behavior tends to recur every year.* ■ The problem with this approach is that the conflict may reoccur because its root cause has not been removed. *The problem with this approach is that the conflict may recur because its root cause has not been removed.* ■ It is even more important that more be done to protect them from the occurrence and reoccurrence of that which precipitates these disorders: sexual abuse. *It is even more important that more be done to protect them from the occurrence and recurrence of that which precipitates these disorders: sexual abuse.*

repay back *repay.*

repeat again (and again) *repeat.* Single-use plans apply to activities that do not repeat again. *Single-use plans apply to activities that do not repeat.* ■ All of this is based on predictable behaviors that are repeated again and again in rather exact ways. *All of this is based on predictable behaviors that are repeated in rather exact ways.*

repeat back *repeat.*

repeat occurrence *recurrence.* What should he do so as not to have a repeat occurrence of this? *What should he do so as not to have a recurrence of this?*

repeat over (and over) *repeat.* A loop is a sequence of commands, the last of which refers the program back to the first so that the commands repeat over and over until stopped. *A loop is a sequence of commands, the last of which refers the program back to the first so that the commands repeat until stopped.*

reply back *reply.* I sent her a letter and then waited two weeks for a reply back. *I sent her a letter and then waited two weeks for a reply.*

report back *report.* The Insurance Division will report back to the high court within 30 days on whether to rehabilitate them in some ways or declare them insolvent. *The Insurance Division will report to the high court within 30 days on whether to rehabilitate them in some ways or declare them insolvent.* ■ Trainees consistently report back that such rehearsals have a profound effect on their actual, on-the-job performance, long after the training ends. *Trainees consistently report that such rehearsals have a profound effect on their actual, on-the-job performance, long after the training ends.*

represents *is.* These numbers represent the washer's inside diameter, outside diameter, and thickness. *These numbers are the washer's inside diameter, outside diameter, and thickness.* ■ Styles represent an easy way to attach a collection of formatting codes to various sections of text at once. *Styles are an easy way to attach a collection of formatting codes to various sections of text at once.* ■ We believe that our offer represents a fair price and is in the best interest of Pennwalt's shareholders. *We believe that our offer is a fair price and is in the best interest of Pennwalt's shareholders.*

require *need.*

requirement *need.*

requisite *need.*

reside *dwell; live.* I am now residing in New York City. *I am now living in New York City.*

residence *home; house.*

residual trace *trace.* She is still beautiful despite residual traces of a massive stroke suffered when she was three-months pregnant. *She is still beautiful despite* *traces of a massive stroke suffered when she was three-months pregnant.*

resiliency *resilience.*

respective (respectively) delete. Microsoft hereby limits the duration of any implied warranty(ies) on the disk or such hardware to the respective periods stated above. *Microsoft hereby limits the duration of any implied warranty(ies) on the disk or such hardware to the periods stated above.*

respond back *respond.* I was disappointed the governor could not have responded back to me personally. *I was disappointed the governor could not have responded to me personally.*

respond in the affirmative *agree; say yes.* We hope he will respond in the affirmative. *We hope he will say yes.*

respond in the negative *disagree; say no.*

restore back *restore.* If something happens to the files on the disk that you back up, you can use the backup copies to restore files back onto it. *If something happens to the files on the disk that you back up, you can use the backup copies to restore files onto it.*

rest up *rest.*

resultant *(n) effect; result.*

resultant effect *effect; result.*

resume again *resume.*

retain ... position as *remain.*

retreat back *retreat.* Having conquered consumer electronics, the Japanese firms are attacking in industrial electronics, and the American firms are once again in the process of retreating back to defense electronics to get those higher returns on investment. *Having conquered consumer electronics, the Japanese firms are attacking in industrial electronics, and the American firms are once again in the process of retreating to defense electronics to get those higher returns on investment.*

return back *return.* In the 1980s, we're returning back to the cultural norm of marriage and family. *In the 1980s, we're returning to the cultural norm of marriage and family.* ■ When it reaches the end of the line, a charge in voltage returns the beam back to the left side of the screen. *When it reaches the end of the line, a charge in voltage returns the beam to the left side of the screen.*

reuse again *reuse.* If you want to create more than one graph for a model so that you can reuse them again, what must you do? *If you want to create more than one graph for a model so that you can reuse them, what must you do?*

revert back *revert.* Some companies that encounter operational problems during an advanced stage may revert back to a previous stage. *Some companies that encounter operational problems during an advanced stage may revert to a previous stage.* ■ It should be noted that the question of whether to revert back to private ownership came up before the unwelcome offer. *It should be noted that the question of whether to revert to private ownership came up before the unwelcome offer.*

right-hand *right.* If the company has a weak competitive position and the market opportunity is not great, then we would find ourselves down in the right-hand corner of this diagram. *If the company has a weak competitive position and the market opportunity is not great, then we would find ourselves down in the right corner of this diagram.*

root cause *cause; reason; root; source.* The agency was unable to pinpoint a common design flaw or manufacturing defect that could be the root cause for these unwanted acceleration incidents. *The agency was unable to pinpoint a common design flaw or manufacturing defect that could be the cause for these unwanted acceleration incidents.* ■ White-collar crimes, not poor economic conditions or deregulation, are the root cause of the S&L crisis. *White-collar crimes, not poor economic conditions or deregulation, are the root of the S&L crisis.*

rough sketch *sketch.* A rough sketch is made to indicate the type of illustration required and the method of reproduction to be used. *A sketch is made to indicate the type of illustration required and the method of reproduction to be used.*

routine procedure *routine.* There is a routine procedure that we follow. *There is a routine that we follow.*

rules and regulations *regulations; rules.* Rules and regulations regarding the use of the library have been posted throughout the building. *Rules regarding the use of the library have been posted throughout the building.* ■ In order to help carry out the provisions of this Lease, the Landlord may issue rules and regulations for the benefit, safety, comfort, and convenience of all occupants of the Building. *In order to help carry out the provisions of this Lease, the Landlord may issue regulations for the benefit, safety, comfort, and convenience of all occupants of the Building.*

run of the mill *average; common; everyday; mediocre; ordinary; typical; usual.*

S

sad to relate (say) *sadly*. Sad to say, politicians who rely on certain familiar locutions to get around the predictable ridicule that this horn-tooting always provokes fare no better. *Sadly, politicians who rely on certain familiar locutions to get around the predictable ridicule that this horn-tooting always provokes fare no better.* ∎ Sad to relate, some bicyclists have become a menace to pedestrian and motor vehicle traffic. *Sadly, some bicyclists have become a menace to pedestrian and motor vehicle traffic.*

satirical *satiric.*

say, for example (for instance) *for example (for instance); say.* She also predicted that readers will begin to see magazine advertisements that talk, say, for example, Lee Iacocca hawking Chrysler cars in his own voice. *She also predicted that readers will begin to see magazine advertisements that talk, for example, Lee Iacocca hawking Chrysler cars in his own voice.* ∎ Say, for example, you use a 12-percent home-equity loan to finance $10,000 of an automobile purchase. *Say you use a 12-percent home-equity loan to finance $10,000 of an automobile purchase.*

scatter in all (every) direction(s) *scatter.*

scream and yell *scream; yell.*

secondarily *second.*

secondly *second.* The emotionally maladjusted person, "the neurotic," is in difficulty, first, because communication within himself has broken down and, secondly, because as a result of this his communication with others has been damaged. *The emotionally maladjusted person, "the neurotic," is in difficulty, first, because communication within himself has broken down and, second, because as a result of this his communication with others has been damaged.*

second of all *also; and; as well; besides; beyond that (this); further; furthermore; in addition; moreover; more than that (this); next; second; still more; too; what is more.*

seeing (as; as how; that) *because; considering; for; in that; since.* Seeing as how I don't have any stamps, I'm going to deliver this myself. *Since I don't have any stamps, I'm going to deliver this myself.*

seek out *seek.* In most cases, we actively seek out foreign investment. *In most cases, we actively seek foreign investment.*

seesaw back and forth (up and down) *seesaw.* The Hang Seng index seesawed back and forth last week as student demonstrations fueled speculation. *The Hang Seng index seesawed last week as student demonstrations fueled speculation.*

see where *see (that).*

(a; the) select number (of) *few; select; two (three).* On occasion, countries impose prohibitions on capital flows and the importation of all, or a select number of, goods. *On occasion, countries impose prohibitions on capital flows and the importation of all, or select, goods.*

select out *choose; pick out; select.* The other approach, selecting out for doctors' treatment those at particularly high risk, is already well established, but it has limitations. *The other approach, selecting for doctors' treatment those at particularly high risk, is already well established, but it has limitations.*

(my)self *(I; me).* Richard and myself are going to lunch. *Richard and I are going to lunch.* ■ Let's hope someone comes along, like myself, to take his place. *Let's hope someone comes along, like me, to take his place.* ■ Very large people like yourself can eat tiny amounts of food and not lose an ounce. *Very large people like you can eat tiny amounts of food and not lose an ounce.* ■ We feel Mr. Roedler's comments do an injustice to collectors like ourselves who currently pay $1,500 to $2,000 for radios of this type. *We feel Mr. Roedler's comments do an injustice to collectors like us who currently pay $1,500 to $2,000 for radios of this type.* ■ Neither the mayor nor myself desires to comment on the status of the matter. *Neither the mayor nor I desire to comment on the status of the matter.*

selfsame *same.*

seminal fluid *semen.* There was a trace of seminal fluid on her clothing. *There was a trace of semen on her clothing.*

(a) sense of *delete.* Our sense of foreboding grew as the afternoon wore on. *Our foreboding grew as the afternoon wore on.* ■ You feel a sense of joy and fulfillment in pursuing your own interests. *You feel joy and fulfillment in pursuing your own interests.* ■ I feel a sense of relief. *I feel relief.* ■ I felt a sense of helplessness when he beat me. *I felt helpless when he beat me.* ■ We all feel a sense of sadness at the loss of my father. *We all feel sad at the loss of my father.* ■ The teachers read to the children, talk with the children, help them observe and adapt to their surroundings, and encourage them to develop a sense of self-confidence. *The teachers read to the children, talk with the children, help them observe and adapt to their surroundings, and encourage them to develop self-confidence.*

(five; many; several) separate *(five; many; several); separate.* The report cites 171 separate studies, most of them conducted during the past decade, as references. *The report cites 171 studies, most of them conducted during the past decade, as references.*

separate and apart *apart; separate.* We agreed that these issues ought to be separate and apart from the treaty. *We agreed that these issues ought to be separate from the treaty.* ■ The government's acquisition regulations provide for a convoluted bid-evaluation scheme wherein bidders submit a price proposal separate and apart from a technical proposal. *The government's acquisition regulations provide for a convoluted bid-evaluation scheme wherein bidders submit a price proposal separate from a technical proposal.*

separate and autonomous *autonomous; separate.*

separate and discrete *discrete; separate.* We found that 58 percent of respondent worksites had a separate and discrete unit that supports end-user computing. *We found that 58 percent of respondent worksites had a discrete unit that supports end-user computing.*

separate and distinct *distinct; separate.* Each of us has four separate and distinct vocabularies: a written, a spoken, a heard, and a visual vocabulary. *Each of us has four distinct vocabularies: a written, a spoken, a heard, and a visual vocabulary.* ■ Initially, the alternatives should be separate and distinct solutions to the problem. *Initially, the alternatives should be separate solutions to the problem.*

separate and independent *independent; separate.* Southern New England Telephone in Connecticut is a separate and independent company. *Southern New England Telephone in Connecticut is an independent company.*

separate and individual *individual; separate.* A Covered Person will be fully insured for benefits under the Policy while taking an airline trip only when the fare has been charged separately and individually to the Basic or Additional Cardmember's enrolled account. *A Covered Person will be fully insured for benefits under the Policy while taking an airline trip only when the fare has been charged separately to the Basic or Additional Cardmember's enrolled account.*

separate apart *separate.*

separate entity *entity; separate.* The artificial separation of these three dimensions is confusing when they are seen as three separate entities. *The artificial separation of these three dimensions is confusing when they are seen as three entities.* ■ For years, our minds and bodies were seen as being separate entities. *For years, our minds and bodies were seen as being separate.*

separate individual *individual; separate.* Astronomers have long studied binary systems in which the stars are far enough apart and bright enough to be seen as separate individuals. *Astronomers have long studied binary systems in which the stars are far enough apart and bright enough to be seen as individuals.*

separate out *separate.* We have a long history of the scientific establishment trying to separate out the research and development of a technology from its social application. *We have a long history of the scientific establishment trying to separate the research and development of a technology from its social application.*

seriously addicted *addicted.* I was never seriously addicted to heroin. *I was never addicted to heroin.*

serve up *serve.* Can I serve you up some quiche? *Can I serve you some quiche?*

seventy-five (75) percent (of) *three-fourths; three-quarters.*

shaken up *shaken.*

share (a; the) common *share.* We have to have people with whom we can share a common view of the world and not have to apologize for it. *We have to have people with whom we can share a view of the world and not have to apologize for it.* ■ Group action is possible in your meeting, even when everyone does not share a common understanding of the subject. *Group action is possible in your meeting, even when everyone does not share an understanding of the subject.*

share ... in common (with) *share.* U.S. research on global change shares something in common with the legendary horseman who roamed the hills of Washington Irving's Sleepy Hollow: They both appear to lack heads. *U.S. research on global change shares something with the legendary horseman who roamed the hills of Washington Irving's Sleepy Hollow: They both appear to lack heads.*

share together *share.* If there is one commitment that defines him, it is the commitment that we share together. *If there is one commitment that defines him, it is the commitment that we share.*

short and sweet *brief; concise; pithy; short; succinct; terse.*

short and to the point *brief; concise; pithy; short; succinct; terse; to the point.*

should ... then *should.* Should the Department of Public Utilities concur that the blame for these plant outages rests with Boston Edison, then the company's stockholders—not the customers—must absorb the costs. *Should the Department of Public Utilities concur that the blame for these plant outages rests with*

Boston Edison, the company's stockholders—not the customers—must absorb the costs.

show (a; the) … (of; to) delete. Figure 14.3 shows a comparison of dimensions in millimeters with those in inches. *Figure 14.3 compares dimensions in millimeters with those in inches.* ■ The respondents preferred to retain but not retrain obsolete older employees and showed a tendency to withhold promotions from older workers. *The respondents preferred to retain but not retrain obsolete older employees and tended to withhold promotions from older workers.*

shown at (in) *at (in).* The aperture cards shown in Figure 18.3 are data processing cards that can be catalogued by a computer. *The aperture cards in Figure 18.3 are data processing cards that can be catalogued by a computer.* ■ Each of the sequences shown at the right is an arithmetic sequence. *Each of the sequences at the right is an arithmetic sequence.*

shuttle back and forth between … and *shuttle between … and.* From July 1987 until June 1988, he shuttled back and forth between San Francisco and the Urbana research facility to study the three bears. *From July 1987 until June 1988, he shuttled between San Francisco and the Urbana research facility to study the three bears.*

sick and tired *annoyed; disgusted; sick; tired.*

side by side (with) *alongside; among; beside; next to; with.*

significance *import; moment.*

significant (substantial) *ample; big; grand; great; heavy; huge; immense; large; many; most; much; vast.* The region began the decade with a significant surplus of power. *The region began the decade with a large surplus of power.* ■ The company believes this market offers substantial opportunities and may experience a 25-percent annual growth rate into the 1990s. *The company believes this market offers many opportunities and may experience a 25-percent annual growth rate into the 1990s.* ■ Substantial benefits result from using any kind of LAN software. *Ample benefits result from using any kind of LAN software.*

(a; the) significant (substantial) amount (of) *a good (great) deal (of); a good (great) many (of); almost all (of); considerable; many (of); most (of); much (of); nearly all (of); vast.* This difficulty is a major stumbling block, costing end users significant amounts of time and money. *This difficulty is a major stumbling block, costing end users much time and money.* ■ A lot of communities are going to want to build new schools, and it will add up to a significant amount of money. *A lot of communities are going to want to build new schools, and it will add up to a great deal of money.*

(a; the) significant (substantial) degree (of) *a good (great) deal (of); considerable; great; much (of); vast.*

(a; the) significant (substantial) element (of) *a good (great) deal (of); a good (great) many (of); considerable; great; many (of); much (of); vast.*

(a; the) significant (substantial) fraction (of) *a good (great) deal (of); a good (great) many (of); almost all (of); (nine) in (ten) (of); many (of); most (of); much (of); nearly all (of); (43) of (48) (of); ... percent (of); three-fourths (two-thirds) (of).* A significant fraction of leading U.S. weapons production specialists met last weekend to discuss the proposal, with predictable results. *Six of ten leading U.S. weapons production specialists met last weekend to discuss the proposal, with predictable results.*

significant importance *consequence; importance; significance.*

significantly (substantially) *a good (great) deal; amply; far; greatly; largely; mostly; much; vastly.* The three studies identified fundamentally different groups of pill users in whom risk appeared significantly elevated. *The three studies identified fundamentally different groups of pill users in whom risk appeared much elevated.* ▪ These results for these groups were substantially the same as for the control group. *These results for these groups were largely the same as for the control group.* ▪ Two of the 13 had slightly higher earnings; only three did substantially better. *Two of the 13 had slightly higher earnings; only three did far better.*

(a; the) significant (substantial) majority (of) *a good (great) deal (of); a good (great) many (of); almost all (of); (nine) in (ten) (of); many (of); most (of); much (of); nearly all (of); (43) of (48); ... percent (of); three-fourths (two-thirds) (of).* A substantial majority think certain reforms would improve the present primary system. *Many think certain reforms would improve the present primary system.* ▪ The survey also indicated a substantial majority of Americans would oppose President Reagan for a third term if he could run again. *The survey also indicated 52 percent of Americans would oppose President Reagan for a third term if he could run again.* ▪ Polls have shown for years that a substantial majority of Japanese want a revision of the antiquated tax system. *Polls have shown for years that most Japanese want a revision of the antiquated tax system.*

(a; the) significant (substantial) minority (of) *almost half (of); fewer than half (of); (one) in (three); less than half (of); nearly half (of); (20) of (48) (of); one-third (one-fifth) (of); ... percent (of).* A significant minority of agents said that they would not sell the type of insurance our researchers requested in the amount they wanted to buy. *Eighteen of fifty agents said that they would not sell the type of insurance our researchers requested in the amount they wanted to buy.* ▪ Even among smokers, a significant minority are happier in smoke-free skies. *Even among smokers, nearly half are happier in smoke-free skies.* ▪ The scientists conclude that SAD represents the extreme end of a spectrum of seasonal mood and behavior changes affecting a substantial minority of the population. *The scientists conclude that SAD represents the extreme end of a spectrum of seasonal mood and behavior changes affecting one-third of the population.*

(a; the) significant (substantial) number (of) *a good (great) many (of); almost all (of); countless; dozens (of); hundreds (of); many (of); millions (of); most (of); nearly all (of); numerous; scores (of); six hundred (twelve hundred) (of); thousands (of).* If all goes as anticipated, Ford will sell a substantial number of expensive, European-made Fords to the Soviets. *If all goes as anticipated, Ford will sell thousands of expensive, European-made Fords to the Soviets.* ■ A significant number of by-pass operations are unnecessary. *Many by-pass operations are unnecessary.* ■ A significant number of adults die from pneumonia each year. *Scores of adults die from pneumonia each year.* ■ We did this because we received a substantial number of reports that the election was unfair. *We did this because we received hundreds of reports that the election was unfair.* ■ If we had an agreement to supply them with a substantial number of copies of the book, we would have to take into consideration their requirements. *If we had an agreement to supply them with 2,000 copies of the book, we would have to take into consideration their requirements.*

(a; the) significant (substantial) part (of) *a good (great) deal (of); a good (great) many (of); almost all (of); (nine) in (ten) (of); many (of); most (of); much (of); nearly all (of); (43) of (48) (of); ... percent (of); three-fourths (two-thirds) (of).* Improvements in computerization would enable financial institutions to bring a substantial part of their services directly into the home. *Improvements in computerization would enable financial institutions to bring many of their services directly into the home.* ■ Businessland Inc. says mice represent a substantial part of its computer accessories sales. *Businessland Inc. says mice represent 8 percent of its computer accessories sales.*

(a; the) significant (substantial) percentage (of) *a good (great) deal (of); a good (great) many (of); almost all (of); (nine) in (ten) (of); many (of); most (of); much (of); nearly all (of); (43) of (48) (of); ... percent (of); three-fourths (two-thirds) (of).* A significant percentage of criminals in New York are on drugs when they commit their crimes. *Three in ten criminals in New York are on drugs when they commit their crimes.* ■ The drug can cause serious kidney damage and other side effects, and a substantial percentage of patients cannot absorb it. *The drug can cause serious kidney damage and other side effects, and many patients cannot absorb it.*

(a; the) significant (substantial) portion (of) *a good (great) deal (of); a good (great) many (of); almost all (of); (nine) in (ten) (of); many (of); most (of); much (of); nearly all (of); (43) of (48) (of); ... percent (of); three-fourths (two-thirds) (of).* The company said that a significant portion of the cuts will be achieved through early retirement. *The company said that most of the cuts will be achieved through early retirement.* ■ A substantial portion of this investment was in the Japan market. *Two-thirds of this investment was in the Japan market.* ■ Other developing nations also destroy substantial portions of their tree canopy each year. *Other developing nations also destroy a good deal of their tree canopy each year.* ■ Known as the Cretaceous-Tertiary (K-T) boundary, this time marks the extinction of a significant portion of living species, including the dinosaurs. *Known as the Cretaceous-Tertiary (K-T) boundary, this time marks the extinction of a great many living species, including the dinosaurs.*

(a; the) significant (substantial) proportion (of) *a good (great) deal (of); a good (great) many (of); almost all (of); (nine) in (ten) (of); many (of); most (of); much (of); nearly all (of); (43) of (48) (of); ... percent (of); three-fourths (two-thirds) (of).* West German and British firms also account for a significant proportion of U.S. patents. *West German and British firms also account for many U.S. patents.* ■ One recent survey of investigators revealed that a substantial proportion of the studies involving clinical trials of a certain unspecified new therapy remained unpublished. *One recent survey of investigators revealed that one-third of the studies involving clinical trials of a certain unspecified new therapy remained unpublished.* ■ The oxygen, carrying an energy of 3.2 trillion electron-volts, deposits a significant proportion of this energy into the excised material, creating the atomic equivalent of a fireball. *The oxygen, carrying an energy of 3.2 trillion electron-volts, deposits much of this energy into the excised material, creating the atomic equivalent of a fireball.*

(a; the) significant (substantial) quantity (of) *a good (great) deal (of); a good (great) many (of); almost all (of); dozens (of); hundreds (of); many (of); millions (of); most (of); nearly all (of); scores (of); six hundred (twelve hundred) (of); thousands (of).*

simple (and) fundamental *fundamental; simple.* We welcome the opportunity to present the following two descriptions of barriers and gateways to communication, in the thought that they may help to bring the problem down to earth and show what it means in terms of simple fundamentals. *We welcome the opportunity to present the following two descriptions of barriers and gateways to communication, in the thought that they may help to bring the problem down to earth and show what it means in terms of fundamentals.*

simply and solely *simply; solely.* She was fired simply and solely on account of her sex. *She was fired solely on account of her sex.*

simultaneously *as one; at once; collectively; concurrently; jointly; together.* A collaborative work group is several people working on the same document simultaneously. *A collaborative work group is several people working on the same document at once.*

simultaneously ... while *while.* A dissemination system must simultaneously develop the capability of people at several levels through staff development and ongoing support while it works to create a context in schools, districts, and states. *A dissemination system must develop the capability of people at several levels through staff development and ongoing support while it works to create a context in schools, districts, and states.*

simultaneous (simultaneously) with *with.* The selection of the media to be used for advertising campaigns needs to be done simultaneously with the development of message, theme, concepts, and copy. *The selection of the media to be used for advertising campaigns needs to be done with the development of message, theme, concepts, and copy.*

(ever) since that time *since; since then.* Since that time, much of what we know about mutation, speciation, and other genetic phenomena has been discovered with populations of fruit flies in nature and in the lab. *Since then, much of what we know about mutation, speciation, and other genetic phenomena has been discovered with populations of fruit flies in nature and in the lab.* ■ Since that time, a lot has changed in my life. *A lot has since changed in my life.*

(ever) since then *since.* Since then several states have passed laws against the misuse of sickle cell screening. *Several states have since passed laws against the misuse of sickle cell screening.* ■ Since then, he and his collaborators have found a second distant, faint galaxy similar to Malin 1 but only half as large. *He and his collaborators have since found a second distant, faint galaxy similar to Malin 1 but only half as large.*

since ... then *since.* Since the suit makes no mention of a sexual relationship, then what we are talking about are the types of things two friends share. *Since the suit makes no mention of a sexual relationship, what we are talking about are the types of things two friends share.*

single best (biggest; fastest; greatest; largest; most) *best (biggest; fastest; greatest; largest; most).* Our single biggest concern is the capacity issue. *Our biggest concern is the capacity issue.* ■ In the next chapter, we discuss planning the meeting, one of the single most important elements of meetings. *In the next chapter, we discuss planning the meeting, one of the most important elements of meetings.* ■ Since the single fastest growing group of all workers is female, it is interesting that day care is not more widespread. *Since the fastest growing group of all workers is female, it is interesting that day care is not more widespread.*

sink down *sink.*

(a; the) -sion (-tion) of (that; to) *-ing.* The essence of consumer finance marketing strategy is the realization that *how* a loan product is explained or delivered is much more significant than *what* the credit product is. *The essence of consumer finance marketing strategy is realizing that* how *a loan product is explained or delivered is much more significant than* what *the credit product is.* ■ Determination of consumer's needs requires greater attention. *Determining consumer's needs requires greater attention.* ■ Their subordinates are nonmanagement workers—the group on which management depends for the execution of their plans. *Their subordinates are nonmanagement workers—the group on which management depends for executing their plans.* ■ Another important analysis using internal customer data is the estimation of the revenue or profit impact of current strategies. *Another important analysis using internal customer data is estimating the revenue or profit impact of current strategies.* ■ Self-improvement and career planning both begin with an identification of your skills. *Self-improvement and career planning both begin with identifying your skills.* ■ It seems to me that our Legislature, which has an interest not only in the preservation of the health of its citizens but also in the prevention of illness, should discuss and develop legislation banning polystyrene for uses that are not essential. *It seems to me that our Legislature, which has an interest not only in preserving the health of its citizens but also in preventing illness, should discuss and develop legislation banning polystyrene for uses that are not essential.*

situated delete. Many of the hospital incinerators are situated in heavily populated areas. *Many of the hospital incinerators are in heavily populated areas.* ■ A smaller basin of about 500 meters is situated behind the main harbor and is the focus of future excavations. *A smaller basin of about 500 meters is behind the main harbor and is the focus of future excavations.*

(a; the) ... situation delete. The robber had no intention of turning it into a hostage situation. *The robber had no intention of taking hostages.* ■ Because of her pregnancy situation, I decided to leave the priesthood. *Because of her pregnancy, I decided to leave the priesthood.* ■ We are in a crisis situation. *We are in a crisis.* ■ This is the normal situation. *This is normal.* ■ It wasn't a love situation. *It wasn't love.* ■ Several factors came together during that decade to create a situation that changed the traditional distribution methods. *Several factors came together during that decade to change the traditional distribution methods.* ■ Situations that may trigger attacks of ulcerative colitis are rape, birth of a deformed child, an operation, moving, divorce, changing jobs, death of a significant other, and school exams. *Rape, birth of a deformed child, an operation, moving, divorce, changing jobs, death of a significant other, and school exams may trigger attacks of ulcerative colitis.* ■ If he doesn't do something, it could be an embarrassing situation for him. *If he doesn't do something, it could be embarrassing for him.*

skilled craftsman (craftswoman) *craftsman (craftswoman).* High wages ensure skilled craftsmen will work on public projects, saving money in the long run on repairing shoddy work. *High wages ensure craftsmen will work on public projects, saving money in the long run on repairing shoddy work.*

skirt around *skirt.*

slight trace *trace.*

(a; the) small (tiny) amount (degree; part; percentage; portion; proportion; quantity) (of) *a couple (of); a few (of); a handful (of); fewer than half (of); hardly any (of); (one) in (ten) (of); less than half (of); not many (of); (9) of (48) (of); one or two (two or three) (of); one-third (one-fifteenth) (of); ... percent (of); scarcely any (of).* Only a very small percentage of people, the innovators, are willing to try the product when it is first available. *Only a few people, the innovators, are willing to try the product when it is first available.* ■ Only a small percentage of the state's bridges will be repaired. *Only one-fourth of the state's bridges will be repaired.* ■ Of the estimated 10 percent of Americans who have a drinking problem at some time in their lives, only a tiny proportion receive treatment. *Of the estimated 10 percent of Americans who have a drinking problem at some time in their lives, only one in twenty receives treatment.*

(a; the) smaller (tinier) amount (degree; part; percentage; portion; proportion; quantity) (of) *less.* The net result is that under the new law, most people will pay a smaller part of their taxable income to the government—although more of their income may be taxable. *The net result is that under the new law, most people will pay less of their taxable income to the government—although more of their income may be taxable.* ■ Americans are spending a smaller percentage of their incomes on food than ever before. *Americans are spending less of their incomes on food than ever before.*

(a; the) smaller (tinier) number (of) *fewer.* One option calls for a smaller number of programs earmarked for "multiyear" funding, a method of saving money over the long haul by spending more money up front. *One option calls for fewer programs earmarked for "multiyear" funding, a method of saving money over the long haul by spending more money up front.* ■ The instructor would back off, slow down, and give students a chance to follow and absorb the development of a smaller number of scientific ideas. *The instructor would back off, slow down, and give students a chance to follow and absorb the development of fewer scientific ideas.*

(a; the) small (tiny) fraction (of) *a couple (of); a few (of); a handful (of); fewer than half (of); hardly any (of); (one) in (ten) (of); less than half (of); not many (of); (9) of (48) (of); one or two (two or three) (of); one-third (one-fifteenth) (of); ... percent (of); scarcely any (of).* His deputy sold only a small fraction of his stock, not one-third as reported. *His deputy sold only one-twelfth of his stock, not one-third as reported.* ■ Robots will replace only a tiny fraction of the estimated 131 million people in the U.S. labor force by 1997. *Robots will replace only 7 percent of the estimated 131 million people in the U.S. labor force by 1997.* ■ Nearly all Americans are aware of the crisis in the nation's savings and loan industry, but only a small fraction are withdrawing their money. *Nearly all Americans are aware of the crisis in the nation's savings and loan industry, but only a few are withdrawing their money.*

(a; the) small (tiny) minority (of) *a couple (of); a few (of); a handful (of); fewer than half (of); hardly any (of); (one) in (ten) (of); less than half (of); not many (of); (9) of (48) (of); one or two (two or three) (of); one-third (one-fifteenth) (of); ... percent (of); scarcely any (of).* His organization, which represents a small minority of farmers, also is concerned that licenses to use transgenic patents may be affordable only to large agribusiness and supermarket chain companies. *His organization, which represents a handful of farmers, also is concerned that* *licenses to use transgenic patents may be affordable only to large agribusiness and supermarket chain companies.* ▪ A small minority may be troubled or are troublemakers. *A few may be troubled or are troublemakers.*

(a; the) small (tiny) number (of) *a couple; a few; hardly any; not many; one or two (two or three); two; scarcely any.* Many observers believe that by the turn of the century only a small number of giant financial supermarkets will cover the range of financial services. *Many observers believe that by the turn of the century only eight giant financial supermarkets will cover the range of financial services.* ▪ Over the last year, only a small number of Arab leaders have been moderate in their views of Israel. *Over the last year, not many Arab leaders have been moderate in their views of Israel.* ▪ Most S&Ls operate only a small number of offices and thus compete in narrow geographic markets. *Most S&Ls operate only two or three offices and thus compete in narrow geographic markets.*

small (tiny) particle *particle.* With the high speeds and small spaces involved, even a small particle can cause the read/write head to crash. *With the high speeds and small spaces involved, even a particle can cause the read/write head to crash.*

small (tiny) peccadillo *peccadillo.*

small-size(d) *small.*

so as to *to.* Salespeople often make their estimates low so as to keep their sales quotas down and make them easier to attain. *Salespeople often make their estimates low to keep their sales quotas down and make them easier to attain.* ▪ The infectious code was written so as to exploit several bugs in two commonly used computer programs. *The infectious code was written to exploit several bugs in two commonly used computer programs.*

sociological *sociologic.*

so consequently *consequently; hence; so; then; therefore; thus.*

some but not all *a few; several; some.* Some studies, but not all, found cancerous tumors in rats and mice fed dye chemicals. *Some studies found cancerous tumors in rats and mice fed dye chemicals.*

some day (time) in the future *at length; eventually; in due time; in the end; in time; later; one day; over the months (years); over time; someday; sometime; ultimately; with time; yet.* If Greek is something that is resented by the American-born generations, the church will remain Greek Orthodox even though the language may be changed some day in the future. *If Greek is something that is resented by the American-born generations, the church will remain Greek Orthodox even though the language may be changed someday.* ▪ Some time in the future, the problems could precipitate a crisis—a run on the dollar, a decline in living standards—the price the United States must pay for its profligacy. *Eventually, the problems could precipitate a crisis—a run on the dollar, a decline in living standards—the price the United States must pay for its profligacy.*

somehow or other *in some way; somehow; someway(s).* Somehow or other, people get used to a system, even if it takes a little time. *Somehow, people get used to a system, even if it takes a little time.*

someplace (somewhere) else *elsewhere.* The meeting should run no more than two or three hours, provide obvious benefits for being there instead of somewhere else, and have built-in breaks at regular intervals. *The meeting should run no more than two or three hours, provide obvious benefits for being there instead of elsewhere, and have built-in breaks at regular intervals.*

something like *or so; some.* Pensions and Social Security may provide, on average, something like 60 percent of the household's prior working income. *Pensions and Social Security may provide, on average, some 60 percent of the household's prior working income.*

something (somewhat) of a *a; delete.* He takes superpower diplomacy seriously, which makes him something of an oddity in the Reagan Administration, and he derives satisfaction from its skillful practice. *He takes superpower diplomacy seriously, which makes him an oddity in the Reagan Administration, and he derives satisfaction from its skillful practice.* ■ He is somewhat of a skeptic. *He is skeptical.* ■ Yale University's School of Organization and Management has become something of an embarrassment to the university. *Yale University's School of Organization and Management has become an embarrassment to the university.*

somewhat *delete.* Following these steps can help make a difficult project somewhat more manageable. *Following these steps can help make a difficult project more manageable.* ■ The reference in the other direction may be somewhat less clear. *The reference in the other direction may be less clear.*

somewhere along the line (the way) *at some point; at some time.* Somewhere along the way, people got the idea that biotechnology is a magic solution to the food problem. *At some point, people got the idea that biotechnology is a magic solution to the food problem.* ■ Since becoming adults, it seems as if somewhere along the line we surrendered independence to predators. *Since becoming adults, it seems as if at some time we surrendered independence to predators.*

somewhere around (round) *or so; some.*

sooner or later *eventually; ultimately; yet.*

sort of *delete.* I'm sort of curious to find out what your thoughts are. *I'm curious to find out what your thoughts are.* ■ America has for 20 years now been seeing sort of a rise in the exploration of roots and examination of cultural traditions. *America has for 20 years now been seeing a rise in the exploration of roots and examination of cultural traditions.*

so therefore *hence; so; then; therefore; thus.*

space-consuming *big; bulky; huge; large; massive.* Second best are fire-resistant, locked files, which are expensive, heavy, and space consuming. *Second best are fire-resistant, locked files, which are expensive, heavy, and bulky.*

speaking to *about; as for; as to; for; in; of; on; over; to; toward; with.*

speciality *specialty.*

specifically prescribe *prescribe; specific.* Verbal and unsigned instructions should be handled in a specifically prescribed manner. *Verbal and unsigned instructions should be handled in a prescribed manner.*

springtime *spring.*

stall for time *stall.*

stand in (marked; sharp) contrast to *clash with; conflict with; contest; contradict; contrast with; differ from; disagree with; dispute; oppose.* That view stands in sharp contrast to those expressed by legislators and state business leaders. *That view sharply differs from those expressed by legislators and state business leaders.*

stand in need of *need; require.* The country stands in need of a strong gesture in support of both science and education. *The country needs a strong gesture in support of both science and education.*

stand in opposition to *conflict with; contest; disagree with; disapprove of; dispute; object to; oppose; protest; resist.*

stand in support of *back; endorse; favor; prefer; support.* With only 8 of the 1,176 voting delegates refusing to stand in support of the election, it appears Lee may have won the mandate he has been seeking. *With only 8 of the 1,176 voting delegates refusing to support the election, it appears Lee may have won the mandate he has been seeking.*

stand in the way of *block; frustrate; hinder; impede; interfere with; obstruct; prevent; thwart.* The public health threat posed by AIDS is so great that we must find ways to overcome social and cultural taboos that stand in the way of improved AIDS prevention. *The public health threat posed by AIDS is so great that we must find ways to overcome social and cultural taboos that thwart improved AIDS prevention.*

start off (out) *start.* Let me start out with you, Ginny. *Let me start with you, Ginny.* ■ It started out as a feud between my mother and wife. *It started as a feud between my mother and wife.*

(a; the) ... state of *delete.* There was a continuous state of turmoil. *There was continuous turmoil.* ■ All cultural dimensions of a society and individuals are in a constant state of flux. *All cultural dimensions of a society and individuals are in constant flux.*

stereotypical *stereotypic.* These theorists believe women have been taught and conditioned in stereotypical role behavior that predisposes them to the development of agoraphobia. *These theorists believe women have been taught and conditioned in stereotypic role behavior that predisposes them to the development of agoraphobia.*

stick-to-it-iveness *determination; perseverance; persistence; resolve; tenacity.* Loyalty, empathy, diligence, and stick-to-it-iveness are highly regarded, whether in a co-worker or a friend. *Loyalty, empathy, diligence, and resolve are highly regarded, whether in a co-worker or a friend.*

still and all *even so; still; yet.*

still continue (endure; last; persevere; persist; prevail; remain; survive) *continue (endure; last; persevere; persist; prevail; remain; survive); still.* The department has set up an internal review process to deal with some of these cases, but problems still persist. *The department has set up an internal review process to deal with some of these cases, but problems persist.* ■ The fact still remains that there is a serious question as to whether there was a valid agreement of option to lease the land. *The fact remains that there is a serious question as to whether there was a valid agreement of option to lease the land.* ■ Unfortunately, that attitude still prevails today. *Unfortunately, that attitude prevails today.* ■ And even after revamping their plans, many hotels still continue to restrict some awards. *And even after revamping their plans, many hotels still restrict some awards.*

still in existence *current; extant; surviving.*

stoical *stoic.*

straight horizontal (vertical) *horizontal (vertical).*

strange to relate (say) *oddly; strangely.* Strange to say, that interest does not seem to be more than a few hundred years old. *Strangely, that interest does not seem to be more than a few hundred years old.*

strangle to death *strangle.*

stressed out *stressed.*

strong point (suit) *forte.*

student body *students.* In the view of the student body, this policy came out of nowhere. *In the view of the students, this policy came out of nowhere.*

study up *study.*

subject area (field; matter) *area; field; subject; theme; topic.* Each new title is arranged by subject area. *Each new title is arranged by subject.* ■ The subject matter is complex and beyond the intended scope of this course. *The topic is complex and beyond the intended scope of this course.* ■ Each Abstract Newsletter cites current materials in the subject area covered by the newsletter. *Each Abstract Newsletter cites current materials in the area covered by the newsletter.* ■ Patents are filed in the Search Room of the PTO by classes and subclasses according to subject matter. *Patents are filed in the Search Room of the PTO by classes and subclasses according to subject.*

subject of conversation (discussion) *subject; theme; topic.* The extraordinary appeal became the main subject of discussion at the summit meeting. *The extraordinary appeal became the main topic at the summit meeting.*

subsequently *after; afterward; later; since (then); then.* Subsequently, I heard a loud screech of brakes. *Afterward, I heard a loud screech of brakes.* ■ We subsequently changed our strategy for the plan you mentioned and ended up with impressive results. *We then changed our strategy for the plan you mentioned and ended up with impressive results.* ■ He resigned his positions in 1963 and was subsequently jailed. *He resigned his positions in 1963 and was later jailed.*

subsequent to (that; this) *after; afterward; later; since (then); then.* Subsequent to that, I had surgery to remove half of my stomach. *Afterward, I had surgery to remove half of my stomach.* ■ The suit stems from Lotus' public announcement last year that Release 3 would ship in the second quarter of 1988, and subsequent to missing the delivery date, that the product would ship no later than December 31, 1988. *The suit stems from Lotus' public announcement last year that Release 3 would ship in the second quarter of 1988, and after missing the delivery date, that the product would ship no later than December 31, 1988.*

subsequent to the time (of; that; when) *after; following.* The stock can be transferred any time subsequent to the time that a person actually receives it. *The stock can be transferred any time after a person actually receives it.*

substantiality *substance.* Jackson has exhibited a remarkable degree of substantiality and common sense. *Jackson has exhibited a remarkable degree of substance and common sense.*

substantiate *back up; confirm; prove; support; verify.* Recent studies clearly substantiate the health and economic advantage of car safety seat belts. *Recent studies clearly confirm the health and economic advantage of car safety seat belts.*

substantive *ample; big; grand; great; heavy; huge; immense; large; many; most; much; vast.* The recent improvement in the economic well-being of most nations occurred without substantive change in the physical bulk or weight of gross national product. *The recent improvement in the economic well-being of most nations occurred without much change in the physical bulk or weight of gross national product.*

succumb to injuries *die.*

such as *like.* Posttraumatic stress disorder is less severe after a natural disaster such as an earthquake or a flood. *Posttraumatic stress disorder is less severe after a natural disaster like an earthquake or a flood.* ■ I have a lot of admiration for actors such as them. *I have a lot of admiration for actors like them.*

such as ... and others (and so forth; and so on; and such; and the like; et al.; etc.) *and others (and so forth; and so on; and such; and the like; et al.; etc.); such as.* You can explore the results of various approaches such as gross margin, markup over cost, and others. *You can explore the results of various approaches such as gross margin and markup over cost.* ■ The MLI commands perform such standard file-handling chores as opening, reading, writing, closing, and so forth. *The MLI commands perform such standard file-handling chores as opening, reading, writing, and closing.* ■ Grass-roots budgeting asks each manager to project his or her unit's need for funds in specific categories—such as wages, salaries, supplies, etc. *Grass-roots budgeting asks each manager to project his or her unit's need for funds in specific categories—wages, salaries, supplies, etc.* ■ One seemingly good argument for a network—several users need to share costly peripherals such as laser printers, plotters, scanning devices, and the like—probably isn't a good argument because of the many codes and protocols with which different software communicate to the same devices. *One seemingly good argument for a network—several users need to share costly peripherals such as laser printers, plotters, and scanning devices—probably isn't a good argument because of the many codes and protocols with which different software communicate to the same devices.*

such as ... for example (for instance) *as; for example (for instance); like; such as.* One of the book's main themes is the "fact" that women were responsible for all the important contributions to the advancement of civilization (such as the development of agriculture, for instance), often despite the arrogance and stupidity of men. *One of the book's main themes is the "fact" that women were responsible for all the important contributions to the advancement of civilization (such as the development of agriculture), often despite the arrogance and stupidity of men.*

such as (your)self *like (you).* It's very rare that we have an opportunity to talk to someone such as yourself. *It's very rare that we have an opportunity to talk to someone like you.*

such is the case *so it is.* Such was the case when Congress sought to save us from a few financial institutions who were unfairly delaying credit for consumer check deposits. *So it was when Congress sought to save us from a few financial institutions who were unfairly delaying credit for consumer check deposits.*

suddenly and without warning *suddenly; without warning.* Survivors said the pier in Butterworth, 180 miles northwest of Kuala Lumpur, collapsed suddenly and without warning yesterday. *Survivors said the pier in Butterworth, 180 miles northwest of Kuala Lumpur, collapsed suddenly yesterday.*

sufficient (sufficiently) *due (duly); enough.* Bright ideas alone are not sufficient. *Bright ideas alone are not enough.* ■ Since responsibility is assigned not to individuals but to the group, members may not devote sufficient time and effort to the task. *Since responsibility is assigned not to individuals but to the group, members may not devote due time and effort to the task.* ■ A proposed design must be sufficiently strong to support the maximum design load that can be anticipated. *A proposed design must be strong enough to support the maximum design load that can be anticipated.* ■ Significant escalations in mortality rates are easily achievable by sufficiently motivated individuals. *Significant escalations in mortality rates are easily achievable by duly motivated individuals.*

(a; the) sufficient amount (of) *due; enough.* Western support of my rule had always been tempered by a need to exercise a sufficient amount of control. *Western support of my rule had always been tempered by a need to exercise due control.* ■ It's time we include a sufficient amount of money in the state budget for snow removal. *It's time we include enough money in the state budget for snow removal.*

sufficient (sufficiently) enough *duly; enough.* All companies involved in foreign marketing must distribute their products in markets that differ sufficiently enough from one another to warrant the development of individualized distribution systems and strategies. *All companies involved in foreign marketing must distribute their products in markets that differ enough from one another to warrant the development of individualized distribution systems and strategies.*

(a; the) sufficient number (of) *enough; five (ninety).* The proposed changes to the Marine Mammal Protection Act would not provide for a sufficient number of federal observers to ride on tuna boats and monitor fishing techniques. *The proposed changes to the Marine Mammal Protection Act would not provide for fifty federal observers to ride on tuna boats and monitor fishing techniques.* ■ If it gains the sufficient number of signatures to qualify, we'll have to watch it even more carefully. *If it gains enough signatures to qualify, we'll have to watch it even more carefully.*

sum (summary) and substance *center; core; crux; essence; gist; heart; pith; substance; sum; summary.* He asked, in summary and substance, whether GAF wanted to have Union Carbide close at a specific price for several days in a row. *He asked, in essence, whether GAF wanted to have Union Carbide close at a specific price for several days in a row.*

summation *sum; total.* The summation of these products is 4320.154. *The sum of these products is 4320.154.* ■ The magnitude of the resultant of the loads is the summation of the vertical downward forces, or the distance from A to D. *The magnitude of the resultant of the loads is the sum of the vertical downward forces, or the distance from A to D.*

summertime *summer.* Even in summertime, snow sometimes occurs high up in rain clouds, and the flakes can terminate the arc of a rainbow. *Even in summer, snow sometimes occurs high up in rain clouds, and the flakes can terminate the arc of a rainbow.*

summing up *in brief; in fine; in short; in sum.* Summing up, I feel strongly that my criteria capture the characteristics of firms that are likely to be successful in the Information Age, i.e., firms that impatiently look for ways to give information users the best that science and technology make possible. *In sum, I feel strongly that my criteria capture the characteristics of firms that are likely to be successful in the Information Age, i.e., firms that impatiently look for ways to give information users the best that science and technology make possible.*

sum total *sum; total.* Women have always commanded over half the sum total of human intelligence and creativity. *Women have always commanded over half the total of human intelligence and creativity.*

sum up *add; sum; total.*

superimpose one ... on top of (over) another (the other) *superimpose.* Overlays allow you to superimpose one data range on top of another. *Overlays allow you to superimpose data ranges.*

surrounded on all sides *surrounded.*

swallow down *swallow.*

switch over *switch.* School systems in Maryland and California tried to switch over after the 1975 legislation and had trouble when students did not receive enough reinforcement outside their classrooms to get acclimated to metric. *School systems in Maryland and California tried to switch after the 1975 legislation and had trouble when students did not receive enough reinforcement outside their classrooms to get acclimated to metric.*

symbolical *symbolic.*

symmetrical *symmetric.*

symptomatize *symptomize.*

systematical *systematic.*

T

tailor-made *custom; tailored.* The event seemed tailor-made to give the vice president the upper hand. *The event seemed tailored to give the vice president the upper hand.* ▪ A growing parade of "new" genetically engineered animals is likely to move from the laboratory to the barnyard in the next decade or so, dramatically altering U.S. farming and bringing tailor-made food products to the table. *A growing parade of "new" genetically engineered animals is likely to move from the laboratory to the barnyard in the next decade or so, dramatically altering U.S. farming and bringing custom food products to the table.*

take account for (of) *allow for; consider; provide for; reckon with; regard; weigh.* But HMO officials say that current reimbursements fail to take account for medical inflation. *But HMO officials say that current reimbursements fail to allow for medical inflation.*

take action (to) *act;* delete. Directors need to be well informed to feel comfortable when taking an action on behalf of the bank. *Directors need to be well informed to feel comfortable when acting on behalf of the bank.* ▪ He said Nicaragua would take action to defend the rights of ambassadors. *He said Nicaragua would defend the rights of ambassadors.* ▪ If we are to save the right whales, we will have to take action. *If we are to save the right whales, we will have to act.* ▪ The Legislature must take action to stop the insurance companies from reaching into our pockets every time they perceive the loss of a dime. *The Legislature must act to stop the insurance companies from reaching into our pockets every time they perceive the loss of a dime.*

take ... action (on; to) *act -(al)ly;* delete. The operator has to determine the cause of the deviation and then take corrective action. *The operator has to determine the cause of the deviation and then correct it.* ▪ In caring relationships, nurses are motivated to take appropriate actions on behalf of clients. *In caring relationships, nurses are motivated to act appropriately on behalf of clients.* ▪ He issued a statement calling on the NRC to take immediate action to correct deficiencies identified in the report. *He issued a statement calling on the NRC to act immediately to correct deficiencies identified in the report.*

take advantage of *abuse; cheat; deceive; exploit; ill-treat; mistreat; misuse; use; victimize; wrong.* He took advantage of her good nature. *He exploited her good nature.* ▪ What was important was that the minority shareholders collectively should not be taken advantage of. *What was important was that the minority shareholders collectively should not be mistreated.*

take advantage of *benefit from; gain; profit by; reap.* Already frustrated over low pay, long hours and limited responsibilities, most work for "pools" to take advantage of flexible hours and to augment their salaries. *Already frustrated over low pay, long hours and limited responsibilities, most work for "pools" to benefit from flexible hours and to augment their salaries.* ■ There are several easy ways to take advantage of Fidelity's expertise in retirement planning. *There are several easy ways to profit by Fidelity's expertise in retirement planning.*

take aim *aim.*

take a ... look (at) *consider; look; regard; view.* We need to examine each, but let's first take a brief look at the foundations of management theory. *We need to examine each, but let's first briefly look at the foundations of management theory.* ■ Let's take a look at the individual who has never really done any conscious planning and at age 55 realizes that it's now or never. *Let's consider the individual who has never really done any conscious planning and at age 55 realizes that it's now or never.*

take a measure of *approximate; estimate.* The balance sheet yields financial data that can be used in various ratio calculations to take a measure of the company's financial health. *The balance sheet yields financial data that can be used in various ratio calculations to estimate the company's financial health.*

take a stand against (in opposition to) *contest; contradict; contrast with; differ from; disagree with; dispute; oppose; resist.*

take a stand for (in favor of; in support of) *back; endorse; favor; prefer; support.* I commend the *Globe* on taking a stand in support of the state's longstanding compassionate treatment of immigrants. *I commend the* Globe *on endorsing the state's longstanding compassionate treatment of immigrants.*

take a (the) ... view (of) *consider; look; regard; view.* Financial institutions can no longer take a passive view of product development. *Financial institutions can no longer regard product development passively.* ■ Our conclusion is that the overwhelming majority of our middle managers take a favorable view of the major restructuring we went through earlier this year. *Our conclusion is that the overwhelming majority of our middle managers view favorably the major restructuring we went through earlier this year.*

take delivery on *receive.*

take enjoyment in *admire; delight in; enjoy; rejoice in; relish; savor.*

take exception to *challenge; complain about; criticize; demur; differ in; disagree with; dispute; find fault with; object to; oppose; protest; question; resent.* I take exception to the statement: "Angiography is not only expensive but also painful and risky." *I disagree with the statement: "Angiography is not only expensive but also painful and risky."* ■ We take exception to the comment that Oki cut prices and stole market share. *We dispute the comment that Oki cut prices and stole market share.* ■ I take very strong exception to that characterization. *I strongly object to that characterization.* ■ Representatives of Guilford and the United Transportation Union took exception to FRA's charges regarding a safety compromise. *Representatives of Guilford and the United Transportation Union protested FRA's charges regarding a safety compromise.*

take (a) hold of *grasp; seize; take.*

take into account *allow for; consider; provide for; reckon with; regard; weigh.* The problem is that this standard profitability equation does not apply well to most home banking projects because it fails to take into account the numerous tactical and strategic benefits involved. *The problem is that this standard profitability equation does not apply well to most home banking projects because it fails to consider the· numerous tactical and strategic benefits involved.* ■ We felt sexuality education programs failed to take into account these gender differences. *We felt sexuality education programs failed to weigh these gender differences.* ■ But taking into account the timing differences in repricing, standard prepayment expectations, and spread relationships, the risk exposure is only 10 percent. *But allowing for the timing differences in repricing, standard prepayment expectations, and spread relationships, the risk exposure is only 10 percent.* ■ It fails to take into account the impact of the U.S. federal budget deficit on U.S. competitiveness. *It fails to regard the impact of the U.S. federal budget deficit on U.S. competitiveness.*

take into (under) consideration *allow for; consider; provide for; reckon with; regard; weigh.* His prior offenses, even though they were in a different state, can be taken into consideration by the court. *His prior offenses, even though they were in a different state, can be weighed by the court.* ■ Another model that takes into consideration the possibility of a trend might be more appropriate. *Another model that allows for the possibility of a trend might be more appropriate.* ■ This is particularly incredible when you take into consideration that she is only 18 years old. *This is particularly incredible when you consider that she is only 18 years old.*

take into custody *arrest; capture; catch; seize.*

take issue (with) *attack; challenge; contradict; demur; differ (with); disagree (with); dispute; object (to); oppose; question.* He also takes issue with the state plan to pay. *He also opposes the state plan to pay.* ■ I take issue with the article's rather cavalier dismissal of American efforts in Japan as paltry and disorganized. *I object to the article's rather cavalier dismissal of American efforts in Japan as paltry and disorganized.* ■ While all biologists affirm that some animal social behaviors are genetically programmed, many take issue with the sociobiology doctrine as applied to humans. *While all biologists affirm that some animal social* *behaviors are genetically programmed, many dispute the sociobiology doctrine as applied to humans.* ■ The activists took issue with the Army for using posters calling on residents in the war-games area to call if they spotted designated enemy troops. *The activists attacked the Army for using posters calling on residents in the war-games area to call if they spotted designated enemy troops.* ■ Although they support many parts of the academy report, members take issue with several important elements. *Although they support many parts of the academy report, members question several important elements.*

take measures (to) *act (to);* delete.

taken by surprise *startled; surprised.* Everyone I talked to today was taken by surprise by his announcement. *Everyone I talked to today was surprised by his announcement.*

take note of *attend to; consider; hearken to; heed; listen to; mind; note; notice; observe; regard; see; tend to; watch; witness.* The United States should take note of the percentage of technical graduates and lawyers in Japan's population. *The United States should note the percentage of technical graduates and lawyers in Japan's population.* ■ It's ludicrous to stick one's head in the sand and say the island isn't as nice as it was in 1940 and not take note of the fact that the island is growing and changing. *It's ludicrous to stick one's head in the sand and say the island isn't as nice as it was in 1940 and not notice the fact that the island is growing and changing.*

take notice of *attend to; consider; hearken; heed; listen to; mind; note; notice; observe; regard; see; tend to; watch; witness.* Clouds in the dry stratosphere were rarely sighted—mostly because they form near the poles only during winter and early spring, when darkness eclipses the sky and few spectators are around to take notice. *Clouds in the dry stratosphere were rarely sighted—mostly because they form near the poles only during winter and early spring, when darkness eclipses the sky and few spectators are around to watch.*

take offense at *disagree with; dislike; object to; resent.* I take offense at the *Globe*'s editorial ("Scorsese and the stone-casters") and will no longer sit by and watch the Christian-bashing continue. *I resent the Globe's editorial ("Scorsese and the stone-casters") and will no longer sit by and watch the Christian-bashing continue.*

take pity on (upon) *pity; sympathize (with).*

take place *happen; occur.*

take pleasure in *admire; delight in; enjoy; rejoice in; relish (in); savor.*

take precedence over *antecede; come before; forego; go before; precede.* Criminals' rights take precedence over the victims'. *Criminals' rights come before the* *victims'.* ■ Because multinationals purchase a host of products and services in different locations, providing services to these customers must take precedence over the needs of the small profit center from the parent bank's point of view. *Because multinationals purchase a host of products and services in different locations, providing services to these customers must precede the needs of the small profit center from the parent bank's point of view.*

take priority over *antecede; come before; forego; go before; precede.* The widow's allowance takes priority over all other debts of your husband's estate, as well as any provisions of his will. *The widow's allowance comes before all other debts of your husband's estate, as well as any provisions of his will.* ■ He says that in women's shoes, fashion always takes priority over comfort. *He says that in women's shoes, fashion always precedes comfort.*

take satisfaction in *admire; delight in; enjoy; rejoice in; relish (in); savor.*

take the position (that) *assert; believe; claim; consider; contend; feel; hold; judge; maintain; regard; say; think; to; view.* He takes the position that, as a meeting leader, you will be more effective if you view yourself "as the servant of the group rather than as its master." *He maintains that, as a meeting leader, you will be more effective if you view yourself "as the servant of the group rather than as its master."*

take the view (that) *assert; believe; claim; consider; contend; feel; hold; judge; maintain; regard; say; think; to; view.*

take the wrong way *misinterpret; misunderstand.*

take to task *admonish; chide; criticize; rebuke; reprimand; reproach; reprove; scold.* He took the project's tenant leaders to task for their selection of an architectural consultant for the remodeling job. *He admonished the project's tenant leaders for their selection of an architectural consultant for the remodeling job.*

take umbrage at (with) *disagree with; dislike; object to; resent.* Some people, such as the NRA, took umbrage with the message of the show. *Some people, such as the NRA, disliked the message of the show.* ■ I took umbrage at that statement, especially since I could name several women within our organization. *I resented that statement, especially since I could name several women within our organization.*

take under advisement *consider; contemplate; reflect on; review; think about; weigh.* Pillsbury's board is taking the franchisee group's protest under advisement. *Pillsbury's board is reviewing the franchisee group's protest.* ■ I'll take the matter under advisement and give you my ruling tomorrow. *I'll consider the matter and give you my ruling tomorrow.*

take under consideration *consider; contemplate; reflect on; review; think about; weigh.* About 1 in 50 products is taken under consideration. *About 1 in 50 products is considered.*

tell the difference *discriminate; distinguish; tell apart.* The reality is that science and technology have made it almost impossible to tell the difference between telecommunications and computers. *The reality is that science and technology have made it almost impossible to distinguish between telecommunications and computers.*

temperature *fever.*

temporary reprieve *reprieve.*

temporary stopgap *stopgap.*

(my) tendency is to *(I) tend to.* Our tendency is to get up a little later each morning and go to sleep a little later each night. *We tend to get up a little later each morning and go to sleep a little later each night.*

tense up *tense.*

term as *term.*

terminate *cancel; cease; conclude; end; finish; halt; stop.* Over a year ago, NERAC terminated its relationship with the University of Connecticut. *Over a year ago, NERAC ended its relationship with the University of Connecticut.* ■ If any primary or contingent Beneficiary shall predecease me, his or her interest and the interest of any of his or her heirs shall then terminate. *If any primary or contingent Beneficiary shall predecease me, his or her interest and the interest of any of his or her heirs shall then stop.* ■ Having no plan at all would be better than terminating one. *Having no plan at all would be better than canceling one.*

test out *test.*

that (this) being the case *consequently; hence; so; then; therefore; thus.* That being the case, the only apparent remedy is for owners of family firms to begin early in earmarking shares of the business for their children. *The only apparent remedy, then, is for owners of family firms to begin early in earmarking shares of the business for their children.*

that (the; this) business of *that (this); delete.* We've got to get over this business of seeing everything in cartoon terms. *We've got to get over seeing everything in cartoon terms.* ■ The Glass-Steagall Act prohibits banks from engaging in the business of underwriting, selling, or distributing securities such as shares of a mutual fund. *The Glass-Steagall Act prohibits banks from engaging in underwriting, selling, or distributing securities such as shares of a mutual fund.*

that (this) fact *that (this).* The world beyond visual range is a haze of anxiety, and the most sophisticated radar sets in the world do not change that fact. *The world beyond visual range is a haze of anxiety, and the most sophisticated radar sets in the world do not change that.*

that (which) happens (occurs; takes place) when *when.* What about the inevitable disappointment that happens when a child doesn't win a trophy? *What about the inevitable disappointment when a child doesn't win a trophy?*

that is delete. This relates to the cost that is incurred by start-up firms. *This relates to the cost incurred by start-up firms.* ■ They chose hardware that was available and reliable. *They chose available, reliable hardware.* ■ The manager must set a level of performance that is attainable. *The manager must set an attainable level of performance.* ■ Data modification can produce results that are not valid. *Data modification can produce invalid results.*

that is (this is; which is) as much as to say *namely; that is; to wit.*

that is (which is) to say (that) *namely; that is; to wit;* delete. That is to say, the person named by the testator in his will will normally be appointed by the court, despite lack of great intelligence or experience. *That is, the person named by the testator in his will will normally be appointed by the court, despite lack of great intelligence or experience.* ■ These suits spring from the same concern that drives the antiabortion position—that is to say, assigning a more elevated moral and legal status to the fetus, granting it personhood separate from the woman carrying it. *These suits spring from the same concern that drives the antiabortion position—namely, assigning a more elevated moral and legal status to the fetus, granting it personhood separate from the woman carrying it.*

that (this) kind (sort; type) of stuff (thing) *it; that (this);* delete. If there's a lot of that kind of thing, I will try to figure out whether things will stay depressed forever. *If there's a lot of that, I will try to figure out whether things will stay depressed forever.* ■ We could take an approach that would take us back to feudal times where you're born into your occupation and that type of thing. *We could take an approach that would take us back to feudal times where you're born into your occupation.*

that (this) juncture (moment; period; point; stage) in time *(just; right) now; that (this) time; then.* Not until that moment in time did I understand what being homeless meant. *Not until then did I understand what being homeless meant.*

that (those) of *-'s.* Toronto's population is close to 3 million, which is slightly larger than that of Boston. *Toronto's population is close to 3 million, which is slightly larger than Boston's.* ■ Thrift A's exposure to rising rates is considerably higher than that of Thrift B. *Thrift A's exposure to rising rates is considerably higher than Thrift B's.* ■ Learn from your own experiences and from those of others. *Learn from your own experiences and from others'.* ■ This is not a viable solution because the medic's role cannot be compared to, or interchanged with, that of the professional nurse. *This is not a viable solution because the medic's role cannot be compared to, or interchanged with, the professional nurse's.* ■ As the more aggrieved party, the victim's rights must take precedence over those of the perpetrator. *As the more aggrieved party, the victim's rights must take precedence over the perpetrator's.*

that (these; this; those) of delete. Another exercise is that of completing the views when some or all of them have missing lines. *Another exercise is completing the views when some or all of them have missing lines.* ■ There are two basic philosophies of stock investment: that of growth and that of investment yield. *There are two basic philosophies of stock investment: growth and investment yield.*

(of) that (these; this; those) delete. For those calculators that do not have a 10x key, the antilogarithm can be found by using the INV or 2nd key. *For calculators that do not have a 10x key, the antilogarithm can be found by using the INV or 2nd key.* ■ Those options with the word *patch* in their titles are especially complicated. *Options with the word* patch *in their titles are especially complicated.*

that (this) time around (round) *that (this) time; then (now).* Such an outcome has a far higher probability this time around. *Such an outcome has a far higher probability now.*

the above *that; this;* delete. Please call me if you have any questions concerning the above. *Please call me if you have any questions concerning this.*

the above-mentioned *that; the above; this;* delete.

the act of delete. The act of making sketches and writing statements about the problem helps to get the designer off dead center. *Making sketches and writing statements about the problem helps to get the designer off dead center.* ■ In the act of listening, the differential between thinking and speaking rates means that our brain works with hundreds of words in addition to those that we hear, assembling thoughts other than those spoken to us. *In listening, the differential between thinking and speaking rates means that our brain works with hundreds of words in addition to those that we hear, assembling thoughts other than those spoken to us.*

the aforementioned *that; the above; this;* delete. The aforementioned argument is without merit, as it fails to consider the important differences which can be found to exist in skills and productivity found in the construction industry. *This argument is without merit, as it fails to consider the important differences which can be found to exist in skills and productivity found in the construction industry.* ■ Each of the aforementioned techniques can be used to solve a specific employee problem in the workplace. *Each of the above techniques can be used to solve a specific employee problem in the workplace.*

the aforesaid *that; the above; this;* delete.

the age of delete. He acknowledged that the Soviet Union has 46,000 registered drug addicts (only a minority of the entire drug-dependent population), most of them under the age of 30. *He acknowledged that the Soviet Union has 46,000 registered drug addicts (only a minority of the entire drug-dependent population), most of them under 30.* ■ It predicts a tightening labor market will force the hiring of more people between the ages of 35 and 45. *It predicts a tightening labor market will force the hiring of more people between 35 and 45.*

the area of (the ... area) delete. The main interest for me is the history area. *The main interest for me is history.* ■ These teams should be granted broad functions, with key roles being played by representatives from the engineering, manufacturing, marketing, and finance areas. *These teams should be granted broad functions, with key roles being played by representatives from engineering, manufacturing, marketing, and finance.* ■ The area of international business is concerned with transactions which involve the transfer of goods, services, and factor inputs across national boundaries. *International business is concerned with transactions which involve the transfer of goods, services, and factor inputs across national boundaries.*

the (this) author (writer) *I; me; my; our; us; we.* Every word processing manual the authors have seen assumes you know what a hanging indent, widow, and running header are. *Every word processing manual we have seen assumes you know what a hanging indent, widow, and running header are.* ■ A practical approach to setting international objectives will, in this writer's view, concentrate first on protecting an existing profit base. *A practical approach to setting international objectives will, in my view, concentrate first on protecting an existing profit base.* ■ He explained to this writer how a London-based Scot beat Morgan Stanley and Goldman Sachs to the punch in their own backyard. *He explained to me how a London-based Scot beat Morgan Stanley and Goldman Sachs to the punch in their own backyard.*

the better part (of) *almost all; most; nearly all.* Manufacturers Hanover Corp. spent the better part of 175 years reaching the top of American banking alongside the Citicorps and Chase Manhattans. *Manufacturers Hanover Corp. spent most of 175 years reaching the top of American banking alongside the Citicorps and Chase Manhattans.*

the biggest (greatest; highest; largest) amount (degree; extent; number; part; percentage; portion; proportion; quantity) of *most.* That's why many analysts argue that boosting energy efficiency and adopting fossil-fuel alternatives will buy the greatest degree of climate insurance for the dollar. *That's why many analysts argue that boosting energy efficiency and adopting fossil-fuel alternatives will buy the most climate insurance for the dollar.* ■ The greatest number of pneumonia deaths occur among people 65 and older—more than 20 times the rate in the 45-to-64 age group. *Most pneumonia deaths occur among people*

65 and older—more than 20 times the rate in the 45-to-64 age group. ■ The concept of calories has been well embedded in the minds of people throughout the largest portion of the twentieth century. *The concept of calories has been well embedded in the minds of people throughout most of the twentieth century.*

the both (of) *both.* I saw the both of them on a talk show today. *I saw both of them on a talk show today.*

the (great) bulk (of) *almost all; most; nearly all.* JETRO has for about a decade been devoting the great bulk of its efforts in the United States to promoting American exports to Japan. *JETRO has for about a decade been devoting most of its efforts in the United States to promoting American exports to Japan.* ■ Unfortunately for the startups, though, a few major players have secured the bulk of the orders. *Unfortunately for the startups, though, a few major players have secured most of the orders.*

the case *right; so; true;* delete. I think that's probably the case. *I think that's probably true.* ■ That's just not the case. *That's just not so.* ■ Consumers have more diversified opportunities for placement of discretionary funds than has been the case in the past. *Consumers have more diversified opportunities for placement of discretionary funds than in the past.* ■ Analysis of the internal data verified that this was the case. *Analysis of the internal data verified that this was right.* ■ Such companies are often durable goods manufacturers, but this is not always the case. *Such companies are often durable goods manufacturers, but not always.*

the character of delete. He played the character of a picaro in the film. *He played a picaro in the film.*

the city (town) of delete. In the city of Chicago, there are a lot of counseling centers. *In Chicago, there are a lot of counseling centers.* ■ A chicken-processing plant closed today in the town of Belfast, Maine. *A chicken-processing plant closed today in Belfast, Maine.*

the color delete. I noticed the predominance of the color green in their costumes. *I noticed the predominance of green in their costumes.*

the ... company delete. In 1986, the Hitachi company displaced General Electric as the firm receiving the most U.S. patents. *In 1986, Hitachi displaced General Electric as the firm receiving the most U.S. patents.*

the concept of delete. The following example illustrates the concept of correlation. *The following example illustrates correlation.* ■ Thatcher added that the concept of a United States of Europe will not happen in her lifetime, or hopefully, ever. *Thatcher added that a United States of Europe will not happen in her lifetime, or hopefully, ever.* ■ When we visited them in Mexico last year, Corona

Beer was interested in the concept of expanding their distribution. *When we visited them in Mexico last year, Corona Beer was interested in expanding their distribution.*

the condition of delete. British companies do not hesitate to go to the market with a share issue when the condition of the balance sheet warrants it. *British companies do not hesitate to go to the market with a share issue when the balance sheet warrants it.* ■ The condition of his health has deteriorated. *His health has deteriorated.*

the continent of (the ... continent) delete. Despite droughts, floods, wars, and low oil and commodity prices, the African continent as a whole is better off now than a year ago. *Despite droughts, floods, wars, and low oil and commodity prices, Africa as a whole is better off now than a year ago.*

the country of delete.

the decade (period; period of time; span of time; time; years) between ... and *between ... and; from ... through (to); to.*

the decade (period; period of time; span of time; time; years) (from) ... through (till; to; until) *between ... and; from ... through (to); to.* But he notes that if you don't count the period from 1929 through 1936, the Republicans emerge with only a very slight edge in annual return. *But he notes that if you don't count from 1929 through 1936, the Republicans emerge with only a very slight edge in annual return.* ■ Her chapters covering the decade from 1923 until 1932, especially, are melanges of miscellaneous topics that remain ill-connected by strained generalizations. *Her chapters covering from 1923 to 1932, especially, are melanges of miscellaneous topics that remain ill-connected by strained generalizations.* ■ The United Nations General Assembly recently declared the decade from 1990 to 2000 to be the International Decade of Natural Disaster Reduction. *The United Nations General Assembly recently declared 1990 to 2000 to be the International Decade of Natural Disaster Reduction.*

the degree of *how much; the;* delete. The closer the value of r to either extreme, the greater the degree of association. *The closer the value of* r *to either extreme, the greater the association.* ■ Business owners and managers must have a way to measure the degree of success or failure of their business or department. *Business owners and managers must have a way to measure the success or failure of their business or department.* ■ I am concerned with the degree of difficulty they're having getting the product out. *I am concerned with how much difficulty they're having getting the product out.*

the degree to which *how; how far; how much.* The degree to which exporters seek to manage and control the marketing and distribution of their products to and in foreign markets varies greatly. *How much exporters seek to manage and control the marketing and distribution of their products to and in foreign markets* *varies greatly.* ■ The GOP's principal concern is the degree to which the law would regulate child-care facilities nationwide. *The GOP's principal concern is how much the law would regulate child-care facilities nationwide.* ■ The degree to which her agency will regulate the new TCB network and its rates has yet to be determined. *How her agency will regulate the new TCB network and its rates has yet to be determined.*

the ... dollar mark *(a) ... dollars.* First-level managers now often find themselves in charge of budgets with assets approaching or surpassing the half million dollar mark. *First-level managers now often find themselves in charge of budgets with assets approaching or surpassing a half million dollars.*

the equal (equivalent) of *equal (equivalent) to; like.* The loss of 1 high-value customer was the equivalent of losing the business of 36 small-value customers. *The loss of 1 high-value customer was equivalent to losing the business of 36 small-value customers.*

the existence of *delete.* The existence of even one extra, undocumented Write statement in a module may change what appears on a user's terminal. *Even one extra, undocumented Write statement in a module may change what appears on a user's terminal.* ■ As the participants learn to accept and deal with their own assumptions and attitudes, and to be more tolerant of the existence of viewpoints different from their own, the case discussions become more succinct and relevant. *As the participants learn to accept and deal with their own assumptions and attitudes, and to be more tolerant of viewpoints different from their own, the case discussions become more succinct and relevant.*

the extent of *how much; delete.* Most people know something about Social Security, but few know the extent of the monthly benefits they will eventually receive when they retire. *Most people know something about Social Security, but few know the monthly benefits they will eventually receive when they retire.* ■ I would fantasize about graduating, or joining the cheerleading team, but that would be the extent of it. *I would fantasize about graduating, or joining the cheerleading team, but that would be it.* ■ The extent of our success can be measured not only by our balance sheet, but by the growing list of customers that rely on the NYNEX family of companies. *Our success can be measured not only by our balance sheet, but by the growing list of customers that rely on the NYNEX family of companies.* ■ Despite early campaign rhetoric, the extent of actual change a new treasurer would attempt is of course unknown. *Despite early campaign rhetoric, how much actual change a new treasurer would attempt is of course unknown.*

the extent to which *how; how far; how much.* The extent to which these facilitating and reconciling capabilities are needed, and how they are developed and structured, depends on the company's involvement in exporting or foreign marketing. *How much these facilitating and reconciling capabilities are needed, and how they are developed and structured, depends on the company's involvement* *in exporting or foreign marketing.* ■ This is especially surprising in view of the extent to which child-care issues have moved close to center stage in American politics. *This is especially surprising in view of how child-care issues have moved close to center stage in American politics.* ■ Eastern cannot predict the extent to which its operations and financial results will continue to be affected by the negative public perception generated by the investigations. *Eastern cannot predict how its operations and financial results will continue to be affected by the negative public perception generated by the investigations.*

the fact that *that.* The fact that she was institutionalized doesn't mean she should have been. *That she was institutionalized doesn't mean she should have been.* ■ This ignores the fact that increased use of kilowatts has significantly decreased our use of oil. *This ignores that increased use of kilowatts has significantly decreased our use of oil.* ■ Possibly the biggest attraction of a Category III product is the fact that it aims for a sizable market that others consider important. *Possibly the biggest attraction of a Category III product is that it aims for a sizable market that others consider important.*

the fact is (that) *actually; indeed; in fact; in faith; in truth; really; truly;* delete. The fact is we have to deal with the public every day. *We have to deal with the public every day.* ■ Computers are an integral part of AT&T's data-networking strategy, and the fact is that the financial results for the first half of this year in our data systems division are on target. *Computers are an integral part of AT&T's data-networking strategy, and in fact, the financial results for the first half of this year in our data systems division are on target.* ■ The fact is that most people confuse a dull presentation with dull ideas. *Actually, most people confuse a dull presentation with dull ideas.* ■ The fact is that the resale value guarantee applies only toward the purchase of another Audi. *In truth, the resale value guarantee applies only toward the purchase of another Audi.* ■ The fact is that Mrs. Eddy doesn't advocate any kind of a positive thinking or "think good, feel good" philosophy. *Indeed, Mrs. Eddy doesn't advocate any kind of a positive thinking or "think good, feel good" philosophy.*

the fact of the matter is (that) *actually; indeed; in fact; in faith; in reality; in truth; really; truly;* delete. The fact of the matter is you cannot copyright an idea. *You cannot copyright an idea.* ■ The fact of the matter is most couples don't talk about sex. *In truth, most couples don't talk about sex.* ■ The fact of the matter is most people in this country are hypocrites. *Most people in this country are hypocrites.* ■ The fact of the matter is there is no evidence of a reintroduction of troops. *Indeed, there is no evidence of a reintroduction of troops.*

the fact remains (that) delete. The fact remains we have the overwhelming support of the Christian and Jewish religions. *We have the overwhelming support of the Christian and Jewish religions.* ■ Economists, psychologists, and feminists can postulate all they want on the effects, but the fact remains that the American dream is fading fast. *Economists, psychologists, and feminists can postulate all they want on the effects, but the American dream is fading fast.*

(what is) the fashion (manner; way) (in which; that) *how.* The path-goal theory of leadership is concerned with the ways in which a leader can influence a subordinate's motivation, goals, and attempts at achievement. *The path-goal theory of leadership is concerned with how a leader can influence a subordinate's motivation, goals, and attempts at achievement.* ■ What do you think about the fashion in which this testing program was introduced into the plant? *What do you think about how this testing program was introduced into the plant?* ■ Health officials say that the viral infection is spread similarly to the manner in which AIDS is spread. *Health officials say that the viral infection is spread similarly to how AIDS is spread.* ■ What do you think about the fashion in which she handled this? *What do you think about how she handled this?* ■ More important than the sample's size is the manner in which the sample is taken. *More important than the sample's size is how the sample is taken.*

the feeling of delete.

the field of delete. This process became known as Boolean algebra and is widely used in the fields of computing and philosophy. *This process became known as Boolean algebra and is widely used in computing and philosophy.* ■ The field of cancer chemotherapy, which has been in the doldrums in recent years, appears poised on the edge of a new era due to the advent of potent drugs that stimulate the growth of white blood cells. *Cancer chemotherapy, which has been in the doldrums in recent years, appears poised on the edge of a new era due to the advent of potent drugs that stimulate the growth of white blood cells.*

the foregoing *that; the above; this;* delete. On top of the foregoing, the recent legislation on extending mandatory retirement further heightens the concern about job performance in the later years. *On top of this, the recent legislation on extending mandatory retirement further heightens the concern about job performance in the later years.*

the forenamed *that; the above; this;* delete.

the function of delete. The function of settling disputes requires the exercise of tact and concern for resolution of conflicts. *Settling disputes requires the exercise of tact and concern for resolution of conflicts.*

the heart of the matter *center; core; crux; essence; gist; heart; pith; substance; sum.*

the history of delete. For the first time in the history of this century, the death penalty is extended beyond the borders of a single country, in spite of the laws of other countries. *For the first time in this century, the death penalty is extended beyond the borders of a single country, in spite of the laws of other countries.*

the hows and (the) whys *aims; causes; goals; motives; purposes; reasons.* Our association has attempted to encourage proactive lending in low-income communities by working with the Fed to educate banks about the hows and whys of these investment opportunities. *Our association has attempted to encourage proactive lending in low-income communities by working with the Fed to educate banks about the aims of these investment opportunities.*

the idea of delete. Bloody revolution and punitive economic sanctions are not necessary if a government is committed to the idea of expanding political and economic freedoms and abolishing the discriminatory system. *Bloody revolution and punitive economic sanctions are not necessary if a government is committed to expanding political and economic freedoms and abolishing the discriminatory system.* ▪ The idea of a federal anti-discrimination law protecting HIV-infected individuals was among the most controversial of the AIDS commission's 597 recommendations. *A federal anti-discrimination law protecting HIV-infected individuals was among the most controversial of the AIDS commission's 597 recommendations.* ▪ A large number of today's teens have actually thought about the idea of suicide. *A large number of today's teens have actually thought about suicide.*

the interesting thing is (that) *interestingly;* delete. The interesting thing is that he never realized what he had done. *He never realized what he had done.*

the issue of delete. We shall first consider the issue of plotting the historical series we want to analyze. *We shall first consider plotting the historical series we want to analyze.* ▪ The issue of computer compatibility is becoming increasingly important now that many firms want to connect all of these individual computers into a network so they can exchange files. *Computer compatibility is becoming increasingly important now that many firms want to connect all of these individual computers into a network so they can exchange files.*

theistical *theistic.*

the language of (the … language) delete. He speaks the Spanish language fluently. *He speaks Spanish fluently.* ▪ Twelve of his novels have been translated into the Russian language. *Twelve of his novels have been translated into Russian.* ▪ His American dream became a nightmare as he learned that his lack of skills and familiarity with the English language relegated him to low-paying jobs. *His American dream became a nightmare as he learned that his lack of skills and familiarity with English relegated him to low-paying jobs.*

the last time *last.* A fifth bit acts as a flag indicating whether the file has been modified since the last time it was backed up. *A fifth bit acts as a flag indicating whether the file has been modified since it was last backed up.*

the length of time *how long; the time.* The purpose of a network is to show all activities needed to complete a project and to enable the planner to calculate the length of time a project will take from start to finish. *The purpose of a network is to show all activities needed to complete a project and to enable the planner to* *calculate the time a project will take from start to finish.* ■ A copyright registration is effective on the date that all required elements are received in the Copyright Office, regardless of the length of time it takes the Office to process the application and mail the certificate of registration. *A copyright registration is effective on the date that all required elements are received in the Copyright Office, regardless of how long it takes the Office to process the application and mail the certificate of registration.*

the lion's share *almost all; most; nearly all.*

the long and (the) short *center; core; crux; essence; gist; heart; pith; substance; sum.*

the manifestation of delete. Looking first at managers, one once again sees the manifestation of the tendency toward caution with age. *Looking first at managers, one once again sees the tendency toward caution with age.*

the matter *it; that; this.* Legislators in six other states are expected to take up the matter in new legislative sessions next year. *Legislators in six other states are expected to take this up in new legislative sessions next year.*

(what is) the means by which *how.* Thus Wednesday's municipal elections, which the government hopes will be a first step toward a constitution under which blacks share power, will provide indicators of the means by which apartheid is ultimately to be dismantled. *Thus Wednesday's municipal elections, which the government hopes will be a first step toward a constitution under which blacks share power, will provide indicators of how apartheid is ultimately to be dismantled.* ■ What is the means by which a nation can increase investment? *How can a nation increase investment?*

the medium of delete.

the method of delete.

the month of delete. Between the months of July and September, only three more ventured-financed firms went public. *Between July and September, only three more ventured-financed firms went public.*

the more (most) *more (most).* Testing can answer which of these two models is the more appropriate. *Testing can answer which of these two models is more appropriate.* ■ What angers small business activists the most is the expeditious altering of S corporation regulations. *What most angers small business activists is the expeditious altering of S corporation regulations.*

then and only then *only then; then.* I suggest that then and only then will people such as Mr. Becker realize that there really is no free lunch. *I suggest that only then will people such as Mr. Becker realize that there really is no free lunch.*

then at that (this) juncture (juncture in time; moment; moment in time; period; period of time; point; point in time; stage; stage in time; time) *then.*

the nature of *like;* delete. Disagreement on the viability of standardization strategies also reflects varying interpretations on the nature of the environment facing the international company. *Disagreement on the viability of standardization strategies also reflects varying interpretations of the environment facing the international company.* ■ In addition to poor education, he cites psychological blocks and misconceptions about the nature of mathematics. *In addition to poor education, he cites psychological blocks and misconceptions about mathematics.*

the notion of delete. He said that the notion of incorporating minimally toxic products into a pest management program is also catching on among some big-time horticulturalists and growers. *He said that incorporating minimally toxic products into a pest management program is also catching on among some big-time horticulturalists and growers.* ■ The notion of punishment for the sins of colleagues is devoid of either justice or practicality. *Punishment for the sins of colleagues is devoid of either justice or practicality.* ■ While not necessarily new, the notion of live-work developments is seeing a revival. *While not necessarily new, live-work developments are seeing a revival.*

then subsequently *then.* Then subsequently he left Digital and started his own business. *Then he left Digital and started his own business.*

theocratical *theocratic.*

the ... of *-'s.* I needed the help of my mother to care for my child. *I needed my mother's help to care for my child.* ■ The task of the analyst is to find the coefficients a and b in Equation 2-2. *The analyst's task is to find the coefficients a and b in Equation 2-2.* ■ The failure to recognize expenses of this type can affect the profitability of a product. *The failure to recognize expenses of this type can affect a product's profitability.*

theological *theologic.*

the one (that) delete. Although there are several approaches, the one we focus on is Greiner's model for organizational change. *Although there are several approaches, we focus on Greiner's model for organizational change.* ■ The one that seems to be the most popular is the use of the pull-down Mac menus for function keys. *The most popular seems to be the use of the pull-down Mac menus for function keys.*

the one best *the best.* The emphasis of scientific management was to try to find the one best way by examining the way work was done, the sequence of steps, and the skills of the workers. *The emphasis of scientific management was to try to* *find the best way by examining the way work was done, the sequence of steps, and the skills of the workers.*

(of) the opposite sex *female; male; man; woman.* He is abandoning his hemline indicator because it tended to offend too many investors of the opposite sex. *He is abandoning his hemline indicator because it tended to offend too many female investors.*

theoretical *theoretic.*

the other way around (round) *the opposite; the reverse.*

the passage of time *time.* Meanwhile, the passage of time has made it increasingly apparent that last year's stock market crash was not the immediate precursor of a corresponding plunge for the economy. *Meanwhile, time has made it increasingly apparent that last year's stock market crash was not the immediate precursor of a corresponding plunge for the economy.* ■ For too long the extent of the problem was downplayed, thereby promoting the mistaken belief that time would somehow correct the situation; instead, the passage of time has only deepened the crisis. *For too long the extent of the problem was downplayed, thereby promoting the mistaken belief that time would somehow correct the situation; instead, time has only deepened the crisis.*

the practice of delete. Japan shares the United States' concern about the practice of using aid funds for export promotion. *Japan shares the United States' concern about using aid funds for export promotion.* ■ One distinctly American ritual is likely to be played out on Election Day this November: the practice of staying away from the polls. *One distinctly American ritual is likely to be played out on Election Day this November: staying away from the polls.* ■ Community groups have charged banks with the practice of "red lining" poor and minority neighborhoods by denying them mortgages, personal and business loans, and other services. *Community groups have charged banks with "red lining" poor and minority neighborhoods by denying them mortgages, personal and business loans, and other services.*

the presence of delete. It is the presence of poverty in the United States that prevents our citizens from describing systematic government-sponsored repression abroad. *It is poverty in the United States that prevents our citizens from describing systematic government-sponsored repression abroad.* ■ Mammography uses an X-ray technique to detect the presence of lesions, such as tumors, within the breast. *Mammography uses an X-ray technique to detect lesions, such as tumors, within the breast.* ■ More recent surveys of fainter sources in that direction now show the presence of a few dim galaxies within the void. *More recent surveys of fainter sources in that direction now show a few dim galaxies within the void.*

(of) the present ... *here; this;* delete. The objective of the present chapter is to discuss these arguments. *The objective here is to discuss these arguments.* ■ In the present chapter, we introduce capital structure theories. *In this chapter, we introduce capital structure theories.* ■ At the beginning of the present decade, only 21 percent of the state's deposits were concentrated in the five largest banks. *At the beginning of the 1980s, only 21 percent of the state's deposits were concentrated in the five largest banks.*

the present author (writer) *I.*

the present day *(just; right) now; nowadays; the present; these days; today.* Ever since MIT economist Rudiger Dornbusch first firmly broached the suggestion, the financial world has been absorbed in the resemblance between 1968 and the present day in macroeconomic terms. *Ever since MIT economist Rudiger Dornbusch first firmly broached the suggestion, the financial world has been absorbed in the resemblance between 1968 and today in macroeconomic terms.*

the present-day *nowaday's; the present's; today's.* Discoveries, innovations, surprises, and complexities of the present-day South multiply beyond what it seemed possible for him to cover. *Discoveries, innovations, surprises, and complexities of today's South multiply beyond what it seemed possible for him to cover.*

the principle of delete.

the problem of delete. Of all the approaches that can be taken to address the problem of fraud, the most important may be a demonstrated intolerance for the problem. *Of all the approaches that can be taken to address fraud, the most important may be a demonstrated intolerance for the problem.*

the procedure of delete. Let's now look at the procedure of how teams are eliminated. *Let's now look at how teams are eliminated.*

(what is) the process by which *how.* We will now examine the process by which natural and global marketing activities are controlled. *We will now examine how natural and global marketing activities are controlled.* ■ The two are very particular when it comes to the ingredients and the process by which their soups are made. *The two are very particular when it comes to the ingredients and how their soups are made.*

the process of delete. The process of selecting the proper school for your child can be hugely exciting. *Selecting the proper school for your child can be hugely exciting.* ■ Staffing initially entails the process of recruiting potential candidates for a job, reviewing the applicants' credentials, and trying to match the job demands with the candidates' abilities. *Staffing initially entails recruiting potential candidates for a job, reviewing the applicants' credentials, and trying to match the job demands with the candidates' abilities.* ■ In the process of further reconceptualizing our department store strategy, we undertook an asset sale program that produced $4.1 billion and reduced our original debt by $3.4 billion. *In further reconceptualizing our department store strategy, we undertook an* *asset sale program that produced $4.1 billion and reduced our original debt by $3.4 billion.*

the purpose of ... is to delete. The purpose of this view is to allow you to work on the outline's organization. *This view allows you to work on the outline's organization.* ■ The purpose of double exponential smoothing is to enable the estimation of a linear trend in a time series. *Double exponential smoothing enables the estimation of a linear trend in a time series.*

the question of delete. Corporate dividend policy deals with the question of how much of the firm's earnings should be paid to its stockholders in cash dividends. *Corporate dividend policy deals with how much of the firm's earnings should be paid to its stockholders in cash dividends.* ■ The question of alcohol is a different matter. *Alcohol is a different matter.* ■ I've talked a lot about pharmaceuticals, but I don't want to ignore the question of medical products. *I've talked a lot about pharmaceuticals, but I don't want to ignore medical products.* ■ They didn't attempt to examine the fundamentals in the markets they studied, so they're agnostic on the question of whether bubble psychology is based on anything concrete at all. *They didn't attempt to examine the fundamentals in the markets they studied, so they're agnostic on whether bubble psychology is based on anything concrete at all.*

therapeutical *therapeutic.*

there delete. This is true for current products where there exists a sales history. *This is true for current products where a sales history exists.*

the (this) reader *I; you;* delete. This book is meant to help the reader learn how to program in C. *This book is meant to help you learn how to program in C.* ■ The reader may also find classical solutions to this equation in several texts on applied mathematics. *You may also find classical solutions to this equation in several texts on applied mathematics.* ■ This reader was dismayed by his cynical and narrow view of the public sector. *I was dismayed by his cynical and narrow view of the public sector.*

thereafter *later; next; then.*

the reality of delete. A key element of an ILP is that students can change their objectives at any time based on current interests and the reality of their academic progress. *A key element of an ILP is that students can change their objectives at any time based on current interests and their academic progress.* ■ Patients facing an ileostomy, colostomy, or urostomy must come to terms with the reality of the disease. *Patients facing an ileostomy, colostomy, or urostomy must come to terms with the disease.*

the realm of delete. Brainstorming has broadened its appeal to the business world and has found widespread acceptance in the realm of business meetings.

Brainstorming has broadened its appeal to the business world and has found widespread acceptance in business meetings.

therefore *hence; so; then; thus.* Therefore if the host program wants to send data to the Mac, it can. *Thus if the host program wants to send data to the Mac, it can.* ■ The front view is more descriptive than the top view; therefore, the front view should be dimensioned. *The front view is more descriptive than the top view, so the front view should be dimensioned.*

the region of delete.

therein *there.*

there is ... (that; who) *is;* delete. There are fifteen people in the group. *Fifteen people are in the group.* ■ There are millions of people who feel the way you do. *Millions of people feel the way you do.* ■ For every discovery that scientists make about Egyptian antiquity, there are hundreds that remain unsolved. *For every discovery that scientists make about Egyptian antiquity, hundreds remain unsolved.* ■ If there is more than one file that begins with the same letter, press that letter repeatedly until the appropriate file is selected. *If more than one file begins with the same letter, press that letter repeatedly until the appropriate file is selected.* ■ There are few among us who could be undaunted or detached when faced with these issues. *Few among us could be undaunted or detached when faced with these issues.* ■ You might be wondering if there is one approach or theory that can be applied to all management situations. *You might be wondering if one approach or theory can be applied to all management situations.*

thereupon *later; next; then.*

the role of delete. The role of research and development is crucial to the future of a nation's economic growth and to the future of an industry and an individual business. *Research and development is crucial to the future of a nation's economic growth and to the future of an industry and an individual business.*

the same (thing) as *equal to; like.* Asserting that the deficit numbers "have no clothes" is not the same thing as saying that all is fine in the nation's economic affairs. *Asserting that the deficit numbers "have no clothes" is not like saying that all is fine in the nation's economic affairs.*

the same exact *just (the); the exact; the same.* These are high-grade municipal bonds, the same exact ones that the banks buy. *These are high-grade municipal bonds, the same ones that the banks buy.*

the same thing *as much; the same.* Looking back, I find I did the same thing. *Looking back, I find I did the same.* ■ The state's consumer chief said she may do the same thing here. *The state's consumer chief said she may do the same here.* ■ Others have discovered the same thing. *Others have discovered as much.*

the same way *as; like.* Normally when you make a printout, it looks the same way it does when displayed on the screen. *Normally when you make a printout, it looks as it does when displayed on the screen.*

the scale of delete.

the scope of delete. The scope of the loss of control over one's body can only be understood through a personal experience. *The loss of control over one's body can only be understood through a personal experience.* ■ The Foreign Technology Abstract Newsletter has dramatically expanded the scope of its coverage, becoming a true newsletter incorporating news of current worldwide developments in foreign technology into its format. *The Foreign Technology Abstract Newsletter has dramatically expanded its coverage, becoming a true newsletter incorporating news of current worldwide developments in foreign technology into its format.*

the single best (biggest; greatest; largest; most) *the best (biggest; greatest; largest; most).* The single most important issue for women is equal pay for equal work. *The most important issue for women is equal pay for equal work.* ■ The single best predictor of reading ability is the number of stories read to that child before he or she gets to school. *The best predictor of reading ability is the number of stories read to that child before he or she gets to school.*

the situation with *right; so; true;* delete. This is often the situation with inexperienced managers, but it can be remedied with management training. *This is often so with inexperienced managers, but it can be remedied with management training.*

the space of delete. Within the space of a few minutes, he was dead. *Within a few minutes, he was dead.*

the state of delete. The state of Massachusetts is considering a similar law. *Massachusetts is considering a similar law.* ■ The 11th district of the Federal Home Loan Bank system includes almost every savings and loan and savings bank in the states of California, Arizona, and Nevada. *The 11th district of the Federal Home Loan Bank system includes almost every savings and loan and savings bank in California, Arizona, and Nevada.*

the state of (the ... state) *the;* delete. Consumers were more confident about the state of the economy in December than during the same month last year. *Consumers were more confident about the economy in December than during the same month last year.* ■ The state of deterioration is so advanced that the government now fears that the approaching typhoon season will be Okinotorishima's last if the massive reclamation project is not completed in time. *The deterioration is so advanced that the government now fears that the approaching typhoon season will be Okinotorishima's last if the massive reclamation project is not completed in time.* ■ Many priests feel celibacy is no greater than the married state. *Many priests feel celibacy is no greater than marriage.*

the subject of delete. Both authors have written widely on the subject of behavioral science research and application. *Both authors have written widely on behavioral science research and application.* ▪ Because of changing societal demands and preferences, there is an increasing public interest in the subject of corporate governance. *Because of changing societal demands and preferences, there is an increasing public interest in corporate governance.*

the sum of *all;* delete.

the time will come when *at length; eventually; in due time; in the end; in time; later; one day; over the months (years); over time; someday; sometime; ultimately; with time; yet.* The time will come when you will appreciate all I've done for you. *One day you will appreciate all I've done for you.*

the topic of delete. Knowledge Center is a library of lessons on the topics of project management, supervisory skills, business writing, computer literacy, strategic planning, forecasting, business math, finance and accounting, and negotiating. *Knowledge Center is a library of lessons on project management, supervisory skills, business writing, computer literacy, strategic planning, forecasting, business math, finance and accounting, and negotiating.* ▪ He spoke on the topic of probate lawyers and fiduciaries at the recent ABA convention in Toronto. *He spoke on probate lawyers and fiduciaries at the recent ABA convention in Toronto.*

the total (of) *all;* delete.

the totality of *all;* delete. If you look at the totality of votes cast, Jackson is very well off. *If you look at all the votes cast, Jackson is very well off.*

the truth is (that) *actually; indeed; in fact; in faith; in truth; really; truly;* delete.

the truth of the matter is (that) *actually; indeed; in fact; in faith; in reality; in truth; really; truly;* delete. The truth of the matter is nobody can deny there's a problem. *Nobody can deny there's a problem.* ▪ The truth of the matter is that glasnost and communism are incompatible. *In truth, glasnost and communism are incompatible.* ▪ The truth of the matter is when the president calls and says I want you to be my Secretary of the Treasury, you do it. *When the president calls and says I want you to be my Secretary of the Treasury, you do it.*

the ... use of *using;* delete. The use of proper line weights greatly improves a drawing's readability and appearance. *Using proper line weights greatly improves a drawing's readability and appearance.* ▪ Would the use of these exacerbate the situation? *Would using these exacerbate the situation?* ▪ This construction is performed with the use of a compass and a straightedge. *This construction is performed with a compass and a straightedge.* ▪ Our extensive curriculum is presented by specialists with years of experience in the use of the techniques they teach. *Our extensive curriculum is presented by specialists with* *years of experience in the techniques they teach.* ■ Verification of the debt's nature is determined through the use of "tracing rules," under which the borrower must provide evidence of claimed expenditures. *Verification of the debt's nature is determined through "tracing rules," under which the borrower must provide evidence of claimed expenditures.*

the way *as.* When the images are the way you want them, you print the document, and the picture files that the codes refer to are merged into the document. *When the images are as you want them, you print the document, and the picture files that the codes refer to are merged into the document.* ■ Look carefully at the results, and try to determine why they behave the way they do. *Look carefully at the results, and try to determine why they behave as they do.*

the why and (the) wherefore (of) *aim; cause; goal; motive; purpose; reason.* We're going to be talking about the whys and the wherefores of his lead. *We're going to be talking about the reasons for his lead.*

the year (of) delete. Nearly 2,500 years ago, in the year 500 B.C., the first object which could project an image was made in ancient China. *Nearly 2,500 years ago, in 500 B.C., the first object which could project an image was made in ancient China.* ■ By the year 2025, China will have an estimated 1.49 billion people, and India 1.44 billion. *By 2025, China will have an estimated 1.49 billion people, and India 1.44 billion.*

(a; the) ... thing delete. It's a tricky thing. *It's tricky.* ■ Censorship is a very dangerous thing. *Censorship is very dangerous.* ■ It's a very complex thing. *It's very complex.* ■ It's an uncomfortable thing to say. *It's uncomfortable to say.* ■ Suicide doesn't seem like such a bad thing anymore. *Suicide doesn't seem so bad anymore.* ■ It's a very difficult thing. *It's very difficult.*

thinking in (my) mind *thinking.* What were you thinking in your mind when you bought the two guns and the knife? *What were you thinking when you bought the two guns and the knife?*

think to myself *think.* As they were yelling at me, I thought to myself, "These can't be my parents." *As they were yelling at me, I thought, "These can't be my parents."*

thirdly *third.*

this coming *next; this.* This coming Wednesday we are having our town fair. *This Wednesday we are having our town fair.*

those individuals (people; persons) *people (persons); those.* Only those people authorized to have access to information are allowed to see it. *Only people authorized to have access to information are allowed to see it.* ■ The program quickly gained popularity among those people who had experience on the

Wang. *The program quickly gained popularity among those who had experience on the Wang.* ▪ Advocates are those people who want change but do not have the power to sponsor it themselves. *Advocates are those who want change but do not have the power to sponsor it themselves.*

through and through *all through; completely; entirely; thoroughly; throughout; totally; wholly.*

throughout ... entire (whole) *entire (whole); throughout.* He was in trouble throughout his entire life. *He was in trouble his entire life.* ▪ This problem doesn't exist throughout the entire race. *This problem doesn't exist throughout the race.*

throughout the length and breadth (of) *all through; completely; entirely; thoroughly; throughout; totally; wholly.*

through (throughout) the course (duration; length) of *during; for; in; over; throughout; when; while; with.* This report is our opportunity to share the insights we have gained throughout the course of the study. *This report is our opportunity to share the insights we have gained throughout the study.* ▪ When we return, we'll have the answers to all the questions we've been posing throughout the course of this broadcast. *When we return, we'll have the answers to all the questions we've been posing during this broadcast.* ▪ They have a great organization, and through the course of the years, they've proven it works. *They have a great organization, and over the years, they've proven it works.*

through the medium of *by; from; in; on; over; through; with.* My basic interest is the lucid communication of ideas through the medium of print. *My basic interest is the lucid communication of ideas through print.*

through the use of *by; in; through; with.* Verbal reasoning is the ability to think, comprehend, and communicate effectively through the use of words. *Verbal reasoning is the ability to think, comprehend, and communicate effectively with words.*

through whatever (whichever) manner (means) *despite how; however.*

through what (which) means (mechanism) *how.*

throw into a rage *enrage.*

throw into doubt *challenge; contradict; dispute; doubt; question.*

throw into jeopardy *endanger; imperil; jeopardize.* The sale, which would have been one of the nation's largest bottling transactions ever, was thrown into jeopardy Friday, when an FTC request for more information for antitrust appraisal pushed the transaction into 1989. *The sale, which would have been one of the* *nation's largest bottling transactions ever, was jeopardized Friday, when an FTC request for more information for antitrust appraisal pushed the transaction into 1989.*

throw into question *challenge; contradict; dispute; doubt; question.*

thusly *thus.*

till (until) after *before; till (until).* Do not delete the first code until after you have made the adjustments. *Do not delete the first code until you have made the adjustments.*

till (until) the juncture (juncture in time; moment; moment in time; period; period in time; point; point in time; stage; stage in time; time) (that; when) *till (until).* Until the time that deposit interest rates were set free to seek levels dictated by the financial markets, the thrift business was uncomplicated. *Until deposit interest rates were set free to seek levels dictated by the financial markets, the thrift business was uncomplicated.*

till (until) ... then *till (until).* Until we realize that all addictive chemical substances are fair game in the war on drugs, then the war cannot be won, much less fought. *Until we realize that all addictive chemical substances are fair game in the war on drugs, the war cannot be won, much less fought.*

till (until) the recent past *till (until) lately; till (until) of late; till (until) recently;* delete. Until the recent past, such courses were taken, often as electives, by advanced undergraduates who already had a certain degree of sophistication. *Until recently, such courses were taken, often as electives, by advanced undergraduates who already had a certain degree of sophistication.*

time after time *frequently; often; recurrently; regularly; repeatedly.* Time after time, the Democrats have turned to the idea of raising taxes. *The Democrats have regularly turned to the idea of raising taxes.*

time and (time) again *frequently; often; recurrently; regularly; repeatedly.* This has been demonstrated time and time again in their subsequent on-the-job experiences. *This has been repeatedly demonstrated in their subsequent on-the-job experiences.*

time-consuming *drawn-out; lengthy; long; prolonged; protracted.* For instruments already in orbit, astronomers can only continue to identify the unwanted data, a time-consuming but manageable task. *For instruments already in orbit, astronomers can only continue to identify the unwanted data, a lengthy but manageable task.*

(a; the) time frame (of) *age; eon; epoch; era; interval; period; time;* delete. Outpacing both, however, were the regional banks, which moved up 29 percent over the same time frame. *Outpacing both, however, were the regional banks, which moved up 29 percent over the same period.* ■ The state investigators have also studied use of pesticides to see if any were used differently during the so-called window of exposure, a time frame of about two years between 1980 and 1982 when a common environmental factor may have been present. *The state investigators have also studied use of pesticides to see if any were used differently during the so-called window of exposure, about two years between 1980 and 1982 when a common environmental factor may have been present.* ■ A confirmed carbon date placing the shroud in the medieval time frame has nothing to do with determining the nature of the image on the cloth. *A confirmed carbon date placing the shroud in the medieval age has nothing to do with determining the nature of the image on the cloth.*

(a; the) time horizon (of) *age; eon; epoch; era; interval; period; time;* delete. Estimates are then made of the values of these factors over an appropriate time horizon. *Estimates are then made of the values of these factors over an appropriate time.* ■ The Income Stock Fund strives to provide income and principal growth at a reasonable rate over a three- to five-year investment time horizon. *The Income Stock Fund strives to provide income and principal growth at a reasonable rate over a three- to five-year investment period.*

(a; the) time interval (of) *interval; period; time.* Float is the time interval between the time a check is written and the time it is finally taken from the check writer's account. *Float is the interval between the time a check is written and the time it is finally taken from the check writer's account.*

time of day *time.*

(a; the) time period (of) *age; eon; epoch; era; interval; period; time;* delete. Income tax regulations allow recognition of certain transactions for tax purposes in time periods other than the period during which the transaction will be recognized in the determination of net income for financial reporting purposes. *Income tax regulations allow recognition of certain transactions for tax purposes in periods other than the period during which the transaction will be recognized in the determination of net income for financial reporting purposes.* ■ The Greek material is similar to stone tools from Hungary and Bulgaria dated to about the same time period. *The Greek material is similar to stone tools from Hungary and Bulgaria dated to about the same age.*

(five) times over *(five)fold.* He was able to increase the conviction of drug traffickers five times over. *He was able to increase the conviction of drug traffickers fivefold.*

(a; the) time span (of) *age; eon; epoch; era; interval; period; time;* delete. He says they would like to achieve 10-millisecond resolution, and adds that audiences can perceive tempo changes within that time span. *He says they would like to achieve 10-millisecond resolution, and adds that audiences can perceive* *tempo changes within that time.* ■ Over the same time span, the savings rate rose from 4.1 to 5.4 percent. *Over the same period, the savings rate rose from 4.1 to 5.4 percent.*

time was when *formerly; long ago; once.*

tiny (little) bit *bit; fragment; hint; piece; shred; speck; trace.* The prosecution attempted to identify the victim through tiny bits of human skin, flesh, and teeth found in a pile of wood chips. *The prosecution attempted to identify the victim through pieces of human skin, flesh, and teeth found in a pile of wood chips.* ■ This tiny bit of code is used by the ProDOS 8 interrupt-handling sub-routine. *This fragment of code is used by the ProDOS 8 interrupt-handling sub-routine.* ■ I think Kroger management is just a tiny bit more relaxed than they were yesterday. *I think Kroger management is just a bit more relaxed than they were yesterday.*

tiny little *little; tiny.*

title *delete.* One of the most successful shows on TV that year happened to be titled "St. Elsewhere." *One of the most successful shows on TV that year happened to be "St. Elsewhere."*

(in order) to accomplish (achieve) that (this) aim (end; goal; objective) *to that (this) end; toward that (this) end.* To accomplish this goal, two special task forces were established. *To this end, two special task forces were established.* ■ In order to achieve that objective, Congress in 1985 authorized the Peace Corps to double its volunteers to 10,000. *Toward that end, Congress in 1985 authorized the Peace Corps to double its volunteers to 10,000.*

to a certain (limited; some) degree *in a sense; in part; less often; less so; more or less; partially; partly; rather; some; somewhat;* delete. To some degree, all three of them may play a role. *All three of them may play some role.* ■ This depends to a limited degree on whether the company follows a global or a national strategy focus. *This partly depends on whether the company follows a global or a national strategy focus.* ■ You can intimidate umpires to a certain degree. *You can intimidate umpires somewhat.* ■ The five manufacturing indus-tries covered by the new rules are gloves and mittens, buttons and buckles, handkerchiefs, embroideries and, to a limited degree, jewelry. *The five manu-facturing industries covered by the new rules are gloves and mittens, buttons and buckles, handkerchiefs, embroideries and, less so, jewelry.*

to a certain (limited; some) extent *in a sense; in part; less so; more or less; partially; partly; rather; some; somewhat;* delete. These are two factors that women can control to some extent. *These are two factors that women can some-what control.* ■ In Germany, and to some extent in Japan, our products are now priced competitively. *In Germany, and less so in Japan, our products are now priced competitively.* ■ I agree with you to a certain extent. *I agree with you in a* *sense.* ■ Besides depending on managers' conceptual skills, all plans rest to some extent on three basic elements: objectives, assumptions, and forecasts. *Besides depending on managers' conceptual skills, all plans rest partly on three basic elements: objectives, assumptions, and forecasts.* ■ It does restrict our movements to some extent. *It does more or less restrict our movements.* ■ The first sort of tendency is countered to some extent by the fear of getting the reputation of not producing work that other scientists can safely use. *The first sort of tendency is partially countered by the fear of getting the reputation of not producing work that other scientists can safely use.*

to a degree *in part; more or less; partially; partly; rather; some; somewhat;* delete. Any choice would have been controversial to a degree. *Any choice would have been somewhat controversial.*

to a ... degree *-(al)ly;* delete. We have reduced our nuclear weaponry to a significant degree. *We have significantly reduced our nuclear weaponry.* ■ To a surprising degree, we find the outlook hopeful. *We find the outlook surprisingly hopeful.* ■ A falling dollar in international exchange markets has to a considerable degree offset the rise in the domestic markets. *A falling dollar in international exchange markets has considerably offset the rise in the domestic markets.*

to a ... extent *-(al)ly;* delete. Economic growth and personal prosperity have increased to a remarkable extent over the past ten years in the OECD countries. *Economic growth and personal prosperity have increased remarkably over the past ten years in the OECD countries.* ■ It's a change that's already been worked out to a considerable extent at the local level. *It's a change that's already been considerably worked out at the local level.*

to a great (large) degree *almost all; chiefly; commonly; generally; greatly; in general; largely; mainly; most; mostly; most often; much; nearly all; normally; overall; typically; usually; well.* The blood supply is exceptionally safe and protected to a great degree by existing screening tests and the self-deferral of individuals at high risk. *The blood supply is exceptionally safe and well protected by existing screening tests and the self-deferral of individuals at high risk.* ■ Because the state will pay for the bulk of building and running the school, it will naturally be involved in the project to a large degree. *Because the state will pay for the bulk of building and running the school, it will naturally be much involved in the project.* ■ In Malaysia, imports are controlled to a great degree by a handful of European commission houses. *In Malaysia, imports are mostly controlled by a handful of European commission houses.*

to a greater (larger) degree (extent) *more; more often; more so.* The risks of radiation are understood to a much greater degree than many other risks we take for granted. *The risks of radiation are understood much more than many other risks we take for granted.* ■ From the perspective of the small company, the increasing use of strategic partnerships will create situations where small companies will be able to exploit technologies to a greater extent than was possible in the past. *From the perspective of the small company, the increasing use of strategic partnerships will create situations where small companies will be able to exploit technologies more often than was possible in the past.* ▪ We've tightened our strategic focus on department stores, and we're emphasizing customer service to a greater extent than ever before. *We've tightened our strategic focus on department stores, and we're emphasizing customer service more than ever before.* ▪ Black males suffer from debilitating health problems to a greater degree than males in other ethnic and racial groups. *More black males suffer from debilitating health problems than males in other ethnic and racial groups.*

to a greater or lesser degree (extent) *in part; in some way; more or less; partially; partly; rather; some; somehow; someway(s); somewhat; to some degree (extent); various; variously; varying; varyingly;* delete. Malamud's subsequent career provides a paradigm of sorts of the transition that has marked the careers of writers who were raised, to a greater or lesser degree, as Jews who lived in America but have spent the greater part of their adult lives as American novelists or playwrights, poets or critics who happen to be Jewish. *Malamud's subsequent career provides a paradigm of sorts of the transition that has marked the careers of writers who were raised, more or less, as Jews who lived in America but have spent the greater part of their adult lives as American novelists or playwrights, poets or critics who happen to be Jewish.*

to a great (large) extent *almost all; chiefly; commonly; generally; greatly; in general; largely; mainly; most; mostly; most often; much; nearly all; normally; overall; typically; usually; well.* That image to a large extent is created by what the U.S. government says the Soviet Union is like. *That image is largely created by what the U.S. government says the Soviet Union is like.* ▪ Its costs are to a great extent measured in foreign currencies without an offsetting increase in revenues. *Its costs are mostly measured in foreign currencies without an offsetting increase in revenues.* ▪ To a large extent, the success of any business venture depends on planning. *The success of any business venture chiefly depends on planning.*

to a lesser (lower; smaller) degree (extent) *less; less often; less so.* Some have been dramatically affected by this pilgrimage; others to a lesser degree. *Some have been dramatically affected by this pilgrimage; others less so.* ▪ It is only in Iowa and, to a lesser extent, in New Hampshire, that candidates meet so many rural Americans. *It is only in Iowa and, less often, in New Hampshire that candidates meet so many rural Americans.* ▪ The tactics are being used in the Pittston coal strike in West Virginia, and to a lesser degree by striking telephone workers at NYNEX. *The tactics are being used in the Pittston coal strike in West Virginia, and less so by striking telephone workers at NYNEX.* ▪ Traders said that other bond issues suffering from depressed prices, although to a far lesser extent, were Circle K, Owens-Illinois, and even UAL. *Traders said that other bond issues suffering from depressed prices, although far less so, were Circle K, Owens-Illinois, and even UAL.*

to all appearances *apparently; appear (to); outwardly; seem (to); seemingly; superficially.*

to all appearances ... appear (seem) *appear (seem).*

to a major or minor degree (extent) *in part; in some way; more or less; partially; partly; rather; some; somehow; someway(s); somewhat; to some degree (extent); various; variously; varying; varyingly;* delete. All of us are involved in the writing of the shows to a major or minor degree. *All of us are somehow involved in the writing of the shows.*

to an extent *in part; more or less; partially; partly; rather; some; somewhat;* delete.

to an increasing degree (extent) *increasingly; more and more.*

to a point *in part; partially; partly; rather; somewhat.* Retin A is effective to a point. *Retin A is somewhat effective.*

to a (the) point of *to.* The business is very close to the point of breaking even. *The business is very close to breaking even.* ■ We do it by putting in ridiculous hours and working ourselves to the point of numbness. *We do it by putting in ridiculous hours and working ourselves to numbness.*

to a (the) point (stage) that (when; where) *so (that); so far (that); so much (that); so that; to; to when; to where;* delete. It got to the point where I didn't leave the house at all for fear of missing her phone call. *It got so that I didn't leave the house at all for fear of missing her phone call.* ■ Because of the mathematics involved, forecasting intimidates some managers to the point that they accept projections at face value. *Because of the mathematics involved, forecasting so intimidates some managers that they accept projections at face value.* ■ Her Parkinson's disease has progressed to a point where she is now semipsychotic. *Her Parkinson's disease has progressed to where she is now semipsychotic.* ■ When temperatures drop to the point where frozen cloud particles form in the stratosphere, the reservoir compounds can suddenly react chemically on the particle surfaces. *When temperatures drop so far that frozen cloud particles form in the stratosphere, the reservoir compounds can suddenly react chemically on the particle surfaces.* ■ As with Marxism in the Soviet Union, the ideology of race has eroded to the point where it can justify nothing but the pragmatic survival of a master class. *As with Marxism in the Soviet Union, the ideology of race has so eroded that it can justify nothing but the pragmatic survival of a master class.* ■ Of course, few contend that American education has deteriorated to the point that it produces only illiterates. *Of course, few contend that American education has deteriorated so much that it produces only illiterates.*

to be *-(al)ly; to;* delete. To be frank, I think their products are inferior to ours. *Frankly, I think their products are inferior to ours.* ■ To be successful, you must work furiously. *To succeed, you must work furiously.* ■ If tobacco were to be declared illegal, I would feel comfortable in predicting a black market in nicotine smuggling. *If tobacco were declared illegal, I would feel comfortable in predicting a black market in nicotine smuggling.*

to begin (start) with *first.* To begin with, I never thought so many people would respond to such an intimate question. *First, I never thought so many people would respond to such an intimate question.*

to be sure *certainly; of course; surely.*

to do delete. Saving money can be difficult to do. *Saving money can be difficult.* ■ We've been fairly aggressive in the number of things we've tried to do. *We've been fairly aggressive in the number of things we've tried.* ■ I have to decide if I should retrace Sherman's route to the South as I originally planned to do. *I have to decide if I should retrace Sherman's route to the South as I originally planned.* ■ Word processors make changes, revisions, and reorganizations so easy to do that you don't have to think on all these levels at the same time. *Word processors make changes, revisions, and reorganizations so easy that you don't have to think on all these levels at the same time.*

together as a team (unit) *as a team (unit); together.* Here, in one location, specialists work together as a team to fulfill all aspects of a patient's needs. *Here, in one location, specialists work together to fulfill all aspects of a patient's needs.*

together ... in combination *in combination; together.* They can even be used together in combination. *They can even be used in combination.*

together with *along with; and; as well as; combined with; coupled with; joined with; paired with; with.* The team included psychiatrists, psychologists, and neurologists from Georgetown and New York universities, together with educators from Central Connecticut State University. *The team included psychiatrists, psychologists, and neurologists from Georgetown and New York universities and educators from Central Connecticut State University.* ■ If they have their product ready months before the dictionary, they won't be able, or will have to wait, to package the book together with the software. *If they have their product ready months before the dictionary, they won't be able, or will have to wait, to package the book with the software.* ■ Morgan proposed construction of a system of five reservoirs together with substantial channel improvements. *Morgan proposed construction of a system of five reservoirs coupled with substantial channel improvements.*

to make (a; the) ... (about; of; on; with) *to; to -(al)ly.* Although it was difficult to make an accurate count of the struck coal mines, it appeared last night that nine Silesian facilities still were occupied by small groups of workers. *Although it was difficult to accurately count the struck coal mines, it appeared last night that* *nine Silesian facilities still were occupied by small groups of workers.* ■ I need to make a correction about something I said yesterday. *I need to correct something I said yesterday.* ■ I wanted to make a comment on his appearance. *I wanted to comment on his appearance.* ■ We will give the audience a chance to make inquiries about this. *We will give the audience a chance to inquire about this.* ■ I will do everything possible to make a thorough evaluation of your application. *I will do everything possible to thoroughly evaluate your application.* ■ Resellers and suppliers will be forced to make a commitment to IC managers. *Resellers and suppliers will be forced to commit to IC managers.* ■ I am eager to make a deal. *I am eager to deal.* ■ I did try to make contact with the people who live in the house where I found it. *I did try to contact the people who live in the house where I found it.*

to one degree (extent) or another *in part; in some way; more or less; partially; partly; rather; some; somehow; someway(s); somewhat; to some degree (extent); various; variously; varying; varyingly;* delete. Competition is present in nearly all of our markets to one extent or another. *Competition is present to some extent in nearly all of our markets.* ■ We try to spend time together, and we succeed to one degree or another. *We try to spend time together, and we succeed in part.* ■ To one degree or another, the writing exhibited here is inconsistent with correct word usage or good sentence structure. *The writing exhibited here is in some way inconsistent with correct word usage or good sentence structure.*

topic of conversation (discussion) *subject; theme; topic.* It was the topic of conversation at our first meeting of the school year. *It was the subject at our first meeting of the school year.* ■ Among the topics of discussion are "Profiting from The Wall Street Journal," "Options—A Fool's Game?" and "Bonds Are No Longer Boring." *Among the topics are "Profiting from The Wall Street Journal," "Options—A Fool's Game?" and "Bonds Are No Longer Boring."*

to (all) practical purposes *essentially; in effect; in essence; practically; virtually.*

to such a degree *so; so far; so much; such.* Newspapers, financial journals, and everyday conversations influence most of us to such a degree that we are tempted to sell when prices are low and buy when prices are high. *Newspapers, financial journals, and everyday conversations so influence most of us that we are tempted to sell when prices are low and buy when prices are high.* ■ Argentine President Raul Alfonsin recently warned that the economic crisis was destabilizing the nation to such a degree that it and other Latin American nations ran the risk of "the emergence of a Hitler or a Mussolini, as in Europe after the First World War." *Argentine President Raul Alfonsin recently warned that the economic crisis was destabilizing the nation so much that it and other Latin American nations ran the risk of "the emergence of a Hitler or a Mussolini, as in Europe after the First World War."* ■ Never have so many crucial issues confronting a president depended to such a degree on science and technology. *Never have so many crucial issues confronting a president depended so much on* *science and technology.* ■ The writings of Thoreau retain importance and vitality to such a degree that a century later they have had significant influence on the greatest leaders of our time. *The writings of Thoreau retain such importance and vitality that a century later they have had significant influence on the greatest leaders of our time.*

to such an extent *so; so far; so much; such.* He believes Americans are deluged to such an extent with health messages that they exist in a state of heightened health consciousness all the time. *He believes Americans are so deluged with health messages that they exist in a state of heightened health consciousness all the time.* ■ The introduction of these services increases the future business risks to the company to such an extent that further delay in the repricing of NET's services cannot be tolerated. *The introduction of these services increases the future business risks to the company so much that further delay in the repricing of NET's services cannot be tolerated.* ■ The American Establishment warmly reciprocated and valued his judgment—to such an extent that he was even asked to join the Committee on the Constitutional System. *The American Establishment warmly reciprocated and valued his judgment—so much that he was even asked to join the Committee on the Constitutional System.*

to summarize (sum up) *in brief; in fine; in short; in sum.*

to take this opportunity delete. I'd like to take this opportunity to commend these women for their courage in sharing their stories. *I'd like to commend these women for their courage in sharing their stories.* ■ I'd like to take this opportunity to thank the students at Phillips Academy for their sizable contribution. *I'd like to thank the students at Phillips Academy for their sizable contribution.* ■ We wish to take this opportunity to clarify our proposed plan for use of a portion of the first floor of this building as an indoor tot play space. *We wish to clarify our proposed plan for use of a portion of the first floor of this building as an indoor tot play space.*

total (totally) delete. He went totally bankrupt. *He went bankrupt.* ■ This person totally destroyed my career. *This person destroyed my career.* ■ Her second pregnancy was a total disaster. *Her second pregnancy was a disaster.* ■ I was totally devastated when I found out he was having an affair. *I was devastated when I found out he was having an affair.* ■ Quality means different things to different people, so what constitutes quality must be a totally subjective evaluation. *Quality means different things to different people, so what constitutes quality must be a subjective evaluation.* ■ I'm the total antithesis of my mother. *I'm the antithesis of my mother.*

total up *add; sum; total.* When you total up the outside and inside executives, you get an overwhelming preponderance of board members with a managerial mindset. *When you total the outside and inside executives, you get an overwhelming preponderance of board members with a managerial mindset.*

to tell (you) the truth *actually; candidly; frankly; honestly; truthfully;* delete. She was a very sweet, kind woman, but to tell you the truth, a few of us worried about her. *She was a very sweet, kind woman, but frankly a few of us worried about her.*

to that (this) degree (extent) *so; so far; so much; such.* I didn't realize women could lose hair to that extent. *I didn't realize women could lose so much hair.*

(something) to that (the; this) effect (that) *affirming; claiming; conveying; declaring; professing; purporting; saying; suggesting.* The *Globe* story goes on to quote some advice from persons working in the area of elderly services, to the effect that elderly couples should hold onto their houses. *The* Globe *story goes on to quote some advice from persons working in the area of elderly services, purporting that elderly couples should hold onto their houses.* ■ A call to its former office in Dallas resulted in a telephone company answer to the effect that "service has been disconnected." *A call to its former office in Dallas resulted in a telephone company answer declaring "service has been disconnected."* ■ But I'm willing to guess that the wording included something to the effect that you could have "tax-free annual earnings." *But I'm willing to guess that the wording included saying that you could have "tax-free annual earnings."* ■ There are some estimates to that effect. *There are some estimates claiming that.* ■ He has never met him, and he produced witnesses to that effect. *He has never met him, and he produced witnesses professing that.*

to the contrary *but; conversely; however; instead; no; not so; rather.* To the contrary, we found there's a strong tendency for counties that have high radon levels to have low lung-cancer rates. *Instead, we found there's a strong tendency for counties that have high radon levels to have low lung-cancer rates.*

... to the contrary *after all; apart; aside; despite; even with; for all; with all.* Appearances to the contrary, he insists he doesn't plan to run for office. *Despite appearances, he insists he doesn't plan to run for office.* ■ Her adolescent frothing to the contrary, the responsibility for lasting job satisfaction at any level rests with the individual. *For all her adolescent frothing, the responsibility for lasting job satisfaction at any level rests with the individual.*

to the degree (that; to which) *as far as; as much as; so far as; so much as.* To the degree that the death benefit is prepaid through nursing care expenses, that will be subtracted from the sum paid to the beneficiaries upon the death of the nursing home resident. *As far as the death benefit is prepaid through nursing care expenses, that will be subtracted from the sum paid to the beneficiaries upon the death of the nursing home resident.* ■ To the degree that Divi Hotels can do so, it has purchased distressed properties at discount prices and has then renovated them. *So far as Divi Hotels can do so, it has purchased distressed properties at discount prices and has then renovated them.* ■ Volume markdowns did not occur to the degree they did last year. *Volume markdowns did not occur as much as they did last year.*

to the degree (extent) of *up to.* In the event of a total loss, the person is self-insured to the extent of one-third of the damage. *In the event of a total loss, the person is self-insured up to one-third of the damage.*

to the extent (that; to which) *as far as; as much as; so far as; so much as.* To the extent that the distribution of income and wealth goes to the heart of a country's political ethic, the United States has grown unfair. *So far as the distribution of income and wealth goes to the heart of a country's political ethic, the United States has grown unfair.* ■ I help out here and there, but maybe not to the extent that she'd like me to. *I help out here and there, but maybe not as much as she'd like me to.* ■ You agree that you will hold all such materials and information in confidence, will not disclose them to any third party, and will not use them other than in preparation of the report, except to the extent that such materials or information are in the public domain or have been rightfully provided to you by a third party. *You agree that you will hold all such materials and information in confidence, will not disclose them to any third party, and will not use them other than in preparation of the report, except so far as such materials or information are in the public domain or have been rightfully provided to you by a third party.*

to the greatest (largest) degree (extent) *as far as; as much as; so far as; so much as.* NYNEX asked the judge to expedite consideration of the request to the greatest extent possible by ordering the DOJ to submit its response within 14 days under special procedures. *NYNEX asked the judge to expedite consideration of the request as much as possible by ordering the DOJ to submit its response within 14 days under special procedures.*

to the point *apt; pertinent; relevant.*

to the purpose *apt; pertinent; relevant.*

to the tune of *by;* delete. It's the lagniappe that members of Congress collect (to the tune of $9.8 million in 1987) in return for talking to special interest groups with money to spend on them. *It's the lagniappe that members of Congress collect ($9.8 million in 1987) in return for talking to special interest groups with money to spend on them.*

toward the direction of *toward.*

toward the east (north; south; west) *eastward (northward; southward; westward).*

to what degree *how; how far; how much.* Privacy provisions in current law leave ambiguous to what degree such information can be shared. *Privacy* *provisions in current law leave ambiguous how much such information can be shared.* ▪ To what degree are you conscious of the theme as you write? *How conscious of the theme are you as you write?* ▪ But "The Question of Hu" also addresses the larger question of how we define madness and to what degree the madhouse was an instrument of social control. *But "The Question of Hu" also addresses the larger question of how we define madness and how much the madhouse was an instrument of social control.*

to whatever degree (extent) *however.*

to what extent *how; how far; how much.* What I would like to know is to what extent this is the result of reduced parental involvement in the child's upbringing. *What I would like to know is how much this is the result of reduced parental involvement in the child's upbringing.* ▪ To what extent they carried that admiration, only they know. *How far they carried that admiration, only they know.* ▪ To what extent can the best corporations be depended upon to set high standards, even to keep an eye out for the public interest—especially when national security is involved? *How much can the best corporations be depended upon to set high standards, even to keep an eye out for the public interest—especially when national security is involved?*

to what length *how far; how much.* Apart from other fascinating aspects of the ménage à trois, we are shown to what lengths some will go to further their objectives. *Apart from other fascinating aspects of the ménage à trois, we are shown how far some will go to further their objectives.*

trace amount *trace.* When the reaction took too long, they attributed this to trace amounts of water and oxygen, as is usually the case. *When the reaction took too long, they attributed this to traces of water and oxygen, as is usually the case.* ▪ He found trace amounts of chemicals in unrinsed containers, probably from the glue used to keep felt on the balls. *He found traces of chemicals in unrinsed containers, probably from the glue used to keep felt on the balls.*

trace back *trace.* The advantage of exploring what-ifs individually is that you can see the relationship between causes and effects more easily because any effects can be traced back to a single cause. *The advantage of exploring what-ifs individually is that you can see the relationship between causes and effects more easily because any effects can be traced to a single cause.* ▪ From dinosaurs to dogs, all land vertebrates trace their ancestry back to the water. *From dinosaurs to dogs, all land vertebrates trace their ancestry to the water.*

track record *record.* He built the company into a fine organization with an excellent track record, until the last three or four years. *He built the company into a fine organization with an excellent record, until the last three or four years.*

tragical *tragic.*

trained expert *expert.*

trivial details (facts; ideas; information; matters; things) *trivia.* Doesn't the state legislature have more important things to work on than to waste time and money on such a trivial matter as having to dial four extra digits on a telephone? *Doesn't the state legislature have more important things to work on than to waste time and money on such trivia as having to dial four extra digits on a telephone?* ■ While withholding such seemingly trivial information as the astronauts' in-orbit menus might appear ridiculous, even that might provide some clues as to the timing of the launch. *While withholding such seeming trivia as the astronauts' in-orbit menus might appear ridiculous, even that might provide some clues as to the timing of the launch.*

(a; the) true fact *a fact; factual; so; the truth; true; truthful.* That's a true fact. *That's a fact.*

true to fact *fact; factual; so; the truth; true; truthful.*

turn and turn about *by turns.*

twelve midnight *midnight.*

twelve noon *noon.*

twenty-five (25) percent (of) *one-fourth (of); one-quarter (of).*

two twins *twins.*

type (of) delete. It was a small, compact type of car. *It was a small, compact car.* ■ It's not a premeditated-type of act. *It's not a premeditated act.* ■ Dungeons and Dragons is a very seductive type of game. *Dungeons and Dragons is a very seductive game.* ■ We're trying to teach policemen there's not one of these type of people on every street corner. *We're trying to teach policemen there's not one of these people on every street corner.* ■ I'm basically a creative-type person. *I'm basically a creative person.* ■ She was in a psychiatric-type hospital for six months. *She was in a psychiatric hospital for six months.* ■ They're facsimile-type maps. *They're facsimile maps.* ■ This is pornographic type of humor. *This is pornographic humor.* ■ Paula has such a devil-may-care type of attitude. *Paula has such a devil-may-care attitude.* ■ We had experimented with different types of material and tested them under Israeli conditions. *We had experimented with different materials and tested them under Israeli conditions.*

U

unaccustomed to *not used to; unused to.* Adults and children who are unaccustomed to caffeine are more likely to be affected than the habitual consumer.

Adults and children who are not used to caffeine are more likely to be affected than the habitual consumer.

unbeknown (unbeknownst) *unknown.* Unbeknownst to most Americans, forest fires are largely responsible for the lush flora enjoyed by the thousands of visitors who trek to the scenic Wyoming retreat each summer. *Unknown to most Americans, forest fires are largely responsible for the lush flora enjoyed by the thousands of visitors who trek to the scenic Wyoming retreat each summer.* ■ Condominium loans were the favored product, but unbeknown to the bank, the market for condos had already peaked. *Condominium loans were the favored product, but unknown to the bank, the market for condos had already peaked.*

under any circumstances (conditions) *altogether; at all; completely; entirely; ever; fully; never; no matter what; not ever; utterly; whatever; wholly.* I will not see him under any circumstances. *I will not see him at all.* ■ I don't feel it's appropriate to take a commission under any circumstances. *I don't feel it's ever appropriate to take a commission.* ■ Ire is a noun, and it cannot be used as a verb under any circumstances. *Ire is a noun, and it can never be used as a verb.*

under certain (some) circumstances (conditions) *at times; every so often; for (in; with) some (of us; people); from time to time; now and again; now and then; occasionally; once in a while; on occasion; some; sometimes;* delete. Although rhizobia normally appear on roots, under certain conditions they live on stems instead. *Although rhizobia normally appear on roots, they sometimes live on stems instead.* ■ Consumed in large quantities, caffeine can certainly make us jumpy and, under some circumstances, may even lead to shaking, nervousness, depression, insomnia, disorientation, headaches, irritability, and rapid and irregular heartbeats. *Consumed in large quantities, caffeine can certainly make us jumpy and, in some people, may even lead to shaking, nervousness, depression, insomnia, disorientation, headaches, irritability, and rapid and irregular heartbeats.* ■ Why does fiber, which fights constipation, also cause constipation under some circumstances? *Why does fiber, which fights constipation, also at times cause constipation?* ■ Under certain circumstances it's all right, and under certain circumstances it isn't. *Sometimes it's all right, and sometimes it isn't.*

underneath *below; beneath.* Here was a perfect chance to demonstrate that the Square had not completely ossified underneath a layer of brick and limestone. *Here was a perfect chance to demonstrate that the Square had not completely ossified beneath a layer of brick and limestone.*

under no circumstances (conditions) *in no way; never; not; not ever; not once.* Under no circumstances is it to be used or considered as an offer to sell, or a solicitation of any offer to buy, any security. *Never is it to be used or considered as an offer to sell, or a solicitation of any offer to buy, any security.*

under obligation *bind; compel; force; obligate; oblige; require; restrict.* The lessee usually has the option to buy the auto at the end of the lease for the assumed residual value but is not under obligation to do so. *The lessee usually has the option to buy the auto at the end of the lease for the assumed residual value but is not obligated to do so.*

under the weather *ill; sick; unwell.*

unfair and inequitable *inequitable.*

unfortunately *sadly;* delete.

unite together *unite.*

universal panacea *panacea.*

unless and (or) until *till; unless; until.*

unless ... then *unless.* Unless we're prepared to say the Japanese are just smarter than we are, then we're looking at motivation and role models and parents encouraging kids to keep their options open. *Unless we're prepared to say the Japanese are just smarter than we are, we're looking at motivation and role models and parents encouraging kids to keep their options open.*

unnecessarily *needlessly.* The Japanese countered that moving part of the wing production to the General Dynamics plant in Fort Worth, Texas, would slow the production schedule and unnecessarily drive up the costs. *The Japanese countered that moving part of the wing production to the General Dynamics plant in Fort Worth, Texas, would slow the production schedule and needlessly drive up the costs.*

unnecessary *unneeded.*

unproven *unproved.* In the context of Western medicine, acupuncture is still unproven, and it is viewed with skepticism by many doctors and psychologists. *In the context of Western medicine, acupuncture is still unproved, and it is viewed with skepticism by many doctors and psychologists.*

unquestionably (so) *yes.*

unsubstantiated *baseless; groundless; unfounded.*

until and (or) unless *till; unless; until.*

until such point (time) as *until.* This coverage is only valid until either the subscriber or the former spouse remarries or until such time as provided by the divorce judgment, whichever occurs first. *This coverage is only valid until either the subscriber or the former spouse remarries or until provided by the divorce judgment, whichever occurs first.* ■ Instead of a 50-percent pay raise, they should have a 50-percent pay cut until such time as they rule with honesty, integrity, and compassion. *Instead of a 50-percent pay raise, they should have a 50-percent pay cut until they rule with honesty, integrity, and compassion.* ■ Discussions will continue until such point as I have something to show on paper. *Discussions will continue until I have something to show on paper.*

(an; the) untold number (of) *countless; endless; infinite; millions (of); myriad; numberless; untold.* If state government fails to actively support one of the world's most promising industries, it will be letting an untold number of jobs and revenue dollars slip through its fingers. *If state government fails to actively support one of the world's most promising industries, it will be letting untold jobs and revenue dollars slip through its fingers.*

up in the air *unanswered; uncertain; unclear; undecided; unresolved; unsettled; unsure.* Plans for an interview with Castro himself remain up in the air, according to a CBS News spokesperson. *Plans for an interview with Castro himself remain uncertain, according to a CBS News spokesperson.*

upon *on.* Do you wish something of the sort had happened when the senate was called upon to ratify ABM? *Do you wish something of the sort had happened when the senate was called on to ratify ABM?* ■ Deregulation was foisted upon us by economists who condemn "protectionism" while relishing their own academic tenure. *Deregulation was foisted on us by economists who condemn "protectionism" while relishing their own academic tenure.*

up till (until) *till (until).* I was a model up until the age of 19. *I was a model until the age of 19.* ■ Does this mean that up until now women and minorities have been uneducated and untrained? *Does this mean that till now women and minorities have been uneducated and untrained?* ■ Up until recently, Drexel lawyers had been saying confidentially that the crux of the government's investigation hinged on the words of Boesky. *Until recently, Drexel lawyers had been saying confidentially that the crux of the government's investigation hinged on the words of Boesky.*

up till (until) that (this) juncture (juncture in time; moment; moment in time; period; period in time; point; point in time; stage; stage in time; time) *so far; thus far; till (until) now (then); to date; up to now (then); (as) yet.* Up until this point, he hasn't been able to show what he stands for. *Until now, he hasn't been able to show what he stands for.* ■ Up until this time, the estimating had been done with a Lotus 1-2-3 spreadsheet. *Up to then, the estimating had been done with a Lotus 1-2-3 spreadsheet.*

up to a maximum of *up to.* If set to Yes, text wraps around the box (up to a maximum of 20 boxes per page). *If set to Yes, text wraps around the box (up to 20 boxes per page).*

up to and including *through.* Every WordStar Professional command, feature, and function up to and including Release 5 is listed and described in detail. *Every*

WordStar Professional command, feature, and function through Release 5 is listed and described in detail.

up to a point *rather; somewhat.*

up to the current (present) (time) *so far; thus far; till now; to date; until now; up to now; (as) yet.*

up to that (this) juncture (juncture in time; moment; moment in time; period; period in time; point; point in time; stage; stage in time; time) *so far; thus far; till now (then); to date; until now (then); up to now (then); (as) yet.* Up to this point, we have discussed these motivation theories relating to the needs of the individual. *Until now, we have discussed these motivation theories relating to the needs of the individual.* ■ I lost touch with the co-op after 1978, but up to that point it was operating without outside (or Peace Corps) support. *I lost touch with the co-op after 1978, but till then it was operating without outside (or Peace Corps) support.*

upward(s) of *more than; over.* They averaged from 792 parts per million to upwards of 1,000 parts per million. *They averaged from 792 parts per million to over 1,000 parts per million.* ■ In 1984, Peru had upwards of 40,000 acres of coca plants; today, it has 600,000 acres. *In 1984, Peru had more than 40,000 acres of coca plants; today, it has 600,000 acres.*

usage *use.* We project that ATM usage will increase to nearly 60 percent by 1995. *We project that ATM use will increase to nearly 60 percent by 1995.* ■ Occasional cocaine use among college students has dropped to 6 percent from 11 percent a year earlier, while occasional usage by friends dropped to 31 percent from 36 percent. *Occasional cocaine use among college students has dropped to 6 percent from 11 percent a year earlier, while occasional use by friends dropped to 31 percent from 36 percent.*

usually but not always *almost always; most often; nearly always; often; usually.*

utility *use; usefulness.* This has resulted in the much needed return to utility of our long-idled bridge. *This has resulted in the much needed return to use of our long-idled bridge.* ■ The article on British/American English is a good one, but at six pages, its utility is questionable. *The article on British/American English is a good one, but at six pages, its usefulness is questionable.*

utilization *use.* Utilization of existing schools in a region could be optimized to reduce variances caused by local population fluctuations. *Use of existing schools in a region could be optimized to reduce variances caused by local population fluctuations.* ■ That must be done through unending training, increased awareness of each person's limitations, and full utilization of everyone's talents, not through some arbitrary elimination program. *That must be done through* *unending training, increased awareness of each person's limitations, and full use of everyone's talents, not through some arbitrary elimination program.*

utilize *employ; use.* If utilizing the master antenna system is impossible, we will devise a plan for running the cable within the building. *If using the master antenna system is impossible, we will devise a plan for running the cable within the building.* ■ Some plate makers utilize alphanumeric forms, creating hybrid messages that could be written entirely in numeric or alphabetic characters. *Some plate makers use alphanumeric forms, creating hybrid messages that could be written entirely in numeric or alphabetic characters.* ■ The Public Broadcasting System utilizes outside experts in creating the format for its program "Wall Street Week." *The Public Broadcasting System employs outside experts in creating the format for its program "Wall Street Week."*

V

(a) valuable asset *(an) asset; valuable.* The company also has the parent company's financial backing, which provides staying power, a valuable asset in the capital-intensive central office marketplace. *The company also has the parent company's financial backing, which provides staying power, an asset in the capital-intensive central office marketplace.* ■ If all employees are recognized as valuable assets, the company will have muscle—and managers won't have to flex theirs. *If all employees are recognized as valuable, the company will have muscle—and managers won't have to flex theirs.* ■ The wasting of this valuable national asset, through neglect and privation, makes no sense. *The wasting of this national asset, through neglect and privation, makes no sense.*

vantage point *vantage.* That it should do so is hardly surprising when one considers the unique vantage point from which he is able to view the historical scene. *That it should do so is hardly surprising when one considers the unique vantage from which he is able to view the historical scene.*

various and sundry *assorted; diverse; sundry; varied; various; varying;* delete.

various different *assorted; countless; different; diverse; extensive; many; numerous; scores of; sundry; varied; various; varying.* Couples have various different ways of splitting their money. *Couples have various ways of splitting their money.*

verbalization *speech; talk.*

verbalize *speak; talk; write.* Request that those who call you regularly put their thoughts in writing instead of verbalizing on the phone. *Request that those who call you regularly put their thoughts in writing instead of talking on the phone.*

very delete. It's a very tragic story. *It's a tragic story.* ■ Were you very deeply religious before the shooting? *Were you deeply religious before the shooting?* ■ She is a very lovely woman. *She is a lovely woman.* ■ The driving conditions are very treacherous. *The driving conditions are treacherous.* ■ I thought her performance was very memorable. *I thought her performance was memorable.*

very much -ed (-en) *much -ed (-en).* I was very much concerned about that. *I was much concerned about that.* ■ Their efficacy as classroom texts would be very much improved if their pedagogical features were more plentiful. *Their efficacy as classroom texts would be much improved if their pedagogical features were more plentiful.*

very much so *yes.*

vestigial remnant *remnant; vestige.* We Americans have only a vestigial remnant of several basic industries—consumer electronics, photography, toymaking, and office equipment to name a few. *We Americans have only a remnant of several basic industries—consumer electronics, photography, toymaking, and office equipment to name a few.*

viable delete. Having an affair is not a viable solution. *Having an affair is not a solution.*

violent explosion *explosion.*

(a; the) vital ... in (of; to) *vital in (to).* We have been very pleased with their performance and have found them to be a vital part of our operation. *We have been very pleased with their performance and have found them to be vital to our operation.* ■ A vital key to increasing our efforts, righting the U.S. trade deficit, and creating new domestic job opportunities will be the rate at which we gain footholds in the developing countries by establishing a physical presence through direct investment. *Vital to increasing our efforts, righting the U.S. trade deficit, and creating new domestic job opportunities will be the rate at which we gain footholds in the developing countries by establishing a physical presence through direct investment.* ■ The price of housing, therefore, becomes a vital factor in maintaining lifestyle. *The price of housing, therefore, becomes vital to maintaining lifestyle.* ■ The Department of Commerce also provides leads to potential overseas contacts, suppliers, distributors, etc., which is a vital element in the success of any export venture. *The Department of Commerce also provides leads to potential overseas contacts, suppliers, distributors, etc., which is vital to the success of any export venture.*

vital necessity *necessity; vital.*

vocalize *express; say; state; tell; voice.*

voice ... (about; for; of; to) delete. The researchers, writing in *Proceedings of the National Academy of Sciences,* voiced hope that the discovery may also explain why some people become addicted to alcohol and how that can be prevented. *The researchers, writing in* Proceedings of the National Academy of Sciences, *hoped that the discovery may also explain why some people become addicted to alcohol and how that can be prevented.* ■ He also voiced strong support for the international effort to make ISDN—Integrated Services Digital Network—the universally accepted worldwide network of the future. *He also strongly supported the international effort to make ISDN—Integrated Services Digital Network—the universally accepted worldwide network of the future.* ■ They voiced doubt that trees will prove to be a bigger source of hydrocarbons than cars in most cities. *They doubted that trees will prove to be a bigger source of hydrocarbons than cars in most cities.*

voice concern (about) *agonize (about; over); brood (on; over); dread; fear; fret (about; over); regret; stew (about; over); worry (about; over).* Although the judge voiced concern that the witnesses could not give a more specific date of the incident at the restaurant, he appears to have excluded the evidence on the ground that Janice made the statements to the defendant and not the witnesses. *Although the judge regretted that the witnesses could not give a more specific date of the incident at the restaurant, he appears to have excluded the evidence on the ground that Janice made the statements to the defendant and not the witnesses.* ■ U.S. officials have voiced concern about possible Chinese sales of newly developed short-range M-9 missiles elsewhere in the Middle East. *U.S. officials have worried about possible Chinese sales of newly developed short-range M-9 missiles elsewhere in the Middle East.*

voice opposition to *contest; criticize; disagree with; disapprove of; dispute; object to; oppose; protest.* Congress in 1986 passed the Montgomery Amendment after several governors voiced opposition to the Reagan administration's Central American policy. *Congress in 1986 passed the Montgomery Amendment after several governors objected to the Reagan administration's Central American policy.* ■ The officials also voiced their opposition to a controversial needle-distribution program that was approved by a majority of a state task force. *The officials also criticized a controversial needle-distribution program that was approved by a majority of a state task force.*

voice skepticism (about) *disbelieve; distrust; doubt; mistrust; question.*

voice sorrow (about) *bemoan; deplore; grieve; lament; moan; mourn; regret.*

wage (a; the) ... delete. Congressmen continue to wage rigorous campaigns for reelection, and every judicial vacancy produces many aspirants willing to subject themselves to any indignity to land on the bench. *Congressmen continue to campaign rigorously for reelection, and every judicial vacancy produces many aspirants willing to subject themselves to any indignity to land on the bench.* ■ The two families waged a bitter wrangle over the largest element in the package: a new automobile. *The two families wrangled bitterly over the largest element in the package: a new automobile.*

wait around *wait.* The key customers are not going to wait around while those issues get resolved. *The key customers are not going to wait while those issues get resolved.*

want to have *want.* We don't want to have the drug in our formulary unless it has a superior patient care advantage. *We don't want the drug in our formulary unless it has a superior patient care advantage.*

warn in advance *warn.*

(the) way (in which) *how;* delete. This overview should give you a feel for the way these programs work and the way you can use them. *This overview should give you a feel for how these programs work and how you can use them.* ■ That's the way people can reduce their blood pressure. *That's how people can reduce their blood pressure.* ■ This review can also examine ways in which American competitiveness can be enhanced in an increasingly demanding world market. *This review can also examine how American competitiveness can be enhanced in an increasingly demanding world market.*

ways and means *means; methods; ways.*

weather conditions *weather.* The adverse weather conditions on Saturday postponed the running of the race until a day later. *The adverse weather on Saturday postponed the running of the race until a day later.* ■ Despite the bad weather conditions, the bus driver did not reduce his speed. *Despite the bad weather, the bus driver did not reduce his speed.* ■ Farmers, caught between the heat and drought, worried about what the weather conditions might do to their crop yield next year. *Farmers, caught between the heat and drought, worried about what the weather might do to their crop yield next year.*

weld together *weld.* Following the analogy of pantheon, Milton welded together pan, "all," and demon, "devil," to create pandemonium, which literally means "a place for all demons." *Following the analogy of pantheon, Milton welded pan, "all," and demon, "devil," to create pandemonium, which literally means "a place for all demons."* ■ They manufactured their samples by welding together two single-crystal gold films. *They manufactured their samples by welding two single-crystal gold films.*

(all) well and fine (good) *all right; fine; good; great; nice; pleasant; pleasing; welcome; well.* Viewing text files is all well and good, of course, but what happens when it comes time to clean out your 1-2-3 directory? *Viewing text files is fine, of course, but what happens when it comes time to clean out your 1-2-3 directory?* ▪ Variety and customization are well and good, but they are low on most consumers' lists of priorities. *Variety and customization are nice, but they are low on most consumers' lists of priorities.*

were it not for *but for; except for.*

what appears (seems) to be *apparent; seeming.* Manchester police also said a bottle of nonprescription pills was found in the room along with what appeared to be a suicide note. *Manchester police also said a bottle of nonprescription pills was found in the room along with an apparent suicide note.*

what ... for *why.* What did you do that for? *Why did you do that?*

what ... happens (occurs; results; takes place) is (that) delete. What happens is you have to reach a 15-percent threshold. *You have to reach a 15-percent threshold.* ▪ What happens with motherhood is you rarely repeat the problems of your own mother. *With motherhood you rarely repeat the problems of your own mother.* ▪ What happens, again and again, is that people with good intentions falter. *Again and again, people with good intentions falter.* ▪ What's happening is that we've got a labored advance since the October crash. *We've got a labored advance since the October crash.*

what have you *whatnot.*

what in God's (heaven's) name *whatever; what ever.* What in God's name does it have to do with the subject of business? *Whatever does it have to do with the subject of business?*

what in the world (on earth) *whatever; what ever.* What on earth are you talking about? *Whatever are you talking about?*

what is ... (is that) *-(al)ly;* delete. What we need is a way to go directly to the partition block. *We need a way to go directly to the partition block.* ▪ This is what is shown in the figure. *This is shown in the figure.* ▪ What we hope to do is increase our inventory and decrease our costs. *We hope to increase our inventory and decrease our costs.* ▪ What's at issue is a federal law that prohibits this kind of solicitation. *At issue is a federal law that prohibits this kind of solicitation.* ▪ What I'm going to do is relax the body. *I'm going to relax the body.* ▪ What we have described is a typical, hierarchical, central-processor-based, on-line architecture. *We have described a typical, hierarchical, central-processor-based, on-line architecture.* ▪ What has brought them to the hospital's overweight program is peer pressure. *Peer pressure has brought them to the hospital's overweight program.* ▪ What is not so clear or commonly accepted is the scope and nature of these obligations. *Not so clear or commonly accepted is the scope and nature of these obligations.* ▪ What is clear is that the Energy

Department should be thinking in terms of a thorough-going down-sizing of America's nuclear arsenal, not a gold-plated rebuilding of its cold-war capacity. *Clearly, the Energy Department should be thinking in terms of a thorough-going down-sizing of America's nuclear arsenal, not a gold-plated rebuilding of its cold-war capacity.* ■ What is more important, it must set standards for not using them. *More important, it must set standards for not using them.*

what is called (known as; named; referred to as; termed) delete. Many municipal and rural developments are located within what is referred to as the flood plain. *Many municipal and rural developments are located within the flood plain.* ■ After a while, a file may end up scattered all over the disk on what are called noncontiguous sectors. *After a while, a file may end up scattered all over the disk on noncontiguous sectors.* ■ Conspicuous consumption is the economist's term for what is referred to as "keeping up with the Joneses." *Conspicuous consumption is the economist's term for "keeping up with the Joneses."*

what is the time frame (time horizon; time period; time span) in which (of) when. What was the time frame in which you had your relationship with President Kennedy? *When did you have your relationship with President Kennedy?*

what is the likelihood (probability) (of) how likely (probable). What is the likelihood of that? *How likely is that?*

what I want to say is delete.

what (whatever; which; whichever) one(s) what (whatever; which; whichever). Which one would be accomplished better or faster with the help of a computer? *Which would be accomplished better or faster with the help of a computer?* ■ Whichever one you select, it will be an improvement on the one you now have. *Whichever you select, it will be an improvement on the one you now have.* ■ Three months later, you won't have to guess which one is the latest version. *Three months later, you won't have to guess which is the latest version.*

whatsoever at all; whatever. As far as I'm concerned, twins have no ESP ability whatsoever. *As far as I'm concerned, twins have no ESP ability whatever.* ■ There's been no action taken with regard to any of our products and there's no truth whatsoever to the allegations. *There's been no action taken with regard to any of our products and there's no truth at all to the allegations.* ■ To me, this is enjoyable work, and I don't feel any danger whatsoever. *To me, this is enjoyable work, and I don't feel any danger whatever.*

what with with. What with the constant change in today's world, financial plans must be continually updated. *With the constant change in today's world, financial plans must be continually updated.* ■ I sometimes wonder if it's worth it to send my kids to school, what with all the time they spend out of it for holidays, in-service days, and so on. *I sometimes wonder if it's worth it to send my kids to* *school with all the time they spend out of it for holidays, in-service days, and so on.*

when all is said and done *all in all; all things considered; all told; altogether; finally; in all; in the end; on the whole; overall.* When all is said and done, Mr. Marshall emerges as a monster by anyone's standards. *All in all, Mr. Marshall emerges as a monster by anyone's standards.*

when and as *as; when.* Late payments are subject to a late-payment charge of 1 1/2 percent per month, and the advertisers agree to pay any such late-payment penalty when and as billed by the publisher. *Late payments are subject to a late-payment charge of 1 1/2 percent per month, and the advertisers agree to pay any such late-payment penalty when billed by the publisher.*

when and (or) if *if; when.* So when and if the discount rate is charged, it could well be interpreted on Wall Street as nothing more than a "catch-up" move. *So if the discount rate is charged, it could well be interpreted on Wall Street as nothing more than a "catch-up" move.*

when and (or) whether *if; when; whether.*

when, as, and if *if; when.*

when compared to (with) *against; alongside; beside; compared to (with); -(i)er than; less; less than; more; more than; next to; over; than; to; versus; vis-à-vis.* There is a 23-percent-higher suicide rate of Vietnam veterans when compared to other persons in the same age group. *There is a 23-percent-higher suicide rate of Vietnam veterans compared to other persons in the same age group.* ■ Decrying the disarray of the Carter presidency, he adds that it now seems a bit tame when compared to the foreign policy babble that followed. *Decrying the disarray of the Carter presidency, he adds that it now seems a bit tamer than the foreign policy babble that followed.* ■ He also notes that the United States continues to have a number of important advantages when compared to most countries. *He also notes that the United States continues to have a number of important advantages over most countries.*

when (a; the) ... done (finished; over; through) *after.*

when it (you) comes (gets) right down to it *all in all; all things considered; all told; altogether; in all; on the whole; overall.*

when it comes to *about; as for; as to; concerning; for; in; of; on; over; regarding; respecting; to; toward; when; with;* delete. She's very shy when it comes to performing in front of an audience. *She's very shy about performing in front of an audience.* ■ When it comes to educating learning disabled and emotionally disturbed children, the system is flawed. *In educating learning disabled and emotionally disturbed children, the system is flawed.* ■ There's still a lot of fear, prejudice, and ignorance in our country when it comes to AIDS. *There's still a lot* *of fear, prejudice, and ignorance in our country regarding AIDS.* ■ Unfortunately, when it comes to safeguarding prosperity, "almost" can never be good enough. *Unfortunately, when safeguarding prosperity, "almost" can never be good enough.* ■ When it comes to financial services, today's consumer is more sophisticated, more aware, and more demanding. *As for financial services, today's consumer is more sophisticated, more aware, and more demanding.* ■ Employers, employees, and society are often in conflict when it comes to dealing with five key issues facing them today in the workplace. *Employers, employees, and society are often in conflict over dealing with five key issues facing them today in the workplace.*

when measured against *against; alongside; beside; compared to (with); -(i)er than; less; less than; more; more than; next to; over; than; to; versus; vis-à-vis.* The size of the Pennwalt takeover offer isn't large when measured against the multibillion-dollar bidding wars that have reshaped 1988 as the year of unprecedented megadeals. *The size of the Pennwalt takeover offer isn't large alongside the multibillion-dollar bidding wars that have reshaped 1988 as the year of unprecedented megadeals.*

whensoever *whenever.*

when ... then *when.* When the detector no longer sounds, then you know you have reached safety. *When the detector no longer sounds, you know you have reached safety.* ■ When you put these three things together, then you end up with excesses. *When you put these three things together, you end up with excesses.* ■ When external market transactions are undesirable because of these problems, then firms will internalize across national boundaries through FDI. *When external market transactions are undesirable because of these problems, firms will internalize across national boundaries through FDI.* ■ When you have chronic cash-flow problems, then your expenditures are too large for your revenues. *When you have chronic cash-flow problems, your expenditures are too large for your revenues.*

whereabouts *where.*

where ... at *where.* We don't really know where we are at. *We don't really know where we are.*

wherefore *why.*

where ... is concerned *about; as for; as to; concerning; for; in; of; on; over; regarding; respecting; to; toward; with;* delete. Bank customers are often less venturesome where their money is concerned. *Bank customers are often less venturesome with their money.* ■ Keep in mind that bigger isn't necessarily better where information is concerned. *Regarding information, keep in mind that bigger isn't necessarily better.* ■ Some ad agency executives question a strategy that depends primarily on high-tech clients at a time when clients are so skittish about conflicts—especially where confidential technology is concerned. *Some ad agency executives question a strategy that depends primarily on high-tech clients at a time when clients are so skittish about conflicts—especially over confidential technology.* ■ It's beginning to show signs of weakness where demand is concerned, but that's true everywhere. *It's beginning to show signs of weakness in demand, but that's true everywhere.*

wheresoever *wherever.*

where ... to *where.*

whereupon *whereon.*

wherewithal *assets; cash; funds; means; money.* The BOCs have the wherewithal to manage their way up through these layers in order to be effective suppliers of voice messaging services. *The BOCs have the means to manage their way up through these layers in order to be effective suppliers of voice messaging services.* ■ He added that the Minnesotan also has the wherewithal to shore up finances during bad times. *He added that the Minnesotan also has the cash to shore up finances during bad times.*

whether and (or) when *if; when; whether.*

whether *if.* A patent can be granted only after the PTO examiners have searched existing patents to determine whether the invention has been previously patented. *A patent can be granted only after the PTO examiners have searched existing patents to determine if the invention has been previously patented.*

whether or not *if; whether.* These differences determine the power of a computer and whether it can execute a given program or not. *These differences determine the power of a computer and whether it can execute a given program.* ■ The first issue that they must consider is whether or not to seek legal protection for these brands. *The first issue that they must consider is whether to seek legal protection for these brands.* ■ With so many choices, the question is not whether or not to buy a server but what to implement as a server. *With so many choices, the question is not whether to buy a server but what to implement as a server.*

which is delete. The Moscow Papyrus dealt with solving practical problems which are related to geometry, food preparation, and grain allowance. *The Moscow Papyrus dealt with solving practical problems related to geometry, food preparation, and grain allowance.* ■ There's a certain enzyme which is lacking in their systems. *There's a certain enzyme lacking in their systems.* ■ Tandy Corp., which is probably the largest U.S. distributor of small business systems, also sells personal computers in its stores. *Tandy Corp., probably the largest U.S. distributor of small business systems, also sells personal computers in its stores.*

whichsoever *whichever.*

while at the same time *as; at the same time; while.* Another approach to solving the problem of meeting different market needs while at the same time maximizing the degree of product uniformity is the modular approach to product development and manufacture. *Another approach to solving the problem of meeting different market needs while maximizing the degree of product uniformity is the modular approach to product development and manufacture.* ■ So the objective of the game within the Administration was to finesse the longer-term implications of SDI while at the same time manipulating the shorter-term impact of the program in such a way as either to advance arms control or to stop it in its tracks. *So the objective of the game within the Administration was to finesse the longer-term implications of SDI while manipulating the shorter-term impact of the program in such a way as either to advance arms control or to stop it in its tracks.* ■ Women's colleges are offering women innovative programs, while at the same time they are opening doors for minorities. *Women's colleges are offering women innovative programs, as they are opening doors for minorities.*

while concurrently *as; while.* Banks have been forced to develop many new asset and liability products intended to meet customers' needs while concurrently lessening their own vulnerability to unexpected rate changes. *Banks have been forced to develop many new asset and liability products intended to meet customers' needs while lessening their own vulnerability to unexpected rate changes.*

while simultaneously *as; while.* A global company needs to coordinate its local and global distribution activities to enhance its competitive advantages while simultaneously achieving its global and local strategic objectives. *A global company needs to coordinate its local and global distribution activities to enhance its competitive advantages while achieving its global and local strategic objectives.* ■ It's a challenge for Borland to push Quattro, Paradox, and Sprint on one hand to corporate customers, while trying simultaneously to create demand for their single-user language and utility products on the other. *It's a challenge for Borland to push Quattro, Paradox, and Sprint on one hand to corporate customers, while trying to create demand for their single-user language and utility products on the other.* ■ While getting signatures, volunteers were simultaneously assessing the degree of support for my candidacy. *While getting signatures, volunteers were assessing the degree of support for my candidacy.*

who in the world (on earth) *who ever.* Who in the world is that? *Who ever is that?*

who is delete. Because the county jails have no room for them, women who are charged with crimes are brought to Framingham. *Because the county jails have no room for them, women charged with crimes are brought to Framingham.* ■ The groups can vary from project associates to laymen who are unfamiliar with the project and its objectives. *The groups can vary from project* *associates to laymen unfamiliar with the project and its objectives.* ■ The current uncritical acceptance of feminist history as valid portrayal of the past damages the historical profession as a whole and is especially detrimental to historians who are women. *The current uncritical acceptance of feminist history as valid portrayal of the past damages the historical profession as a whole and is especially detrimental to women historians.*

whole (wholly) delete. Never in my whole life have I ever seen such a thing. *Never in my life have I ever seen such a thing.* ■ We have a whole new house to furnish. *We have a new house to furnish.* ■ They have not talked a whole lot about radiation yet. *They have not talked a lot about radiation yet.* ■ There's a whole plethora of new technologies emerging. *There's a plethora of new technologies emerging.* ■ He gave me a whole slew of dates to work with. *He gave me a slew of dates to work with.* ■ Behind this growth has been a whole host of forces, including unprecedented growth in communications networks. *Behind this growth has been a host of forces, including unprecedented growth in communications networks.* ■ This emerging technology opens up a whole new world of opportunities. *This emerging technology opens up a new world of opportunities.*

whomsoever *whomever.*

whosoever *whoever.*

why in the world (on earth) *why ever.* Why in the world would liberals oppose the idea? *Why would liberals ever oppose the idea?* ■ But why on earth would you use cocaine? *But why would you ever use cocaine?*

(many) widely varying *assorted; broad; countless; different; diverse; extensive; many; numerous; scores of; sundry; varied; various; varying.* If a distributor bases its application programs on the Unix operating system, it can choose among many widely varying computers. *If a distributor bases its application programs on the Unix operating system, it can choose among various computers.*

widow (widower) of the late *widow (widower) of.*

widow woman *widow.*

window of opportunity *chance; opportunity.* Interviews with government scientists and physicians suggest a critical window of opportunity was missed. *Interviews with government scientists and physicians suggest a critical opportunity was missed.*

wintertime *winter.* In the wintertime, however, the sun's weaker rays generate less heat energy near the Earth's surface. *In the winter, however, the sun's weaker rays generate less heat energy near the Earth's surface.*

-wise delete. He has a lot of sense, businesswise. *He has a lot of business sense.* ■ I don't know that that would be very effective, costwise. *I don't know that that would be very cost effective.* ■ A teenager is in no position, maturity-wise, to care for a baby. *A teenager is not mature enough to care for a baby.*

with a (the) thought of (to) (-ing) *for (-ing); so as to; to.* We assume that they wish to examine their consumption patterns with a thought to increase their savings rate. *We assume that they wish to examine their consumption patterns so as to increase their savings rate.*

with a (the) view of (to) (-ing) *for (-ing); so as to; to.* From the time Macmillan's management realized that the company might be raided, it began to focus on the information unit, not so much with a view to keeping it independent or owned by the employees but with a view to grabbing control of it for a handful of senior executives. *From the time Macmillan's management realized that the company might be raided, it began to focus on the information unit, not so much to keep it independent or owned by the employees but to grab control of it for a handful of senior executives.* ■ All categories of terms have been reviewed and in some areas an entirely new approach has been adopted with a view to making the book more useful for the reader. *All categories of terms have been reviewed and in some areas an entirely new approach has been adopted so as to make the book more useful for the reader.*

with few (rare) exception(s) *almost all; almost every; most; nearly all; nearly every.* With rare exception, the people we see here have never been homeless before and can't believe it's happening to them. *Most of the people we see here have never been homeless before and can't believe it's happening to them.* ■ With a few exceptions, nominees to the federal bench, over the years, have been men and women respected in the legal field for scholarship and integrity. *Nearly all nominees to the federal bench, over the years, have been men and women respected in the legal field for scholarship and integrity.* ■ With few exceptions, federal and state policies are not aimed at upgrading the technology of existing firms. *Almost all federal and state policies are not aimed at upgrading the technology of existing firms.*

with increasing frequency *increasingly; more and more.* With increasing fre-quency, designers, critics, and executives alike are attacking the entire premise of America's response to trade competition. *Increasingly, designers, critics, and executives alike are attacking the entire premise of America's response to trade competition.* ■ Women are dating younger men with increasing frequency. *More and more women are dating younger men.*

without a (any) question (shadow) of a doubt *certainly; doubtless; no doubt; surely; without (a; any) doubt.*

without basis in fact *baseless; groundless; unfounded.*

without (a; any) doubt *certainly; doubtless; no doubt; surely.*

without equal *matchless; novel; peerless; singular; special; unequaled; unique; unmatched; unrivaled.*

without exception *all; always; consistently; constantly; every; everybody; everyone; every time; invariably; unfailingly;* delete. Without exception, consumers should be aware that caveat emptor is an understatement in this field. *Consumers should always be aware that caveat emptor is an understatement in this field.* ■ Without exception, the leaders and members of various congregations report a new attitude from the Soviet leadership that promises a reason for optimism. *All the leaders and members of various congregations report a new attitude from the Soviet leadership that promises a reason for optimism.* ■ People who are collector-oriented and buy coins because they like them have, without exception, done quite well. *People who are collector-oriented and buy coins because they like them have unfailingly done quite well.* ■ Without exception, no agency of your size, or bigger, or smaller, does what you propose. *No agency of your size, or bigger, or smaller, does what you propose.*

without foundation *baseless; groundless; unfounded.* Most allegations of men abusing their children are totally without foundation. *Most allegations of men abusing their children are totally unfounded.*

without number *countless; endless; infinite; millions (of); myriad; numberless; untold.*

without peer *matchless; novel; peerless; singular; special; unequaled; unique; unmatched; unrivaled.* He is the entrepreneur extraordinaire; he is without peer. *He is the entrepreneur extraordinaire; he is peerless.*

without (a) question *certainly; doubtless; no doubt; surely.*

with reference to *about; as for; as to; concerning; for; in; of; on; over; regarding; respecting; to; toward; with;* delete. With reference to the stereo, I think she should have put it in storage. *Concerning the stereo, I think she should have put it in storage.* ■ With reference to your article on the World Bank, the Bank has no plans to issue commodity bonds or to make commodity-indexed loans. *As for your article on the World Bank, the Bank has no plans to issue commodity bonds or to make commodity-indexed loans.* ■ You're assuming the husband and wife can get along and can make joint decisions with reference to their children. *You're assuming the husband and wife can get along and can make joint decisions about their children.* ■ Only infrequently can we use any of these adjectives with reference to a book on so treacherous a subject. *Only infrequently can we use any of these adjectives for a book on so treacherous a subject.*

with regard to *about; as for; as to; concerning; for; in; of; on; over; regarding; respecting; to; toward; with;* delete. The evidence is mixed with regard to the existence of an optimal capital structure. *The evidence is mixed on the existence of an optimal capital structure.* ■ Three points should be made with regard to these findings. *Three points should be made regarding these findings.* ■ With regard to foreign competition, this last factor is likely more important over the long term than the weakened dollar. *Concerning foreign competition, this last factor is likely more important over the long term than the weakened dollar.* ■ Forecasts are the expectations that planners formulate with regard to the likely or probable state of events or conditions at some time in the future. *Forecasts are the expectations that planners formulate about the likely or probable state of events or conditions at some time in the future.* ■ With regard to the first rationalization, how can a manager know how far is too far? *As to the first rationalization, how can a manager know how far is too far?* ■ The growing internationalization of life, particularly with regard to travel and communications, may present opportunities for firms able to present a coherent and consistent image on a worldwide basis. *The growing internationalization of life, particularly in travel and communications, may present opportunities for firms able to present a coherent and consistent image on a worldwide basis.*

with relation to *about; as for; as to; concerning; for; in; of; on; over; regarding; respecting; to; toward; with;* delete. There are conflicting reports with relation to the altitude of the Iranian airliner. *There are conflicting reports about the altitude of the Iranian airliner.* ■ In writing on "professional priorities in art criticism," I was asked to survey current practices and the current state of affairs in order to properly discuss sound policy with relation to art criticism. *In writing on "professional priorities in art criticism," I was asked to survey current practices and the current state of affairs in order to properly discuss sound policy on art criticism.*

with respect to *about; as for; as to; concerning; for; in; of; on; over; regarding; respecting; to; toward; with;* delete. Something very interesting was said with respect to gender differences. *Something very interesting was said about gender differences.* ■ SDS made a complete investigation of Amtron and its technology and drove a hard bargain with respect to contract terms, etc. *SDS made a complete investigation of Amtron and its technology and drove a hard bargain on contract terms, etc.* ■ Each Licensee hereunder shall have the following rights with respect to the Licensed Software. *Each Licensee hereunder shall have the following rights concerning the Licensed Software.* ■ There are efforts being made to substantially increase the pool from which Harvard promotes and hires its faculty and nonfaculty with respect to blacks. *There are efforts being made to substantially increase the pool from which Harvard promotes and hires its black faculty and nonfaculty.* ■ I hereby revoke all prior designations, if any, made by me with respect to this account. *I hereby revoke all prior designations, if any, made by me regarding this account.* ■ The floodway within communities that have adopted flood-plain regulations is usually subject to strong restrictions with respect to building. *The floodway within communities that have adopted flood-plain regulations is usually subject to strong building restrictions.*

with the exception of (that) *apart from; aside from; barring; besides; but for; except; except for; excepting; excluding; other than; outside of.* With the exception of their paper, these studies found a link between financial structure and industry class. *Except for their paper, these studies found a link between financial structure and industry class.* ■ With the exception of certain correspondent banking services, many commercial banks did not purchase or sell significant amounts of services or assets from or to other institutions. *Aside from certain correspondent banking services, many commercial banks did not purchase or sell significant amounts of services or assets from or to other institutions.* ■ Author shall be paid as billed with the exception that the final payment of $5,000 shall be paid within ten weeks of delivery of the manuscript. *Author shall be paid as billed except that the final payment of $5,000 shall be paid within ten weeks of delivery of the manuscript.* ■ With the exception of the brand name, the subsidiaries were given considerable latitude in deciding on the local marketing mix. *But for the brand name, the subsidiaries were given considerable latitude in deciding on the local marketing mix.* ■ Overall, bears and other stuffed animals, with the exception of dinosaurs, are out. *Overall, bears and other stuffed animals, other than dinosaurs, are out.*

with the exclusion of (that) *apart from; aside from; barring; besides; but for; except; except for; excepting; excluding; other than; outside of.*

with the intent of -ing (to) *for (-ing); so as to; to.* The Intra-Arterial Cardiac Support System 8000 is being designed with the intent to expand the use of nonsurgical cardiac support systems by providing significantly greater support to the heart than is possible with clinically available non-surgical systems. *The Intra-Arterial Cardiac Support System 8000 is being designed to expand the use of non-surgical cardiac support systems by providing significantly greater support to the heart than is possible with clinically available nonsurgical systems.*

with the passage of time *at length; eventually; in due time; in the end; in time; later; one day; over the months (years); over time; someday; sometime; ultimately; with time; yet.* The claim is often made that the handicap decreases in importance with the passage of time. *The claim is often made that the handicap decreases in importance over the years.* ■ The distinctions that now exist between stationary and mobile communications will disappear with the passage of time. *The distinctions that now exist between stationary and mobile communications will ultimately disappear.* ■ With the passage of time, I think he'll be more and more reluctant to pay me $75,000 a year. *With time, I think he'll be more and more reluctant to pay me $75,000 a year.* ■ He did not improve with the passage of time. *He did not improve over time.*

with the purpose of -ing *for (-ing); so as to; to.* For the most part, the book consists of a rewriting of history, from the dawn of time, with the purpose of demonstrating two main themes. *For the most part, the book consists of a rewriting of history, from the dawn of time, so as to demonstrate two main themes.*

with the result (that) *so (that)*.

worthy of attention *considerable; newsworthy; noteworthy*. To give the media pride of place reinforces the impression that any event is worthy of attention only to the extent that a cameraman is blocking our view. *To give the media pride of place reinforces the impression that any event is noteworthy only to the extent that a cameraman is blocking our view.*

worthy of blame *blamable; blameworthy*.

worthy of commendation *admirable; commendable; praiseworthy*. The fact that her article presents the Palestinian as well as the Israeli viewpoint is worthy of commendation. *The fact that her article presents the Palestinian as well as the Israeli viewpoint is commendable.*

worthy of (my) consideration *considerable; newsworthy; noteworthy*.

worthy of gratitude (thanks) *thankworthy*.

worthy of note *considerable; newsworthy; noteworthy; outstanding*. One change worthy of note has been made in the condominium form. *One noteworthy change has been made in the condominium form.*

worthy of praise *admirable; commendable; praiseworthy*.

worthy of trust *honest; trustworthy*.

would appear (guess; hope; imagine; seem; submit; suggest; suspect; think) *appear (guess; hope; imagine; seem; submit; suggest; suspect; think)*. It would seem that there are a lot of adults exercising but very few children. *It seems there are a lot of adults exercising but very few children.* ■ The stock market's reaction would appear to indicate that the stakes have grown too large for casual deadlines. *The stock market's reaction appears to indicate that the stakes have grown too large for casual deadlines.* ■ I would suspect that the greatest gains would be from teaching the existing users to make even better use of current machines. *I suspect that the greatest gains would be from teaching the existing users to make even better use of current machines.* ■ I would hope that's what he meant. *I hope that's what he meant.* ■ I would submit that a number of shaky S&Ls could be salvaged over the next few years. *I submit that a number of shaky S&Ls could be salvaged over the next few years.*

written communication (correspondence) *correspondence; letter; memo; note; report*. Written correspondence is answered within a week, and phone calls are returned within 24 hours. *Letters are answered within a week, and phone calls are returned within 24 hours.* ■ Just as important, outsiders make judgments about your organization based upon the written communications they receive. *Just as important, outsiders make judgments about your organization based upon the correspondence they receive.*

X

X-ray photograph *X-ray.*

Y

year in (and) year out *annually; always; ceaselessly; consistently; constantly; endlessly; eternally; everlastingly; every year; forever; invariably; never ending; perpetually; routinely; unfailingly; yearly.* Eighty percent of what retailers are ordering are classic lines whose demand is stable year in and year out. *Eighty percent of what retailers are ordering are classic lines whose demand is always stable.*

years (old) delete. The study began in 1981–82 with a statewide survey of a sample of women 45 to 55 years old. *The study began in 1981–82 with a statewide survey of a sample of women 45 to 55.* ■ The academy's Committee on Nutrition recommends cholesterol tests for all children older than 2 years with a parent, sibling, grandparent, uncle, or aunt who has hyperlipidemia. *The academy's Committee on Nutrition recommends cholesterol tests for all children older than 2 with a parent, sibling, grandparent, uncle, or aunt who has hyperlipidemia.*

years of age delete. She is 10 years of age. *She is 10.* ■ I have committed my life to public service since I was 29 years of age. *I have committed my life to public service since I was 29.* ■ The suggestion made by our study and other studies was that for children under 2 years of age, care outside of the home is an important factor for acquiring lower respiratory tract illness. *The suggestion made by our study and other studies was that for children under 2, care outside of the home is an important factor for acquiring lower respiratory tract illness.*

yell and scream *scream; yell.* My wife and I yell and scream at each other about a lot of things, and we have a very healthy marriage. *My wife and I yell at each other about a lot of things, and we have a very healthy marriage.*

you know? delete.

you know what I mean? delete.

you know what I'm saying? delete.

young child (infant) *child (infant); young.*

Z

zero in on *focus on; pinpoint.* It zeroes in on the problem of how expectations are formed—and changed. *It pinpoints the problem of how expectations are formed—and changed.*

zoological *zoologic.*

zoological garden *zoo.*